THE HUMBLER POETS.

THE HUMBLER POETS

A COLLECTION OF

NEWSPAPER AND PERIODICAL VERSE

1870 TO 1885

BY SLASON THOMPSON

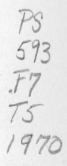
Granger Index Reprint Series

BOOKS FOR LIBRARIES PRESS
FREEPORT, NEW YORK

First Published 1885
Reprinted 1970

INTERNATIONAL STANDARD BOOK NUMBER:
0-8369-6206-0

LIBRARY OF CONGRESS CATALOG CARD NUMBER:
74-133076

PRINTED IN THE UNITED STATES OF AMERICA

EXPLANATORY.

———◆◆◆———

IT has been said that "he is no common benefactor who shrewdly gathers from the world's manifold literature its words of finest wit and maturest wisdom for our entertainment, instruction, and inspiration." But it is not well at all times to partake of the richest dishes or to drink the rarest wines. The finest wit and the maturest wisdom may be read too oft. There come hours to every lover of poetry when he wishes for "some simple and heart-felt lay," something that shall speak from out a mind feeling the every-day cares of life amid the multitude, and not from the heights to which the masters "proudly stooped." It was this feeling that, some fifteen years ago, led me, a prose-thinker, to begin collecting from newspapers and the ephemeral literature of the day such verses as suited my mood, or which seemed the utterance of a soul that had put its thoughts into song. Upon the fly-leaf of my first scrap-book, surrounded by some now faded natural leaves of oak, maple, bilberry, and Virginia creeper, and two withered sprays of trailing arbutus, I find the misquotation from *Love's Labor's Lost*, "As though he had been at a feast of languages and stolen the scraps." The succeeding pages show that it was not from a feast of languages, but from the daily board of wayfaring humanity, that such scraps were gleaned. In the course of years, and during successive changes of residence from the extreme East to San Francisco and back, the collection grew until it contained over a thousand poems. A friend suggested the collocation of the most valuable into some permanent form. My sister, far removed from me as the crow flies, but near in sentiment and appreciation of the songs that "quiet the restless pulse of care," offered the use of her contemporaneous collection for the work. To her I am indebted for some eighty of the more truly poetical pieces included in this volume. Two friends in Chicago placed their collections at my disposal, from which I was able to add some twoscore poems to my store. These independent sources served a further purpose to establish the character and fairly exhaustive scope of my own collection.

Then came the difficult task of selection. My scraps bore no patent of nobility, no royal stamp to show they came from the mint of poetic inspiration. Hundreds of them were without a sign to afford a clew to their parentage. Where the estimate of time, popular favor, and literary criticism has served as a guide-post to other collectors, the very nature of this collection denied it to me; therefore I have been forced to fix an arbitrary standard of my own by which every separate piece was judged. The invariable question has been, "Does this poem or narrative in verse contain anything worth rescuing from oblivion?" Under this rule it will readily be perceived I could not exact anything like the approach to perfection demanded in a collection making claim to represent the best specimens of English verse. I could not require that each piece should contain what was best worth preserving, but only that it should contain something worth preserving at all. The latitude admitted by such a principle of selection will account for the unevenness of this collection as a whole. Some of the pieces are full-fledged poems, complete in form, spirit, and finish, and undoubtedly deserve to rank higher up than in *The Humbler Poets*. Some are mere snatches of song and story "wedded to rhyme," while others are little more than suggestions of beautiful ideas struggling through halting metre and homely jingles. Several are only the rude setting for one or two good lines or happy thoughts. Some of these hedgerow poems contain the germ for others by master hands. Who now can say that Longfellow did not borrow the thought — even some of the very words — for his description of the baby, in *The*

Hanging of the Crane, from as lowly a source as *My Lost Baby,* page 47, when he wrote, —

> " He ruleth by the right divine
> Of helplessness, so lately born
> In purple chambers of the morn,
> As sovereign over thee and thine " ?

It may be asked upon what principle I have drawn the line of exclusion from this volume. My answer is that it has been drawn almost arbitrarily along the line of the collected works of the Lesser Poets, — as Bret Harte, R. H. Stoddard, Helen Hunt Jackson, Celia Thaxter, Austin Dobson, Frederick Locker, W. W. Story, R. W. Gilder, Mary Mapes Dodge, Theodore Tilton, Joaquin Miller, Louisa M. Alcott, Elizabeth Akers Allen, Paul H. Hayne, William Winter, Harriet Prescott Spofford, Benjamin, F. Taylor, Lucy Larcom, Ella Wheeler, Louise Chandler Moulton, Dinah Mulock Craik, H. C. Bunner, Mary Clemmer, T. B. Aldrich, J. T. Fields, and others, may without offence be called. It is possible, and even probable, that this volume may contain some fugitives from between the covers of the works of these contributors to the periodical poetry of the day, or even from higher sources. But I have taken what the lawyers would call the reasonable care of a reasonable man to reduce the chances of such a fault. The range of poetry in the English tongue is now so vast as to put it beyond the study of a lifetime to possess the memory of everything in it.

That my rule has not been lived up to in one or two instances will find excuse, I trust, in the character of the pieces in whose favor the exceptions have been made. The selections credited to Francis W. Bourdillon are notable instances where I have let down the fence to admit poetry that found its way into my scrap-books before the author thought to call it within an enclosure of his own.

Less than twenty selections found in the numerous standard collections, which have been consulted industriously, have been retained in this. No apology seems necessary for the retention of *The Burial of Moses, Tired Mothers, The Blue and the Gray, Our Last Toast, Light,* and *The King's Picture.* They fall naturally into the companionship of this volume, and are not generally accessible to a large body of readers of poetry. *Rain on the Roof* is included for the reason assigned in an accompanying note. *The Water-Mill* has been a fugitive without a father so long, that this opportunity was taken to name its author. William Cullen Bryant had the courage to give the *Beautiful Snow* a place in his *Library of Poetry and Song*, although denied sanctuary by Dana and other editors. As it appears in this volume the last verse has been restored. Some readers may be interested in comparing it with the *Beautiful Snow* written by Major Sigourney, who was long credited with the authorship of the more famous poem.

As the reader comes to the end of poem after poem in this collection well worthy the pen of a master, but without a sign to show whence it came, he must remark the result of one of the most inexcusable faults of modern journalism. Some newspapers make it a rule not to publish the names of their own writers who contribute poetry, while others systematically reprint verses with only the name of the publication from which they are clipped, ignoring the signature appended to the original verse. From the blank spaces at the foot of the unclaimed poems in this volume there rises an appeal to the publishers of newspapers to do a small justice to the minor poets of the English tongue. It says with irresistible logic, "If a poem is worth publishing at all, its author is worthy of recognition."

Little more remains to be said. It is not pretended that all the selections herein were written within the years mentioned on the titlepage. Indeed, some of them are "old vagrants," and the date of many more it is impossible to fix, for newspaper poetry travels in cycles, the same piece turning up in the same "Poet's Corner" about once in seven years. Unlike standard collections from the best authors, this volume contains a very small percentage of poems to be found elsewhere. It preserves many that would otherwise have perished by the wayside, — lost for want of a collector. It is *sui generis*. Perhaps it may inspire future editions to which a more exacting standard of excellence can be applied. If in its pages there is shown the possession of a discriminating judgment regarding the treasures " more golden than gold," irrespective of their lowly source, let it be attributed to an early study of Mr. Francis Turner Palgrave's *Golden Treasury*, which I regret to say some ill-equipped editor has attempted to gild with modern alloy.

If the pleasure I have taken in collecting my scraps here, there, and everywhere, and the labor I have bestowed in bringing them within the compass of this volume, — the doubting judgment respecting some and the regret of rejecting others, — if this shall be the means of preserving many of the better fugitive verses of the period; if to any man or woman, youth or maiden, it shall give a worthy book to take from the shelf when the tasks for the day are all done ; if any shall find herein some familiar but mislaid verse ; if its pages shall recall forgotten scenes to some and whisper in the ear of "uneventful toil " some strains of the music that is everywhere ; if its leaves shall bring a balm of hope, encouragement, and sweet content to some despondent heart ; if its final moral shall teach some frail and weary wight that love, truth, and mirth are unfailing comforters, comrades, friends, — I shall be satisfied.

S. T.

CHICAGO, *October*, 1885.

CONTENTS.

—◆◇◆—

INDEX OF TITLES.

PART I.

Of Poets and Poetry.

If to embody in a breathing word
Tones that the spirit trembled when it heard;
To fix the image all unveiled and warm,
And carve in language its ethereal form,
So pure, so perfect, that the lines express
No meagre shrinking, no unlaced excess;
To feel that art, in living truth, has taught
Ourselves, reflected in the sculptured thought; —
If this alone bestow the right to claim
The deathless garland and the sacred name;
Then none are poets, save the saints on high,
Whose harps can murmur all that words deny.

    .   .   .   .

So every grace that plastic language knows
To nameless poets its perfection owes.
The rough-hewn words to simplest thoughts confined
Were cut and polished in their nicer mind;
Caught on their edge, imagination's ray
Splits into rainbows, shooting far away; —
From sense to soul, from soul to sense, it flies,
And through all nature links analogies;
He who reads right will rarely look upon
A better poet than his lexicon.

OLIVER WENDELL HOLMES.

THE HUMBLER POETS.

Of Poets and Poetry.

AN INVOCATION TO POESY.

STAY with me, Poesy! playmate of childhood!
  Friend of my manhood! delight of my youth!
Roamer with me over valley and wildwood,
  Searching for loveliness, groping for Truth.
Stay with me, dwell with me, spirit of Poesy;
  Dark were the world if thy bloom should depart;
Glory would cease in the sunlight and starlight,
  Freshness and courage would fade from my heart.

Stay with me, comfort me, now more than ever,
  When years stealing over me lead me to doubt
If men, ay, and women, are all we believed them
  When we two first wandered the green earth about!
Stay with me, strengthen me, soother, adorner,
  Lest knowledge, not wisdom, should cumber my brain,
And tempt me to sit in the chair of the scorner,
  And say, with sad Solomon, all things are vain.

Stay with me, lend me thy magical mirror,
  Show me the darkness extinguished in light;
Show me to-day's little triumph of Error
  Foiled by to-morrow's great triumph of Right!
Stay with me, nourish me, robe all creation
  In colors celestial of amber and blue;
Magnify littleness, glorify commonness,
  Pull down the false and establish the true.

Stay with me, Poesy!   Let me not stagnate!
 Despairing with fools, or believing with knaves,
That men must be either the one or the other, —
 Victors or victims, oppressors or slaves!
Stay with me, cling to me, while there is life in me!
 Lead me, assist me, direct and control!
Be in the shade what thou wert in the sunshine,
 Source of true happiness, light of my soul!

Belgravia.   CHARLES MACKAY.

THE POETIC MYSTERY.

(SUGGESTED BY "ALICE IN WONDERLAND.")

"POET, sit and sing to me;
 Sing of how you make your rhymes,
Tweedledum and tweedledee,
 I have tried it fifty times.
When I have a perfect sense,
 Then I have imperfect sounds;
Vice versa!   Tell me whence
 You get both, I neither."   "Zounds!"

Cried the poet, "Don't you see
 Easy 't is as rolling log,
Holding eel or catching flea,
 Meeting friend or leaving grog!
No such matter should annoy,
 Deep the poet never delves;
Take care of the sense, my boy,
 And the sounds care for themselves."

NOCTURNE.

(AN ECHO OF CHOPIN.)

"When we seek to explain our musical emotions, we look about for images calculated to excite similar emotions, and strive to convey through these images to others the effect produced by music on ourselves." — HAWEIS, *Music and Morals.*

WIND, and the sound of a sea
 Heard in the night from afar,
Spending itself on an unknown shore,
Feeling its way o'er an unseen floor
 Lighted by moon nor star;

Telling a tale to the listening ear
Of wounds and woes that the rolling year
  Hath brought to the human heart;
Telling of passion and innermost pain,
Sinking and swooning, and growing again,
  As the wind and the waves take part;
Lifting a voice to the voiceless skies,
Tender entreaties that faint for replies,
Pauses of sorrow that pass into sighs
  Born of a secret despair;
Fluttering back on the clear tide of tone,
Gathering in force till the melody 's grown
Strong to interpret the accents unknown
  Haunting the dark fields of air;
Speaking the longings of life, the full soul's
Hidden desires in music that rolls
  Wave-like in search of a shore;
Eddies of harmony, floating around,
Widen in circles of lessening sound,
Die in the distance, till silence is found
  And earth redemands us once more.

All the Year Round.

POETRY AND THE POOR.

" The world is very beautiful!" I said,
  As, yesterday, beside the brimming stream,
  Glad and alone, I watched the tremulous gleam
Slant through the wintry wood, green carpeted
With moss and fern and curving bramble spray,
  And bronze the thousand russet margin-reeds,
And in the sparkling holly glint and play,
  And kindle all the brier's flaming seeds.

" The world is very horrible!" I sigh,
  As, in my wonted ways, to-day I tread
Chill streets, deformed with dim monotony,
  Hiding strange mysteries of unknown dread, —
The reeking court, the breathless fever-den,
  The haunts where things unholy throng and brood:
Grim crime, the fierce despair of strong-armed men,
  Child infamy, and shameless womanhood.

And men have looked upon this piteous thing, —
  Blank lives unvisited by beauty's spell, —
And said, " Let be: it is not meet to bring
  Dreams of sweet freedom to the prison cell;
Sing them no songs of things all bright and fair,
  Paint them no visions of the glad and free,
  Lest with purged sights their miseries they see,
And through vain longings pass to blank despair."

O brother, treading ever-darkening ways,
  O sister, whelmed in ever-deepening care,
Would God we might unfold before your gaze
  Some vision of the pure and true and fair !
Better to know, though sadder things be known,
  Better to see, though tears half blind the sight,
Than thraldom to the sense, and heart of stone,
  And horrible contentment with the night.

Oh, bring we then all sweet and gracious things
  To touch the lives that lie so chill and drear,
  That they may dream of some diviner sphere,
Whence each soft ray of love and beauty springs !
Each good and perfect gift is from above,
  And there is healing for earth's direst woes ;
God hath unsealed the springs of light and love,
  To make the desert blossom as the rose.

The Spectator.   W. WALSHAM STOWE,
                                      Bishop of Bedford.

———◆———

THE RAIN UPON THE ROOF.

LONG ago a poet dreaming,
  Weaving fancy's warp and woof,
Penned a tender, soothing poem
  On the " Rain upon the Roof."

Once I read it, and its beauty
  Filled my heart with memories sweet;
Days of childhood fluttered round me,
  Violets sprang beneath my feet.
And my gentle, loving mother
  Spoke again in accents mild,
Curbing every wayward passion
  Of her happy, thoughtless child.
Then I heard the swallows twittering
  Underneath the cabin eaves,
And the laughing shout of Willie
  Up among the maple leaves.
Then I blessed the poet's dreaming —
  Blessed his fancy's warp and woof,
And I wept o'er memories treasured,
  As the rain fell on the roof.

Years ago I lost the poem,
  But its sweetness lingered still,
As the freshness of the valley
  Marks where flowed the springtime rill.
Lost to reach, but not to feeling ;
  For the rain-drop never falls

O'er my head with pattering music,
  But it peoples memory's halls
With the old familiar faces
  Loved and treasured long ago,
Treasured now as in life's springtime,—
  For no change my heart can know.
And I live again my childhood
  In the home far, far away;
Roam the woodland, orchard, wildwood,
  With my playmates still at play;
Then my gray hairs press the pillow,
  Holding all the world aloof,
Dreaming sweetly as I listen
  To the rain upon the roof.

Every pattering drop that falleth
  Seemeth like an angel's tread,
Bringing messages of mercy
  To the weary heart and head.
Pleasant thoughts of years departed,
  Pleasant soothings for to-day,
Earnest longings for to-morrow,
  Hoping for the far away;
For I know each drop that falleth
  Comes to bless the thirsty earth,
Making seed to bud and blossom,
  Springing all things into birth.
As the radiant bow that scattereth
  All our faithlessness with proof
Of a seedtime and a harvest,
  So the rain upon the roof.

MRS. F. B. GAGE.

RAIN ON THE ROOF.

WHEN the humid shadows hover
  Over all the starry spheres,
And the melancholy darkness
  Gently weeps in rainy tears,
What a joy to press the pillow
  Of a cottage-chamber bed,
And to listen to the patter
  Of the soft rain overhead!

Every tinkle on the shingles
  Has an echo in the heart,
And a thousand dreamy fancies
  Into busy being start;

And a thousand recollections
  Weave their air-threads into woof,
As I listen to the patter
  Of the rain upon the roof.

Now in memory comes my mother
  As she used in years agone,
To survey her darling dreamers
  Ere she left them till the dawn:
Oh! I see her leaning o'er me,
  As I list to this refrain
Which is played upon the shingles
  By the patter of the rain.

Then my little seraph sister,
  With her wings and waving hair,
And her bright-eyed cherub brother —
  A serene, angelic pair! —
Glide around my wakeful pillow,
  With their praise or mild reproof,
As I listen to the murmur
  Of the soft rain on the roof.

And another comes to thrill me
  With her eyes' delicious blue;
And forget I, gazing on her,
  That her heart was all untrue:
I remember that I loved her
  As I ne'er may love again,
And my heart's quick pulses vibrate
  To the patter of the rain.

There is nought in art's bravuras
  That can work with such a spell
In the spirit's pure deep fountains,
  Whence the holy passions swell,
As that melody of Nature,
  That subdued, subduing strain,
Which is played upon the shingles
  By the patter of the rain.

                                    COATES KINNEY.

NOTE. — This charming poem was so long a vagrant that its text became
very much corrupted until the author furnished a version for publication in
which the last verse read as follows: —

          Art hath nought of tone or cadence
            That can work with such a spell
          In the soul's mysterious fountains,
            Whence the tears of rapture well,
          As that melody of Nature,
            That subdued, subduing strain,
          Which is played upon the shingles
            By the patter of the rain.

It also contained several minor differences in reading from the original. Where considered improvements, they have been adopted; but as a poet's first thoughts are often his best thoughts, I have taken the liberty to follow original "copy" where it seemed to chime best with the patter of the rain. I was the more emboldened to do this by the fact that poets are proverbially unsafe revisers of their own work.[1] William Cullen Bryant edited the life out of many of his younger passages, while Tennyson in later days has retouched the spirit and force out of some of his earlier work.

A DEED AND A WORD.

A LITTLE stream had lost its way
 Amid the grass and fern;
A passing stranger scooped a well,
 Where weary men might turn;
He walled it in, and hung with care
 A ladle at the brink;
He thought not of the deed he did,
 But judged that all might drink.
He passed again, and lo! the well,
 By summer never dried,
Had cooled ten thousand parching tongues,
 And saved a life beside.

A nameless man, amid a crowd
 That thronged the daily mart,
Let fall a word of hope and love,
 Unstudied, from the heart;
A whisper on the tumult thrown,
 A transitory breath —
It raised a brother from the dust,
 It saved a soul from death.
O germ! O fount! O word of love!
 O thought at random cast!
Ye were but little at the first,
 But mighty at the last.

CHARLES MACKAY.

---

[1] Here, on reading the note in manuscript, Mr. Francis F. Browne interjected the query, "*Is* it a fact?" and quoted the following verses from Gautier, as translated by Austin Dobson: —

> "O Poet! then forbear
> The loosely-sandalled verse;
> Choose rather thou to wear
> The buskin, straight and terse.
>
> "Leave to the tyro's hand
> The limp and shapeless style;
> See that thy form demand
> The labor of the file."

THE KING'S PICTURE.

The king from the council chamber
  Came, weary and sore of heart;
He called to Iliff, the painter,
  And spoke to him thus apart:
I 'm sickened of the faces ignoble,
  Hypocrites, cowards, and knaves;
I shall shrink in their shrunken measure,
  Chief slave in a realm of slaves.

Paint me a true man's picture,
  Gracious, and wise, and good,
Dowered with the strength of heroes
  And the beauty of womanhood.
It shall hang in my inmost chamber,
  That, thither when I retire,
It may fill my soul with its grandeur,
  "And warm it with sacred fire."

So the artist painted the picture,
  And it hung in the palace hall;
Never a thing so lovely
  Had garnished the stately wall.
The king, with head uncovered,
  Gazed on it with rapt delight,
Till it suddenly wore strange meaning —
  Baffled his questioning sight.

For the form was the supplest courtier's,
  Perfect in every limb;
But the bearing was that of the henchman
  Who filled the flagons for him;
The brow was a priest's, who pondered
  His parchment early and late;
The eye was the wandering minstrel's,
  · Who sang at the palace gate.

The lips, half sad and half mirthful,
  With a fitful trembling grace,
Were the very lips of a woman
  He had kissed in the market-place;
But the smiles which her curves transfigured,
  As a rose with its shimmer of dew,
Was the smile of the wife who loved him,
  Queen Ethelyn, good and true.

Then, "Learn, O King," said the artist,
  "This truth that the picture tells —
That in every form of the human
  Some hint of the highest dwells;

That, scanning each living temple
  For the place that the veil is thin,
We may gather by beautiful glimpses
  The form of the God within."

HELEN B. BOSTWICK.

UNSPOKEN WORDS.

THE kindly words that rise within the heart,
  And thrill it with their sympathetic tone,
But die ere spoken, fail to play their part,
  And claim a merit that is not their own.
The kindly word unspoken is a sin, —
  A sin that wraps itself in purest guise,
And tells the heart that, doubting, looks within,
  That not in speech, but thought, the virtue lies.

But 't is not so; another heart may thirst
  For that kind word, as Hagar in the wild —
Poor banished Hagar! — prayed a well might burst
  From out the sand to save her parching child.
And loving eyes that cannot see the mind
  Will watch the unexpected movement of the lips.
Ah! can you let its cutting silence wind
  Around that heart and scathe it like a whip?

Unspoken words like treasures in a mine
  Are valueless until we give them birth;
Like unfound gold their hidden beauties shine,
  Which God has made to bless and gild the earth.
How sad 't would be to see the master's hand
  Strike glorious notes upon a voiceless lute!
But oh, what pain when, at God's own command,
  A heart-string thrills with kindness, but is mute!

Then hide it not, the music of the soul,
  Dear sympathy expressed with kindly voice,
But let it like a shining river roll
  To deserts dry — to hearts that would rejoice.
Oh, let the symphony of kindly words
  Sound for the poor, the friendless, and the weak,
And He will bless you! He who struck the chords
  Will strike another when in turn you seek.

IT IS COMMON.

So are the stars and the arching skies,
So are the smiles in the children's eyes:
Common the life-giving breath of the spring;
So are the songs which the wild birds sing, —
    Blessed be God, they are common.

Common the grass in its glowing green;
So is the water's glistening sheen:
Common the springs of love and mirth;
So are the holiest gifts of earth.

Common the fragrance of rosy June;
So is the generous harvest moon,
So are the towering, mighty hills,
So are the twittering, trickling rills.

Common the beautiful tints of the fall;
So is the sun which is over all:
Common the rain, with its pattering feet;
So is the bread which we daily eat, —
    Blessed be God, it is common.

So is the sea in its wild unrest,
Kissing forever the earth's brown breast;
So is the voice of undying prayer,
Evermore piercing the ambient air.

So unto all are the "promises" given,
So unto all is the hope of heaven:
Common the rest from the weary strife;
So is the life which is after life, —
    Blessed be God, it is common.

———◆———

RECIPE FOR A POEM.

Take for your hero some thoroughbred scamp, —
Miner, or pilot, or jockey, or tramp, —
Gambler (of course), drunkard, bully, and cheat,
Facile princeps, in way of deceit;
So fond of the ladies, he's given to bigamy
(Better, perhaps, if you make it polygamy);
Pepper his talk with the raciest slang,
Culled from the haunts of his rude, vulgar gang;
Seasoned with blasphemy — lard him with curses;
Serve him up hot in your "dialect" verses —
Properly dished, he'd excite a sensation,
And tickle the taste of our delicate nation.

Old Mother English has twaddle enough;
Give us a language that 's ready and tough!
Who cares, just now, for a subject Miltonian?
Who is n't bored by a style Addisonian?
Popular heroes must wear shabby clothes!
What if their diction is cumbered with oaths!
That 's but a feature of life Occidental,
Really, at heart, they are pious and gentle.
Think, for example, how solemn and rich is
The sermon we gather from dear " Little Breeches "!
Is n't it charming — that sweet baby talk
Of the urchin who " chawed " ere he fairly could walk?

Sure, 't is no wonder bright spirits above
Singled him out for their errand of love!
I suppose I 'm a " fogy," — not up to the age, —
But I can't help recalling an earlier stage,
When a real inspiration (*divinus afflatus*)
Could be printed without any saving hiatus;
When humor was decently shrouded in rhyme,
As suited the primitive ways of the time,
And we all would have blushed had we dreamed of the rules
Which are taught us to-day in our " dialect " schools.

It may be all right, though I find it all wrong,
This queer prostitution of talent and song;
Perhaps, in our market, gold sells at a loss, —
And the public will pay better prices for dross, —
Well! 't were folly to row 'gainst a tide that has turned,
And the lesson that 's set us has got to be learned;
But I 'll make one more desperate pull to be free
Ere I swallow the brood of that " Heathen Chinee."

New York Evening Post.

PART II.

Among the Little Folk.

So every little child I see,
  With brow and spirit undefiled,
And simple faith and frolic glee,
  Finds still in me another child.

J. G. HOLLAND.

PART II.

Among the Little Folk.

—◦◦◦—

BABY-LAND.

" How many miles to Baby-land?"
  "Any one can tell;
    Up one flight,
    To the right;
  Please to ring the bell."

" What can you see in Baby-land?"
  "Little folks in white —
    Downy heads,
    Cradle-beds,
  Faces pure and bright!"

" What do they do in Baby-land?"
  "Dream and wake and play,
    Laugh and crow,
    Shout and grow;
  Jolly times have they!"

" What do they say in Baby-land?"
  "Why, the oddest things;
    Might as well
    Try to tell
  What a birdie sings!"

" Who is the Queen of Baby-land?"
  "Mother, kind and sweet;
    And her love,
    Born above,
  Guides the little feet."

GEORGE COOPER.

NELLY TELLS HOW BABY CAME.

THERE'S no use of your talking, for mamma told me so,
And if there's any one that does, my mamma ought to know;
For she has been to Europe and seen the Pope at Rome,
Though she says that was before I came to live with her at
　　　home.

You see we had no baby, — unless you call me one,
And I have grown so big, you know, 't would have to be in fun, —
When I went to see grandma, about two weeks ago,
And now we've one, a little one, that squirms and wiggles so.

And mamma says an angel came down from heaven above,
And brought this baby to her for her and me to love;
And it's got the cunningest of feet, as little as can be,
And shining eyes and curly hair, and hands you scarce can see.

And then it never cries a bit, like some bad babies do;
And papa says it looks like me — I don't think so, do you?
For I'm a girl and it's a boy, and boys I can't endure;
Unless they're babies like our own, they'll plague and tease
　　　you, sure.

But you say the angel did n't come: now you just tell me why;
The Bible says there's angels in heaven, and that's up in the
　　　sky;
And Christ loves little babies, and God made everything,
And if the angels did n't, who did our baby bring?

You can't tell: no, I guess you can't, but mamma ought to
　　　know,
For it's her baby — hers and ours — and mamma told me so;
And they don't make any cunning things like him on earth, you
　　　see,
For no wax doll, with real hair, is half so nice as he.

I know an angel brought him, and I think one brought me too;
Though I don't just now remember, and so can't tell, can you?
But mamma knows; and this I know, — the baby was n't home
When I went away, and now he is.　If you want to see him,
　　　come.

For mamma says if I am good I can kiss him every day,
And we'll kiss him now, and then go out and have a nice long
　　　play;
And if anybody asks you how babies come and go,
Why, tell them it's the angels, for mamma told me so.

　　　　　　　　　　　　　THOMAS S. COLLIER.

WELCOME, LITTLE STRANGER.

(By a Displaced Three-year-old.)

MOZZER bought a baby,
 'Ittle bitsey sing;
Sinks I mos' could put him
 Frou my yubber ying.
Ain't he awful ugly?
 Ain't he awful pink?
" Just come down from heaven " —
 Yat 's a fib, I sink.

Doctor tol' anozzer
 Great big awful lie;
Nose ain't out o' joint, zen,
 Yat ain't why I cry.
Mamma stays up in bedroom —
 Guess he makes her sick.
Frow him in the gutter,
 Beat him wiz a stick.

Cuddle him and love him!
 Call him " Blessed sing "!
Don't care if my kite ain't
 Got a bit of string!
Send me off with Bridget
 Every single day, —
" Be a good boy, Charley,
 Run away and play."

Said " I ought to love him "!
 No, I won't! no zur!
Nassy cryin' baby,
 Not got any hair.
Got all my nice kisses,
 Got my place in bed, —
Mean to take my drumsticks
 And beat him on the head.

    CHARLES FOLLEN ADAMS.

———◆———

ONLY A BABY.

(To a Little One just a Week Old.)

ONLY a baby
 'Thout any hair,
'Cept just a little
 Fuzz here and there.

Only a baby,
  Name you have none,
Barefooted and dimpled,
  Sweet little one.

Only a baby,
  Teeth none at all;
What are you good for,
  Only to squall?

Only a baby,
  Just a week old;
What are you here for,
  You little scold?

BABY'S REPLY.

Only a baby!
  What sood I be?
Lots o' big folks
  Been little like me.

Ain't dot any hair?
  'Es I have, too;
S'pos'n' I had n't,
  Dess it tood drow.

Not any teeth—
  Would n't have one;
Don't dit my dinner
  Gnawin' a bone.

What am I here for?
  'At 's petty mean;
Who 's dot a better right
  'T ever you 've seen?

What am I dood for,
  Did you say?
Eber so many sings
  Ebery day.

Tourse I squall at times,
  Sometimes I bawl;
Zey dassn't spant me,
  Taus I 'm so small.

Only a baby!
  'Es, sir, 'at 's so;
'N' if you only tood,
  You 'd be one, too.

'At 's all I 've to say,
  You 're mos' too old;
Dess I 'll det into bed,
  Toes dettin' cold.

———◆———

THE LAST ARRIVAL.

THERE came to port last Sunday night
  The queerest little craft,
Without an inch of rigging on;
  I looked and looked — and laughed!
It seemed so curious that she
  Should cross the unknown water
And moor herself within my room —
  My daughter! oh, my daughter!

Yet by these presents witness all
  She 's welcome fifty times,
And comes consigned in hope and love
  And common-metre rhymes.
She has no manifest but this;
  No flag floats o'er the water;
She 's rather new for our marine —
  My daughter! oh, my daughter!

Ring out, wild bells, and tame ones too!
  Ring out the lover's moon!
Ring in the little worsted socks!
  Ring in the bib and spoon!
Ring out the muse!   Ring in the nurse!
  Ring in the milk and water!
Away with paper, pen, and ink!
  My daughter! oh, my daughter!

GEORGE W. CABLE.

———◆———

THE "COMING MAN."

A PAIR of very chubby legs
  Encased in scarlet hose;
A pair of little stubby boots
  With rather doubtful toes;

A little kilt, a little coat,
  Cut as a mother can,
And lo! before us strides in state
  The Future's "coming man."

His eyes, perchance, will read the stars,
  And search their unknown ways;
Perchance the human heart and soul
  Will open to their gaze;
Perchance their keen and flashing glance
  Will be a nation's light, —
Those eyes that now are wistful bent
  On some "big fellow's" kite.

That brow where mighty thought will dwell
  In solemn, secret state;
Where fierce ambition's restless strength
  Shall war with future fate;
Where science from now hidden caves
  New treasures shall outpour, —
'T is knit now with a troubled doubt,
  Are two, or three cents, more?

Those lips that, in the coming years,
  Will plead, or pray, or teach;
Whose whispered words, on lightning flash,
  From world to world may reach;
That, sternly grave, may speak command,
  Or, smiling, win control, —
Are coaxing now for gingerbread
  With all a baby's soul!

Those hands — those little busy hands —
  So sticky, small, and brown,
Those hands, whose only mission seems
  To pull all order down, —
Who knows what hidden strength may lie
  Within their future grasp,
Though now 't is but a taffy-stick
  In sturdy hold they clasp?

Ah, blessings on those little hands,
  Whose work is yet undone!
And blessings on those little feet,
  Whose race is yet un-run!
And blessings on the little brain
  That has not learned to plan!
Whate'er the Future hold in store,
  God bless the "coming man"!

THE BALD-HEADED TYRANT.

OH! the quietest home on earth had I,
  No thought of trouble, no hint of care;
Like a dream of pleasure the days flew by,
  And peace had folded her pinions there.
But one day there joined in our household band
A bald-headed tyrant from No-man's-land.

Oh the despot came in the dead of night,
  And no one ventured to ask him why;
Like slaves we trembled before his might,
  Our hearts stood still when we heard him cry;
For never a soul could his power withstand,
That bald-headed tyrant from No-man's-land.

He ordered us here, and he sent us there, —
  Though never a word could his small lips speak, —
With his toothless gums and his vacant stare,
  And his helpless limbs so frail and weak;
Till I cried, in a voice of stern command,
"Go up, thou bald-head from No-man's-land!"

But his abject slaves they turned on me;
  Like the bears in Scripture they 'd rend me there,
The while they worshipped on bended knee
  The ruthless wretch with the missing hair;
For he rules them all with relentless hand,
This bald-headed tyrant from No-man's-land.

Then I searched for help in every clime,
  For peace had fled from my dwelling now,
Till I finally thought of old Father Time,
  And now before him I made my bow:
"Wilt thou deliver me out of his hand,
This bald-headed tyrant from No-man's-land?"

Old Time he looked with a puzzled stare,
  And a smile came over his features grim:
"I 'll take the tyrant under my care;
  Watch what my hour-glass does for him.
The veriest humbug that ever was planned
Is this same bald-head from No-man's-land!"

Old Time is doing his work full well:
  Much less of might does the tyrant wield;
But, ah! with sorrow my heart will swell
  And sad tears fall as I see him yield.
Could I stay the touch of that shrivelled hand,
I would keep the bald-head from No-man's-land.

For the loss of peace I have ceased to care;
　Like other vassals I 've learned, forsooth,
To love the wretch who forgot his hair
　And hurried along without a tooth;
And he rules me too with his tiny hand,
This bald-headed tyrant from No-man's-land.

MARY E. VANDYNE.

A HINT.

OUR Daisy lay down
　In her little nightgown,
And kissed me again and again,
　On forehead and cheek,
　On lips that would speak,
But found themselves shut to their gain.

Then foolish, absurd,
　To utter a word,
I asked her the question so old,
　That wife and that lover
　Ask over and over,
As if they were surer when told.

There, close at her side,
　"Do you love me?" I cried;
She lifted her golden-crowned head,
　A puzzled surprise
　Shone in her gray eyes —
" Why, that 's why I kiss you !" she said.

OUR DARLING.

BOUNDING like a football,
　Kicking at the door;
Falling from the table-top,
　Sprawling on the floor;
Smashing cups and saucers,
　Splitting dolly's head;
Putting little pussy cat
　Into baby's bed;
Building shops and houses,
　Spoiling father's hat;
Hiding mother's precious keys
　Underneath the mat;

Jumping on the fender,
  Poking at the fire;
Dancing on his little legs, —
  Legs that never tire;
Making mother's heart leap
  Fifty times a day;
Aping everything we do,
  Every word we say;
Shouting, laughing, tumbling,
  Roaring with a will,
Anywhere and everywhere,
  Never, never still;
Present — bringing sunshine;
  Absent — leaving night;
That 's our precious darling,
  That 's our heart's delight.

———◆———

THE NEW BABY.

I 'se a poor little sorrowful baby,
  For Bidget is way down tairs,
The titten has statched my finder,
  And dolly won't say her payers.
Ain't seen my bootiful mamma
  Since ever so long adoe,
And I ain't her tunningest baby
  No longer, for Bidget says so.

My mamma 's dot a new baby;
  Dod dived it, he did, yesterday;
And it kies, and it kies, *so* defful,
  I wish he would tate it away.
Don't want no sweet little sister,
  I want my dood mamma, I do,
I want her to tis me, and tis me,
  And tall me her pessus Lulu.

Oh, here tums nurse wis the baby!
  It sees me yite out of its eyes;
I dess we will keep it, and dive it
  Some tandy whenever it kies;
I dess I will dive it my dolly
  To play wis 'most every day;
And I dess, I dess — say, Bidget,
  Ask Dod not to tate it away.

WASHING–DAY.

WHILE mother is tending baby
  We 'll help her all we can ;
For I 'm her little toddlekins,
  And you 're her little man.
And Nell will bring the basket,
  For she 's the biggest daughter,
And I 'll keep rubbing, rubbing,
  And you 'll pour in the water.
And now we 'll have to hurry,
  Because it 's getting late ;
Poor dolly is n't dressed yet,
  But dolly 'll have to wait.
I 'll pour, and you can rub 'em,
  Whichever you had rather ;
But seems to me, if I keep on,
  We 'll get a quicker lather.
Maybe when mother sees us
  Taking so much troubles,
She 'll let us put our pipes in
  And blow it full of bubbles.
But now we 'll have to hurry,
  Because it 's getting late;
And dolly is n't dressed yet,
  But dolly 'll have to wait.

Hearth and Home.

————◆————

BABY'S LETTER.

DEAR ole untle, I dot oor letter :
My ole mammy, she ditten better.
She every day little bit stronger,
Don't mean to be sick berry much longer.

Daddy 's so fat, can't hardly stagger ;
Mammy says he jinks too much lager.
Dear little baby had a bad colic,
Had to take tree drops nassy paleygolic.

Toot a dose of tatnip, felt worse as ever.
Sha'n't take no more tatnip, never !
Wind on stomit, felt pooty bad,
Worse fit of sickness ever I had !

Ever had belly-ate, ole untle Bill ?
'T ain't no fun now, say what oo will.
I used to sleep all day and cry all night ;
Don't do so now, 'cause 't ain't yite.

But I 'm growin', gettin' pooty fat,
Gains 'most two pounds, only tink o' dat!
Little flannen blankets was too big before,
Nurse can't pin me in 'em no more.

Skirts so small, baby so stout,
Had to let the plaits in 'em all out.
Got a head of hair jes' as black as nite;
And big boo eyes, yat ook mighty bite.

My mammy says, never did see
Any ozzer baby half as sweet as me.
Grandma comes often, Aunt Sarah too;
Baby loves yem, baby loves oo.

Baby sends a pooty kiss to his untles all,
Aunties and cousins, — big folks and small.
Can't yite no more, so dood-by,
Bully ole untle with a glass eye.

———◆———

MY LOST BABY.

COMES little Maud and stands by my knee,
    Her soft eyes filled with a troubled joy;
And her wondering heart is perplexed to see
    Her babyhood lost in our baby boy.

For Maud was a babe but a week ago, —
    A gentle, lovable, clinging thing;
Now we are saddened but pleased to know
    The queen is dethroned and there reigns a king, —

A tiny king, with a cheek like down;
    With dark, indefinite-colored eyes;
With hair of the softest satiny brown;
    Who doubles his fists and hiccoughs and cries;

Who groans, grimaces, and paws the air,
    And twists his mouth in a meaningless smile;
Who fixes his eyes in a winkless stare,
    And seems in the deepest thought the while;

A wee small king with a comical face,
    Whom one moment we laugh at, the next caress;
A little monarch who holds his place
    By the wondrous might of his helplessness.

Come hither, my Maud, with your wistful eyes;
  Come hither, I 'll lay the small tyrant down;
I 'll gather you up in a glad surprise,
  And press to my bosom your head of brown.

Nestle down close to your mother's breast,
  Poor little babe of a week gone by;
Find for a moment a haven of rest, —
  Clasping my neck with a satisfied sigh.

Alas! I have lost her, she is no more
  The baby girl that I loved to press
Close to my heart; she 's a woman before
  This animate atom of helplessness.

My heart is sad for my girl to-day;
  In a moment babyhood's privileged years
Have passed from her life forever away, —
  We see them vanish through misty tears.

Farewell, sweet babe of a week agone!
  Thou hast reached the land of the nevermore,
And Maud's little feet are standing on
  The perilous heights of childhood's shore.

A BABY'S RATTLE.

I.

ONLY a baby's rattle,
  And yet if you offered me gold
More than my heart could dream of,
  Or jewels my hand could hold,

For that worthless toy, I should answer,
  You cannot buy the tears
Of love and joy, the remembrance
  Of all that it means for all years.

The old associations
  Of the years that have waned and fled
Lie there with the childish token
  That was clasped by a hand that is dead.

And beyond all earthly treasures
  That prowess or brain could win,
I prize that worn old plaything
  For the memories shrined therein.

There may be hope in the future
  With its dreams too bright to last,
But they lack the consecration
  That clings round thoughts of the past.

II.

She came when the May-time scattered
  May-buds upon holt and lea :
And the glint of the sunshine seemed sweeter,
  And a new song was sung by the sea.

'T was a page from the book of Creation,
  With an imprint I knew was divine,
And I felt the infinite yearning
  For the new life sprung from mine.

Ah me ! how we loved our blossom !
  And it scarce seems days ago
That she crowed and laughed in the summer,
  And faded in winter snow.

It seems like a vision remembered
  Of a death in unrestful sleep,
When fearsome thoughts come upon you
  As storms brood over the deep.

And whenever I hear the laughter
  That rings from a child at play,
I think of our dear dead snowdrop, —
  And it seems but yesterday.

III.

The May-time had changed to summer,
  And the roses of autumn come,
The birds sung blithe in the branches,
  But blither the birdie at home.

The cynic may sneer at the feeling,
  For a cold, hard creed is rife;
But I know that my love for my darling
  Was my purest thought in life.

She grew with the summer's fruitage,
  But in warm autumnal days,
She faded, it seemed like the leaflets
  That strewed the woodland ways.

4

It was hard to mark, and still harder
    To think that the hopes we kept
Must be buried away with old fancies,
    And dreams that in silence slept.

Were we never to see her joyous
    In childhood's innocent play?
Ah, no! she was called, and left us —
    And it seems but yesterday.

IV.

At last — how well I remember
    The long and lingering night,
When we watched by the tiny cradle
    Till the morning's earliest light;

And then when the desolate morning
    Shone cold through the winter bars,
Lo! God had taken our snowdrop
    To blossom beyond the stars.

It was hard to bow in submission
    When we thought of the vacant place,
And there within the cradle
    The white little baby face.

Only one thought could comfort,
    The echo of words divine,
That, tender as any mother,
    By the waters of Palestine,

He spake, who bade the children
    Draw near on the sacred sod,
When he stretched out hands of blessing, —
    "Of such is the kingdom of God"

------◆------

WATCHING FOR PAPA.

SHE always stood upon the steps
    Just by the cottage door,
Waiting to kiss me when I came
    Each night home from the store.
Her eyes were like two glorious stars,
    Dancing in heaven's own blue —
"Papa," she 'd call like a wee bird,
    "*I's looten out for oo!*"

Alas! how sadly do our lives
  Change as we onward roam!
For now no birdie voice calls out
  To bid me welcome home.
No little hands stretched out for me,
  No blue eyes dancing bright,
No baby face peeps from the door
  When I come home at night.

And yet there's comfort in the thought
  That when life's toil is o'er,
And passing through the sable flood
  I gain the brighter shore,
My little angel at the gate,
  With eyes divinely blue,
Will call with birdie voice, " Papa,
  I's looten out for oo!"

MATTIE'S WANTS AND WISHES.

I WANTS a piece of talito
  To make my doll a dress;
I does n't want a big piece —
  A yard 'll do, I guess.

I wish you 'd fred my needle,
  And find my fimble, too —
I has such heaps o' sowin',
  I don't know what to do.

My Hepsy tored her apron
  A tum'lin' down the stair;
And Cæsar 's lost his pantaloons,
  And needs anozzer pair.

I wants my Maud a bonnet,
  She has n't none at all;
And Fred must have a jacket,
  His uzzer one 's too small.

I wants to go to grandma's,
  You promised me I might;
I know she 'll like to see me —
  I wants to go to-night.

She lets me wash the dishes,
  And see in grandpa's watch —
Wish I 'd free, four pennies,
  To buy some butter-scotch.

I wants some newer mittens,
　I wish you 'd knit me some,
'Cause 'most my fingers freezes,
　They leak so in the fum.

I wored it out last summer
　A-pullin' George's sled ;
I wish you would n't laugh so —
　It hurts me in my head.

I wish I had a cooky —
　I 'm hungry 's I can be ;
If you has n't pretty large ones,
　You 'd better bring me free.

───◆───

GRAN'MA AL'US DOES.

I WANTS to mend my wagon,
　And has to have some nails ;
Just two, free will be plenty ;
　We 're goin' to haul our rails.
The splendidest cob fences
　We 're makin' ever was !
I wis' you 'd help us find 'em —
　Gran'ma al'us does.

My horse's name is " Betsey ; "
　She jumped and broke her head,
I put her in the stable
　And fed her milk and bread ;
The stable 's in the parlor, —
　We did n't make no muss ;
I wis' you 'd let it stay there —
　Gran'ma al'us does.

I 's goin' to the cornfield
　To ride on Charlie's plough,
I spect he 'd like to have me —
　I wants to go right now.
Oh, won't I " gee-up " awful,
　And " whoa " like Charlie whoas !
I wis' you would n't bozzer —
　Gran'ma never does.

I wants some bread and butter,
　I 's hungry worstest kind ;
But Freddy must n't have none —
　'Cause he would n't mind.
Put plenty of sugar on it ;
　I 'll tell you what I knows :
It 's right to put on sugar —
　Gran'ma al'us does.

THE UNFINISHED PRAYER.

"Now I lay," — repeat it, darling.
 "Lay me," lisped the tiny lips
Of my daughter, kneeling, bending
 O'er her folded finger-tips.

"Down to sleep" — "To sleep," she murmured,
 And the curly head bent low;
"I pray the Lord," I gently added;
 You can say it all, I know.

"Pray the Lord" — the sound came faintly,
 Fainter still — "My soul to keep;"
Then the tired head fairly nodded,
 And the child was fast asleep.

But the dewy eyes half opened
 When I clasped her to my breast,
And the dear voice softly whispered,
 "Mamma, God knows all the rest."

Oh, the trusting, sweet confiding
 Of the child heart ! Would that I
Thus might trust my Heavenly Father,
 He who hears my feeblest cry.

"NOW I LAY ME DOWN TO SLEEP."

GOLDEN head so lowly bending,
 Little feet so white and bare,
Dewy eyes, half shut, half opened,
 Lisping out her evening prayer.

Well she knows when she is saying,
 "Now I lay me down to sleep,"
'T is to God that she is praying, —
 Praying him her soul to keep.

Half asleep, and murmuring faintly,
 "If I should die before I wake," —
Tiny fingers clasped so saintly, —
 "I pray the Lord my soul to take."

Oh the rapture, sweet, unbroken,
  Of the soul who wrote that prayer!
Children's myriad voices floating
  Up to heaven record it there.

If, of all that has been written,
  I could choose what might be mine,
It should be that child's petition,
  Rising to the throne divine.

---◆---

IN THE FIRELIGHT.

THE fire upon the hearth is low,
  And there is stillness everywhere;
  Like troubled spirits, here and there
The firelight shadows fluttering go.
And as the shadows round me creep,
  A childish treble breaks the gloom,
  And softly from a further room
Comes: "Now I lay me down to sleep."

And, somehow, with that little prayer
  And that sweet treble in my ears,
  My thought goes back to distant years,
And lingers with a dear one there;
And as I hear the child's amen,
  My mother's faith comes back to me, —
  Crouched at her side I seem to be,
And mother holds my hands again.

Oh for an hour in that dear place!
  Oh for the peace of that dear time!
  Oh for that childish trust sublime!
Oh, for a glimpse of mother's face!
Yet, as the shadows round me creep,
  I do not seem to be alone, —
  Sweet magic of that treble tone
And "Now I lay me down to sleep!"

                              EUGENE FIELD.

---◆---

THAT BOY.

Is the house turned topsy-turvy?
  Does it ring from street to roof?
Will the racket still continue,
  Spite of all your mild reproof?
Are you often in a flutter?
  Are you sometimes thrilled with joy?
Then I have my grave suspicions
  That you have at home — that Boy.

Are your walls and tables hammered?
  Are your nerves and ink upset?
Have two eyes, so bright and roguish,
  Made you every care forget?
Have your garden beds a prowler
  Who delights but to destroy?
These are well-known indications
  That you have at home — that Boy.

Have you seen him playing circus
  With his head upon the mat,
And his heels in mid-air twinkling —
  For his audience, the cat?
Do you ever stop to listen,
  When his merry pranks annoy, —
Listen to a voice that whispers,
  You were once just like — that Boy?

Have you heard of broken windows,
  And with nobody to blame?
Have you seen a trousered urchin
  Quite unconscious of the same?
Do you love a teasing mixture
  Of perplexity and joy?
You may have a dozen daughters,
  But I know you 've got — that Boy.

THE CHILDREN'S BEDTIME.

THE clock strikes seven in the hall,
  The curfew of the children's day,
That calls each little pattering foot
  From dance and song and livelong play;
Their day, that in our wider light
Floats like a silver day-moon white,
Nor in our darkness sinks to rest,
But sinks within a golden west.

Ah, tender hour that sends a drift
  Of children's kisses through the house,
And cuckoo-notes of sweet "Good-night,"
  And thoughts of home and heaven arouse;
And a soft stir of sense and heart,
As when the bee and blossom part;
And little feet that patter slower,
Like the last droppings of the shower.

And in the children's rooms aloft
  What blossom shapes do gayly slip
Their dainty sheaths, and rosy run
  From clasping hand and kissing lip.
A naked sweetness to the eye —
Blossom and babe and butterfly
In witching one so dear a sight !
An ecstasy of life and light.

And, ah, what lovely witcheries
  Bestrew the floor, — an empty sock,
By vanished dance and song left loose
  As dead bird's throat ; a tiny smock
That, sure, upon some meadow grew,
And drank the heaven-sweet rains ; a shoe
Scarce bigger than an acorn-cup ;
Frocks that seem flowery meads cut up.

Then lily-drest in angel-white
  To mother's knee they trooping come ;
The soft palms fold like kissing shells,
  And they and we go shining home, —
Their bright heads bowed and worshipping
As though some glory of the spring,
Some daffodil that mocks the day,
Should fold his golden palms and pray.

And gates of Paradise swing wide
  A moment's space in soft accord,
And those dread angels, Life and Death,
  A moment veil the flaming sword,
As o'er the weary world forlorn
From Eden's secret heart is borne
That breath of Paradise most fair,
Which mothers call the " children's prayer."

Ah, deep, pathetic mystery !
  The world's great woe unconscious hung,
A rain-drop on a blossom's lip,
  White innocence that woos our wrong,
And love divine that looks again,
Unconscious of the cross and pain,
From sweet child-eyes, and in that child
Sad earth and heaven reconciled.

Then, kissed, on beds we lay them down,
  As fragrant-white as clover's sod ;
And all the upper floors grow hushed
  With children's sleep, and dews of God.
And as our stars their beams do hide,
The stars of twilight, opening wide,
Take up the heavenly tale at even,
And light us on to God and heaven.

THE CHILDREN'S MUSIC.

WE asked where the magic came from
  That made her so wondrous fair,
As she stood with the sunlight touching
  Her gloss of golden hair.
And her blue eyes looked toward heaven
  As though they could see God there.
"Hush!" said the child, "can't you hear it,
  The music that 's everywhere?"

God help us! we could not hear it,
  Our hearts were heavy with pain;
We heard men toiling and wrangling,
  We heard the whole world complain;
And the sound of a mocking laughter
  We heard again and again,
But we lost all faith in the music,
  We had listened so long in vain.

"Can't you hear it?" the young child whispered,
  And sadly we answered, "No.
We might have fancied we heard it
  In the days of long ago;
But the music is all a delusion,
  Our reason has told us so,
And you will forget that you heard it,
  When you know the sound of woe."

Then one spoke out from among us
  Who had nothing left to fear;
Who had given his life for others,
  And been repaid with a sneer.
And his face was lit with a glory,
  And his voice was calm and clear;
And he said, "I can hear the music
  Which the little children hear."

                                F. M. OWEN.

CREEPING UP THE STAIRS.

IN the soft falling twilight
  Of a weary, weary day,
With a quiet step I entered
  Where the children were at play;
I was brooding o'er some trouble
  Which had met me unawares,
When a little voice came ringing:
  "Me is creeping up the stairs."

Ah, it touched the tenderest heart-strings
　　With a breath and force divine,
And such melodies awakened,
　　As no wording can define.
And I turned to see our darling, —
　　All forgetful of my cares,
When I saw the little creature
　　Slowly creeping up the stairs.

Step by step she slowly clambered
　　On her little hands and knees,
Keeping up a constant chatter,
　　Like a magpie in the trees,
Till at last she reached the topmost,
　　When, o'er all her world's affairs,
She, delighted, stood a victor
　　After creeping up the stairs.

Fainting heart, behold an image
　　Of man's brief and struggling life,
Whose best prizes must be captured
　　With a noble, earnest strife;
Onward, upward, reaching ever,
　　Bending to the weight of cares,
Hoping, fearing, still expecting,
　　We go creeping up the stairs.

On their steps may be no carpet,
　　By their side may be no rail,
Hands and knees may often pain us,
　　And the heart may almost fail;
Still above there is the glory
　　Which no sinfulness impairs,
With its rest and joy forever,
　　After creeping up the stairs.

Burlington Hawkeye.　　　　　　REV. W. S. McFETRIDGE.

LITTLE GOLDENHAIR.

GOLDENHAIR climbed upon grandpapa's knee!
Dear little Goldenhair! tired was she —
All the day busy as busy could be!

Up in the morning as soon as 't was light —
Up with the birds and butterflies bright,
Skipping about till the coming of night.

Grandpapa toyed with the curls on her head;
" What has my darling been doing?" he said,
" Since she rose, with the sun, from her bed?"

" Pitty much ! " answered the sweet little one ;
" I cannot tell — so much things I have done :
Played with my dolly and feeded my bun.

" And then I jumped with my little jump-rope,
And I made bubbles out of some water and soap —
Bootiful worlds ! mamma's castles of hope !

" I afterwards readed in my picture-book ;
And Bella and I we went out to look
For the smooth little fishes by the side of the brook.

" And then I came home and eated my tea,
And climbed up on grandpapa's knee ;
And I jes as tired as tired can be ! "

Lower and lower the little head pressed,
Until it had dropped upon grandpapa's breast !
Dear little Goldenhair ! sweet be thy rest !

We are but children ; the things that we do
Are as sports of a babe to the Infinite view,
That marks all our weakness, and pities it, too.

God grant that when night overshadows our way,
And we shall be called to account for our day,
He shall find us as guileless as Goldenhair lay !

And oh ! when aweary, may we be so blest
As to sink like the innocent child to our rest,
And to feel ourselves clasped to the Infinite breast !

F. BURGE SMITH.

BEAUTIFUL GRANDMAMMA.

GRANDMAMMA sits in her quaint arm-chair, —
Never was lady more sweet and fair !
Her gray locks ripple like silver shells,
And her brow its own calm story tells
Of a gentle life and a peaceful even,
A trust in God and a hope in heaven !

Little girl Mary sits rocking away
In her own low seat, like some winsome fay ;
Two dolly babies her kisses share,
And another one lies by the side of her chair.
Mary is fair as the morning dew —
Cheeks of roses and ribbons of blue !

" Say, grandmamma," says the pretty elf,
" Tell me a story about yourself.
When you were little what did you play?
Was you good or naughty, the whole long day?
Was it hundreds and hundreds of years ago?
And what makes your soft hair as white as snow?

" Did you have a mamma to hug and kiss?
And a dolly like this, and this, and this?
Did you have a pussy like my little Kate?
Did you go to bed when the clock struck eight?
Did you have long curls and beads like mine?
And a new silk apron, with ribbons fine? "

Grandmamma smiled at the little maid,
And laying aside her knitting, she said:
" Go to my desk and a red box you 'll see;
Carefully lift it and bring it to me."
So Mary put her dollies away and ran,
Saying, " I 'll be as careful as ever I can."

Then grandmamma opened the box: and lo!
A beautiful child with throat like snow,
Lips just tinted like pink shells rare,
Eyes of hazel and golden hair,
Hands all dimpled, and teeth like pearls —
Fairest and sweetest of little girls!

" Oh, who is it? " cried winsome May;
" How I wish she was here to-day!
Would n't I love her like everything,
And give her my new carnelian ring!
Say, dear grandmamma, who can she be? "
" Darling," said grandmamma, " that child was me! "

May looked long at the dimpled grace,
And then at the saint-like, fair old face.
" How funny! " she cried, with a smile and a kiss,
" To have such a dear little grandma as this!
Still," she added, with a smiling zest,
" I think, dear grandma, I like *you* best! "

So May climbed on the silken knee,
And grandma told her her history —
What plays she played, what toys she had,
How at times she was naughty, or good, or sad.
" But the best thing you did," said May, " don't you see?
Was to grow a beautiful grandma for me! "

THE BABY OVER THE WAY.

ACROSS in my neighbor's window,
  With its drapings of satin and lace,
I see, 'neath a crown of ringlets,
  A baby's innocent face.
His feet in their wee red slippers
  Are tapping the polished glass,
And the crowd in the street look upward,
  And nod and smile as they pass.

Just here in *my* cottage window,
  In the rays of the noonday sun,
With a patch on his faded apron,
  Stands my own little one.
His face is as pure and handsome
  As the baby's over the way,
And he keeps my heart from breaking
  At my toiling every day.

Sometimes when the day is ended,
  And I sit in the dusk to rest,
With the face of my sleepy darling
  Hugged close to my lonely breast,
I pray that my neighbor's baby
  May not catch heaven's roses, all;
But that some may crown the forehead
  Of my loved one as they fall.

And when I draw the stockings
  From his little tired feet,
And kiss the rosy dimples
  In his limbs so round and sweet,
I think of the dainty garments
  Some little children wear,
And frown that my God withholds them
  From *mine*, so pure and fair.

May God forgive my envy,
  I knew not what I said;
My heart is crushed and humbled:
  My neighbor's boy is dead.
I saw the little coffin
  As they carried it out to-day;
A mother's heart is breaking
  In the mansion over the way.

The light is fair in my window,
  The blossoms bloom at my door;
My boy is chasing the sunbeams
  That dance on the cottage floor;

The roses of health are blushing
  On my darling's cheek to-day;
But baby is *gone* from the window
  Of the house that's over the way.

REV. WASHINGTON GLADDEN.

FRED ENGLEHARDT'S BABY.

DRU as I leev, most efry day
I laugh me wild to saw der way
My schmall young baby dries to play —
        Dot funny leetle baby.

When I look of dem leetle toes,
Und saw dot funny leetle nose,
Und hear der way dot rooster crows —
        I schmile like I vas grazy.

Sometimes der comes a leetle shquall,
Dots ven der vindy vind does crawl
Right in his leetle shtomach schmall —
        Dot's too bad for der baby.

Dot makes him sing at night so shweet,
Und gorryparric he must eat,
Und I must chump shpry on my feet
        To help dot leetle baby.

He bulls my nose und kicks my hair,
Und crawls me ofer everywhere,
Und schlobber me — but what I care?
        Dot vas my schmall young baby.

Around my head dot leetle arm
Vas shquozh me all so nice und warm.
Oh, may dere never come some harm
        To dot schmall leetle baby.

CHARLES FOLLEN ADAMS.

LEEDLE YAWCOB STRAUSS.

I HAF a vunny leedle poy
  Vat gomes schust to my knee;
Der queerest schap, der greatest rogue
  As efer you did see.
He runs und jumps und smashes dings
  In all parts of der house, —
But what of dot? He vas mine son,
  Mine leedle Yawcob Strauss.

He get der measles und der mumbs,
   Und eferyding dot 's out ;
He spills mine glass of lager beer,
   Puts schnuff into mine kraut ;
He fills mine pipe with Limburg cheese —
   Dot vas der roughest chouse ;
I 'd dake dot from no oder poy
   But leedle Yawcob Strauss.

He dakes der milkpan for a drum,
   Und cuts mine cane in dwo,
To make der shticks to beat it mit —
   Mine cracious, dot vas drue !
I dinks mine head vas schplit abart,
   He kicks up such a touse, —
But nefer mind, der poys vas few
   Like dot schmall Yawcob Strauss.

He asks me questions sooch as dese .
   Who baints mine nose so red ?
Who vas it cut dot schmoot blace oudt
   Vrom der hair upon my head ?
Und vere der plaze goes vrom der lamp
   Vene'er der glim I douse ? —
How gan I all dese tings eggsblain
   To dot schmall Yawcob Strauss ?

I somedimes dink I schall go vild
   Mid sooch a grazy poy,
Und vish vonce more I gould haf rest
   Und beaseful dimes enshoy ;
But ven he vas aschleep in bed,
   So quiet as a mouse,
I brays der Lord, " Dake anydings,
   But leaf dot Yawcob Strauss."

Indianapolis Sentinel.   CHARLES FOLLEN ADAMS.

—◆—

THE GOODEST MOTHER.

EVENING was falling, cold and dark,
   And people hurried along the way
As if they were longing soon to mark
   Their own home candle's cheering ray.

Before me toiled in the whirling wind
   A woman with bundles great and small,
And after her tugged, a step behind,
   The Bundle she loved the best of all.

A dear little rolly-poly boy
  With rosy cheeks, and a jacket blue,
Laughing and chattering full of joy,
  And here 's what he said — I tell you true :

" You 're the goodest mother that ever was."
  A voice as clear as a forest bird's ;
And I 'm sure the glad young heart had cause
  To utter the sweet of the lovely words.

Perhaps the woman had worked all day
  Washing or scrubbing ; perhaps she sewed ;
I knew, by her weary footfall's way,
  That life for her was an uphill road.

But here was a comfort. Children dear,
  Think what a comfort you might give
To the very best friend you can have here,
  The lady fair in whose house you live,

If once in a while you 'd stop and say, —
  In task or play for a moment pause,
And tell her in sweet and winning way,
  " You 're the GOODEST mother that ever was."

THE COB HOUSE.

WILLY and Charley, eight and ten,
  Were under the porch in the noonday heat ;
I could see and hear the little men,
  Unseen, myself, in the window-seat.

Will on a cob house was hard at work,
  With a zeal that was funny enough to me.
At eight one has hardly learned to shirk ;
  That comes later, — as you will see.

For Charley, by virtue of riper age,
  Did nothing but stand and criticise ;
His hands in his pockets, stage by stage
  He watched the tottering castle rise.

" And now, after all your fuss," says he,
  " S'posin' it tumbles down again ? "
" Oh," Will answers as cool as could be,
  " Of course I should build it better then."

Charley shook sagely his curly head,
  Opened his eyes of dancing brown,
And then for a final poser said,
  " But s'posin' it always kept tumblin' down ? "

Will, however, was not of the stuff
  At a loss to be taken so.
"Why, then," he answered ready enough,
  "I should keep on building it better, you know."

And, seeing the wise world's wisest knot
  Cut at a stroke with such simple skill,
Older people than Charley, I thought,
  Might learn a lesson of Master Will.

KATE PUTNAM OSGOOD.

CARD HOUSES.

My little niece and I — I read
  My Plato in my easy-chair;
And she was building on the floor
  A pack of cards with wondrous care.

We worked in silence, but alas!
  Among the cards a mighty spill,
And then the little ape exclaimed,
  "Well! Such is life! Look, Uncle Will!"

I gave a start and dropped my book, —
  It was the "Phædo" I had read, —
A sympathetic current thrilled
  Like lightning through my heart and head.

I eyed with curious awe the child,
  The unconscious Sibyl, where she sat,
Whose thoughtless tongue could babble forth
  Strange parables of life and fate.

Yet such is life! a Babel house,
  A common doom hath tumbled all,
King, queen, and knave, and plain and trump, —
  A motley crew in motley fall!

We rear our hopes, no Pharaoh's tomb,
  Nor brass, could build so sure a name,
But, soon or late, a sad collapse,
  And great the ruin of the same.

Ah, such is life! Oh, sad and strange
  That love and wisdom so ordain!
Some ere the builder's hands have yet
  One card against another lain;

Some when the house is tiny still ;
　　Some when you 've built a little more ;
And some when patience hath achieved
　　A second, third, or higher floor.

Or should you win the topmost stage,
　　Yet is the strength but toil and pain —
And here the tiny voice rejoined,
　　" But I can build it up again."

My height of awe was reached. Can babes
　　Behold what reason scans in vain ?
Ah, childhood is divine, I thought, —
　　Yes, Lizzie, build it up again.

New York Graphic.

BERTIE'S PHILOSOPHY.

Small boy Bertie,
　　Drumming on the pane,
Looking at the chickens
　　Draggled with the rain.

Little philosopher
　　Wrinkles his brow,
Says, " I wonder —
　　I don't see how.

" Where do chickens come from ?
　　Mamma, please to tell.
Yes, I know they come from eggs,
　　Know *that* very well.

"Course the old hen hatched 'em,
　　I know *that ;* but then —
Won't you tell me truly,
　　Where 'd they get the hen ?

" S'posin' you were my boy,
　　All the one I had,
And big folks would n't tell you things,
　　Should n't you feel bad ?

" Every single thing you say
　　I knew years ago ;
Where that first hen came from,
　　Is what I want to know."

Providence Journal.　　　　　　　　　　Eva M. Tappan

BOYS' RIGHTS.

I WONDER now if any one
  In this broad land has heard
In favor of downtrodden boys
  One solitary word?
We hear enough of " woman's rights,"
  And " rights of workingmen,"
Of " equal rights," and " nation's rights,"
  But pray just tell us when
Boys' Rights were ever spoken of?
  Why, we've become so used
To being snubbed by every one,
  And slighted and abused,
That when one is polite to us,
  We open wide our eyes,
And stretch them in astonishment
  To nearly twice their size !
Boys seldom dare to ask their friends
  To venture in the house ;
It don't come natural at all
  To creep round like a mouse.
And if we should forget ourselves
  And make a little noise,
Then ma or auntie sure would say,
  " Oh, my ! those dreadful boys !"
The girls bang on the piano
  In peace, but if the boys
Attempt a tune with fife and drum,
  It 's " Stop that horrid noise !"
" That horrid noise !" just think of it,
  When sister never fails
To make a noise three times as bad
  With everlasting " scales."
Insulted thus, we lose no time
  In beating a retreat ;
So off we go to romp and tear
  And scamper in the street.
No wonder that so many boys
  Such wicked men become ;
'T were better far to let them have
  Their plays and games at home.
Perhaps that text the teacher quotes
  Sometimes, — " Train up a child," —
Means only, train the little girls,
  And let the boys run wild.
But patience, and the time shall come
  When we will all be men,
And when it does, I rather think
  Wrongs will be righted then.

CARRIE MAY.

ROSEBUD'S FIRST BALL.

"'T is really time you were out, I think,"
  Said Lady Rose to her daughter small;
"So I 'll send my invitations round,
  And give you, my dear, a splendid ball.

"We 'd best decide on your toilet first;
  Your sister Jacqueminot wore dark red;
But you are so much smaller than she,
  I think you must wear pale pink instead.

"Then, whom to invite: we can't ask all,
  And yet it 's hardest of all to tell
The flowers from weeds.   Indeed, last year
  I snubbed Field Daisy, and now she 's a belle.

"We 'll ask the Pansies, they 're always in
  The best society everywhere;
The Lilies, Heliotropes, and Pinks,
  Geraniums, Fuchsias, must sure be there.

"Miss Mignonette is so very plain,
  A favorite, though, — I 'll put her down;
The Violets, I think, are away;
  They 're always the first to leave for town.

"The Larkspurs are such old-fashioned things
  It 's not worth while asking them to come;
The Zinnias are coarse, Bergamots stiff,
  The Marigolds better off at home.

"Miss Morning Glory I 'd like to ask,
  But then, she never goes out at night;
She 's such a delicate thing, she says,
  She scarce can bear a very strong light.

"The Verbenas, I know, will be put out
  If we don't ask them; the Petunias, too.
They are not quite *au fait*, but then, my dear,
  They 're such near neighbors, what 's one to do?

"I 'll make out my list at once, for there
  A butterfly is coming this way;
I 'll send my invitations by him, —
  He 'll go the rounds without delay.

"Dear! dear! to think that to-morrow night
  You 'll really be out.   Now listen, my child:
Don't go much with your cousin Sweet Brier;
  He 's very nice, but inclined to be wild."

New York Star.

THE LITTLE CONQUEROR.

" 'T WAS midnight ; not a sound was heard
    Within the " — " Papa, won't 'ou 'ook
An' see my pooty 'ittle house ?
    I wis' 'ou would n't wead 'ou book — "

" Within the palace where the king
    Upon his couch in anguish lay — "
" Papa, pa-pa, I wis' 'ou 'd tum
    An' have a 'ittle tonty play — "

" No gentle hand was there to bring
    The cooling draught, or cool his brow ;
His courtiers and his pages gone — "
    " Tum, papa, tum ; I want 'ou now — "

Down goes the book with needless force,
    And with expression far from mild ;
With sullen air and clouded brow
    I seat myself beside my child.

Her little trusting eyes of blue
    With mute surprise gaze in my face,
As if in its expression stern
    Reproof and censure she could trace.

Anon her little bosom heaves,
    Her rosy lips begin to curl ;
And with a quivering chin she sobs,
    " Papa don't love his 'ittle dirl ! "

King, palace, book, are all forgot ;
    My arms are round my darling thrown, —
The thundercloud has burst, and lo !
    Tears fall and mingle with her own.

" LULU."

" MIDGET, gypsy, big-eyed elf, little Kitty Clover,
What have you been playing at for this hour and over ?
Where have you been wandering, in the name of wonder ?
Were n't you frightened at the wind ? Are you fond of thunder ?
Were you in a fairies' cave while the rain was falling,
With your ears sewn tightly up, not to hear me calling ?
    Who has taught your hair to curl ?
    Where 's your apron, dirty girl ? "

"Now my brains is all mussed up, got too big a headful;
Fifteen questions at a time mixes me up dreadful.
Course I been a visiting, me and Rainy Weather, —
Sure to find the birds at home when we go together;
Guess my ears was full of songs so I did n't hear you,
Else because you stayed at home I got too far from near you.
    Once some little thing said low,
      'Mamma wants you, Lu, I know.'

"'Spect it was that funny bird that kept and kept a singing,
While the rain was coming down and thunder-bells was ringing.
'Oh, you goosie-bird,' I said, 'rains like sixty-seven,
And your song 'll get so wet it can't fly up to heaven;
Did you swallow it one day when you was a drinking?
Is it all the talk you 've got, or only just your thinking?
      Or do songs come up and sprout,
        And rain makes 'em blossom out?'

"Then the bird came close to me, — mamma, he did, truly, —
Said, 'I never told before, but I 'll tell you, Luly:
One day God got tired of heaven and the angels' singing,
Thought their harps were out of tune, made such awful dinging;
So he sang a piece of song, put some feathers round it,
Then he threw it in a tree, where some bird's name found it;
      And he mixed the song and name
        Till they grew the very same.'

"Mamma, what you smiling at? Had n't you better hold me?
I 'll be tired a saying through what the birdie told me:
God sends word down by the rain when he wants to hear him, —
That is why the whisper-drops tinkle by so near him.
Should you think his song would lose? I can tell you better!
It don't have so far to go as my grandma's letter;
      Earth and heaven 's so close apart,
        God can catch it in his heart.

"'T was the wind that curled my hair, — did n't he fix it funny?
Combed and twisted it like this 'thout a spec' of money;
Where 's my apron? Let me see! I must think it over —
'Fraid you 've got a naughty girl for your Kitty Clover,
'Cause I gave that to the brook with the big stones in it,
Where it has to run across every little minute;
      Covered 'em all dry and neat,
        So my brook won't wet its feet!"

                                        CARRIE W. THOMPSON.

BABY IN CHURCH.

AUNT NELLIE had fashioned a dainty thing
    Of hamburg and ribbon and lace,
And mamma had said, as she settled it round
    Our Baby's beautiful face,

Where the dimples play and the laughter lies
Like sunbeams hid in her violet eyes, —
" If the day is pleasant, and Baby is good,
She may go to church and wear her new hood."

Then Ben, aged six, began to tell,
　In elder-brotherly way,
How very, very good she must be
　If she went to church next day.
He told of the church, the choir, and the crowd,
And the man up in front who talked so loud ;
But she must not talk, nor laugh, nor sing,
But just sit as quiet as anything.

And so, on a beautiful Sabbath in May,
　When the fruit-buds burst into flowers
(There was n't a blossom on bush or tree
　So fair as this blossom of ours),
All in her white dress, dainty and new,
Our Baby sat in the family pew.
The grand, sweet music, the reverent air,
The solemn hush, and the voice of prayer,

Filled all her baby soul with awe,
　As she sat in her little place,
And the holy look that the angels wear
　Seemed pictured upon her face.
And the sweet words uttered so long ago
Came into my mind with a rhythmic flow, —
" Of such is the kingdom of heaven," said He,
And I knew He spake of such as she.

The sweet-voiced organ pealed forth again,
　The collection-box came around,
And Baby dropped her penny in,
　And smiled at the chinking sound.
Alone in the choir Aunt Nellie stood,
Waiting the close of the soft prelude,
To begin her solo.　High and strong
She struck the first note ; clear and long

She held it, and all were charmed, but one
　Who, with all the might she had,
Sprang to her little feet and cried,
　" Aunt Nellie, you 's being bad ! "
The audience smiled, the minister coughed,
The little boys in the corner laughed,
The tenor shook like an aspen-leaf,
And hid his face in his handkerchief.

And poor Aunt Nellie could never tell
    How she finished that terrible strain,
But says nothing on earth could tempt
    Her to go through the scene again.
So we have decided, perhaps 't is best,
For her sake, and ours, and all the rest,
That we wait, may be a year or two,
Ere our Baby re-enter the family pew.

WHO'LL TEND BABY?

" WHO'LL take care of the baby ? "
Says Joe to Sam, in fierce debate
    Upon the woman question ;
" You 've answered well all other points,
    Now here 's my last suggestion :
When woman goes to cast her vote, —
    Some miles away, it may be, —
Who, then, I ask, will stay at home
    To rock and tend the baby ? "

Quoth Sam : " I own you 've made my case
    Appear a little breezy ;
I hoped you 'd pass this question by,
    And give me something easy.
But since the matter seems to turn
    On this one as its axis,
Just get the one who rocked it when
    She went to pay her taxes ! "

                                        E. E

HER NAME.

IN search from "A" to "Z" they passed,
And "Marguerita" chose at last;
But thought it sounded far more sweet
To call the baby "Marguerite."
When grandma saw the little pet,
She called her "darling Margaret."
Next Uncle Jack and Cousin Aggie
Sent cup and spoon to "little Maggie."
And grandpapa the right must beg
To call the lassie "bonnie Meg;"
(From "Marguerita" down to "Meg")
And now she 's simply "little Peg."

WHY?

WHAT did the baby come for?
  That was the question trite
The neighbors asked of each other
  That stormy winter night.
What was the need of children?
  'T was hard enough before
To keep care out of the window, —
  The gray wolf from the door.

Out of the wintry barren,
  Over the sleeping town,
Out of the cold, dark heaven
  Drifted the snow-flakes down.
Within the low, old cottage
  Flickered the candle's flame
In the dusk of the early dawning,
  But never an answer came.

What did the baby come for?
  A woman's heart could tell:
At touch of the tiny fingers,
  Like to a fairy spell,
A heart that was hard with doubting,
  A soul that was barred with sin,
Opened a tide from God's ocean,
  The mother-love swept in.

What did the baby come for?
  A strong man's heart had grown,
Through poverty's constant grinding,
  As hard as the nether stone.
Only a baby's prattle,
  And yet, O wonderful song
That made a man's heart grow lighter,
  Made a man's hands grow strong!

Was ever a spring or summer
  That vanished on wings so fleet?
Ah! 't was a joy to labor,
  When living had grown so sweet!
Care never came near the window,
  And poverty, gaunt and grim,
Never stepped over the threshold, —
  There was no place for him.

                              MAUD MOORE.

"ONLY A BIT OF CHILDHOOD THROWN AWAY."

WHAT did the baby go for ?
  Softly the summer night
Fell like a benediction
  On the baby, shrouded white.
Only two golden summers !
  'T was not a life, we say,
" Only a bit of childhood
  The great God threw away."

Out on the dusky meadow,
  Over the slumbering town,
Out of the silent heaven
  Brightly the stars looked down.
What did the baby go for?
  Flickered the dawning's flame
Into the cottage window,
  But never an answer came.

What did the baby go for?
  Oh, thou shadow of death !
Oh, thou angel ! thou demon
  Icy of touch and breath !
We cry to the sunlit heavens,
  And no voice answereth.

Will there ever come a morning
  When, with our tears all dried,
Resting in fair green pastures
  The river of life beside,
We shall know, beyond all doubting,
  Just why the baby died?

Oh, thank God for the children !
  Ay, give thanks, — though we lay
Under the " sod of the valley "
  The fairest of all away.
Thank Him for those that leave us,
  Thank Him for those that stay.

MAUD MOORE.

PART III.

For Christmas Tide.

Ring out, ye crystal spheres,
Once bless our human ears,
* If ye have power to touch our senses so ;*
And let your silver chime
Move in melodious time,
* And let the bass of heaven's deep organ blow ;*
And with your ninefold harmony,
Make up full consort to angelic symphony.

                                        MILTON.

PART III.

For Christmas Tide.

———

MERRY CHRISTMAS.

In the rush of the merry morning,
  When the red burns through the gray,
And the wintry world lies waiting
  For the glory of the day;
Then we hear a fitful rushing
  Just without upon the stair,
See two white phantoms coming,
  Catch the gleam of sunny hair.

Are they Christmas fairies stealing
  Rows of little socks to fill?
Are they angels floating hither
  With their message of good-will?
What sweet spell are these elves weaving,
  As like larks they chirp and sing?
Are these palms of peace from heaven
  That these lovely spirits bring?

Rosy feet upon the threshold,
  Eager faces peeping through,
With the first red ray of sunshine,
  Chanting cherubs come in view;
Mistletoe and gleaming holly,
  Symbols of a blessed day,
In their chubby hands they carry,
  Streaming all along the way.

Well we know them, never weary
  Of this innocent surprise;
Waiting, watching, listening always
  With full hearts and tender eyes,
While our little household angels,
  White and golden in the sun,
Greet us with the sweet old welcome, —
  " Merry Christmas, every one ! "

FAIRY FACES.

Out of the mists of childhood,
  Steeped in a golden glory,
Come dreamy forms and faces,
  Snatches of song and story;
Whispers of sweet, still faces;
  Rays of ethereal glimmer,
That gleam like sunny heavens,
  Ne'er to grow colder or dimmer:
Now far in the distance, now shining near,
Lighting the snows of the shivering year.

Faces there are that tremble,
  Bleared with a silent weeping,
Weird in a shadowy sorrow,
  As if endless vigil keeping.
Faces of dazzling brightness,
  With childlike radiance lighted,
Flashing with many a beauty,
  Nor care nor time had blighted.
But o'er them all there's a glamour thrown,
Bright with the dreamy distance alone.

Aglow in the Christmas halo,
  Shining with heavenly lustre,
These are the fairy faces
  That round the hearthstone cluster.
These the deep, tender records,
  Sacred in all their meetness,
That, wakening purest fancies,
  Soften us with their sweetness;
As, gathered where flickering fagots burn,
We welcome the holy season's return.

———◆———

A CHRISTMAS SONG.

The oak is a strong and stalwart tree,
  And it lifts its branches up,
And catches the dew right gallantly
  In many a dainty cup;
And the world is brighter and better made
  Because of the woodman's stroke,
Descending in sun, or falling in shade,
  On the sturdy form of the oak.
But stronger, I ween, in apparel green,
  And trappings so fair to see,
With its precious freight for small and great,
  Is the beautiful Christmas Tree.

The elm is a kind and goodly tree,
  With its branches bending low;
The heart is glad when its form we see,
  And we list to the river's flow.
Ay, the heart is glad and the pulses bound,
  And joy illumines the face,
Whenever a goodly elm is found,
  Because of its beauty and grace.
But kinder, I ween, more goodly in mien,
  With branches more drooping and free,
The tint of whose leaves fidelity weaves,
  Is the beautiful Christmas Tree.

The maple is supple and lithe and strong,
  And claimeth our love anew,
When the days are listless and quiet and long,
  And the world is fair to view;
And later, — as beauties and graces unfold, —
  A monarch right regally drest,
With streamers aflame, and pennons of gold,
  It seemeth of all the best.
More lissome, I ween, the brightness and sheen,
  And the coloring sunny and free,
And the banners soft, that are held aloft
  By the beautiful Christmas Tree.

St. Nicholas.   MRS. HATTIE S. RUSSELL.

A CHRISTMAS CAMP ON THE SAN GABR'EL.

LAMAR and his Rangers camped at dawn on the banks of the
    San Gabr'el,
Under the mossy live-oaks, in the heart of a lonely dell;
With the cloudless Texas sky above, and the musquite grass
    below,
And all the prairie lying still, in a misty, silvery glow.

The sound of the horses cropping grass, the fall of a nut, full
    ripe,
The stir of a weary soldier, or the tap of a smoked-out pipe,
Fell only as sounds in a dream may fall upon a drowsy ear,
Till the Captain said, "'T is Christmas Day! so, boys, we'll
    spend it here;

"For the sake of our homes and our childhood, we'll give the
    day its dues."
Then some leaped up to prepare the feast, and some sat still
    to muse,
And some pulled scarlet yupon-berries and wax-white mistle-
    toe,
To garland the stand-up rifles, — for Christmas has no foe.

And every heart had a pleasant thought, or a tender memory,
Of unforgotten Christmas Tides that nevermore might be;
They felt the thrill of a mother's kiss, they heard the happy
    psalm,
And the men grew still, and all the camp was full of a gracious
    calm.

"Halt!" cried the sentinel; and lo! from out of the brush-
    wood near
There came, with weary, fainting step, a man in mortal fear, —
A brutal man, with a tiger's heart, and yet he made this plea:
"I am dying of hunger and thirst, so do what you will with me."

They knew him well: who did not know the cruel San Sabatan, —
The robber of the Rio Grande, who spared not any man?
In low, fierce tones they spoke his name, and looked at a coil
    of rope;
And the man crouched down in abject fear — how could he dare
    to hope?

The Captain had just been thinking of the book his mother read,
Of a Saviour born on Christmas Day, who bowed on the cross
    his head;
Blending the thought of his mother's tears with the holy
    mother's grief, —
And when he saw San Sabatan, he thought of the dying thief.

He spoke to the men in whispers, and they heeded the words
    he said,
And brought to the perishing robber, water and meat and
    bread.
He ate and drank like a famished wolf, and then lay down to rest,
And the camp, perchance, had a stiller feast for its strange
    Christmas guest.

But, or ever the morning dawned again, the Captain touched
    his hand:
"Here is a horse, and some meat and bread; fly to the Rio
    Grande!
Fly for your life! We follow hard; touch nothing on your
    way —
Your life was only spared because 't was Jesus Christ's birth-
    day."

He watched him ride as the falcon flies, then turned to the
    breaking day;
The men awoke, the Christmas berries were quietly cast away;
And, full of thought, they saddled again, and rode off into the
    west —
May God be merciful to them, as they were merciful to their
    guest!

AMELIA BARR.

CHRISTMAS TREASURES.

I count my treasures o'er with care:
    The little toy that baby knew,
    A little sock of faded hue,
A little lock of golden hair.

Long years ago this Christmas time
    My little one, my all to me,
    Sat robed in white upon my knee,
And heard the merry Christmas chime.

"Tell me, my little golden-head,
    If Santa Claus should come to-night,
    What shall he bring my baby bright,
What treasure for my boy?" I said.

And then he named the little toy,
    While in his honest, mournful eyes
    There came a look of sweet surprise,
That spoke his quiet, trustful joy.

And as he lisped his evening prayer,
    He asked the boon with childish grace,
    Then, toddling to the chimney-place,
He hung his little stocking there.

That night, as lengthening shadows crept,
    I saw the white-winged angels come
    With heavenly music to our home,
And kiss my darling as he slept.

They must have heard his baby prayer,
    For in the morn, with smiling face,
    He toddled to the chimney-place,
And found the little treasure there.

They came again one Christmas Tide,
    That angel host so fair and white,
    And, singing all the Christmas night,
They lured my darling from my side.

A little sock, a little toy,
    A little lock of golden hair,
    The Christmas music on the air,
A watching for my baby boy.

But if again that angel train
    And golden head come back to me
    To bear me to eternity,
My watching will not be in vain.

EUGENE FIELD.

6

CHRISTMAS OUTCASTS.

CHRIST died for all; and on the hearts of all
   Who gladly decorate their cheerful homes
At Christmas Tide, this blessed truth should fall,
That they may mix some honey with the gall
   Of those to whom a Christmas never comes.

The poor are everywhere in Nature's course,
   Yet they may still control some sweetened crumbs,
No matter what they lack in hearts or purse;
But there are those whose better fate is worse,
   To whom no day of Christmas ever comes.

The man who wildly throws away his chance,
   An outcast from all cheerful hearts and homes,
Who may not mingle where the happy dance,
Nor gain from loving eyes one kindly glance,
   Is he to whom no Christmas ever comes.

The man condemned in hidden ways to grope,
   At sight of whom each kindly voice is dumb,
Or he whose life is shortened in its scope,
Who waits for nothing but the hangman's rope,
   Is he to whom a Christmas cannot come.

Christ died for all; he came to find the lost,
   Whether they bide in palaces or slums, —
No matter how their lines of life are crossed.
And they who love him best will serve him most
   By helping those to whom no Christmas comes.

New York Sun.

CHRISTMAS BELLS.

THERE are sounds in the sky when the year grows old,
   And the winds of the winter blow —
When night and the moon are clear and cold,
   And the stars shine on the snow,
Or wild is the blast and the bitter sleet
   That beats on the window-pane;
But blest on the frosty hills are the feet
   Of the Christmas time again !
      Chiming sweet when the night wind swells,
      Blest is the sound of the Christmas Bells !

Dear are the sounds of the Christmas chimes
  In the land of the ivied towers,
And they welcome the dearest of festival times
  In this Western world of ours !
Bright on the holly and mistletoe bough
  The English firelight falls,
And bright are the wreathed evergreens now
    That gladden our own home walls !
      And hark ! the first sweet note that tells,
      The welcome of the Christmas Bells !

The owl that sits in the ivy's shade,
  Remote from the ruined tower,
Shall start from his drowsy watch afraid
  When the clock shall strike the hour ;
And over the fields in their frosty rhyme
  The cheery sounds shall go,
And chime shall answer unto chime
    Across the moonlit snow !
      How sweet the lingering music dwells, —
      The music of the Christmas Bells.

It fell not thus in the East afar
  Where the Babe in the manger lay :
The wise men followed their guiding star
  To the dawn of a milder day ;
And the fig and the sycamore gathered green,
  And the palm-tree of Deborah rose ;
'T was the strange first Christmas the world had seen —
    And it came not in storm and snows.
      Not yet on Nazareth's hills and dells
      Had floated the sound of Christmas Bells.

The cedars of Lebanon shook in the blast
  Of their own cold mountain air ;
But nought o'er the wintry plain had passed
  To tell that the Lord was there !
The oak and the olive and almond were still,
  In the night now worn and thin ;
No wind of the winter-time roared from the hill
    To waken the guests at the inn ;
      No dream to them the music tells
      That is to come from the Christmas Bells !

The years that have fled like the leaves on the gale
  Since the morn of the Miracle-Birth,
Have widened the fame of the marvellous tale
  Till the tidings have filled the earth !
And so in the climes of the icy North,
  And the lands of the cane and the palm,
By the Alpine cotter's blazing hearth,
    And in tropic belts of calm,
      Men list to-night the welcome swells,
      Sweet and clear, of Christmas Bells !

They are ringing to-night through the Norway firs,
  And across the Swedish fells,
And the Cuban palm-tree dreamily stirs
  To the sound of those Christmas Bells !
They ring where the Indian Ganges rolls
  Its flood through the rice-fields wide ;
They swell the far hymns of the Lapps and Poles
  To the praise of the Crucified.
        Sweeter than tones of the ocean's shells
        Mingle the chimes of the Christmas Bells !

The years come not back that have circled away
  With the past of the Eastern land,
When He plucked the corn on the Sabbath day
  And healed the withered hand ;
But the bells shall join in a joyous chime
  For the One who walked the sea,
And ring again for the better time
  Of the Christ that is to be !
        Then ring ! — for earth's best promise dwells
        In ye, O joyous Prophet Bells !

Ring out at the meeting of night and morn
  For the dawn of a happier day !
Lo, the stone from our faith's great sepulchre torn
  The angels have rolled away !
And they come to us here in our low abode,
  With words like the sunrise gleam, —
Come down and ascend by that heavenly road
  That Jacob saw in his dream.
        Spirit of love, that in music dwells,
        Open our hearts with the Christmas Bells !

Help us to see that the glad heart prays
  As well as the bended knees ;
That there are in our own as in ancient days
  The Scribes and the Pharisees ;
That the Mount of Transfiguration still
  Looks down on these Christian lands,
And the glorified ones from that holy hill
  Are reaching their helping hands.
        These be the words our music tells
        Of solemn joy, O Christmas Bells !

CHRISTMAS SHADOWS.

THE needles have dropped from her nerveless hands,
  As she watches the dying embers glow ;
For out from the broad old chimney-place
  Come ghostly shadows of "long ago," —

Shadows that carry her back again
  To the time of her childhood's artless joy;
Shadows that show her a tiny row
  Of stockings awaiting the Christmas toy;

Shadows that show her the faces loved
  Of many a half-forgotten friend,
And the Christmas Eve, it is passing by,
  While Past and Present in shadows blend.
Alone in the dear old homestead now,
  With only the shadows of "Auld Lang Syne,"
The clock is ticking the moments on,
  While the tears in her aged eyes still shine.

If only out from the silent world,
  The world of shadows which mocks her so,
One might return to his vacant chair,
  To sit with her in the firelight's glow!
If only — Was that a white, white hand
  That seemed to beckon her out of the gloom?
Or was it the embers' last bright flash
  That startled the shadows round the room?

The Christmas Eve, it has passed at length;
  A glorious day from the night is born;
The shadows are gone from earth away,
  And the bells are ringing for Christmas morn.
But, ah! by the broad old chimney-place
  The angel of death keeps watch alone,
For straight to the Christ-child's beckoning arms
  A longing spirit hath gladly flown.

———◆———

UPON THE THRESHOLD.

ONCE more we stand with half-reluctant feet
  Upon the threshold of another year;
That line where Past and Present seem to meet
  In stronger contrast than they do elsewhere.

Look back a moment. Does the prospect please,
  Or does the weary heart but sigh regret?
Can Recollection smile, or, ill at ease
  With what is past, wish only to forget?

Say, canst thou smile when Memory's lingering gaze
  Once more recalls the dying year to sight?
Wouldst thou live o'er again those changing days,
  Or bid them fade forever into night?

A solemn question, and the faltering heart
  Scarce dare say "Yes," yet will not quite say "No;"
For joy and sadness both have played their part
  In making up the tale of "long ago."

Here Memory sees the golden sunlight gleam
  Across the path of life and shine awhile;
And now the picture changes like a dream,
  And sorrow dims the eyes and kills the smile.

So — it has gone — where all has gone before;
  The moaning wind has sung the dead year's dirge,
Time's waves roll on against the crumbling shore,
  And sinks the worn-out bark beneath the surge.

Here ends the checkered page of prose and verse,
  Of shapely words and lines writ all awry,
There they must stand for better or for worse;
  So shut the book and bid the year good-by!

Chambers's Journal.   G. E.

A NEW YEAR.

OVER the threshold a gallant new-comer
  Steppeth with tread that is royal to see;
White as the winter-time, rosy as summer,
  Hope in his eyes, and his laugh ringeth free.
Lo! in his hands there are gifts overflowing,
  Promises, prophecies, come in his train;
O'er him the dawn in its beauty is glowing,
  Flee from his presence the shadows of pain.

How shall we welcome him?   Shall we remember
  One who as royally came to our door
Twelve months ago when the winds of December
  Moaned in the tree-tops and raved on the shore?
He, too, had largess of bounty to offer;
  He was as smiling, as gracious of mien;
Only the beautiful sought he to proffer,
  Only such looks as were calm and serene.

Now he has fled; and our hopes that have perished,
  Lovely ideals which never were found,
Dreams that we followed and plans that we cherished,
  Lie, like the autumn leaves, dead on the ground.
So wilt thou cheat us with sign and with token, —
  So wilt thou woo us to follow thee on,
Till thy last sigh, through a lute that is broken,
  Till thy last vision is faded and gone.

Nay! we are thankless indeed if we borrow
   Only the weary libretto of pain;
Find in the retrospect nothing but sorrow,
   Count up our year in the tones that complain.
Surely we're stronger through faith and endeavor;
   Surely are richer in courage and love;
Surely are nearer the Infinite ever, —
   Nearer the dear ones who wait us above.

Welcome, then, New Year, with stainless white pages,
   Though we may blot them ere long with our tears;
So it has been through the long passing ages,
   Worn with the footprints of close crowding years.
Welcome, sweet year! may the full-handed hours
   Find us like servants who wait for their Lord;
Using with earnest devotion our powers,
   Looking for him, and obeying his word.

TURNING OVER THE NEW LEAF.

THE year begins.   I turn the leaf,
   All over writ with good resolves;
Each to fulfil will be in chief
   My aim while earth its round revolves.
How many a leaf I've turned before,
   And tried to make the record true;
Each year a wreck on Time's dull shore
   Proved much I dared, but little knew.

Ah, bright resolve!   How high you bear
   The future's hopeful standard on;
How brave you start; how poor you wear;
   How soon are hope and courage gone!
You point to deeds of sacrifice,
   You shun the path of careless ease;
Lentils and wooden shoes?   Is this
   The fare a human soul to please?

What wonder, then, if men do fall
   Where good is ever all austere;
While vice is fair and pleasant all,
   And turns the leaf to lead the year?
Yet still once more I turn the leaf,
   And mean to walk the better way;
I struggle with old unbelief,
   And strive to reach the perfect day.

Why should the road that leads to heaven
  Be all one reach of sterile sand?
Why not, just here and there, be given
  A rose to deck the dreary land?
But why repine? Others have trod,
  With sorer feet and heavier sins,
Their painful pathway toward their God —
  My pilgrimage anew begins.

Failure and failure, hitherto,
  Has time inscribed upon my leaves;
I've wandered many a harvest through
  And never yet have gathered sheaves;
Yet once again the leaf I turn,
  Hope against hope for one success;
One merit-mark at least to earn,
  One sunbeam in the wilderness.

PART IV.

Under the Open Sky.

Here haply too, at vernal dawn,
  Some musing bard may stray,
And eye the smoking dewy lawn,
  And misty mountain gray;
Or by the reaper's nightly beam,
  Mild-checkering through the trees,
Rave to my darkly dashing stream,
  Hoarse swelling on the breeze.

Let lofty firs, and ashes cool,
  My lowly banks o'erspread,
And view, deep bending in the pool,
  Their shadows' watery bed!
Let fragrant birks in woodbine drest
  My craggy cliffs adorn;
And, for the little songster's nest,
  The close-embowering thorn.

                                        BURNS

PART IV.

Under the Open Sky.

———•◦•———

ROBIN'S COME.

FROM the elm-tree's topmost bough,
  Hark! the robin's early song!
Telling one and all that now
  Merry springtime hastes along;
Welcome tidings dost thou bring,
Little harbinger of spring:
          Robin's come.

Of the winter we are weary,
  Weary of the frost and snow;
Longing for the sunshine cheery,
  And the brooklet's gurgling flow;
Gladly then we hear thee sing
The joyful reveille of spring:
          Robin's come.

Ring it out o'er hill and plain,
  Through the garden's lonely bowers,
Till the green leaves dance again,
  Till the air is sweet with flowers!
Wake the cowslips by the rill,
Wake the yellow daffodil:
          Robin's come.

Then, as thou wert wont of yore,
  Build thy nest and rear thy young
Close beside our cottage door,
  In the woodbine leaves among;
Hurt or harm thou need'st not fear,
Nothing rude shall venture near:
          Robin's come.

Singing still in yonder lane,
  Robin answers merrily;
Ravished by the sweet refrain,
  Alice clasps her hands in glee,
Calling from the open door,
With her soft voice o'er and o'er,
            Robin's come.
                    WILLIAM W. CALDWELL.

NESTLINGS.

O LITTLE bird! sing sweet among the leaves,
Safe hid from sight, beside thy downy nest;
The rain falls, murmuring to the drooping eaves
A low refrain, that suits thy music best.
Sing sweet, O bird! thy recompense draws nigh,—
Four callow nestlings 'neath the mother's wing.
So many flashing wings that by and by
Will cleave the sunny air.   Oh, sing, bird, sing!

(Sing, O my heart!   Thy callow nestlings sleep,
Safe hidden 'neath a gracious folding wing,
Until the time when from their slumbers deep
They wake, and soar in beauty.   Sing, heart, sing!)

O little bird, sing sweet!   Though rain may fall,
And though thy callow brood thy care require,
Behind the rain-cloud, with its trailing pall,
Shineth, undimmed, the gracious, golden fire.
Sing on, O bird! nor of the cloud take heed;
For thou art heritor of glorious spring;
And every field is sacred to thy need —
The wealth, the beauty thine.   Oh, sing, bird, sing!

(Sing, O my heart! sing on, though rain may pour;
Sing on, for unawares the winds will bring
A drift of sunshine to thy cottage door,
And arch the clouds with rainbows.   Sing, heart, sing!)

O bird! sing sweet.   What though the time be near
When thou shalt sit upon the swaying bough,
With no sweet mate, no nestling by, to hear
The bubbling song thou sing'st to glad them now!
Thy task was done, fulfilled in sweet spring days —
In golden summer, when thy brood take wing,
Shalt thou not still have left a hymn of praise
Because thy work is over?   Sing, bird, sing!

(Sing, O my heart!   What if thy birds have flown?
Thou hadst the joy of their awakening,
A thousand memories left thee for thine own ;
Sing thou for task accomplished.   Sing, heart, sing!)

F. C. A.

---◆---

THE CHIMNEY NEST.

A DAINTY, delicate swallow-feather
    Is all that we now in the chimney trace
Of something that days and days together
    With twittering bird-notes filled the place.

Where are you flying now, swallow, swallow?
    Where are you waking the spaces blue?
How many little ones follow, follow,
    Whose wings to strength in the chimney grew?

Deep and narrow, and dark and lonely,
    The sooty place that you nested in ;
Over you one blue glimmer only, —
    Say, were there many to make the din?

This is certain, that somewhere or other
    Up in the chimney is loosely hung
A queer-shaped nest, where a patient mother
    Brooded a brood of tender young.

That here, as in many deserted places,
    Brimming with life for hours and hours,
We miss with the hum a thousand graces,
    Valued the more since no more ours.

Ah! why do we shut our eyes half blindly,
    And close our hearts to some wee things near,
Till he who granted them kindly, kindly
    Gathers them back, that we see and hear,

And know, by loss of the same grown dearer,
    Nought is so small of his works and ways,
But, holding it tenderly when 't was nearer,
    Has added a joy to our vanished days?

So, little, delicate swallow-feather,
    Fashioned with care by the Master's hand,
I 'll hold you close for your message, whether
    Or not the whole I may understand.

MARY B. DODGE.

THE CAPTIVE HUMMING–BIRD.

Fleet-flying gem, of burnished crest
　　And silver-tipped wing,
With azure, gold, and sapphire breast;
　　Æolian captive thing !

Tell me the secret of thy song,
　　And whence thy robe of beams,
If to the earth thou dost belong,
　　Or Paradise of dreams.

Born for one season of a ray,
　　To banquet 'mid the bowers,
Or wilt thou chant another May,
　　Sweet minstrel of the flowers?

The coyest honeysuckles still
　　Their daintiest buds unfold,
For thee to kiss, with honeyed bill,
　　Their nectar lips of gold.

The lily opes its snowy cells,
　　The pink, its crimson door.
" Sip !" whispers every fond bluebell,
　　" My honey to the core."

While blushing flowers for thee all fling
　　Their fragrance on the air,
The purple morning-glories cling
　　On high in beauty bare.

The tiny chalice of the thyme,
　　And daisies, plead below,
Each dewy-eyed, too small to climb,
　　" Come, kiss me ere you go."

Away on thy melodious wing
　　To Love's mysterious bowers,
Still thy free band of minstrels bring
　　To revel 'mid the flowers.

Breathe on their bosoms fair and sweet,
　　And rosy lips apart,
And give and take, in Love's retreat,
　　The honey of the heart.

Joel T. Hart

THE YELLOW–HAMMER'S NEST.

THE yellow-hammer came to build his nest
High in the elm-tree's ever-nodding crest;
All the day long, upon his task intent,
Backward and forward busily he went;

Gathering from far and near the tiny shreds
That birdies weave for little birdies' beds, —
Now bits of grass, now bits of vagrant string,
And now some queerer, dearer sort of thing.

Far on the lawn, where he was wont to come
In search of stuff to build his pretty home,
We dropped one day a lock of golden hair,
Which our wee darling easily could spare.

And close beside it tenderly we placed
A lock that had the stooping shoulders graced
Of her old grandsire; it was white as snow,
Or cherry-trees when they are all ablow.

Then throve the yellow-hammer's work apace;
Hundreds of times he sought the lucky place
Where, sure, he thought, in his bird fashion dim,
Wondrous provision had been made for him.

Both locks, the white and golden, disappeared;
The nest was finished and the brood was reared;
And then there came a pleasant summer day
When the last yellow-hammer flew away.

Ere long, in triumph, from its leafy height
We bore the nest so wonderfully dight,
And saw how prettily the white and gold
Made warp and woof of many a gleaming fold.

But when again the yellow-hammers came,
Cleaving the orchard with their pallid flame,
Grandsire's white locks and baby's golden head
Were lying low, both in one mossy bed.

And so more dear than ever is the nest
Taken from the elm-tree's ever-nodding crest.
Little the yellow-hammer thought how rare
A thing he wrought of white and golden hair.

JOHN W. CHADWICK.

THE BIRD ON THE TELEGRAPH WIRE.

THE long lines stretched from west to east,
　The bird was a dot 'gainst the wide blue sky,
And I, full of summer gladness and joy,
　Wrote of the bird as he swung on high.

So free from all care and sorrow and toil !
　So fearless 'mid music of countless spheres !
So true to its instincts, though under its feet
　Passed "the news of the world " and the labor of years !

He trilled a song to his patient mate ;
　Not a note was made less loud and sweet
By a thought of the wounded and dying men,
　Though the news of the battle passed under his feet.

He sang of his birdies — one, two, three,
　Of his nest in the apple-tree over the way,
While the wires were bearing the death of a prince, —
　How a kingdom's throne was empty that day.

A lovely sight, with his breast of gold,
　His glossy wings and beaded eyes ;
One of life's beautiful things, I thought,
　O'erlying its deeper mysteries.

Little cared he for battles or thrones,
　While the air was so soft and the sun so bright ;
His nestful and mate were enough for him,
　And he taught me a lesson, — to trust in God's might.

On the earth which sages and martyrs have trod
　He teaches us how to build our nest ;
Through trials, temptations, and mysteries strange,
　He teaches us, trusting, to say, " It is best."

PANSIES.

I SEND thee pansies while the year is young,
　Yellow as sunshine, purple as the night ;
Flowers of remembrance, ever fondly sung
　By all the chiefest of the Sons of Light ;
And if in recollection lives regret
　For wasted days and dreams that were not true,
I tell thee that the " pansy freaked with jet "
　Is still the heart's-ease that the poets knew.
Take all the sweetness of a gift unsought,
And for the pansies send me back a thought.

SARAH DOUDNEY.

THE WATER-LILY.

"O STAR on the breast of the river !
    O marvel of bloom and grace !
Did you fall right down from heaven,
    Out of the sweetest place ?
You are white as the thoughts of an angel,
    Your heart is steeped in the sun :
Did you grow in the Golden City,
    My pure and radiant one ? "

" Nay, nay, I fell not out of heaven ;
    None gave me my saintly white :
It slowly grew from the darkness,
    Down in the dreary night.
From the ooze of the silent river
    I won my glory and grace.
White souls fall not, O my poet,
    They rise — to the sweetest place."

MARY FRANCES BUTTS.

THE ROSE-BUSH.

THERE was a rose-bush in a garden growing,
    Its tender leaves unfolding day by day ;
The sun looked on, and his down-going
    Left it amid the starlit dusk of nights of May.

The dew-drop came and kissed it in the gloaming ;
    It gathered sweetness in the morning hours ;
The bee beheld it as he went a roaming,
    And thought, " What honey will be hidden in its flowers ! "

The light grew richer and the days grew long ;
    The May-time deepened into June ;
The air was laden with the robin's song,
    The light wind touched the leaves and set them all atune.

And now a tiny bud appeared, and then another —
    Bright promises of radiant flowers ;
The breezes, whispering, told it to each other,
    The rose-bush heard them in the gladsome hours.

New hope awoke and thrilled in all its veins ;
    Life is so sweet that culminates in flowers !
It smiled and grew in misty summer rains,
    And caught the freshness of the evening showers.

And oft the gardener came and stood beside ;
   He tended it alway with zealous care,
Watching lest any evil should betide,
   Or blight creep o'er the leaves that grew so fair.

He crushed the buds and dropped them on the ground ;
   The rose-bush felt a chill in every vein ;
It drooped, as if to hide each bitter wound —
   This strange experience was its earliest thought of pain.

" Poor little plant," the gardener thought,
   " Thou art too young, too young to know
That few buds unto flowers are brought, —
   It is by pruning thou must grow."

And still the summer smiled and shone,
   And other roses bloomed and died.
" Mine would more beauteously have blown,"
   The little rose-bush sadly sighed.

Again the gardener sought his flowers,
   Where he had watched his treasures blow :
The autumn blast had swept the bowers,
   The winds and storms had laid them low !

Though sad of heart, the rose-bush still was green ;
   It lifted up its drooping head ;
" The life that would have filled the buds may still be seen,
   'T is folded in its heart," he said.

He stooped and took it from the ground
   All trembling with its vague alarms,
And quick and tenderly he wrapped it round,
   And kindly bore it in his arms.

And now, where soft the sunshine flows,
   Within a fair, immortal bower,
In all its fragrant beauty blooms the rose,
   Its every bud grown into perfect flower.

THE PHANTOM OF THE ROSE.

Sweet lady, let your lids unclose, —
   Those lids by maiden dreams caressed ;
I am the phantom of the rose
   You wore last night upon your breast.
Like pearls upon my petals lay
   The weeping fountain's silver tears,
Ere in the glittering array
   You bore me proudly 'mid your peers.

O lady, 't was for you I died —
    Yet have I come and will I stay;
My rosy phantom by your side
    Will linger till the break of day.
Yet fear not, lady; nought claim I —
    Nor mass, nor hymn, nor funeral prayer;
My soul is but a perfumed sigh,
    Which pure from Paradise I bear.

My death is as my life was — sweet ;
    Who would not die as I have done?
A fate like mine who would not meet,
    Your bosom fair to lie upon?
A poet on my sentient tomb
    Engraved this legend with a kiss:
"Here lies a rose of fairest bloom ;
    E'en kings are jealous of its bliss."

JEROME A. HART.
(*From Théophile Gautier.*)

NOTE. — A scholar who criticises the second half of Mr. Hart's second verse as diverging unnecessarily from the spirit of Gautier, suggests this much less poetical quatrain in its place : —

    Yet fear not, neither mass nor prayer
      Nor holy funeral hymn I claim, —
    My soul is but a perfume rare,
      And pure from Paradise it came.

THE MESSAGE OF THE ROSE.

ONLY a rose in a glass,
    Set by a sick man's bed ;
The day was weary, the day was long,
But the rose it spoke with a voice-like song,
    And this is what it said : —

"I know that the wind is keen,
    And the drifted snows lie deep;
I know that the cruel ice lies spread
O'er the laughing brook and the lake's blue bed,
    And the fountain's rush and leap.

"I know, I know all this ;
    Yet here I sit — a rose !
Smiling I sit and I feel no fear,
For God is good and the spring is near,
    Couched in the shrouding snows.

"Canst thou not smile with me?
  Art thou less strong than I?
Less strong at heart than a feeble flower
Which lives and blossoms but one brief hour,
  And then must droop and die?

"Surely, thou canst endure
  Thy little pains and fears,
Before whose eyes, all fair and bright,
In endless vistas of delight,
  Stretch the eternal years!"

Then o'er the sick man's heart
  Fell a deep and hushed repose;
He turned on his pillow and whispered low,
That only the listening flower might know:
  "I thank thee, Rose, dear Rose."

———◆———

BEAN–BLOSSOMS.

WHERE grass grows short and the meadows end,
And hedged fields slowly the hill ascend,
To the gentle breezes bending low,
Lazily bending, the bean-flowers blow.

In winter the steaming horses toil
With the bright plough deep in the loamy soil;
In spring the sower goes forth to sow:
Sweet in the summer the bean-flowers blow.

Thither the bee with his ceaseless hum,
Thither the maids with their lovers come.
Pity that beauty cannot last!
Pity the blossoms fade so fast!

Oh, sweet the scent of the garden rose:
As sweet on the hill the bean-flower blows.
The bean to the threshing-floor shall come,
But the rose is not at the harvest home.

Maiden, what do the bean-flowers say?
"Beauty but lasts for a little day;
Who learns the lesson our blossoms tell,
May be sweet and lovely and good as well."

St. James Gazette.

TRAILING ARBUTUS.

In spring, when branches of woodbine
　　Hung leafless over the rocks,
And the fleecy snow in the hollows
　　Lay in unshepherded flocks,

By the road where the dead leaves rustled,
　　Or damply matted the ground,
While over me gurgled the robin
　　His honeyed passion of sound,

I saw the trailing arbutus
　　Blooming in modesty sweet,
And gathered store of its richness
　　Offered and spread at my feet.

It grew under leaves, as if seeking
　　No hint of itself to disclose,
And out of its pink-white petals
　　A delicate perfume rose,

As faint as the fond remembrance
　　Of joy that was only dreamed ;
And like a divine suggestion
　　The scent of the flower seemed.

I had sought for love on the highway,
　　For love unselfish and pure,
And had found it in good deeds blooming,
　　Though often in haunts obscure.

Often in leaves by the wayside,
　　But touched with a heavenly glow,
And with self-sacrifice fragrant,
　　The flowers of great love grow.

O lovely and lowly arbutus !
　　As year unto year succeeds,
Be thou the laurel and emblem
　　Of noble, unselfish deeds.

The Academy. Henry Abbey.

---◆---

A FLOWER FROM THE CATSKILLS.

The orchards that climb the hillsides,
　　That lie in the valley below,
Are white in the soft May sunshine,
　　And fragrant with May-day snow.
The violets wakened by April
　　Their watch in the meadow yet keep,
The golden spurs of the columbine
　　Are hung where the lichens creep.

Still gleams by the sluggish waters
  Some loitering marigold,
Where ferns, late greeting the sunshine,
  Their downy green plumes unfold.
And just by the wooded waysides
  Faint glows the azalea's blush, —
The dawn of the coming summer,
  The morning's awakening flush !

But there where the wind-rent rain-clouds
  O'ershadow the Catskills' crest,
There blossoms one flower more precious,
  Far sweeter than all the rest.
Where scarcely a leaf has opened,
  The promise of summer to give,
Where the lingering winds of winter
  For the sleet and the snow-drift grieve,

Where the trees grow scant and stunted,
  And scarcely a shadow is cast,
There nestles the trailing arbutus
  Close, close to the hill's cold breast.
The storm-winds give to it courage,
  The skies give it power to bless,
And it giveth to all its loving
  In its happy thankfulness.

Now pink as the lip of the sea-shell,
  Now white as the breakers' foam,
It spreadeth its stainless treasure
  To brighten its rugged home.
Low trailing amid the mosses
  Its delicate blossoms lie, —
Giving the earth its beauty,
  Its worship giving the sky.

Though bleak be the home that reared it,
  And rough be its lullaby,
Gathering strength from the tempest,
  And grace from the fair blue sky,
It waiteth with patient longing,
  In the snow's embrace held fast,
Still trusting, with faith unbroken,
  The sun to welcome at last, —

To welcome with loving greeting
  The soft falling step of spring,
Scarce felt on the northern hill-slopes,
  Where the lingering snow-drifts cling;
And faint on the winds up-sweeping
  Is wafted its perfume rare,
Like the incense of worship ascending, —
  The mountains' low, unspoken prayer !

O brave little blossom! still teach us
  Through love to be patient and strong,
Though the spring be laggard in coming,
  And the days be dark and long.
Like thy bloom by the rude ways scattered,
  Each day some life may we bless,
Till our souls, like thy fragrance ascending,
  Reach heavenly perfectness.

E. W.

HEART'S-EASE.

WHILE o'er my life still hung the morning star,
  Dreamy and soft in tender-lighted skies,
While care and sorrow held themselves afar,
  And no sad mist of tears had dimmed my eyes,
    I saw Love's roses blowing,
    With scent and color glowing,
  And so I wished for them with longing sighs.

The brightest hung so high, and held aloft
  Their crimson faces, passionately bright;
The gay, rich, golden ones escaped me oft,
  And hedged with sharpest thorns the lofty white;
    From all my eager pleading
    They turned away, unheeding;
  Among Love's roses none were mine of right.

Yet, of sweet things, those roses seemed most sweet
  And most desirable, until a voice,
Soft as sad music, said, "Lo, at thy feet
  A little flower shall make thy heart rejoice."
    And so, the voice obeying,
    I saw, in beauty straying,
  A wealth of heart's-ease, waiting for my choice.

Great purple pansies, each with snowy heart,
  And golden ones, with eyes of deepest blue;
Some "freaked with jet," some pure white ones apart,
  But all so sweet and fresh with morning dew,
    I could not bear to lose them,
    I could not help but choose them,
  For sweet Content sat singing where they grew.

So, now, Love's roses shake their scented leaves,
  But tempt me not to their enchanted quest;
I gather "heart's-ease," set in dewy leaves,
  And am *content*, — for me it is the best.
    Be glad if, sweet and glowing,
    You find Love's roses blowing —
  I sing through life with heart's-ease at my breast.

HELIOTROPE.

How strong they are, those subtile spells
That lurk in leaves and flower-bells,
    Rising from faint perfumes;
Or, mingling with some olden strain,
Strike through the music shafts of pain,
    And people empty rooms.

They come upon us unaware,
In crowded halls and open air,
    And in our chambers still;
A song, an odor, or a bird
Evokes the spell and strikes the chord,
    And all our pulses thrill.

I wandered but an hour ago,
With lagging footsteps tired and slow,
    Along the garden walk;
The summer twilight wrapped me round,
Through open windows came the sound
    Of song and pleasant talk.

The odor-stealing dews lay wet
And heavy on the mignonette
    That crept about my feet;
Upon the folded mossy vest
That clothed the ruby rose's breast
    It fell in droppings sweet.

It fell on beds of purple bloom,
From whence arose the rare perfume
    Of dainty heliotrope;
Which smote my heart with sudden power, —
My favorite scent, my favorite flower,
    In olden days of hope!

Ah, me! the years have come and gone,
Each with its melody or moan,
    Since that sunshiny hour,
When, for the sake of hands that brought,
And for the lesson sweet it taught,
    I chose it for my flower.

Faint-scented blossoms! Long ago
Your purple clusters came to show
    My life had wider scope;
They spoke of love that day — to-night
I stand apart from love's delight,
    And wear no heliotrope.

Between to-night and that far day
Lie life's bright noon and twilight gray, —
    But I have lived through both ;
And if before my paling face
The midnight shadows fall apace,
    I see them, nothing loath.

Only to-night that faint perfume
Reminds me of the lonely gloom
    Of life outliving hope ; —
I wish I had been far to-night
What time the dew fell, silver-white,
    Upon the heliotrope !

THE CLOVER.

SOME sings of the lily, and daisy, and rose,
And the pansies and pinks that the summer-time throws
In the green grassy lap of the medder that lays
Blinkin' up at the skies through the sunshiny days ;
But what is the lily and all of the rest
Of the flowers to a man with a heart in his breast
That has dipped brimmin' full of the honey and dew
Of the sweet clover-blossoms his babyhood knew ?

I never set eyes on a clover-field now,
Or fool round a stable, or climb in the mow,
But my childhood comes back, just as clear and as plain
As the smell of the clover I 'm sniffin' again ;
And I wander away in a barefooted dream,
Where I tangle my toes in the blossoms that gleam
With the dew of the dawn of the morning of love
Ere it wept o'er the graves that I 'm weepin' above.

And so I love clover — it seems like a part
Of the sacredest sorrows and joys of my heart ;
And wherever it blossoms, oh, there let me bow,
And thank the good God as I 'm thankin' him now ;
And I pray to him still for the strength, when I die,
To go out in the clover and tell it good-by,
And lovingly nestle my face in its bloom,
While my soul slips away on a breath of perfume.

JAMES WHITCOMB RILEY.

THE VIOLET'S GRAVE.

THE woodland, and the golden wedge
    Of sunshine slipping through ;
And there, beside a bit of hedge,
    A violet so blue !

So tender was its beauty, and
    So douce and sweet its air,
I stooped, and yet withheld my hand —
    Would pluck, and yet would spare.

Now which was best? For spring will pass,
    And vernal beauty fly —
On maiden's breast or in the grass,
    Where would you choose to die?

                  FROM THE SICILIAN OF VICORTARI.

THE LILY AND THE LINDEN.

FAR away under skies of blue,
    In the pleasant land beyond the sea,
Bathed with sunlight and washed with dew,
    Budded and bloomed the fleur-de-lis.

Through mists of morning, one by one,
    Grandly the perfect leaves unfold,
And the dusky glow of the sinking sun
    Flushed and deepened its hues of gold.

She saw him rise o'er the rolling Rhine,
    She saw him set in the western sea,
" Where is the empress, garden mine,
    Doth rule a realm like the fleur-de-lis?

" The forest trembles before the breath,
    From the island oak to the northern pine,
And the blossoms pale with the hue of death
    When my anger rustles the tropic vine.

" The lotus wakes from its slumbers lone,
    To waft its homage unto me,
And the spice-groves lay before my throne
    The tribute due to the fleur-de-lis ! "

So hailed she vassals far and wide,
    Till her glance swept over a hemisphere,
But noted not, in her queenly pride,
    A slender sapling growing near.

Slow uprising o'er glade and glen,
    Its branches bent in the breezes free,
But its roots were set in the hearts of men,
    Who gave their life to the linden-tree.

" Speak, O seer of the mighty mien !
Answer, sage of the mystic air !
What is the lot of the linden green ?
What is the fate of the lily fair ? "

" Hear'st thou the wail of the winter wake ?
Hear'st thou the roar of the angry sea ?
Ask not, for heaven's own thunders break
On the linden fair and the fleur-de-lis ! "

.   .   .   .   .

The storm-clouds fade from the murky air,
Again the freshening breezes blow,
The sunbeams rest on the garden rare,
But the lily lies buried beneath the snow !

From the ice-locked Rhine to the western sea
Mournfully spreads the wintry pall,
Cold and still is the fleur-de-lis,
But the linden threatens to shadow all !

Frowning down on the forest wide,
Darkly loometh his giant form,
Alone he stands in his kingly pride,
And mocks at whirlwind and laughs at storm.

" Speak, O sage of the mystic air !
Answer, seer of the mighty mien !
Must all thy trees of the forest fair
Fall at the feet of the linden green ? "

" Wouldst thou the scroll of the future see ?
Thus I divine the fate of all !
A worm is sapping the linden-tree,
The pride that goeth before a fall.

" For shame may come to the haughty crest,
A storm may sweep from the northern sea,
And winds from the east and winds from the west
May blow in wrath o'er the linden-tree !

" Here, where the voice of the winter grieves,
The lily hath lain its regal head ;
Bright was the gleam of the golden leaves,
But the lily was flecked with spots of red.

" Behind the clouds of the battle strife
The glow of resurrection see !
Lo ! I proclaim a newer life,
The truer birth of the fleur-de-lis ! "

Thus saith the seer of the mighty mien,
　Thus saith the sage of the mystic air,
The sunshine fell from the linden green
　And gilded the grave of the lily fair.

Stewart's Quarterly.　　　　　　　Dr. Fred Crosby.

--◆--

RAIN.

Millions of massive rain-drops
　Have fallen all around;
They have danced on the house-tops,
　They have hidden in the ground.

They were liquid like musicians
　With anything for keys,
Beating tunes upon the windows,
　Keeping time upon the trees.

--◆--

PROMISE.

There is a rainbow in the sky,
　Upon the arch where tempests trod;
God wrote it ere the world was dry —
　It is the autograph of God.

Note. — This quatrain was cut from the body of a poem which contained
little else of worth, and the very title of which is now forgotten.

--◆--

WHAT THEY DREAMED AND SAID.

Rose dreamed she was a lily,
　Lily dreamed she was a rose;
Robin dreamed he was a sparrow,
　What the owl dreamed no one knows.

But they all woke up together
　As happy as could be.
Said each one : " You 're lovely, neighbor,
　But I 'm very glad I 'm me."

M. E.

--◆--

THE WANDERER.

Upon a mountain height, far from the sea,
　I found a shell ;
And to my listening ear this lonely thing
Ever a song of ocean seemed to sing, —
　Ever a tale of ocean seemed to tell.

How came this shell upon the mountain height ?
    Ah, who can say
Whether there dropped by some too careless hand,
Whether there cast when oceans swept the land,
    Ere the Eternal had ordained the day ?

Strange, was it not ?   Far from its native deep,
    One song it sang :
Sang of the awful mysteries of the tide,
Sang of the storied sea, profound and wide, —
    Ever with echoes of old ocean rang.

And as the shell upon the mountain height
    Sang of the sea,
So do I ever, leagues and leagues away,
So do I ever, wandering where I may,
    Sing, O my home ! sing, O my home, of thee !

                  EUGENE FIELD.

METEORS.

TEARS of gold the heavens wept ;
They fell and were by billows swept
Into the sea, 'mid coral caves,
Where roll the ever-restless waves.

And thus they lay, till they were found
By mermaids on the ocean's ground.
The sea-nymphs took the gems so rare,
And wound them in their sea-green hair.

And often now some summer's night
The ocean gleams with golden light
Caused by the mermaids sporting there
With tears of gold in flowing hair.

              ANNA PH. EICHBERG.

A BROOK SONG.

I 'M hastening from the distant hills
    With swift and noisy flowing ;
Nursed by a thousand tiny rills,
    I 'm ever onward going.
The willows cannot stay my course,
    With all their pliant wooing ;
I sing and sing till I am hoarse,
    My prattling way pursuing.
I kiss the pebbles as I pass,
    And hear them say they love me,

I make obeisance to the grass
  That kindly bends above me.
So onward through the meads and dells
  I hasten, never knowing
The secret motive that impels,
  Or whither I am going.

A little child comes often here
  To watch my quaint commotion
As I go tumbling swift and clear
  Down to the distant ocean;
And as he plays upon my brink,
  So thoughtless like and merry
And full of noisy song, I think
  The child is like me, very.
Through all the years of youthful play,
  With ne'er a thought of sorrow,
We, prattling, speed upon our way,
  Unmindful of the morrow;
Aye, through these sunny meads and dells
  We gambol, never trowing
The solemn motive that impels,
  Or whither we are going.

And men come here to say to me:
  "Like you, with weird commotion,
O little singing brooklet, we
  Are hastening to the ocean;
Down to a vast and misty deep,
  With fleeting tears and laughter
We go, nor rest until we sleep
  In that profound Hereafter.
What tides may bear our souls along,
  What monsters rise appalling,
What distant shores may hear our song
  And answer to our calling?
Ah, who can say! Through meads and dells
  We wander, never knowing
The awful motive that impels,
  Or whither we are going!"

                              EUGENE FIELD.

———◆———

THE PRAIRIE PATH.

UPON the brown and frozen sod
  The wind's wet fingers shake the rain;
The bare shrubs shiver in the blast
  Against the dripping window-pane.
Inside, strange shadows haunt the room,
  The flickering firelights rise and fall,
And make I know not what strange shapes
  Upon the pale gray parlor wall.

I feel, but do not see these things, —
  My soul stands under other skies;
There is a wondrous radiance comes
  Between my eyelids and my eyes.
I seem to pull down on my feet
  God's gentian flowers, as on I pass
Through a great prairie, still and sweet
  With growing vines and blowing grass.

And then — ah! whence can he have come? —
  I feel a small hand touching mine;
Our voices first are like the breath
  That sways the grass and scented vine.
But clearer grow the childish words
  Of Egypt and of Hindostan;
And Archie's telling me again
  Where he will go when he's a man.

The smell of pines is strangely blent
  With sandal-wood, and broken spice,
And cores of calamus; the flowers
  Grow into gems of wondrous price.
We sit down in the grass and dream;
  His face grows strangely bright and fair;
I think it is the amber gleam
  Of sunset in his pale gold hair.

But while I look I see a path
  Across the prairie to the light;
And Archie, with his small, bare feet,
  Has almost passed beyond my sight.
Upon my heart there falls a smile,
  Upon my ears a soft adieu:
I see the glory in his face,
  And know his dreams have all come true.

Some day I shall go hence and home, —
  We shall go hence, I mean to say;
And as we pass the shoals of time,
  " My brother," I shall, pleading, say,
" There was upon the prairie wide
  A spot so dear to thee and me,
I fain would see it ere we walk
  The fields of Immortality."

———◆———

A SUMMER PICTURE.

FROM saffron to yellow, from purple to gray,
Slow fades on the mountain the beautiful day;
I sit where the roses are heavy with bloom,
And wait for the moonlight to whiten the gloom.

Far down the green valley I see through the night
The lamps of the village shine steady and bright ;
But on my sweet silence there creeps not a tone
Of labor or sorrow, of pleading or moan.

Low sings the glad river along its dark way,
An echo by night of its chiming by day;
And tremulous branches lean down to the tide,
To dimple the waters that under them glide.

The night moths are flitting about in the gloom,
Their wings from the blossoms shake dainty perfume ,
I know where the cups of the lilies are fair,
By the breath of their sweetness that floats on the air.

I sit in the shadow ; but lo ! in the west
The mountains in garments of glory are drest !
And slowly the sheen of their brightness drops down
To rest on the hills in a luminous crown.

The dew glitters clear where the shadows are green ;
In ranks of white splendor the lilies are seen ;
And the roses above me sway lightly to greet
Their shadowy sisters, afloat at my feet.

Low sings the glad river; its waters alight,
A pathway of silver, lead on through the night;
And fair as the glorified isles of the blest
Lies all the sweet valley, the valley of rest.

———◆———

AUTUMN.

'T is the golden gleam of an autumn day,
With the soft rain raining as if in play;
And a tender touch upon everything,
As if autumn remembered the days of spring.

In the listening woods there is not a breath
To shake their gold to the sward beneath;
And a glow as of sunshine on them lies,
Though the sun is hid in the shadowed skies.

The cock's clear crow from the farmyard comes,
The muffled bell from the belfry booms,
And faint and dim, and from far away,
Come the voices of children in happy play.

O'er the mountains the white rain draws its veil,
And the black rooks, cawing, across them sail;
While nearer the swooping swallows skim
O'er the steel-gray river's fretted brim.

No sorrow upon the landscape weighs,
No grief for the vanished summer days;
But a sense of peaceful and calm repose
Like that which age in autumn knows.

The springtime longings are past and gone,
The passions of summer no longer are known,
The harvest is gathered, and autumn stands
Serenely thoughtful, with folded hands.

Over all is thrown a memorial hue,
A glory ideal the real ne'er knew;
For memory sifts from the past its pain,
And suffers its beauty alone to remain.

With half a smile and half a sigh
It ponders the past that has hurried by:
Sees it and feels it and loves it all,
Content it has vanished beyond recall.

O glorious autumn, thus serene,
Thus living and loving all that has been!
Thus calm and contented let me be
When the autumn of age shall come to me.

Blackwood.

---◆---

WINTER.

WHERE are the flowers? where the leaves?
    Where the sweet zephyrs' gentle breath?
Where mellowed fruits and golden sheaves?
    Dead, dead; all icy bound in death!
Is Love too dead? Hence, needless pain!
Love only sleeps to wake again.
Love dead? Ah, no, not so with Love!
Love only dies to live above.

---◆---

WINTER.

THOU dark-robed man with solemn pace,
And mantle muffled round thy face,
Like the dim vision seen by Saul,
Upraised by spells from Death's dark hall;

8

Thou sad, small man, — face thin and old,
Teeth set, and nose pinched blue and cold, —
Ne'er mind! Thy coat, so long and black,
And fitting round thee all so slack,
Has glorious spangles, and its stars
Are like a conqueror's fresh from wars.
Who wove it in Time's awful loom
With woof of glory, warp of gloom?
Jove's planet glitters on thy breast;
The morning star adorns thy crest;
The waxing or the waning moon
Clings to thy turban late or soon;
Orion's belt is thine, — thy thigh
His jewelled sword hangs briefly by;
The Pleiades seven, the Gypsy's star,
Shine as thy shoulder-knots afar;
And the great Dog-star, bright, unknown,
Blazes beside thee like a throne.
Take heart! Thy coat, so long and black,
Sore worn, and fitting round thee slack,
Is broidered by the Northern Lights,
Those silvery arrows shot by sprites, —
Is powdered by the Milky Way
With awful pearls unknown to day,
Which well make up for all the hues
Proud Summer, bridegroom-like, may use.

Proud Summer, with his roses' sheen,
And dress of scarlet, blue, and green,
Floods us with such a sea of light
We miss the faint, far isles of Night,
And thoughtless dance, while he with lutes
Beguiles us or assists to fruits;
But like a shade from Spirit-land
Dim Winter beckons with his hand, —
He beckons; all things darker grow,
Save white-churned waves and wreathing snow.
We pause; a chill creeps through our veins;
We dare not thank him for his pains;
We fear to follow, and we creep
To candle-light, to cards, to sleep.

Yet when we follow him, how deep
The secret he has got to keep!
How wonderful! how passing grand!
For, peering through his storms, there stand
The eternal cities of the sky,
With stars like street-lamps hung on high;
No angel yet can sum their worth,
Though angels sang when they had birth.

OCTOBER.

THERE comes a month in the weary year, —
    A month of leisure and healthful rest ;
When the ripe leaves fall and the air is clear, —
    October, the brown, the crisp, the blest.

My life has little enough of bliss ;
    I drag the days of the odd eleven,
Counting the time that shall lead to this, —
    The month that opens the hunter's heaven.

And oh ! for the mornings crisp and white,
    With the sweep of the hounds upon the track ;
The bark-roofed cabin, the camp-fire's light,
    The break of the deer, and the rifle's crack !

Do you call this trifling ?   I tell you, friend,
    A life in the forest is past all praise ;
Give me a dozen such months on end,
    You may take my balance of years and days.

For brick and mortar breed filth and crime,
    And a pulse of evil that throbs and beats ;
And men grow withered before their prime,
    With the curse paved in on the lanes and streets ;

And lungs are choked, and shoulders are bowed,
    In the smoking reek of mill and mine ;
And Death stalks in on the struggling crowd,
    But he shuns the shadow of oak and pine.

And of all to which the memory clings,
    There is nought so sweet as the sunny spots
Where our shanties stood by the crystal springs,
    The vanished hounds and the lucky shots.

——◆——

OCTOBER.

OH, haunting dreams of a sweet summer dead !
    Ye bring me heart-ache in your whispers low, —
Echoes of song I may not hear again,
    Voices whose tones were silent long ago ;
Visions of orchards crowned with bridal bloom,
    Where apple-blossoms scent the air of May,
And from the sloping hillside comes the sound
    Of sweet-voiced children at their happy play.

There is a low, sad rustle in the air,
  Among the yellow banners of the corn;
The faded sunflower droops her heavy head,
  The garden border of its wealth is shorn.
A subtile stillness broods o'er all the scene,
  The benediction of the year has come;
The sheaves are garnered from the fading field,
  The husbandman has sung the "Harvest Home."

In faded meadows, where the partridge trills
  His clear, loud song to call his wandering mate,
The streams are shallow and the grasses brown,
  Where scarlet poppies flecked the field but late.
There is a whisper in the falling stream,
  A sigh through all the aisles of forest trees,
A tremulous vibration in the songs
  The wild birds pour upon the evening breeze.

The sweet, dead days will come to us no more;
  New summers may bring harvests of delight,
Fair days may dawn with eyes of splendid hue,
  They cannot shine so infinitely bright
As the sweet, vanished hours which we have lost;
  Or are they only garnered safe and sure,
To wait for us in some far, future world,
  Where summers shall eternally endure?

The rustling leaves drop softly at my feet,
  Warm airs caress my cheeks with loving kiss,
No chill of autumn shivers in the air,
  Yet something indefinable I miss.
O Summer sweet, if never more on earth
  I may rejoice in all your beauty rare,
I cannot say farewell, for we shall meet
  Where you will bloom more infinitely fair.

Church's Musical Visitor.   D. M. JORDAN.

---◆---

LATE OCTOBER.

How peacefully the sunlight fell
  Across the woodland's pleasant reaches,
And like a shower of gilded rain
  The leaves dropped from the golden beeches!
Far down the shadowy aisles I heard
  An undertone of plaintive sighing,
As if the waning Summer wept
  For all her glories dead and dying.

The golden-rod, with drooping plume,
  Had lost its aureole of gladness;
The starless mullein by the road
  Dropped down its seeds like tears of sadness;

The far-off hill, veiled like a bride,
Seemed wedded to the sky immortal;
And through the sunset's golden gate
There flashed the gleam of heaven's portal.

O peaceful hour, O faith renewed,
That touched the fading earth with sweetness,
And lifted up my heart in thanks
For life's glad measure of completeness!
Though dead leaves rustle at my feet,
And all the fields are brown and sober,
The heart may blossom with new hope
Beneath the gray skies of October.

Cincinnati Commercial.   D. M. JORDAN.

MOON AND DAWN.

THE bluest gray — the grayest blue,
Where golden, gleaming stars are set;
A moon whose glorious yellow waves
Make fair the rippled rivulet.

Night has her curtain over all;
The firs show dark against the sky;
The only sound is in the song ·
Of a late nightingale close by.

The wooded walks, which seemed so sweet
Seen in the morning's fairy light,
Now, dim and shadowy, hold no charm
Save the mysterious charm of night.

One swallow stirs, the gold stars fade,
In the cold sky a chill wind wakes;
The gray clouds frighten out the morn,
And through pale mist the new day breaks.

Good-morn — good-night — which is the best?
God grant some day that I may find
Both true: good-morn to joy begun,
Good-night to sorrows left behind.

Sunday Magazine.

"WHEN THE FROST IS ON THE PUNKIN."

WHEN the frost is on the punkin and the fodder 's in the shock,
And you hear the kyouck and gobble of the struttin' turkey-
cock,
And the clackin' of the guineys, and the cluckin' of the hens,
And the rooster's hallelooyer as he tiptoes on the fence,

Oh, it 's then 's the time a feller is a feelin' at his best,
With the risin' sun to greet him from a night of gracious rest,
As he leaves the house bareheaded and goes out to feed the
    stock,
When the frost is on the punkin and the fodder 's in the shock.

There 's somepin kind o' hearty-like about the atmosphere
When the heat of summer 's over and the coolin' fall is here.
Of cours we miss the flowers, and the blossoms on the trees,
And the mumble of the hummin'-birds and the buzzin' of the bees;
But the air 's so appetizin', and the landscape through the haze
Of a crisp and sunny morning of the early autumn days
Is a picture that no painter has the colorin' to mock,
When the frost is on the punkin and the fodder 's in the shock.

The husky, rusty rustle of the tassels of the corn,
And the raspin' of the tangled leaves as golden as the morn;
The stubble in the furries — kind o' lonesome like, but still
A preachin' sermons to us of the barns they growed to fill;
The straw-stack in the medder, and the reaper in the shed,
The hosses in their stalls below, the clover overhead, —
Oh, it sets my heart a clickin' like the tickin' of a clock,
When the frost is on the punkin and the fodder 's in the shock.

JAMES WHITCOMB RILEY.

IN SNOW-TIME.

How should I choose to walk the world with thee,
Mine own beloved ? When green grass is stirred
By summer breezes, and each leafy tree
Shelters the nest of many a singing bird ?
In time of roses, when the earth doth lie
Dressed in a garment of midsummer hues,
Beneath a canopy of sapphire sky,
Lulled by a soft wind's song ? Or should I choose
To walk with thee along a wintry road,
Through flowerless fields, thick-sown with frosty rime,
Beside an ice-bound stream, whose waters flowed
In voiceless music all the summer-time ?
In winter dreariness, or summer glee,
How should I choose to walk the world with thee ?

The time of roses is the time of love,
Ah, my dear heart ! but winter fires are bright,
And in the lack of sunshine from above
We tend more carefully love's sacred light.
The path among the roses lieth soft
Sun-kissed and radiant under youthful feet ;
But on a wintry way true hands more oft
Do meet and cling in pressure close and sweet.

There is more need of love's supporting arm
Along life's slippery pathway, in its frost;
There is more need for love to wrap us warm
Against life's cold, when summer flowers are lost.
Let others share thy life's glad summer glow,
But let me walk beside thee in its snow.

THE TROUT–BROOK.

You see it first near the dusty road,
Where the farmer stops with his heavy load,
 At the foot of a weary hill;
There the mossy trough it overflows,
Then away, with a leap and a laugh, it goes
 At its own sweet, wandering will.

It flows through an orchard gnarled and old,
Where in spring the dainty buds unfold
 Their petals pink and white;
The apple-blossoms, so sweet and pure,
The streamlet's smiles and songs allure
 To float off on its ripples bright.

It winds through the meadow, scarcely seen,
For o'er it the flowers and grasses lean
 To salute its smiling face.
And thus, half hidden, it ripples along,
The whole way singing its summer song,
 Making glad each arid place.

Just there, where the water, dark and cool,
Lingers a moment in yonder pool,
 The dainty trout are at play;
And now and then one leaps in sight,
With sides aglow in the golden light
 Of the long, sweet summer day.

Oh, back to their shelves those books consign,
And look to your rod and reel and line,
 Make fast the feathered hook;
Then away from the town with its hum of life,
Where the air with worry and work is rife,
 To the charms of the meadow brook.

 Carl Waring

THE CLOUD.

A CLOUD came over a land of leaves
   (Oh, hush, little leaves, lest it pass you by!) —
How they had waited and watched for the rain,
Mountain and valley, and vineyard and plain,
   With never a sign from the sky!
Day after day had the pitiless sun
   Looked down with a lidless eye.

But now!   On a sudden a whisper went
   Through the topmost twigs of the poplar spire;
Out of the east a light wind blew;
(All the leaves trembled, and murmured, and drew
   Hope to the help of desire);
It stirred the faint pulse of the forest tree,
   And breathed through the brake and the brier.

Slowly the cloud came, and then the wind died,
   Dumb lay the land in its hot suspense;
The thrush on the elm-bough suddenly stopped,
The weather-warned swallow in mid-flying dropped,
   The linnet ceased song in the fence; —
Mute the cloud moved, till it hung overhead,
   Heavy, big-bosomed, and dense.

Ah, the cool rush through the dry-tongued trees,
   The patter and plash on the thirsty earth,
The eager bubbling of runnel and rill,
The lisping of leaves that have drunk their fill,
   The freshness that follows the dearth!
New life for the woodland, the vineyard, the vale,
   New life with the world's new birth!

PART V.

Love, Sentiment, and Friendship.

The fountains mingle with the river,
  And the rivers with the ocean,
The winds of heaven mix forever
  With a sweet emotion;
Nothing in the world is single;
  All things by a law divine
In one another's being mingle —
  Why not I with thine?

See the mountains kiss high heaven,
  And the waves clasp one another;
No sister flower would be forgiven
  If it disdained its brother:
And the sunlight clasps the earth,
  And the moonbeams kiss the sea, —
What are all these kissings worth,
  If thou kiss not me?

SHELLEY.

PART V.

Love, Sentiment, and Friendship.

———◆◆———

CHALCEDONY.

AGES long since, upon the desert waste,
Within the hollow rock a gem was formed;
Liquid at first, it hardened age by age, —
The rock slow crumbling into sand, the gem remained.

Nourished within my heart, intensest love
Of one fine nature, earnest, simple, rare —
Grew crystalline, and evermore shall live,
Outlasting that poor home wherein it grew.

EMMA POMEROY GREENOUGH.

———◆———

WHEN WILL LOVE COME?

SOME find Love late, some find him soon,
  Some with the rose in May,
Some with the nightingale in June,
  And some when skies are gray;
Love comes to some with smiling eyes,
  And comes with tears to some;
For some Love sings, for some Love sighs,
  For some Love's lips are dumb.
How will you come to me, fair Love?
  Will you come late or soon?
With sad or smiling skies above,
  By light of sun or moon?
Will you be sad, will you be sweet,
  Sing, sigh, Love, or be dumb?
Will it be summer when we meet,
  Or autumn ere you come?

PAKENHAM BEATTY.

A LOVE'S LIFE.

'T WAS springtime of the day and year;
    Clouds of white fragrance hid the thorn.
My heart unto her heart drew near,
    And ere the dew had fled the morn,
        Sweet Love was born.

An August noon, an hour of bliss,
    That stands amid my hours alone,
A word, a look, then — ah, that kiss!
    Joy's veil was rent, her secret known:
        Love was full-grown.

And now this drear November eve,
    What has to-day seen done, heard said?
It boots not; who has tears to grieve
    For that last leaf yon tree has shed,
        Or for Love dead?

Chambers's Journal.

THIS YEAR — NEXT YEAR.

THIS year — next year — sometime — never,
    Gayly did she tell;
Rose-leaf after rose-leaf ever
    Eddied round and fell.

This year — and she blushed demurely;
    That would be too soon;
He could wait a little, surely,
    'T is already June.

Next year — that's almost too hurried,
    Laughingly said she;
For when once a girl is married,
    She no more is free.

Sometime — that is vague — long waiting
    Many a trouble brings;
'Twixt delaying and debating
    Love might use its wings.

Never — word of evil omen,
    And she sighed, heigh-ho, —
'T is the hardest lot for women
    Lone through life to go.

Next year — early in the May-time,
    Was to be the day;
Looked she sweetly toward that gay time
    Gleaming far away.

Never — fair with bridal flowers
    Came that merry spring ;
Ere those bright and radiant hours
    She had taken wing.

This year — hearts are bound by sorrow ;
    Next year — some forget ;
Sometime — comes that golden morrow ;
    Never — earth say yet.

———◆———

LIGHT.

THE night has a thousand eyes,
    And the day but one ;
Yet the light of the bright world dies
    With the dying sun.

The mind has a thousand eyes,
    And the heart but one ;
Yet the light of a whole life dies
    When love is done.

                FRANCIS W. BOURDILLON

———◆———

LOVE AND PITY.

LOVE came a beggar to her gate,
The night was drear, the hour was late,
And through the gloom she heard his moan
Where at the gate he stood alone.

His rounded form in rags was clad,
His weeping eyes were wan and sad ;
But hid beneath his garb of woe
He bore his arrows and his bow.

She wept to see the beggar weep,
She bade him on her bosom sleep,
His wretched plight allayed her fears,
She kissed and bathed him with her tears.

The merry eyes began to glow,
The rosy hand essayed the bow,
The rough disguise was cast aside,
And laughing Love for mercy cried.

Love came a beggar to her gate,
More wisely than with pomp and state ;
For who hath woman's pity won
May count love's siege and battle done.

COULD N'T KEEP A SECRET.

I TOLD my secret to the sweet wild roses,
    Heavy with dew, new waking in the morn;
And they had breathed it to a thousand others
    Before another day was slowly born.
" Oh, fickle roses," said I, " you shall perish ! "
    So plucked them for my lady sweet to wear
In the pure silence of her maiden bosom,
    The curled luxuriance of her chestnut hair.

I told the secret to a bird new building
    Her nest at peace within the spreading tree ;
And ere her children had begun to chatter,
    She told it o'er and o'er right joyously.
" Oh, traitor bird," I whispered, " stay thy singing,
    Thou dost not know, there in thy nest above,
That secrets are not made to tell to others,
    That silence is the birthright of true love."

I told the secret to my love, my lady ;
    She held it closely to her darling breast.
Then, as I clasped her, came a tiny whisper :
    " The birds and flowers told me all the rest,
Nor shouldst thou chide them that they spake the secret;
    The whole world is a chord of love divine,
And birds and flowers but fulfil their mission
    In telling secrets sweet as mine and thine."

All the Year Round.

WHAT MY LOVER SAID.

By the merest chance, in the twilight gloom,
    In the orchard path he met me,
In the tall wet grass with its faint perfume,
And I tried to pass, but he made no room ;
    Oh, I tried, but he would not let me !
So I stood and blushed till the grass grew red,
    With my face bent down above it,
While he took my hand, as he whispering said —
How the clover lifted its pink, sweet head,
To listen to all that my lover said !
    Oh, the clover in bloom ! I love it.

In the high, wet grass went the path to hide,
    And the low wet leaves hung over ;
But I could not pass on either side,
For I found myself, when I vainly tried,
    In the arms of my steadfast lover.

And he held me there and he raised my head,
  While he closed the path before me,
And he looked down into my eyes and said —
How the leaves bent down from the boughs o'erhead,
To listen to all that my lover said,
  Oh, the leaves hanging lowly o'er me !

I am sure he knew, when he held me fast,
  That I must be all unwilling;
For I tried to go, and I would have passed,
As the night was come with its dews at last,
  And the skies with stars was filling.
But he clasped me close, when I would have fled,
  And he made me hear his story,
And his soul came out from his lips, and said —
How the stars crept out, when the white moon led,
To listen to all that my lover said.
  Oh, the moon and the stars in glory !

I know that the grass and the leaves will not tell,
  And I 'm sure that the wind, precious rover,
Will carry his secret so safely and well
  That no being shall ever discover
One word of the many that rapidly fell
  From the eager lips of my lover.
And the moon and the stars that looked over
Shall never reveal what a fairy-like spell
They wove round about us that night in the dell,
  In the path through the dew-laden clover ;
Nor echo the whispers that made my heart swell
  As they fell from the lips of my lover.
                         HOMER GREENE.

———◆———

LOVE'S TRANSFIGURATION.

O STRANGE sweet loveliness ! O tender grace,
  That in the light of passion's dayspring threw
Soft splendor on a fair familiar face,
  Changing it, yet unchanged and old, yet new !
Perfect the portrait in my heart, and true,
  Which traced the smile about the flower-like mouth,
And those gray eyes with just a doubt of blue,
  Yet darkened with the passion of the South.
And the white arch of thoughtful forehead crowned
With meeting waves of hair ; — but still I found
Some undreamt light of tenderness that fell
  From the new dawn, and made more fair to see
What was so fair, that now no song can tell
  How lovely seemed thy love-lit face to me.
Chambers's Journal.

LOVE'S BELIEF.

I.

I BELIEVE if I should die,
And you should kiss my eyelids where I lie
Cold, dead, and dumb to all the world contains,
The folded orbs would open at thy breath,
And, from its exile in the Isles of Death,
Life would come gladly back along my veins.

II.

I believe if I were dead,
And you upon my lifeless heart should tread, —
Not knowing what the poor clod chanced to be, —
It would find sudden pulse beneath the touch
Of him it ever loved in life so much,
And throb again, warm, tender, true to thee.

III.

I believe if in my grave,
Hidden in woody deeps all by the wave,
Your eyes should drop some warm tears of regret,
From every salty seed of your deep grief
Some fair, sweet blossom would leap into leaf,
To prove that death could not make my love forget.

IV.

I believe if I should fade
Into that realm where light is made,
And you should long once more my face to see,
I would come forth upon the hills of night
And gather stars like fagots, till thy sight,
Fed by the beacon-blaze, fell full on me.
I believe my love for thee
(Strong as my life) so nobly placed to be,
It could as soon expect to see the sun
Fall like a dead king from his heights sublime,
His glory stricken from the throne of time,
As thee unworthy the worship thou hast won.

V.

I believe who has not loved
Hath half the treasure of his life unproved,
Like one who, with the grape within his grasp,
Drops it, with all its crimson juice unpressed,
And all its luscious sweetness left unguessed,
Out of his careless and unheeding grasp.
I believe love, pure and true,
Is to the soul a sweet, immortal dew

That gems life's petals in the hour of dusk;
The waiting angels see and recognize
The rich crown-jewel love of Paradise,
When life falls from us like a withered husk.

———◆———

LIGHT AND LOVE.

Iʄ light should strike through every darkened place,
   How many a deed of darkness and of shame
Would cease, arrested by its gentle grace,
   And striving virtue rise, unscathed by blame!
The prisoner in his cell new hopes would frame,
The miner catch the metal's lurking trace,
The sage would grasp the ills that harm our race,
   And unknown heroes leap to sudden fame.
If love but one short hour had perfect sway,
   How many a rankling sore its touch would heal,
How many a misconception pass away,
   And hearts long hardened learn at last to feel:
What sympathies would wake, what feuds decay
If perfect love might reign but one short day!

The Academy.

———◆———

FRIEND OR FOE?

Patter! patter! running feet!
Something stirring in the street!
Does it come, or does it go?
Patter! patter!   Friend or foe?

Love, the merry tricksy sprite,
In my lantern sits to-night.
Be it coming, friend or foe,
Love will "show him up" I know.

Patter! patter! nearer still;
Shall I? — no — I — yes — I will.
"Who goes there?" — "It's only me!"
Ah! my little pet Marie!

Merry, loving, fond, and fair,
In the dark I see you there.
Still the sentry I will play:
"There's a password, love, to say."

What!   She cannot answer me?
Has she lost her tongue, may be?
Never mind, love; face full well
Tells what lips refuse to tell!

9

Passwords, questions, little one,
We can quite well leave alone.
Other folks than we, I know,
Shall solve our riddle : Friend or foe ?

F. E. WEATHERLY.

LOVE'S LOGIC.

I. HER RESPECTABLE PAPA'S.

"MY dear, be sensible ! Upon my word
This — for a woman even — is absurd ;
His income 's not a hundred pounds, I know.
He 's not worth loving." — "But I love him so."

II. HER MOTHER'S.

" You silly child, he is well made and tall ;
But looks are far from being all in all.
His social standing 's low, his family 's low.
He 's not worth loving." — "And I love him so."

III. HER ETERNAL FRIEND'S.

" Is that he picking up the fallen fan ?
My dear ! he 's such an awkward, ugly man !
You must be certain, pet, to answer ' No.'
He 's not worth loving." — " And I love him so."

IV. HER BROTHER'S.

" By Jove ! were I a girl — through horrid hap —
I would n't have a milk-and-water chap.
The man has not a single spark of ' go.'
He 's not worth loving." — " Yet I love him so."

V. HER OWN.

" And were he everything to which I 've listened :
Though he were ugly, awkward (and he is n't),
Poor, low-born, and destitute of ' go,'
He is worth loving, for I love him so."

Chambers's Journal.

"YES."

THEY stood above the world,
    In a world apart ;
And she drooped her happy eyes,
And stilled the throbbing pulses
    Of her happy heart.

And the moonlight fell above her,
Her secret to discover;
    And the moonbeams kissed her hair,
As though no human lover
    Had laid his kisses there.

"Look up, brown eyes," he said,
    "And answer mine;
Lift up those silken fringes
That hide a happy light
    Almost divine."
The jealous moonlight drifted
To the finger half uplifted,
    Where shone the opal ring —
Where the colors danced and shifted
    On the pretty, changeful thing.

Just the old, old story
    Of light and shade,
Love like the opal tender,
Like it may be to vary —
    May be to fade.
Just the old tender story,
Just a glimpse of morning glory
    In an earthly Paradise,
With shadowy reflections
    In a pair of sweet brown eyes.

Brown eyes a man might well
    Be proud to win !
Open to hold his image,
Shut under silken lashes,
    Only to shut him in.
O glad eyes, look together,
For life's dark, stormy weather
    Grows to a fairer thing
When young eyes look upon it
    Through a slender wedding ring.

R. D. Blackmore.

——◆——

REUNITED LOVE.

"I dreamed that we were lovers still,
    As tender as we used to be
When I brought you the daffodil,
    And you looked up and smiled at me."

"True sweethearts were we then, indeed,
    When youth was budding into bloom;
And now the flowers are gone to seed,
    And breezes have left no perfume."

"Because you ever, ever will
   Take such a crooked view of things,
Distorting this and that, until
   Confusion ends in cavillings."

"Because you never, never will
   Perceive the force of what I say ;
As if I always reasoned ill —
   Enough to take one 's breath away ! "

"But what if riper love replace
   The vision that enchanted me,
When all you did was perfect grace,
   And all you said was melody ? "

"And what if loyal heart renew
   The image never quite foregone,
Combining, as of yore, in you
   A Samson and a Solomon ? "

"Then to the breezes will I toss
   The straws we split with temper's loss ;
Then seal upon your lips anew
   The peace that gentle hearts ensue."

"Oh, welcome then, ye playful ways,
   And sunshine of the early days ;
And banish to the clouds above
   Dull reason, that bedarkens love ! "

Blackwood.   R. D. BLACKMORE.

THE SEA'S LOVE.

ONCE in the days of old,
   In the years of youth and mirth,
The Sea was a lover bright and bold,
   And he loved the golden Earth.
The Sun, in his royal raiment clad,
   Loved her and found her sweet,
But the Sea was content and glad
   Only to be at her feet.
       Ah! that the bards should sing,
          And wail for the golden years !
       Love was and is but an idle thing,
       'T is but a wind that veers.

And Earth in her beauty and pride
   Held her lips to the wooing Sun ;
He said, "Thou art fair, O my bride,"
   And she sang, "I am thine alone."

The faithful Sea at her faithless feet
  Rolled with a broken moan;
"O Sun!" he cried, "but thy bride is sweet,
  And I am alone, alone!"
    Ah! that the bards, etc.

Oft would the Sun depart,
  And his bride in her gloom made moan,
And the Sea would cry that her loving heart
  Should be left to pine alone.
And his voice is strange and sad and sweet,
  "O love, not mine! not mine!
I am content to lie at thy feet,
  And love thee in storm and shine."
    Ah! that the bards should sing,
      And wail for the golden years!
    Love was and is but an idle thing,
      'T is but a wind that veers.

F. E. WEATHERLY.

INDECISION.

  Do I love her?
Dimpling red lips at me pouting,
Dimpling shoulders at me flouting;
  No, I don't!

  Do I love her?
Prisoned in those crystal eyes
Purity forever lies;
  Yes, I do!

  Do I love her?
Little wild and wilful fiction,
Teasing, torturing contradiction;
  No, I don't!

  Do I love her?
With kind acts and sweet words she
Aids and comforts poverty;
  Yes, I do!

  Do I love her?
Quick she puts her cuirass on,
Stabs with laughter, stings with scorn;
  No, I don't!

  Do I love her?
No! Then to my arms she flies,
Filling me with glad surprise;
  Ah, yes, I do!

FRENCH WITH A MASTER.

Aimer, aimer ; c'est à vivre.
("To love, to love ; this it is to live.")

TEACH you French ?   I will, my dear !
Sit and con your lesson here.
What did Adam say to Eve ?
Aimer, aimer ; c'est à vivre.

Don't pronounce the last word long ;
Make it short to suit the song ;
Rhyme it to your flowing sleeve,
Aimer, aimer ; c'est à vivre.

Sleeve, I said, but what 's the harm
If I really meant your arm ?
Mine shall twine it (by your leave),
Aimer, aimer ; c'est à vivre.

Learning French is full of slips ;
Do as I do with the lips ;
Here 's the right way, you perceive,
Aimer, aimer ; c'est à vivre.

French is always spoken best
Breathing deeply from the chest ;
Darling, does your bosom heave ?
Aimer, aimer ; c'est à vivre.

Now, my dainty little sprite,
Have I taught your lesson right ?
Then what pay shall I receive ?
Aimer, aimer ; c'est à vivre.

Will you think me overbold
If I linger to be told
Whether you yourself believe
Aimer, aimer ; c'est à vivre ?

Pretty pupil, when you say
All this French to me to-day,
Do you mean it, or deceive ?
Aimer, aimer ; c'est à vivre.

Tell me, may I understand,
When I press your little hand,
That our hearts together cleave ?
Aimer, aimer ; c'est à vivre.

Have you in your tresses room
For some orange-buds to bloom ?
May I such a garland weave ?
Aimer, aimer ; c'est à vivre.

Or, if I presume too much,
Teaching French by sense of touch,
Grant me pardon and reprieve!
Aimer, aimer ; c'est à vivre.

Sweetheart, no! you cannot go!
Let me sit and hold you so;
Adam did the same to Eve, —
Aimer, aimer ; c'est à vivre.

THEODORE TILTON.

NOTE. — This dainty little love-poem was read by the Hon. William M.
Evarts to the jury in the celebrated Beecher-Tilton case. The poem and
its reading was received with the warmest applause, in which court, counsel,
and spectators joined. Even the weary jury could not forbear to smile.

AFEARED OF A GAL.

OH, darn it all! — afeared of her,
    And such a mite of a gal ;
Why, two of her size rolled into one
    Won't ditto sister Sal!
Her voice is sweet as the whippoorwill's,
    And the sunshine 's in her hair ;
But I 'd rather face a redskin's knife,
    Or the grip of a grizzly bear.
Yet Sal says, " Why, she 's such a dear,
    She 's just the one for you."
Oh, darn it all! — afeared of a gal,
    And me just six feet two!

Though she ain't any size, while I 'm
    Considerable tall,
I 'm nowhere when she speaks to me,
    She makes me feel so small.
My face grows red, my tongue gets hitched,
    The cussed thing won't go ;
It riles me, 'cause it makes her think
    I 'm most tarnation slow.
And though folks say she 's sweet on me,
    I guess it can't be true.
Oh, darn it all! — afeared of a gal,
    And me just six feet two!

My sakes! just s'pose if what the folks
    Is saying should be so!
Go, Cousin Jane, and speak to her,
    Find out and let me know ;
Tell her the gals should court the men,
    For is n't this leap-year?
That 's why I 'm kind of bashful like,
    A waiting for her here.

And should she hear I 'm scared of her,
You 'll swear it can't be true.
Oh, darn it all ! — afeared of a gal,
And me just six feet two !

A CONCEIT.

OH, touch that rosebud ! it will bloom —
        My lady fair !
A passionate red in dim green gloom,
A joy, a splendor, a perfume
        That sleeps in air.

You touched my heart ; it gave a thrill
        Just like a rose
That opens at a lady's will ;
Its bloom is always yours, until
        You bid it close.

MORTIMER COLLINS.

L'ENVOY.

DRAW down thy curtains close, O heart !
Shut out the rays that, beaming bright,
        Reveal my darkening sorrow ;
Our paths diverge, our paths now part,
And mine drifts out into the night —
        A night without a morrow.

I, dreaming, waited long and loved,
Nor spoke one word of germèd fire ;
        Deep hidden, slept my passion ;
While, side by side, we onward moved,
Calm friendship yours, mine, fond desire —
        Love met with cold compassion.

Now, merry, merry clash the bells ;
Bring sheeny robes and ivy leaf ;
        Bring crown of orange-flowers :
He in thy smile forever dwells,
While I drift on through clouds of grief,
        Gold fringed with happy bygone hours.

Love, Love, farewell ; and ne'er again,
In all the drear and empty realm
        That bounds my heart so weary,
Shall Love rebuild to him a fane ;
And loveless, drifting without helm,
        My life will float, so dreary.

RANDOLPH.

THE MILLER AND THE MAID.

ACROSS the heath and down the hill,
  Aback of patient Dobbin,
The farmer's daughter rides to mill,
  And mocks the thrush and robin.

For saddle she's a sack of grain,
  She sidewise sits and chirrups;
A finger in old Dobbin's mane
  Is good as forty stirrups.

The miller comes — a merry blade! —
  And doffs his hat and greets her:
"What wish you here, my pretty maid?"
  "I've brought a sack of wheat, sir."

"And have you gold to give for grist?"
  "Not I, we're poor, alack! sir;
But take your toll — a tenth, I wist —
  From what is in my sack, sir."

He lifts her lightly from her seat,
  And laughs — a merry miller!
"I cannot take my toll in wheat,
  I must have gold or siller.

"But since you've brought nor coin nor scrip,"
  He smiles and fondly eyes her —
"I'll ask no toll but from your lip —
  One kiss! who'll be the wiser?"

The maiden blushed and bowed her head,
  And with her apron fingered,
And pouted out her lips of red
  Where countless kisses lingered.

"A single kiss?" (She smiled in glee,
  As who would say, "I've caught you.")
"My father said your toll would be
  A tenth of what I brought you."

The mill-stream shouted to the sands:
  "He kissed the farmer's daughter!"
But the grim old wheel stretched out its hands
  And spanked the saucy water.

F. N. SCOTT.

A KISS IN THE RAIN.

ONE stormy morn I chanced to meet
    A lassie in the town ;
Her locks were like the ripened wheat,
    Her laughing eyes were brown.
I watched her, as she tripped along,
    Till madness filled my brain,
And then — and then — I knew 't was wrong —
    I kissed her in the rain.

With rain-drops shining on her cheek,
    Like dew-drops on a rose,
The little lassie strove to speak,
    My boldness to oppose ;
She strove in vain, and, quivering,
    Her finger stole in mine ;
And then the birds began to sing,
    The sun began to shine.

Oh, let the clouds grow dark above,
    My heart is light below ;
'T is always summer when we love,
    However winds may blow ;
And I 'm as proud as any prince,
    All honors I disdain ;
She says I am her rain-beau since
    I kissed her in the rain.

TÊTE–À–TÊTE.

I.

A BIT of ground, a smell of earth,
    A pleasant murmur in the trees,
The chirp of birds, an insect's hum,
    And, kneeling on their chubby knees,

Two neighbors' children at their play ;
    Who has not seen a hundred such ?
A head of gold, a head of brown,
    Bending together till they touch.

II.

A country school-house by the road,
    A spicy scent of woods anear,
And all the air with summer sounds
    Laden for who may care to hear.

So do not two, a boy and girl,
 Who stay, when all the rest are gone,
Solving a problem deeper far
 Than one they seem intent upon.

Dear hearts, of course they do not know
 How near their heads together lean ;
The bee that wanders through the room
 Has hardly space to go between.

III.

Now darker is the head of brown,
 The head of gold is brighter now,
And lines of deeper thought and life
 Are written upon either brow.

The sense that thrills their being through
 With nameless longings vast and dim
Has found a voice, has found a name,
 And where he goes she follows him.

Again their heads are bending near,
 And bending down in silent awe
Above a morsel pure and sweet,
 A miracle of love and law.

How often shall their heads be bowed
 With joy or grief, with love and pride,
As waxeth strong that feeble life,
 Or slowly ebbs its falling tide!

IV.

A seaward hill where lie the dead
 In dreamless slumber deep and calm ;
Above their graves the roses bloom,
 And all the air is full of balm.

They do not smell the roses sweet ;
 They do not see the ships that go
Along the far horizon's edge ;
 They do not feel the breezes blow.

Here loving hands have gently laid
 The neighbors' children, girl and boy
And man and wife ; head close to head
 They sleep, and know nor pain nor joy.

Christian Union.

WEDDED.

Some quick and bitter words we said,
  And then we parted.   How the sun
Swam through the sullen mist of gray !
A chill fell on the summer day,
Life's best and happiest hours were done ;
  Friendship was dead.

How proud we went our separate ways,
  And spake no word and made no moan !
She braided up her flowing hair,
That I had always called so fair,
Although she scorned my loving tone,
  My word of praise.

And I ! I matched her scorn with scorn,
  I hated her with all my heart,
Until — we chanced to meet one day ;
She turned her pretty head away ;
I saw two pretty tear-drops start,
  Lo ! love was born.

Some fond, repenting word I said,
  She answered only with a sigh ;
But when I took her hand in mine
A radiant glory, half divine,
Flooded the earth and filled the sky —
  Now we are wed.

———◆———

MUSIC IN THE SOUL.

Over my soul the great thoughts roll
  Like the waves of a mighty sea ;
But clear through the rushing and surging there sounds
  A wonderful music to me.
    So sweet, so low, the harmonies flow ;
    They rise and they fall, they come and they go ;
    Wonderful, beautiful, soft, and slow.

Not here, not there, not in this calm air,
  Nor born of the silver sea ;
Immortal — beyond all the music of man —
  It is love that is singing to me.
    So sweet, so low, the harmonies flow ;
    They rise and they fall, they come and they go ;
    Wonderful, beautiful, soft, and slow.

Not mine alone this melting tone —
  The soul of it comes from thee —
For thou in thy bosom art singing of love,
  And the music flows over to me.
    So sweet, so low, the harmonies flow;
    They rise and they fall, they come and they go;
    Wonderful, beautiful, soft, and slow.

———◆———

YES?

Is it true, then, my girl? did you mean it —
  The word spoken yesterday night?
Does that hour seem so sweet now between it
  And this has come day's sober light?
Have you woke from a moment of rapture
  To remember, regret, and repent,
And to hate, perchance, him who has trapped your
  Unthinking consent?

Who was he, last evening — this fellow
  Whose audacity lent him a charm?
Have you promised to wed Punchinello?
  For life taken Figaro's arm?
Will you have the Court fool of the papers,
  The clown in the journalist's ring,
Who earns his scant bread by his capers,
  To be your heart's king?

A Modoc — a Malay — a Kaffir
  ("Bohemian" puts it too mild);
By profession a poor paragrapher,
  Light Laughter's unrecognized child;
At the best but a Brummagem poet,
  Inspired of tobacco and beer,
Altogether off color — I know it;
  I 'm all that, my dear.

When we met quite by chance at the theatre,
  And I saw you home under the moon,
I 'd no thought, love, that mischief would be at her
  Tricks with my tongue quite so soon;
That I should forget fate and fortune,
  Make a difference 'twixt Sêvres and delf;
That I 'd have the calm nerve to importune
  You, sweet, for yourself.

It 's appalling, by Jove, the audacious
  Effrontery of that request!
But you — you grew suddenly gracious,
  And hid your sweet face on my breast.

Why you did it I cannot conjecture;
  I surprised you, poor child, I dare say,
Or perhaps — does the moonlight affect your
  Head often that way?

It was glorious for me, but what pleasure
  Could you find in such wooing as this?
Were my arms not too ursine in pressure,
  Was no flavor of clove in my kiss?
Ah, your lips I profaned when I made with
  Their dainty divinity free, —
Twin loves never meant to be played with
  By fellows like me.

   .   .   .   .   .

You 're released! With some wooer replace me
  More worthy to be your life's light;
From the tablet of memory efface me,
  If you don't mean your "yes" of last night.
But unless you are anxious to see me a
  Wreck of the pipe and the cup
In my birthplace and graveyard, Bohemia —
  Love, don't give me up.

Puck.   H. C. BUNNER.

———◆———

YES!

"Is it true?" — that 's the doubtful suggestion
  I 've made to myself ever since;
Did I misinterpret your question?
  Is joy, then, so hard to convince?
"Is it true?" For my part, yes, completely,
  And, if I may answer for you,
I 'll add it is wondrously, sweetly,
  Entrancingly true.

Oh, dear, if I make a confession,
  You 'll admit you have tempted it forth;
If I own you have long had possession,
  You 'll not deem the prize of less worth?
If I say that a lifetime of pleasure
  Last evening was brimmed in my cup,
And that you poured the liberal measure,
  You won't give *me* up?

Ere ever I saw you I knew you,
  I watched for your song and your jest,
And fancy in bright colors drew you
  My hero, my Bayard, my best.
Nor was it mere fancy anointed
  Yourself as my bosom's high priest;
When we met I was not disappointed —
  No, love, not the least.

Last night! — and I'm owning already
　　The secrets of nearly a year.
They tell me you're fast, scarcely steady,
　　In short, a Bohemian, dear.
Well, those are not faults that need hurt you;
　　They'll do to pair off with my own —
You have all a Bohemian's virtue,
　　The rest I condone.

But I — how was I ever worthy
　　Of winning so precious a prize?
My thoughts, dear, are of the earth, earthy,
　　While yours soar away to the skies.
If all that you hint at were real, —
　　The jest, the despite, and the fleer,
The world could not dim my ideal,
　　Nor make you less dear.

So, darling, though you are above me
　　In intellect, knowledge, and worth,
Sufficient for me that you love me, —
　　I'll follow you over the earth.
Sufficient for me that you deem me a
　　Soul not unworthy to sup
The joys of your wondrous Bohemia —
　　I *can't* give you up.

　　　　　　　　　　　　GEORGE H. JESSOP.
*Written for the San Francisco Bohemian Club,
　as a reply to Bunner's " Yes ?"*

———◆———

ANTONY AND CLEOPATRA.

I AM dying, Egypt, dying!
　　Ebbs the crimson life-tide fast,
And the dark Plutonian shadows
　　Gather on the evening blast.
Let thine arm, O Queen, support me;
　　Hush thy sobs and bow thine ear!
Hearken to the great heart secrets
　　Thou, and thou alone, must hear.

Though my scarred and veteran legions
　　Rear their eagles high no more,
And my wrecked and scattered galleys
　　Strew dark Actium's fatal shore;
Though no glittering guards surround me,
　　Prompt to do their master's will,
I must perish like a Roman —
　　Die the great Triumvir still!

Let not Cæsar's servile minions
  Mock the lion thus laid low;
'T was no foeman's arm that felled him;
  'T was his own that dealt the blow —
His, who, pillowed on thy bosom,
  Turned aside from glory's ray —
His, who, drunk with thy caresses,
  Madly threw a world away.

Should the base plebeian rabble
  Dare assail my fame in Rome,
Where my noble spouse, Octavia,
  Weeps within her widowed home,
Seek her! Say the gods have told me —
  Altars, augurs, circling wings —
That her blood with mine commingled
  Yet shall mount the throne of kings!

As for thee, star-eyed Egyptian!
  Glorious sorceress of the Nile!
Light the path to Stygian horrors
  With the splendors of thy smile.
Give to Cæsar crowns and arches,
  Let his brow the laurel twine,
I can scorn the Senate's triumphs,
  Triumphing in love like thine.

I am dying, Egypt, dying!
  Hark! the insulting foeman's cry!
They are coming! Quick, my falchion!
  Let me front them ere I die.
Ah! no more amid the battle
  Shall my heart exulting swell;
Isis and Osiris guard thee —
  Cleopatra — Rome — farewell.
                    GEN. WILLIAM H. LYTLE.

CLEOPATRA TO ANTONY.

SPREAD a feast with choicest viands —
  Friends, 't will be my very last;
Bring the rarest flowers to grace it —
  Haste, my sands of life flow fast;
Place an asp beneath the lotus
  That shall light me to the grave
With its starry petals' splendor;
  Weep not, let your hearts be brave.

Speed, Octavia, with thy minions —
  Fire thy heart with deadly hate!
Thou wilt miss the royal victim —
  Cleopatra rules her fate!

She defies Rome's conquering legions!
  Let them triumph in her fall!
What is earthly pomp or greatness? —
  Love, thy love outweighs it all!

Thrones and sceptres are but trifles
  To my spirit's yearning pain;
What were fortune's gifts without *thee*
  I would lose the world to gain?
Let no base heart tell our story;
  Ages, speak, when time unurns
These dull ashes, say to Ages,
  Soul to soul their love still burns.

Fatal asp, thy sleep 's not endless,
  That the morrow's dawn will prove;
I shall reign in lands elysian,
  Antony's proud Queen of Love!
Isis and Osiris, hear me!
  Hear me, gods of boundless power!
Ye have tasted deathless passion!
  Ye will guide me to his bower!

Pardon, mighty ones, the error
  If Octavia I have wronged,
Judged by higher laws supernal;
  Ah! how earthly passions thronged.
Overpowering heart and reason,
  Nature, answering Nature's call,
Rushed as cloud responsive rushes
  On to cloud, to meet and — fall.

Antony, my love, I 'm dying!
  Curdles fast life's crimson tide,
But no dark Plutonian shadows
  Fall between us to divide.
Hark! the Stygian waters swelling,
  Call me, love, with thee to rest, —
Death I fear not since thou braved it,
  Pillowed on my aching breast.

Strange emotions fill my bosom
  As I near the vast unknown;
Yet my heart still throbs in dying,
  Antony, for thee alone.
Oh! "I feel immortal longings," —
  I can brave stern Pluto's frown, —
Robe me in my regal garments,
  Deck with jewels, sceptre, crown.

Antony! I 'm coming! coming!
  Open, open wide thine arms!
Ah! the blissful hope of union
  Robs the grave of its alarms.

See ! the glorious heroes beckon
 O'er the Stygian water's swell.
I shall have immortal crowning !
 Egypt — dear old Nile ! — farewell.
                    SARAH DOUDNEY.

———◆———

CLEOPATRA'S SOLILOQUY.

WHAT care I for the tempest ?   What care I for the rain ?
If it beat upon my bosom, would it cool its burning pain, —
This pain that ne'er has left me since on his heart I lay,
And sobbed my grief at parting as I 'd sob my soul away ?
O Antony ! Antony ! Antony ! when in thy circling arms
Shall I sacrifice to Eros my glorious woman's charms,
And burn life's sweetest incense before his sacred shrine,
With the living fire that flashes from thine eyes into mine ?
Oh, when shall I feel thy kisses rain down upon my face,
As a queen of love and beauty I lie in thine embrace,
Melting, melting, melting, as a woman only can
When she 's a willing captive in the conquering arms of man,
As he towers a god above her — and to yield is not defeat,
For love can own no victor if love with love shall meet !
I still have regal splendor, I still have queenly power,
And, more than all, unfaded is woman's glorious dower.
But what care I for pleasure ? what 's beauty to me now,
Since Love no longer places his crown upon my brow ?
I have tasted its elixir, its fire has through me flashed,
But when the wine glowed brightest, from my eager lips 't was
          dashed.
And I would give all Egypt but once to feel the bliss
Which thrills through all my being whene'er I meet his kiss.
The tempest wildly rages, my hair is wet with rain,
But it does not still my longing or cool my burning pain.
For Nature's storms are nothing to the raging of my soul
When it burns with jealous frenzy beyond a queen's control.
I fear not pale Octavia, that haughty Roman dame,
My lion of the desert, my Antony, can tame.
I fear no Persian beauty, I fear no Grecian maid ;
The world holds not the woman of whom I am afraid.
But I 'm jealous of the rapture I tasted in his kiss,
And I would not that another should share with me that bliss.
No joy would I deny him, let him cull it where he will,
So mistress of his bosom is Cleopatra still ;
So that he feels forever, when he Love's nectar sips,
'T was sweeter, sweeter, sweeter when tasted on my lips ;
So that all other kisses, since he has drawn in mine,
Shall be unto my loved as " water after wine."
Awhile let Cæsar fancy Octavia's pallid charms
Can hold Rome's proudest consul a captive from these arms.
Her cold embrace but brightens the memory of mine,
And for my warm caresses he in her arms shall pine.

'T was not for love he sought her, but for her princely dower;
She brought him Cæsar's friendship, she brought him kingly
    power.
I should have bid him take her, had he my counsel sought,—
I 've but to smile upon him, and all her charms are nought;
For I would scorn to hold him by but a single hair
Save his own longing for me when I 'm no longer there;
And I will show you, Roman, that for one kiss from me
Wife, fame, and even honor to him shall nothing be!

Throw wide the window, Isis, fling perfumes o'er me now,
And bind the lotus-blossoms again upon my brow.
The rain has ceased its weeping, the driving storm is past,
And calm are Nature's pulses that lately beat so fast.
Gone is my jealous frenzy, and Eros reigns serene,
The only god e'er worshipped by Egypt's haughty queen.
With Antony, my loved, I 'll kneel before his shrine
Till the loves of Mars and Venus are nought to his and mine;
And down through coming ages, in every land and tongue,
With them shall Cleopatra and Antony be sung.
Burn sandal-wood and cassia; let the vapor round me wreathe,
And mingle with the incense the lotus-blossoms breathe;
Let India's spicy odors and Persia's perfumes rare
Be wafted on the pinions of Egypt's fragrant air.
With the singing of the night breeze, the river's rippling flow,
Let me hear the notes of music in cadence soft and low.
Draw round my couch its curtains; I 'd bathe my soul in sleep;
I feel its gentle languor upon me slowly creep.
Oh, let me cheat my senses with dreams of future bliss,
In fancy feel his presence, in fancy taste his kiss,
In fancy nestle closely against his throbbing heart,
And throw my arms around him, no more, no more to part.
Hush! hush! his spirit's pinions are rustling in my ears;
He comes upon the tempest to calm my jealous fears;
He comes upon the tempest in answer to my call,—
Wife, fame, and even honor, for me he leaves them all;
And royally I 'll welcome my lover to my side.
I have won him, I have won him from Cæsar and his bride.

The Galaxy.　　　　　　　　　　　　　MARY BAYARD CLARK.

---◆---

CLEOPATRA'S DREAM.

Lo, by Nilus' languid waters
    Fades the dreamy summer day,
Where, on couch of gold and crimson,
    Egypt's royal daughter lay,—
Dreaming lay, while palm and pillar
    Cast their lengthening shadows now,
And the lotus-laden zephyrs
    Lightly kissed her queenly brow.

Soft the evening steals upon her,
     As behind the curtained west
Sinks the day-god in his splendor —
     Folds his wooing arms to rest.
Drowsy shades of dusky Egypt
     Homeward, slow, their burdens bear,
While the boatman's lazy challenge
     Falls upon the quivering air.

Dreams she of her Roman lover,
     He who cast a crown away,
Country, kindred, fame, and honor,
     In her captive arms to lay?
Ay! of Antony her hero,
     Sharer of her heart and throne,
He whose ships, now homeward sailing,
     Bear her all of love alone.

Starts she in her sleeping glory,
     And her brown arms, jewelled, bare,
Round and rich in queenly beauty,
     Wildly cleave the slumberous air.
Beads of perspiration gather
     On her matchless woman's brow,
While her parted lips in anguish
     Tell of heart-pangs none may know.

Sure some vision, dire and dreadful,
     Palls upon her eyes and brain,
Piercing to her being's centre
     With a fiery shaft of pain.
Like a sea her full-orbed bosom
     Swells and falls with pent-up ire;
Then her spirit breaks its thraldom,
     And she shrieks in wild despair: —

"Charmian, quick, unloose my girdle,
     Give me breath! I faint! I die!
Ho! slaves, bring my royal galley,
     Let us hence to Egypt fly.
Oh for vengeance on the traitor,
     And upon his Roman bride!
Let him never dare — ah, Charmian,
     Stand you closely by my side.

"Do I dream?   Is this my palace —
     Yon my sweetly flowing Nile?
Ah, I see — O great Osiris,
     How I thank thee for thy smile!
Oh, I've had such fearful vision —
     He, my Antony, untrue;
And my heart was nigh to bursting
     With its fearful weight of woe.

" But 't is over; yet I tremble —
  On what brink of fate I stand;
What prophetic bird of evil
  Hovers o'er this sacred land!
What if true should come my dreaming,
  And no more my love return!
Ah, the thought my heart's blood freezes,
  While my brain with madness burns."

.   .   .   .   .

Then she listened, gazing outward
  Toward a dim futurity —
And the Nile forever onward
  Bears its burdens to the sea;
And she catches from its whispers —
  Echoing whispers in her soul —
That her reign of love is ended,
  And her life is near its goal.

                    J. J. Owens.

STORY OF THE GATE.

Across the pathway, myrtle-fringed,
Under the maple, it was hinged —
  The little wooden gate;
'T was there within the quiet gloam,
When I had strolled with Nelly home,
  I used to pause and wait

Before I said to her good-night,
Yet loath to leave the winsome sprite
  Within the garden's pale;
And there, the gate between us two,
We 'd linger as all lovers do,
  And lean upon the rail.

And face to face, eyes close to eyes,
Hands meeting hands in feigned surprise,
  After a stealthy quest, —
So close I 'd bend, ere she 'd retreat,
That I 'd grow drunken from the sweet
  Tuberose upon her breast.

We 'd talk — in fitful style, I ween —
With many a meaning glance between
  The tender words and low;
We 'd whisper some dear, sweet conceit,
Some idle gossip we 'd repeat,
  And then I 'd move to go.

"Good-night," I 'd say ; "good-night — good-by ! "
"Good-night " — from her with half a sigh —
  "Good-night ! " "*Good*-night ! "   And then —
And then I do *not* go, but stand,
Again lean on the railing, and —
    Begin it all again.

Ah ! that was many a day ago —
That pleasant summer-time — although
    The gate is standing yet ;
A little cranky, it may be,
A little weather-worn — like me —
    Who never can forget

The happy — "End"?   My cynic friend,
Pray save your sneers — there was no "end."
    Watch yonder chubby thing !
That is our youngest, hers and mine ;
See how he climbs, his legs to twine
    About the gate and swing.

Scribner's Magazine.   HARRISON ROBERTSON.

IN THE HAMMOCK.

THE lazy, languid breezes sweep
  Across a fluttered crowd of leaves ;
The shadows fall so dim, so deep,
Ah, love, 't is good to dream and sleep
  Where nothing jars or nothing grieves.

My love she lies at languid ease
  Across her silken hammock's length ;
Her stray curls flutter in the breeze
That moves amidst the sunlit trees,
  And stirs their gold with mimic strength.

So calm, so still, the drowsy noon ;
  So sweet, so fair, the golden day ;
Too sweet that it should turn so soon
From set of sun to rising moon,
  And fade and pass away.

Her eyes are full of happy dreams,
  And languid with unuttered bliss ;
The calm of unstirred mountain streams,
The light of unforgotten scenes,
  Live in her thoughts of that or this.

A year, a month, a week, a day ;
  The meaning of some look or word,
Swift, sudden as a sunbeam's ray, —
Do these across her memory stray
  As if again she looked or heard ?

It may be so.   I would it were,
  For I who love and she who dreams;
The world to me is only her.
Can my heart's cry to pity stir
  Her heart that silent seems?

O deep eyes, lose your gentle calm;
  O fair cheek, lose your tint of rose;
O heart, beat swift with love's alarm,
That I may win with chain and charm,
  And hold you till life close.

Lo, sweet, I stand, and gaze and faint
  Beneath the wonder of your eyes,
Whose beauty I can praise and paint
Till words and fancy lose restraint,
  And fear forgotten dies.

London Society.

THE RING'S MOTTO.

A LOVER gave the wedding ring
  Into the goldsmith's hand;
"Grave me," he said, "a tender thought
  Within the golden band."
        The goldsmith graved
        With careful art,
        "Till death us part."

The wedding bell rang gladly out;
  The husband said, "O wife,
Together we shall share the grief,
  The happiness of life.
        I give to thee
        My hand, my heart,
        Till death us part."

'T was she that lifted now his hand,
  (O love, that this should be!)
Then on it placed the golden band,
  And whispered tenderly:
        "Till death us join,
        Lo, thou art mine,
        And I am thine.

"And when death joins, we nevermore
  Shall know an aching heart,
The bridal of that better love
  Death has no power to part.
        That troth will be,
        For thee and me,
        Eternity."

So up the hill and down the hill,
　　Through fifty changing years,
They shared each other's happiness,
　　They dried each other's tears.
　　　　Alas, alas,
　　　　That death's cold dart
　　　　Such love can part!

But one sad day — she stood alone
　　Beside his narrow bed;
She drew the ring from off her hand,
　　And to the goldsmith said:
　　　　"O man who graved
　　　　With careful art,
　　　　'Till death us part,'

"Now grave four other words for me, —
　　'Till death us join.'"　He took
The precious golden band once more,
　　With solemn, wistful look,
　　　　And wrought with care,
　　　　For love, not coin,
　　　　"Till death us join."

———◆———

ASKING.

HE stole from my bodice a rose,
　　My cheek was its color the while;
But, ah, the sly rogue! he well knows,
　　Had he asked it, I must have said no.

He snatched from my lips a soft kiss;
　　I tried at a frown — 't was a smile;
For, ah, the sly rogue! he knows this:
　　Had he asked it, I must have said no.

That "asking" in love 's a mistake,
　　It puts one in mind to refuse;
'T is best not to ask, but to take;
　　For it saves one the need to say no.

Yet, stay — this is folly I 've said;
　　Some things should be asked if desired;
My rogue hopes my promise to wed;
　　When he asks me, I will not say no.

AN OLD RHYME.

"I DARE not ask a kisse,
   I dare not beg a smile,
Lest having that or this,
   I might grow proud the while.
No, no, the utmost share
   Of my desire shall be
Only to kisse the aire
   That lately kissèd thee."

———◆———

THE FRIVOLOUS GIRL.

HER eyes were bright and merry,
   She danced in the mazy whirl ;
She took the world in its sunshine,
   For she was a frivolous girl.

She dressed like a royal princess,
   She wore her hair in a curl ;
The gossips said, " What a pity
   That she 's such a frivolous girl ! "

(TWENTY YEARS LATER.)

She 's a wife, a mother, a woman,
   Grand, noble, and pure as a pearl ;
While the gossips say, " Would you think it,
   Of only a frivolous girl ? "

Steubenville Herald.

———◆———

WHERE IGNORANCE IS BLISS.

Is love contagious ? — I don't know ;
But this I am prepared to say,
That I have felt for many a day
A great desire to make it so.

Does she vouchsafe a thought of me ?
Sometimes I think she does ; and then
I 'm forced to grope in doubt again,
Which seems my normal state to be.

Why don't I ask, and asking know?
I grant perhaps it might be wise;
But when I look into her eyes,
And hear her voice which thrills me so,

I think that on the whole I won't;
I 'd rather doubt than know she don't.

———◆———

AN EXPLANATION.

HER lips were so near
That — what else could I do?
You 'll be angry, I fear,
But her lips were so near —
Well, I can't make it clear,
Or explain it to you,
But — her lips were so near
That — what else could I do?

Scribner's Magazine.   WALTER LEARNED.

———◆———

THINE EYES.

THOU hast diamonds and pearls of rare beauty,
Thou hast all that the heart can admire;
Thine eyes shine far brighter than jewels —
What more can my darling desire?

On thine eyes, bright as stars of the evening,
Have I written and tuned to my lyre
Whole volumes of rapturous sonnets —
What more can my darling desire?

With thine eyes of unquenchable splendor
Hast thou kindled my heart into fire,
And forced me to kneel as thy suitor —
What more can my darling desire?

JOHN F. BALLANTYNE.
(From the German of Heine.)

———◆———

HYMN TO SANTA RITA,

THE PATRON SAINT OF THE IMPOSSIBLE.

HAVE you heard of Santa Rita?
Patron of the hopeless, she;
Fleeting dreams of pleasure fleeter
Under her protection be;

Idle wish and aspiration,
   Fruitless hope and gray despair,
Crave alike her mediation, —
   Santa Rita! hear my prayer

Long have I, with ardor leal,
   Sought the maiden of my dreams,
Chasing still my bright ideal,
   Like a marsh-light's taunting gleams.
Candles sweet and incense sweeter
   Do I vow thee, week by week, —
Give me, lovely Santa Rita!
   The ideal girl I seek.

Rich fair eyes, like summer twilight
   Ere the stars glint through the blue,
Beaming with a soft and shy light,
   Hiding summer lightnings too;
Rich brown hair in wayward cluster,
   Rippling down in heavy fold,
Giving in the sunset's lustre
   Here and there a gleam of gold;

Fair, sweet face, whose quick expression
   Mirrors well the thoughts that flit, —
Soft now with love's shy confession,
   Brightened now by fire of wit;
Fair, sweet nature, were I bolder
   To dispel the doubts that spring,
I would touch her angel shoulder,
   Just to feel the budding wing!

Silver voice to charm and fill me
   With an ecstasy of sound;
Springing, buoyant step to thrill me
   In the waltz's dazing round;
Mind as bright as rainbow's prism,
   Wit as keen as archer's dart,
And, to work the mechanism,
   Just a little mite of heart.

This my longing, Santa Rita!
   This the girl for whom I wait.
Tell me, tell me, shall I meet her
   Ere I die disconsolate?
Are my dreams but idle fancy?
   Lives there such a maiden rare?
I invoke thy necromancy, —
   Santa Rita! hear my prayer!

ALVEY A. ADEE

WE LOVE BUT FEW.

OH, yes, we mean all kind words that we say
  To old friends and to new;
Yet doth this truth grow clearer day by day:
  We love but few.

We love! we love!   What easy words to say,
  And sweet to hear,
When sunrise splendor brightens all the way,
  And, far and near,

Are breath of flowers and carolling of birds,
  And bells that chime;
Our hearts are light: we do not weigh our words
  At morning time!

But when the matin music all is hushed,
  And life's great load
Doth weigh us down, and thick with dust
  Doth grow the road,

Then do we say less often that we love.
  The words have grown!
With pleading eyes we look to Christ above,
  And clasp our own.

Their lives are bound to ours by mighty bands
  No mortal strait,
Nor Death himself, with his prevailing hands,
  Can separate.

The world is wide, and many friends are dear,
  And friendships true;
Yet do these words read plainer, year by year:
  We love but few.

A SONG FOR THE GIRL I LOVE.

I.

A SONG for the girl I love —
  God love her!
A song for the eyes that tender shine,
And the fragant mouth that melts on mine,
The shimmering tresses uncontrolled
That clasp her neck with tendrils of gold;
And the blossom mouth and the dainty chin,
And the little dimples out and in —
    The girl I love —
      God love her!

II.

A song for the girl I loved —
    God loved her!
A song for the eyes of faded light,
And the cheek whose red rose waned to white,
And the quiet brow, with its shadow and gleam,
And the dark lashes drooped in a long, deep dream,
And the small hands cros·ed for their churchyard rest,
And the lilies dead on her sweet dead breast.
      The girl I loved —
        God loved her!
           FREDERICK LANGBRIDGE.

UNDOWERED.

THOU hast not gold? Why, this is gold
    All clustering round thy forehead white;
And were it weighed, and were it told,
    I could not say its worth to-night!

Thou hast not wit? Why, what is this
    Wherewith thou capturest many a wight,
Who doth forget a tongue is his,
    As I well-nigh forgot to-night?

Nor station? Well, ah, well! I own
    Thou hast no place assured thee quite;
So now I raise thee to a throne;
    Begin thy reign, my Queen, to-night.

Scribner's Magazine.   HARRIET McEWEN KIMBALL.

THE SILENCE OF LOVE.

I HOLD that we are wrong to seek
    To put in words our deepest thought;
    The purer things by Nature taught
Are turned to coarser when we speak.
The flower whose perfume charms the sense
    Grows hard and common to the touch,
    And love that's wordy overmuch
Is marred by its experience;
For love, like sympathy, hath bands
    More strong in silence than in speech,
    And hearts speak loudest, each to each,
Through meeting lips and clasp of hands.
Nor could I hope for fitting word
    To form in speech the thoughts that start;
    The inner core of every heart
Hath yearnings that are never heard.

They are too subtile, and transcend
　　The power of words to speak them right;
　　We therefore shut them out of sight,
To burn in silence to the end.
Yet even as the Magi held
　　Their sun as sacred, so I hold
　　My love is holy, sacred-souled,
And pure as sacred fire of eld.
Nor dare I stain with word or pen
　　This inner purer love to thee
　　Whose higher nature raiseth me
Beyond the common line of men.

HAMILTON DRUMMOND.

AH! ME.

THE fairest flower upon the vine —
　　So far above my reach it grows
I ne'er can hope to make it mine —
　　Smiles in the sun, — a peerless rose.
The wind is whispering soft and low
　　Fond praises of its loveliness;
　　Its sweetness I can only guess,
　　　　But never know.

On beauteous lips — as far away
　　As is the rose — a kiss there lies,
And on those lips that kiss must stay,
　　Though I may look with longing eyes;
A cruel fate hath willed it so,
　　Not mine that crimson mouth to press;
　　Its sweetness I can only guess,
　　　　But never know.

JUBILATE.

BEYOND the light-house, standing sentinel
　　Just where the line of earth and ocean meet,
The foam-crowned rollers slowly rose and fell
　　Upon the low reef with a murmurous beat.

And sweeping far away, like rippled gold,
　　Lay the wide bosom of the restless sea,
Where a brave ship down to the sky-line rolled,
　　Bearing afar the one most dear to me.

Slowly the broad moon dipped into the west,
　　And for a moment hung the waves above;
While borne along the ocean's lighted breast
　　The stout ship swiftly 'fore the strong wind drove.

Right in the sinking sphere she sailed at last,
 Her tall sails bearing her right bravely on ;
Out flashed a radiance, gilding hull and mast,
 And in a moment ship and moon were gone.

And seeing this, my heart grew glad and light.
 Though storms may roar along the restless main,
I know there is a limit to their might,
 And I shall have my sweetheart's kiss again.

———◆———

MY JOSIAR.

THINGS has come to a pretty pass
 The whole wide country over,
When every married woman has
 To have a friend or lover ;
It ain't the way that I was raised,
 And I hain't no desire
To have some feller pokin' round
 Instead of my Josiar.

I never kin forget the day
 That we went out a walkin',
An' sot down on the river-bank,
 An' kep' on hours a talkin' ;
He twisted up my apron-string
 An' folded it together,
An' said he thought for harvest time
 'T was cur'us kind o' weather.

The sun went down as we sot there —
 Josiar seemed uneasy ;
An' mother she began to call :
 " Looweezy, oh, Looweezy ! "
An' then Josiar spoke right up,
 As I was just a startin',
An' said, " Looweezy ! what's the use
 Of us two ever partin' ? "

It kind o' took me by surprise,
 An' yet I knew 't was comin' ;
I 'd heard it all the summer long
 In every wild bee's hummin' ;
I 'd studied out the way I 'd act, —
 But law ! I could n't do it ;
I meant to hide my love from him,
 But seems as if he knew it.
An' lookin' down into my eyes
 He must have seen the fire, —
An' ever since that hour I 've loved
 An' worshipped my Josiar.

I can't tell what the women mean
    Who let men fool around 'em,
Believin' all the nonsense that
    They only say to sound 'em;
I know, for one, I 've never seen
    The man that I 'd admire
To have a hangin' after me
    Instead of my Josiar.

THE CONSTANT FRIEND.

HUMAN hopes and human creeds
Have their root in human needs,
    And I would not wish to strip
    From that washerwoman's lip
Any song that she may sing,
Any hope that she can bring;
    For the woman has a friend
    That will keep her to the end.

E. F. WARE.

FRIENDSHIP.

FRIENDSHIP needs no studied phrases,
    Polished face, or winning wiles;
Friendship deals no lavish praises,
    Friendship dons no surface smiles.

Friendship follows Nature's diction,
    Shuns the blandishments of Art,
Boldly severs truth from fiction,
    Speaks the language of the heart.

Friendship favors no condition,
    Scorns a narrow-minded creed,
Lovingly fulfils its mission,
    Be it word or be it deed.

Friendship cheers the faint and weary,
    Makes the timid spirit brave,
Warns the erring, lights the dreary,
    Smooths the passage to the grave.

Friendship — pure, unselfish friendship,
    All through life's allotted span,
Nurtures, strengthens, widens, lengthens
    Man's affinity with man.

FRIENDSHIP, LOVE, AND TRUTH.

FRIENDSHIP doth bind, with pleasant ties,
    The heart of man to man, and age
But strengthens it — it never dies
    Till finished is life's final page.

Love is the sacred link which binds
    Hearts joined by friendship firmer still;
Who once has felt it, in it finds
    Joys which his soul with pleasure fill.

Truth only can complete the chain,
    Its links enduring strength can give;
With this unbroken 't will remain
    While e'er the human soul shall live.

DOLCE FAR NIENTE.

MY friend, my chum, my trusty crony!
    We are designed, it seems to me,
To be two happy lazzaroni,
On sunshine fed, and macaroni,
    Far off by some Sicilian sea.

From dawn to eve in the happy land,
    No duty on us but to lie —
Straw-hatted on the shining sand,
With bronzing chest and arm and hand —
    Beneath the blue Italian sky.

There, with the mountains idly glassing
    Their purple splendors in the sea —
To watch the white-winged vessels passing
(Fortunes for busier fools amassing),
    This were a heaven to you and me.

Our meerschaums coloring cloudy brown,
    Two young girls coloring with a blush,
The blue waves with a silver crown,
The mountain shadows dropping down,
    And all the air in perfect hush.

Thus should we lie in the happy land,
    Nor fame, nor power, nor fortune miss;
Straw-hatted on the shining sand,
With bronzing chest and arms and hand, —
    Two loafers couched in perfect bliss.

CHARLES GRAHAM HALPINE.
    (Miles O'Reilly.)

11

A BIRTHDAY GREETING.

WHAT shall I wish thee for the coming year?
Twelve months of dream-like ease? no care? no pain?
Bright spring, calm summer, autumn without rain
Of bitter tears? Wouldst have it thus, my friend?
What lesson, then, were learnt at the year's end?

What shall I wish thee, then? God knoweth well
If I could have my way no shade of woe
Should ever dim thy sunshine; but I know
Strong courage is not learnt in happy sleep,
Nor patience sweet by eyes that never weep.

Ah, would my wishes were of more avail
To keep from thee the many jars of life!
Still let me wish thee courage for the strife, —
The happiness that comes of work well done, —
And, afterwards, the peace of victory won!

                                        M. E. F.

OLD FRIENDS.

WE just shake hands at meeting
  With many that come nigh,
We nod the head in greeting
  To many that go by.
But we welcome through the gateway
  Our few old friends and true;
Then hearts leap up and straightway
  There's open house for you,
      Old friends,
Wide-open house for you.

The surface will be sparkling,
  Let but a sunbeam shine,
But in the deep lies darkling
  The true life of the wine.
The froth is for the many,
  The wine is for the few;
Unseen, untouched of any,
  We keep the best for you,
      Old friends,
The very best for you.

"The many" cannot know us,
  They only pace the strand
Where at our worst we show us,
  The waters thick with sand;

But out beyond the leaping
  Dim surge " 't is clear and blue,"
And there, old friends, we 're keeping
  A waiting calm for you,
    Old friends,
A sacred calm for you.

———◆———

SOMETIMES.

SOMETIMES — not often — when the days are long,
  And golden lie the ripening fields of grain,
Like cadence of some half-forgotten song,
  There sweeps a memory across my brain.
I hear the handrail far among the grass,
  The drowsy murmur in the scented lanes;
I watch the radiant butterflies that pass,
  And I am sad and sick at heart sometimes —
      Sometimes.

Sometimes, when royal winter holds his sway,
  When every cloud is swept from azure skies,
And frozen pool and lighted hearth are gay
  With laughing lips and yet more laughing eyes,
·From far-off days an echo wanders by,
  That makes a discord in the Christmas chimes;
A moment in the dance or talk I sigh,
  And seem half lonely in the crowd sometimes —
      Sometimes.

Not often, not for long. O friend, my friend,
  We were not lent our life that we might weep:
The flower-crowned May of earth hath soon an end;
  Should our fair spring a longer sojourn keep?
Comes all too soon the time of fading leaves,
  Come on the cold short days. We must arise
And go our way, and garner home our sheaves,
  Though some far faint regret may cloud our eyes
      Sometimes.

Sometimes I see a light almost divine
  In meeting eyes of two that now are one.
Impatient of the tears that rise to mine,
  I turn away to seek some work undone.
There dawns a look upon some stranger face;
  I think, " How like, and yet how far less fair!"
And look, and look again, and seek to trace
  A moment more your fancied likeness there —
      Sometimes.

O sad, sweet thoughts! O foolish, vain regrets!
  As wise it were, what time June roses blow,
To weep because the first blue violet
  We found in spring has faded long ago.
O love, my love, if yet by song of bird,
  By flower-scent, by some sad poet's rhymes,
My heart, that fain would be at peace, is stirred,
  Am I to blame that still I sigh sometimes?—
            Sometimes?

And sometimes know a pang of jealous pain,
  That, while I walk all lonely, other eyes
May haply smile to yours that smile again
  Beneath the sun and stars of Southern skies.
The past is past; but is it sin, if yet
  I, who in calm content would seek to dwell,
Who will not grieve, yet cannot quite forget,
  Still send a thought to you, and wish you well
            Sometimes?

                              LOUISA F. STORY.

PART VI.

Echoes of the Past.

Break, break, break,
  On thy cold gray stones, O Sea!
And I would that my tongue could **utter**
  The thoughts that arise in me.

Oh well for the fisherman's boy,
  That he shouts with his sister at play!
Oh well for the sailor lad,
  That he sings in his boat on the bay!

And the stately ships go on
  To their haven under the hill;
But oh for the touch of a vanish'd hand,
  And the sound of a voice that is still!

Break, break, break,
  At the foot of thy crags, O Sea!
But the tender grace of a day that is dead
  Will never come back to me.

TENNYSON.

PART VI.

Echoes of the Past.

———•◦•———

THE LOVE OF THE PAST.

As sailors watch from their prison
 For the long, gray line of the coasts,
I look to the past re-arisen,
 And joys come over in hosts
 Like the white sea-birds from their roosts.

I love not the delicate present,
 The future 's unknown to our quest ;
To-day is the life of the peasant,
 But the past is a haven of rest, —
 The joy of the past is the best.

The rose of the past is better
 Than the rose we ravish to-day ;
'T is holier, purer, and fitter
 To place on the shrine where we pray, —
 For the secret thoughts we obey.

There are no deceptions nor changes,
 There all is as placid and still ;
No grief nor fate that estranges,
 Nor hope that no life can fulfil ;
 But ethereal shelter from ill.

The coarse delights of the hour
 Tempt and debauch and deprave ;
And we joy in a poisonous flower,
 Knowing that nothing can save
 Our flesh from the fate of the grave.

But surely we leave them returning
 In grief to the well-loved nest,
Filled with an infinite yearning,
 Knowing the past to be rest, —
 That the things of the past are the best.

The Spectator.

THE DAYS THAT ARE NO MORE.

O MEMORIES of green and pleasant places,
  Where happy birds their woodnotes twittered low!
O love that lit the dear familiar faces
  We buried long ago!

From barren heights their sweetness we remember,
  And backward gaze with wistful, yearning eyes,
As hearts regret, mid snow-drifts of December,
  The summer's sunny skies.

Glad hours that seemed their rainbow tints to borrow
  From some illumined page of fairy lore;
Bright days that never lacked a bright to-morrow,
  Days that return no more.

Fair gardens, with their many-blossomed alleys,
  And red, ripe roses breathing out perfume;
Deep violet nooks in green, sequestered valleys
  Empurpled o'er with bloom.

Sunset that lighted up the brown-leaved beeches,
  Turning their dusky glooms to glittering gold;
Moonlight that on the river's fern-fringed beaches
  Streamed white-rayed, silvery cold.

O'er moorlands bleak we wander weary-hearted,
  Through many a tangled, wild, and thorny maze,
Remembering as in dreams the days departed,
  The bygone, happy days.

————◆————

MEMORY.

I.

O DREADFUL Memory! why dost thou tread
  From out the secret chambers of my life?
Thou livest with the dead — go to thy dead!
  Nor break my peaceful carelessness with strife.

Thy chains are heavy; thou hast bound me fast.
  I bend beneath the weight I have to bear;
Leave me the Present, thou hast all the Past!
  Unbind me — go! I keep the smallest share.

Art thou not weary of thy ceaseless chase?
  Day after day hast thou not followed me?
Thou wert relentless to pursue the race,
  Until thy chains had bound me hopelessly.

I am thy captive; I am weak, thou strong!
　　Be merciful ; cease to torment me more.
Spare me some pangs of torture, grief, and wrong;
　　Unloose my chains, thy wounds are deep and sore !

II.

O faint, delicious Memory, I call :
　　Come very near; there is no friend like thee !
See, I have nothing left, and thou hast all !
　　For one short hour give it back to me.

Give me my charming summer skies again,
　　The fragrance of my spring and autumn breeze,
The moon that I have watched the rise and wane,
　　The birds I love to hear among the trees.

Sweet eyes, lost in the distance, draw more near;
　　Dear hands, clasp mine — clasp closer yet, I pray ;
Beloved voices, speak that I may hear ;
　　Most precious Memory, go not away !

Without thee I am lonely ; it is strange,
　　Nothing is left that I can call my own.
The world is new, passing from change to change ;
　　My nest is empty, all my birds have flown.

Depart not yet, thy tones are very sweet,
　　Echoes of faith and hope and victory !
And is it true, ye lost, that we shall meet?
　　Canst thou restore thy treasures, Memory ?

People's Magazine.

MEMORIES.

THERE dawn dear memories of the past
　　To charm us as we muse alone,
Still as the hues on rivers cast
　　When long, bright days have almost flown ;
Sometimes they come and fill the mind
　　As stars the heavens when clouds are few ;
And there a cherished welcome find, —
　　Though old, yet seeming ever new.

They are the treasures time has made
　　To shadow forth the bygone years ;
Though dim betimes, they cannot fade,
　　For each some hallowed beauty bears.
Long-slumbering joys each gently wakes,
　　Forms of the past each gently weaves, —
E'en as a cloudless sunset makes
　　A cool, red splendor 'mong green leaves.

They are the day-dreams of a time
    Ere life had felt the touch of care;
Loved like some sweet bell's holy chime
    That faints upon the Sabbath air.
They are the echoes of the past,
    And with us, when alone, they dwell;
For all their wondrous beauties last,
    Like sounds of ocean in a shell.

ONE BY ONE.

ONE by one the old-time fancies
    Fall like blossoms in the blast;
One by one girlhood's romances
    Fade from present into past.

One by one the rosy cloudlets,
    Tinted with the hues of dawn,
Lose the brightness and the beauty
    That belong alone to morn.

Very fair the cherished visions
    That enchant the halls of youth;
Earthly scenes seem then Elysian,
    And the mirage is as truth.

One by one the visions vanish
    In the light experience brings;
But though truth the unreal banish,
    Still remain the living springs.

Though may fade the sparkling fountain
    Glittering in the morning ray,
Still upon life's rugged mountain
    Streams perennial take their way.

Then, my soul, be not disheartened
    If thy castles fade in air,
And thy sunny sky be darkened
    With unwonted shades of care.

Still be thine to choose and cherish
    All things beautiful and bright,
Though thy fancy's garlands perish
    In earth's disenchanting light.

Still be thine to see the rainbow
    Spanning life's most dreary slope;
And to dream of deathless beauty
    In the garden of thy hope.

HAUNTED CHAMBERS.

In the old and ruined mansion
   Where no joyous voices call,
And the gloomy shadows linger
   Like a solemn funeral pall ;
In some dim deserted passage
   Into ruin falling fast,
Aye, they say, the chamber 's haunted
   With the spirits of the past.

When the shades of night have gathered,
   There with deep, majestic gloom
Are these chambers clothed, while spectres
   Gather hither from the tomb.
Not with loud, unhallowed sounding,
   Not with vain, unanswered call,
Are they gathered, but in silence, —
   Mystic, mournful silence all.

Forms that once were bright with being,
   Faces wan that once were fair,
Sadly come amid the silence
   That at midnight reigneth there.
There they love to linger lightly
   Till the stars have ceased to glow, —
Linger lonely in the places
   That were joyous " long ago."

There are chambers, haunted chambers,
   Which we each may call our own,
Where are present forms and faces
   That in other days were known.
In the silence of the midnight
   We, from busy life apart,
Glance in sadness and in sorrow
   At the chambers of the heart.

Ah, what forms are these to haunt us
   When alone with thought at night !
Ah, what faces look upon us
   That we deemed were lost to sight !
Some are bright as when we knew them,
   Others wan and filled with woe ;
All awake the thoughts that slumbered
   Of the days of " long ago."

Ah, the haunted, haunted chambers
   Of the weary human heart ;
They are filled with mournful visions
   That can nevermore depart

Till that heart has ceased its throbbing
  In the sorrow-laden breast,
And the visions of the vanished
  Are forevermore at rest.

———◆———

OUR CHILDHOOD'S HOME.

THERE is one spot on all the earth,
  Where'er in after life we rove,
To which the heart will ever turn
  With an unchanging, deathless love.
Seas may perchance roll far between,
  To distant lands the feet may roam,
But memory turns with yearning back
  To it, our loved, our childhood's home.

Our childhood's home — who can forget
  The many happy, happy years
Spent there when all the world seemed bright,
  And all unknown were cares and tears?
The morning sun beamed brightly down
  On tranquil brows, and never care
Had traced a line, nor sorrow stamped
  Its desolating impress there.

But swiftly flew the summer hours
  With laugh and jest and guileless song,
And in a pathway strewed with flowers
  We sped our happy way along;
We revelled in a sea of love, —
  A perfect Eden of delight;
And years flew on and brought no change,
  For all was pure and all was bright.

How different now!　No more we see
  The pleasant home we loved so well;
No more we hear in silvery tones
  The simple song of evening swell.
We miss the father's kind caress,
  The mother's kiss and accents mild;
The sister's smile, the brother's clasp, —
  All that was valued when a child.

What have we gained in lieu of these?
  We sought for wealth, perchance a name;
But what is wealth compared with love,
  And who can climb the steep of Fame?
With weary heart and throbbing brow,
  And mind with many cares oppressed,
Night after night we seek our couch,
  And "sink to sleep but not to rest."

And still through all the busy strife,
  Through all the cares and maddening fears
Of life, the heart will wander back
  To those beloved and happy years;
And we shall say, in all the earth,
  No matter where the feet may roam,
We may not find the stainless truth
  That blessed our childhood's happy home.

Friendship is but a hollow mask,
  Ambition but an empty name,
And disappointment waits on him
  Who follows in pursuit of fame.
And then at last we drop and fade
  Like autumn leaves, and fall and die,
With no kind hand to raise the head,
  And gently close the dying eye.

Followed by strangers to the grave,
  Few our departure to deplore,
The clay falls coldly on the breast,
  The mound is raised, and all is o'er!
And yet not all; for in that land
  Where tears and trials never come,
Thank God! we yet may join the band
  Who shared with us our childhood's home.

                                        R. S.

A RAINY DAY.

How tired one grows of a rainy day,
  For a rainy day brings back so much;
Old dreams revive that are buried away,
  And the past comes back to the sight and touch.

When the night is short and the day is long,
  And the rain falls down with ceaseless beat,
We tire of our thoughts as we tire of a song
  That over and over is played in the street.

When I woke this morning and heard the splash
  Of the rain-drop over the tall elm's leaves,
I was carried back in a lightning flash
  To the dear old home with the sloping eaves.

And you and I, in the garret high,
  Were playing again at hide-go-seek;
And bright was the light of your laughing eye,
  And rich the glow of your rounded cheek.

And again I was nestled in my white bed
   Under the eaves, and hearing above
The feet of the rain-steeds over my head,
   While I dreamed sweet dreams of you, my love.

Love, my lover, with eyes of truth, —
   O beautiful love of the vanished years,
There is no other love like the love of youth,
   I say it over and over with tears.

Wealth and honor and fame may come, —
   They cannot replace what is taken away;
There is no other home like the childhood's home,
   No other love like the love of May.

Though the sun is bright in the mid-day skies,
   There cometh an hour when the sad heart grieves
With a lonely wail, like a lost child's cry,
   For the trundle-bed and the sloping eaves;

When, with vague unrest and nameless pain,
   We hunger and thirst for a voice and touch
That we never on earth shall know again —
   Oh, a rainy day brings back so much !

UNFINISHED STILL.

A BABY's boot and a skein of wool,
   Faded and soiled and soft;
Odd things, you say, and I doubt you're right,
Round a seaman's neck, this stormy night,
   Up in the yards aloft.

Most likely it's folly; but, mate, look here !
   When first I went to sea,
A woman stood on yon far-off strand
With a wedding ring on the small soft hand
   Which clung close to me.

My wife, — God bless her ! — the day before
   Sat she beside my foot;
And the sunlight kissed her yellow hair,
And the dainty fingers, deft and fair,
   Knitted a baby's boot.

The voyage was over; I came ashore;
   What think you I found there?
A grave the daisies had sprinkled white,
A cottage empty and dark at night,
   And this beside the chair.

The little boot, 't was unfinished still ;
   The tangled skein lay near ;
But the knitter had gone away to her rest,
With the babe asleep on her quiet breast,
   Down in the churchyard drear.

A VAGRANT.

I CANNOT check my thought these days,
   When incense lingers in the air,
But with unwearied wing it strays,
   I know not how or where.

I know not where the blossoms hide
   That throw their lures across its flight ;
How stars can fling their gates so wide,
   To give my thought delight.

There is no door close barred and sealed
   Where cowers suffering or sin,
But will to touch or whisper yield,
   And let this vagrant in.

It bears no passport, no parole,
   But, free and careless as the air,
My thought despises all control,
   And wanders everywhere.

Its warrant from the Throne of thrones,
   Its duty to the King of kings,
Through heights, and depths, and circling zones
   It soars on seraph wings.

What canst thou bring from yon fair height,
   What bring me from the deepening sea ?
What gather for thy own delight
   That is not wealth to me ?

Scribner's Magazine.   JOSEPHINE POLLARD.

DREAMS.

> Good-night ? ah ! no ; the hour is ill
>   Which severs those it should unite ;
> Let us remain together still,
>   Then it will be *good*-night.
>   SHELLEY.

THE night hours wane, the bleak winds of December
   Sweep through the branches of the singing pine,
And while I watch each slowly dying ember
   I dream of joys that never may be mine.

The vacant chair, the room so sad and lonely,
  Bring visions of a home 'neath other skies,
A home created by my fancy only,
  My heart's true rest, my earthly paradise.

In the night watches when my hands are folded
  In weary calm upon my hopeless breast,
These bright creatures, by my heart's love moulded,
  Quicken its beat, and rise all unrepressed.

Roof-tree and tower and portal rise unaided ;
  Aladdin like, their instant birth I see ;
And at love's shrine, by doubtings uninvaded,
  I offer up my wild idolatry.

Only the fire's warm heart, intensely glowing,
  Sends languid throbs of brightness through the gloom,
And gorgeous flowers, with tropic life o'erflowing,
  Pour on the peaceful air their sweet perfume.

Now clasp I in my arms my long-sought treasure,
  Now a dear head is pillowed on my breast ;
And with a joy no earthly tongue can measure,
  Warm, trembling lips to mine are fondly pressed.

For *thou* art with me, with thy presence blessing,
  Thou dearest, best, my first love and my last ;
Within thy arms, thy purest love possessing,
  Darkness is gone, and night is overpast.

O rapturous kisses ! passionate caressing !
  O heart's quick beating with a wild delight !
O murmured words, our mutual love confessing !
  Parted no more, at last it is good-night.

------◆------

AN OLD SONG.

You laugh as you turn the yellow page
  Of that queer old song you sing,
And wonder how folks could ever see
A charm in the simple melody
  Of such an old-fashioned thing.

That yellow page was fair to view,
That quaint old type was fresh and new,
That simple strain was our delight
When here we gathered night by night,
And thought the music of our day
An endless joy to sing and play,

In our youth, long, long ago.
A joyous group we loved to meet,
When hope was high and life was **sweet** ;
When romance shed its golden light,
That circled, in a nimbus bright,
   O'er Time's unwrinkled brow.

The lips are mute that sang these words ;
The hands are still that struck these chords ;
   The loving heart is cold.
From out the circle, one by one,
Some dear companion there has gone.
While others stay to find how true
That life has chord and discord too,
   And all of us are old.

'T is not alone when music thrills,
The power of thought profound **that fills**
   The soul ! 'T is not all art !
The old familiar tones we hear
Die not upon the listening ear ;
   They vibrate in the heart.

And now you know the reason, dear,
Why I have kept and treasured here
   This song of bygone years.
You laugh at the old-fashioned strain ;
It brings my childhood back again,
   And fills my eyes with tears.

THE BOAT-HORN.

OH, list the boat-horn's wild refrain,
   O'er eve's still waters stealing clear !
So softly sweet, so sad a strain
   Ne'er woke before to charm the ear.
From out the past it brings once more,
   As waking echoes of a dream,
The tree-clad hills, the isles and shore,
   Of wild Ohio's winding stream.

Out on the wave while sweeping down
   The boatman trod his little deck,
And dreamed, while lay his all around,
   Of strange adventure, storm, and **wreck.**
That strain he wound his way to cheer
   In dewy eve and golden morn ;
The startled Indian paused to hear,
   In echoes sweet, that simple horn.

He came, rough courier of the men,
  The thronging thousands pressing on,
With axes ringing in the glen,
  And camps the gleaming hills upon.
Gone are the forests, gone the race,
  The dusky shadows of the shore;
The hum of busy life keeps pace
  To music of the steamer's roar.

O boatman, wind thy horn again,
  The simple music of the heart;
What memories live along its strain,
  And into being softly start!
The wood-crowned hills, the isles, the stream,
  In sweetest musings wide expand;
I see as in a summer's dream
  The romance of my native land.

THE OLD DEACON'S LAMENT.

YES, I 've been a deacon of our church
  Nigh on to fifty year,
Walked in the way of dooty, too,
  And kep' my conscience clear.
I 've watched the children growin' up,
  Seen brown locks turnin' gray,
But never saw sech doin's yet
  As those I 've seen to-day.

This church was built by godly men
  To glorify the Lord,
In seventeen hundred eighty-eight;
  Folks could n't then afford
Carpets, cushings, and sech like —
  The seats were jest plain wood,
Too narrer for the sleepy ones;
  In prayer we allus stood.

And when the hymns were given out,
  I tell you it was grand
To hear our leader start the tunes,
  With tunin'-fork in hand!
Then good old "China," "Mear," and all,
  Were heard on Sabbath days,
And men and women, boys and girls,
  J'ined in the song of praise.

But that old pulpit was my pride —
  Jest eight feet from the ground
They 'd reared it up — on either side
  A narrer stairs went down;

The front and ends were fitly carved
   With Scripter stories all, —
Findin' of Moses, Jacob's dream,
   And sinful Adam's fall.

Just room inside to put a cheer,
   The Bible on the ledge
(I 'll own I did git narvous when
   He shoved it to the edge).
There week by week the parson stood
   The Scripter to expound ;
There, man and boy, I 've sot below,
   And not a fault was found.

Of course I 've seen great changes made,
   And fought agenst 'em too ;
And first a choir was interdooced,
   Then cushings in each pew ;
Next, boughten carpet for the floor ;
   And then, that very year,
We got our new melodeon
   And the big shandyleer.

Well, well ! I tried to keep things straight —
   I went to ev'ry meetin'
And voted " No " to all they said,
   And found my influ'nce fleetin'.
At last the worst misfortin' fell —
   I must blame Deacon Brown ;
He helped the young folks when they said
   The pulpit should come down.

They laughed at all those pious scenes
   I 'd found so edifyin' ;
Said, " When the parson rose to preach,
   He looked a'most like flyin' ; "
Said that " Elijah's chariot
   Jest half-way up had tarried ; "
And Deacon Brown sot by and laughed, —
   And so the p'int was carried.

This was last week. The carpenters
   Have nearly made an end —
Excoose my feelin's. Seems to me
   As ef I 'd lost a friend.
" It made their necks ache, lookin' up,"
   Was what the folks did say ;
More lookin' up would help us all
   In this degin'rate day.

The church won't never seem the same
   (I 'm half afraid) to me,
Under the preachin' of the truth
   I 've ben so used to be.

And now to see our parson stand,
 Like any common man,
With jest a railin' round his desk —
 I don't believe I can !

MRS. E. T. CORBETT.

——◆——

FOREVER.

FOREVER and ever the reddening leaves
 Float to the sodden grasses,
Forever and ever the shivering trees
Cower and shriek to the chilling breeze
That sweeps from the far-off sudden seas,
 To wither them as it passes.

Forever and ever the low gray sky
 Stoops o'er the sorrowful earth ;
Forever and ever the steady rain
Falls on bare bleak hill and barren plain,
And flashes on roof and window-pane,
 And hisses upon the hearth.

Forever and ever the weary thoughts
 Are tracing the selfsame track
Forever and ever, to and fro,
On the old unchanging road they go,
Through dreaming and waking, through joy and woe,
 Calling the dead hours back.

Forever and ever the tired heart
 Ponders o'er the evil done ;
Forever and ever through cloud and gleam,
Tracing the course of the strong life-stream,
And dreary and dull as the broken dream,
 Forever the rain rains on.

——◆——

THE WANDERER.

(Lines written on recrossing the Rocky Mountains in winter after many years.)

LONG years ago I wandered here,
In the midsummer of the year —
 Life's summer too.
A score of horsemen here we rode,
The mountain world its glories showed,
 All fair to view.

These scenes, in glowing colors drest,
Mirrored the life within my breast, —
 Its world of hope.

The whispering woods and fragrant breeze
That stirred the grass in verdant seas
      On billowy slope,

And glistening crag in sunlit sky,
'Mid snowy clouds piled mountains high,
      Were joys to me;
My path was o'er the prairie wide,
Or here on grander mountain side,
      To choose, all free.

The rose that waved in morning air,
That spread its dewy fragrance there
      In careless bloom,
Gave to my heart its ruddiest hue,
O'er my glad life its color threw,
      And sweet perfume.

Now changed the scene and changed the eyes
That here once looked on glowing skies
      Where summer smiled;
These riven trees and wind-swept plain
Now show the winter's dread domain —
      Its fury wild.

The rocks rise black from storm-packed snow,
All checked the river's pleasant flow,
      Vanished the bloom;
These dreary wastes of frozen plain
Reflect my bosom's life again,
      Now lonesome gloom.

The buoyant hopes and busy life
Have ended all in hateful strife
      And thwarted aim.
The world's rude contact kills the rose,
No more its radiant color shows
      False roads to fame.

Backward amid the twilight glow
Some lingering spots yet brightly show
      On hard roads won
Where still some grand peaks mark the way,
Touched by the light of parting day
      And memory's sun.

But here thick clouds the mountains hide,
The dim horizon, bleak and wide,
      No pathway shows.
And rising gusts and darkening sky
Tell of "the night that cometh" nigh
      The brief day's close.

Littell's Living Age.   ANONYMOUS.
                              (*Ascribed by the N. Y. Evening Post
                                 to General John C. Fremont.*)

REST.

Love, give me one of thy dear hands to hold,
　　Take thou my tired head upon thy breast,
Then sing me that sweet song we loved of old,
　　The dear, soft song about our little nest.
We knew the song before the nest was ours ;
　　We sang the song when first the nest we found ;
We loved the song in happy after-hours
　　When peace came to us and content profound
Then sing that olden song to me to-night,
　　While I, reclining on thy faithful breast,
See happy visions in the frail firelight,
　　And my whole soul is satisfied with rest.
Better than all our bygone dreams of bliss
Are deep content and rest secure as this.

What though we missed love's golden summer-time,
　　His autumn fruits were ripe when we had leave
To enter joy's wide vineyard in our prime,
　　Good guerdon for our waiting to receive.
Love gave us no frail pledge of summer flowers,
　　But side by side we reaped the harvest field ;
Now side by side we pass the winter hours,
　　And day by day new blessings are revealed.
The heyday of our youth, its roseate glow,
　　Its high desires and cravings manifold,
The raptures and delights of long ago,
　　Have passed ; but we have truer joys to hold.
Sing me the dear old song about the nest,
Our blessed home, our little ark of rest.

———◆———

THE LOST BABIES.

Come, my wife, put down the Bible,
　　Lay your glasses on the book ;
Both of us are bent and aged —
　　Backward, mother, let us look.
This is still the same old homestead
　　Where I brought you long ago,
When the hair was bright with sunshine
　　That is now like winter's snow.
Let us talk about the babies,
　　As we sit here all alone ;
Such a merry troop of youngsters, —
　　How we lost them one by one.

Jack, the first of all our party,
   Came to us one winter's night.
Jack, you said, should be a parson,
   Long before he saw the light.
Do you see the great cathedral,
   Filled the transept and the nave,
Hear the organ gladly pealing,
   Watch the silken hangings wave?
See the priest in robes of office,
   With the altar at his back, —
Would you think that gifted preacher
   Could be our own little Jack?

Then, a girl with curly tresses
   Used to climb upon my knee
Like a little fairy princess,
   Ruling at the age of three.
With the years there came a wedding —
   How your fond heart swelled with pride
When the lord of all the country
   Chose your baby for his bride!
Watch that stately carriage coming,
   And the form reclining there, —
Would you think that brilliant lady
   Could be our own little Clare?

Then, the last, a blue-eyed youngster, —
   I can hear him prattling now, —
Such a strong and sturdy fellow,
   With his broad and honest brow.
How he used to love his mother!
   Ah! I see your trembling lip!
He is far off on the water,
   Captain of a royal ship.
See the bronze upon his forehead,
   Hear the voice of stern command, —
That's the boy who clung so fondly
   To his mother's gentle hand.

Ah! my wife, we 've lost the babies,
   Ours so long and ours alone.
What are we to those great people,
   Stately men and women grown?
Seldom do we even see them ;
   Yes, a bitter tear-drop starts
As we sit here in the firelight,
   Lonely hearth and lonely hearts.
All their lives are full without us ;
   They 'll stop long enough one day
Just to lay us in the churchyard,
   Then they 'll each go on his way.

GONE.

WHEN the morning fair and sweet
   Glimmers through the dusky pane,
For the tread of pattering feet,
   Ah! I list in vain.
Not an echo haunts the hall —
Oh, each gladsome, light footfall;
Not an echo wakes the stair —
Silence, silence everywhere;
         They are gone!

When I leave my sleepless bed,
   Passing from the chambered gloom,
No red cheek and flower-like head
   Lift to me their bloom;
Only darkness in the hall
Lingers like a clouded pall;
Round the threshold, o'er the stair —
Darkness, darkness everywhere;
         They are gone!

When from out the toilsome mart,
   Hopeless, weary, I return,
Oh, these wasting fires at heart —
   How they burn — they burn!
Passionate grief *seemed* sunk in dearth,
But beside my ruined hearth
All the anguish, all the pain,
Bursts in flaming woe again —
         They are gone!

When the twilight hour comes down,
   Of all hours the calmest, best,
Hovering like an angel's crown
   O'er the day's unrest,
Whence this alien, brooding air?
Whence this whisper of despair?
'T is but Heartbreak's hollow tone
Muttering, "Canst thou live alone?
         They are gone!"

Gone! In silences of night
   Hapless hands I stretch to find
Vacant spaces left and right,
   Vacant as the wind.
While a mother's moan is heard,
Low, as if some wounded bird,
Sore of wing and sore of breast,
Wailed above her shattered nest:
        All are gone!

MOTHER.

When she undid her hair at night,
  About the time for lying down,
She came and knelt. I was so small,
There in my bed, her curls did fall
  All over me, light gold and brown.

I fell asleep amid her prayers.
  Her fair young face (far off it seems),
Her girlish voice, her kisses sweet,
The patter of her busy feet,
  Passed with me into charming dreams.

And when I woke at merry morn,
  Through her gold hair I saw the sun
Flame strong, shine glad, and glorify
The great, good world. Oh, never can I
  Forget her words, " My darling one ! "

Ah! checkered years since then have crept
  Past her and me, and we have known
Some sorrow and much tempered joy.
Far into manhood stands her boy,
  And her gold hair snow-white is blown.

The world has changed by slow degrees,
  And as old days recede, alas !
So much of trouble have the new,
Those rare, far joys grow dim seen through
  Sad times as through a darkened glass.

But just this morning when I woke,
  How lovingly my lips were kissed !
How chaste and clear the sunlight shone
On mother's hair, like gold-dust sown
  Athwart thin clouds of silver mist !

———◆———

AT SEA.

Worn voyagers, who watch for land
  Across the endless wastes of sea,
Who gaze before and on each hand,
  Why look ye not to what ye flee ?

The stars by which the sailors steer
  Not always rise before the prow;
Though forward nought but clouds appear,
  Behind, they may be breaking now.

What though we may not turn again
　　To shores of childhood that we leave,
Are those old signs we followed vain?
　　Can guides so oft found true deceive?

Oh, sail we to the south or north,
　　Oh, sail we to the east or west,
The port from which we first put forth
　　Is our heart's home, is our life's best.

F. W. BOURDILLON

MY LOST LOVE.

WHEN the silence of the midnight
　　Closes round my lonely room,
And faintly struggling through the curtains
　　Mystic moonbeams light the gloom;
When above the fevered fancies
　　Of the weary heart and brain
Kindly slumber, creeping near me,
　　Reasserts her welcome reign;
　　　　In the seeming
　　　　Of my dreaming,
In all the glow that used to be,
My lost love comes back to me.

When the fair, delusive phantom
　　Fades before the wakening dawn,
And the rosy smile of sunrise
　　Gleams athwart the dew-drenched lawn;
Gazing from the open lattice,
　　Yearning memory pictures there,
Shadowed by enlacing branches,
·　Sweet blue eyes and golden hair;
　　　　And the sunlight
　　　　Takes the one light
That it had for me erewhile
In my lost love's happy smile.

In the glory of the noontide,
　　Her low ringing laugh I hear;
In the whispering of the leaflets,
　　Her light footstep springing near;
In each snow-white lily's swaying
　　Is reflection of her grace;
In each rose's opening beauty
　　Shines for me her fair young face;
　　　　Till through the falling
　　　　Shadows calling,
As even darkens hill and plain,
I hear my lost love's voice again.

So the hours are peopled for me
  Through the haunted days and nights;
While fancy mocks my lonely vigils
  With the ghost of dead delights;
And I let loud life sweep by me,
  Dreaming by the silent hearth,
Where the vision of my darling
  Gives old gladness back to earth:
    While through each gloaming
    Softly coming,
In sweet, false lights of joy and truth,
My lost love gives me back my youth.

All the Year Round.

RETROSPECTION.

WHEN we see our dream-ships slipping
  From the verge of youth's green slope —
Loosening from the transient moorings
  At the golden shore of hope —
Vanishing, like airy bubbles,
  On the rough, tried sea of care,
Then the soul grows sick with longing
  That is almost wild despair.

Far behind lies sunny childhood —
  Fields of flowers our feet have trod
When our vision-bounded Eden
  Held no mystery but God;
When in dreams we spoke with angels,
  When awake, with brooks and birds,
Reading in the breeze and sunshine
  Love's unspoken, tender words.

When the stars were lighted candles
  Shining through God's floor of blue,
And the moon was but a window
  For the angels to look through;
Clouds took shape of wondrous seeming,
  Fairies hid themselves in flowers;
Morning-rise and sunset glories
  Were but doors to heaven's bowers.

Ah! the sweet conceits and fancies
  With which sunny childhood teems!
'T is not strange the sickened spirit
  Clasps the shadows of such dreams;
That, when life is stern and real,
  Hope is crowded out by fears,
Love grown wearied of her vigils,
  Back we look with bitter tears.

Life is but a rugged hillside
　　When cool science puts to flight
Childhood's treasured love of dreaming
　　Tinted all with rosy light.
For though years may bring us wisdom,
　　Distrust poisons holy truth;
So we turn, soul-sick with yearning,
　　To the sweet beliefs of youth!

And sometimes we question sadly,
　　Wherefore all life's bitter pain?
Are our dreams of hope and gladness —
　　Are our strivings all in vain?
Shall we find the scattered roses
　　That our careless hands have lost?
Wander to the thornless pathways
　　That our feet so thoughtless crossed?

And the answer, deep and solemn,
　　Seems to vibrate through all space:
Life is but a course of trial,
　　Childhood starts and ends the race.
For the harvests faithful gathered
　　Through the strife of toil and tears,
For the burdens borne in patience,
　　Joy will crown the endless years.

THE PASTOR'S REVERIE.

THE pastor sits in his easy-chair,
　　With the Bible upon his knee:
From gold to purple the clouds in the west
　　Are changing momently;
The shadows lie in the valleys below,
　　And hide in the curtain's fold;
And the page grows dim whereon he reads,
　　"I remember the days of old."

"Not clear nor dark," as the Scripture saith,
　　The pastor's memories are;
No day that is gone is shadowless,
　　No night was without its star:
But mingled bitter and sweet hath been
　　The portion of his cup;
"The hand that in love hath smitten," he saith,
　　"In love hath bound us up."

Fleet flies his thought over many a field
　　Of stubble and snow and bloom,
And now it trips through a festival,
　　And now it halts at a tomb;

Young faces smile in his reverie
  Of those that are young no more,
And voices are heard that only come
  With the winds from a far-off shore.

He thinks of the day when first, with fear
  And faltering lips, he stood
To speak in the sacred place the Word
  To the waiting multitude ;
He walks again to the house of God,
  With the voice of joy and praise,
With many whose feet long time have pressed
  Heaven's safe and blessed ways.

He enters again the homes of toil,
  And joins in the homely chat ;
He stands in the shop of the artisan ;
  He sits where the Master sat,
At the poor man's fire and the rich man's feast.
  But who to-day are the poor,
And who are the rich ?   Ask Him who keeps
  The treasures that ever endure.

Once more the green and grove resound
  With the merry children's din ;
He hears their shout at the Christmas Tide,
  When Santa Claus stalks in.
Once more he lists while the camp-fire roars
  On the distant mountain-side,
Or, proving apostleship, plies the brook
  Where the fierce young troutlings hide.

And now he beholds the wedding train
  To the altar slowly move,
And the solemn words are said that seal
  The sacrament of love.
Anon at the font he meets once more
  The tremulous youthful pair,
With a white-robed cherub crowing response
  To the consecrating prayer.

By the couch of pain he kneels again ;
  Again the thin hand lies
Cold in his palm, while the last far look
  Steals into the steadfast eyes ;
And now the burdens of hearts that break
  Lie heavy upon his own, —
The widow's woe, and the orphan's cry,
  And the desolate mother's moan.

So blithe and glad, so heavy and sad,
  Are the days that are no more ;
So mournfully sweet are the sounds that float
  With the winds from a far-off shore.

For the pastor has learned what meaneth the word
    That is given him to keep, —
" Rejoice with them that do rejoice,
    And weep with them that weep."

It is not in vain that he has trod
    This lonely and toilsome way,
It is not in vain that he has wrought
    In the vineyard all the day;
For the soul that gives is the soul that lives,
    And bearing another's load
Doth lighten your own, and shorten the way,
    And brighten the homeward road.

REV. WASHINGTON GLADDEN.

HAWTHORN.

I SEE her where the budding May
Throws shadows on the grassy way
    And flecks her robe of white;
Unseen I watch her as she stands,
With fragrant hawthorn in her hands,
    A vision of delight.

She stays, but will not tarry long
To hear the thrush's vernal song
    In blossom-boughs above;
And in my sheltered garden-seat
I too can hear the carol sweet
    Of songster's happy love.

From out the leaves that shade my face
I watch her in her girlish grace,
    The daughter of my friend,
On whose sweet life, for whose sweet sake,
Love hath such precious things at stake,
    In whom such heart ties blend.

My May-day maiden, thought runs back
O'er that long-trodden, sunlit track,
    My own evanished youth,
When I, like her, was young and fair,
Like her, untouched by worldly care,
    Unscarred by broken truth.

Like her, with sunshine on my way,
With scented blossoms of life's May
    Plucked ready for my hand;
Like her, embarked on life's full tide
For joy's glad port, and by my side
    True love at my command.

But shadows dimmed my summer day,
The blossoms of my early May
   Lie buried in a grave.
Hope's tide ebbed out afar from port,
And left my little bark the sport
   Of fortune's wind and wave.

Ah, well! the thrush's song is done,
And she steps forward in the sun,
   She comes toward my bower,
To glad my weary, tear-dimmed eyes,
To lay before me as a prize
   Her spray of hawthorn flower.

Dear heart! she brings me more than May ;
The sunlight of a far-off day
   Shines on me from her face.
Her heart renews for mine the truth,
The hope and springtide of its youth
   In all their early grace.

She looks at me with eyes of love
Like those the turf has lain above
   For many a weary day ;
God bless her! for she brings again,
Across a lifetime's silent pain,
   My unforgotten May.

All the Year Round.

———◆———

THE ORCHARD–LANDS OF LONG AGO.

THE orchard-lands of Long Ago!
O drowsy winds, awake and blow
The snowy blossoms back to me,
And all the buds that used to be!
Blow back along the grassy ways
Of truant feet, and lift the haze
Of happy summer from the trees
That trail their tresses in the seas
Of grain that float and overflow
The orchard-lands of Long Ago!

Blow back the melody that slips
In lazy laughter from the lips
That marvel much if any kiss
Is sweeter than the apple's is.
Blow back the twitter of the birds —
The lisp, the titter, and the words
Of merriment that found the shine
Of summer-time a glorious wine
That drenched the leaves that loved it so
In orchard-lands of Long Ago!

O memory! alight and sing
Where rosy-bellied pippins cling,
And golden russets glint and gleam
As in the old Arabian dream
The fruits of that enchanted tree
The glad Aladdin robbed for me!
And, drowsy winds, awake and fan
My blood as when it overran
A heart ripe as the apples grow
In orchard-lands of Long Ago.

JAMES WHITCOMB RILEY.

———◆———

LAVENDER.

How prone we are to hide and hoard
Each little treasure time has stored,
    To tell of happy hours!
We lay aside with tender care
A tattered book, a lock of hair,
    A bunch of faded flowers.

When death has led with silent hand
Our darlings to the "Silent Land,"
    Awhile we sit bereft;
But time goes on; anon we rise,
Our dead are buried from our eyes,
    We gather what is left.

The books they loved, the songs they sang,
The little flute whose music rang
    So cheerily of old;
The pictures we had watched them paint,
The last plucked flower, with odor faint,
    That fell from fingers cold.

We smooth and fold with reverent care
The robes they living used to wear;
    And painful pulses stir
As o'er the relics of our dead,
With bitter rain of tears, we spread
    Pale purple lavender.

And when we come in after years,
With only tender April tears
    On cheeks once white with care,
To look on treasures put away
Despairing on that far-off day,
    A subtile scent is there.

Dew-wet and fresh we gathered them,
These fragrant flowers; now every stem
    Is bare of all its bloom:
Tear-wet and sweet we strewed them here
To lend our relics, sacred, dear,
    Their beautiful perfume.

The scent abides on book and lute,
On curl and flower, and with its mute
    But eloquent appeal
It wins from us a deeper sob
For our lost dead, a sharper throb
    Than we are wont to feel.

It whispers of the "long ago;"
Its love, its loss, its aching woe,
    And buried sorrows stir;
And tears like those we shed of old
Roll down our cheeks as we behold
    Our faded lavender.

WHILE WE MAY.

THE hands are such dear hands;
They are so full; they turn at our demands
So often; they reach out,
With trifles scarcely thought about,
So many times; they do
So many things for me, for you —
  If their fond wills mistake,
  We well may bend, not break.

They are such fond, frail lips
That speak to us.   Pray, if love strips
  Them of discretion many times,
  Or if they speak too slow, or quick, such crimes
We may pass by; for we may see
Days not far off when those small words may be
  Held not as slow, or quick, or out of place, but dear,
  Because the lips are no more here.

They are such dear, familiar feet that go
Along the path with ours, — feet fast or slow,
And trying to keep pace, — if they mistake,
Or tread upon some flower that we would take
  Upon our breast, or bruise some reed,
  Or crush poor Hope until it bleed,
    We may be mute,
Not turning quickly to impute

13

Grave fault; — for they and we
Have such a little way to go, — can be
Together such a little while along the way,
    We will be patient while we may.

    So many little faults we find,
        We see them ; for not blind
Is Love.   We see them, but if you and I
Perhaps remember them some *by and by*,
        They will not be
Faults then — grave faults to you and me,
But just odd ways, — mistakes, or even less, —
        Remembrances to bless.
Days change so many things, — yes, hours,
We see so differently in sun and showers.
        Mistaken words to-night
        May be so cherished by to-morrow's light.
        We may be patient ; for we know
        There 's such a little way to go.

                        SUSAN COOLIDGE.

------ ◆ ------

THE BOTTOM DRAWER.

IN the best chamber of the house,
    Shut up in dim, uncertain light,
There stood an antique chest of drawers,
    Of foreign wood, with brasses bright.
One day a woman, frail and gray,
    Stepped totteringly across the floor —
" Let in," said she, " the light of day,
    Then, Jean, unlock the bottom drawer."

The girl, in all youth's loveliness,
    Knelt down with eager, curious face;
Perchance she dreamt of Indian silks,
    Of jewels, and of rare old lace.
But when the summer sunshine fell
    Upon the treasures hoarded there,
The tears rushed to her tender eyes,
    Her heart was solemn as a prayer.

" Dear Grandmamma," she softly sighed,
    Lifting a withered rose and palm ;
But on the elder face was nought
    But sweet content and peaceful calm.
Leaning upon her staff, she gazed
    Upon a baby's half-worn shoe;
A little frock of finest lawn ;
    A hat with tiny bows of blue;

A ball made fifty years ago;
  A little glove; a tasselled cap;
A half-done "long division" sum;
  Some school-books fastened with a strap.
She touched them all, with trembling lips—
  "How much," she said, "the heart can bear!
Ah, Jean! I thought that I should die
  The day that first I laid them there.

"But now it seems so good to know
  That through these weary, troubled years
Their hearts have been untouched by grief,
  Their eyes have been unstained by tears.
Dear Jean, we see with clearer sight
  When earthly love is almost o'er;
Those children wait me in the skies,
  For whom I locked that sacred drawer."

MARY A. BARR.

PART VII.

In the Twilight.

When the hours of Day are numbered,
  And the voices of the Night
Wake the better soul, that slumbered,
  To a holy, calm delight;

Ere the evening lamps are lighted,
  And, like phantoms grim and tall,
Shadows from the fitful firelight
  Dance upon the parlor wall;

Then the forms of the departed
  Enter at the open door;
The beloved, the true-hearted,
  Come to visit me once more.

LONGFELLOW.

PART VII.

In the Twilight.

———•◦•———

TWILIGHT'S HOUR.

THE sunlight on a waveless sea —
  The softened radiance fadeth slowly;
The folded flower, the mist-crowned tree,
  Proclaim the gathering twilight holy.

It is the hour when passion bows;
  A solemn stillness round us lingers;
And on our wildly throbbing brows
  We feel the touch of angel fingers.

It is the hour when lovers fond
  (For love its native air is breathing)
Drape with fair hopes life's drear beyond,
  Gay garlands for the future wreathing.

It is the hour when in far land
  The wanderer, tired of ceaseless roaming,
Longs for the clasp of kindred hand,
  And the dear home enwrapt in gloaming.

It is the hour when mankind hears,
  Amid earth's mingled moans and laughter,
Chords which will swell when unborn years
  Are buried in the great hereafter.

Chambers's Journal.   W. F. E. L.

———•———

THE AFTERMATH.

THE glamour of the after-light
  Lay clear and fair along the sky,
And made the pathway eerie bright
  As home we wandered — thou and I.

The meadow mists were lying low,
　　A shadow held the river-side,
The water took the western glow,
　　And peace, gray peace, spread far and wide.

A sober-heartedness was ours —
　　So still the earth, the sky so strange ;
And we had given in sunny hours
　　Our youthful hearts their widest range.

We lingered in the meadow path,
　　Touched by the twilight's silent spell,
While from the sun's fleet aftermath
　　A subtile glory rose and fell.

Dim, wistful thoughts within us grew,
　　Forebodings of the life to be,
Till with a sudden thrill we knew
　　Time's touch of immortality.

For all the wonder and the awe,
　　Far-widening within the west,
Seemed with a mystic power to draw
　　Our hearts into its kindly rest.

Yet still it faded, faded fast,
　　And night crept up the eastern slope ;
But o'er our lives a strength had passed,
　　And left us with a larger hope.

So home we wandered — thou and I —
　　That night, sweet wife, so long ago,
And still we watch the western sky,
　　And strengthen in its mystic glow.

Good Words.   JAMES HENDRY

———◆———

TWILIGHT DREAMS.

THEY come in the quiet twilight hour,
　　When the weary day is done,
And the quick light leaps from the glowing heaps
　　Of wood on the warm hearthstone.

When the household sounds have died away,
　　And the rooms are silent all,
Save the clock's brief tick, and the sudden click
　　Of the embers as they fall ;

They come, those dreams of the twilight hour,
 To me with their noiseless tread,
A tearful band by the guiding hand
 Of a grave-eyed spirit led.

There is no voice within the hall,
 No footstep on the floor ;
The children's laughter is hushed, there is
 No hand at the parlor door.

Like fingers tapping eagerly
 Against the shuttered frame,
Where the trailing rose its long branch throws,
 Beat the great drops of rain.

But my heart heeds not the rustling leaves,
 Nor the rain-fall's fitful beat,
Nor the wind's low sigh as it hurries by
 On its pauseless path and fleet ;

For now in the dusk they gather round,
 The visions of the past,
Arising slow in the dim red glow
 By the burning pine-brands cast.

My brow is calm as with the touch
 Of an angel's passing wing ;
They breathe no word, yet my soul is stirred
 By the messages they bring.

Some in their grasp impalpable
 Bear Eden's cultured flowers,
That sprang in gloom from the tear-bathed tomb
 Of hope's long-buried hours.

Some from the font of memory,
 Lasting, and pure, and deep,
Bring waters clear, though many a year
 Has saddened their first fresh sweep;

And some in their hands of shadow bear,
 From the shrine of prayerful thought,
A fragrance blest to the stricken breast,
 With balm and healing fraught.

The night wears on, the hearth burns low,
 The dreams have passed away ;
But the heart and brow are strenghtened now
 For the toil of coming day.

Chambers's Journal.

YEARNING.

OVER the west the glory dies away,
  Faint rose-flecks gleaming in the darkening sky;
And the low sounds that mark the close of day
  Rise up from wood and upland — rise and die;
Soft silence falls o'er meadow, hill, and grove,
And in the hush I want you, oh, my love.

In the gay radiance of the morning hour,
  In the warm brooding glory of the noon,
When man and Nature, in their prime of power,
  With the day's fulness blend in eager tune,
The rush of life forbids the pulse to move
That now, in yearning passion, wants you, love.

Wants you to watch the crimson glow and fade
  Through the great branches of the broadening lime;
Wants you to feel the soft, gray, quiet shade
  Lap the tired world in blessed eventime;
Wants you to whisper : " Come, your power to prove,
The gloaming needs its angel; come, my love."

All the Year Round.

THE MOTHER'S BLESSING.

THERE in her high-backed chair she sits,
  Sad-eyed dame with the silver hair;
The shadows lengthen, the daylight flits,
And she seems to listen, as still she knits,
  For the sound of the step on the silent stair.

The lamps flash out in the twilight street,
  And many a neighboring casement gleams,
A beacon of home to hurrying feet;
But the white-haired dame in the high-backed seat
  Heeds them not, as she knits and dreams —

Dreams of a boy, long years ago,
  Clasped her neck on a summer day,
Begged her blessing, kissed her, and so
Fled with the speed of a hunted doe
  Down to the sea and sailed away!

A boy with an eye as blue and bright
  As the cloudless noon of a tropic sky;
A fair haired lad, and his heart was right —
Was it ten ? Yes, ten long years to-night!
  Shall I bless him again before I die ?

" Here at my knee his prayer he said :
  ' Our Father, all hallowed be thy name;
Give us this day our daily bread,'
Passing my hand o'er his golden head,
  While oft the tears in his blue eyes came."

Hark ! a step on the silent stair !
  A soft, quick step, and a breathing light !
A form kneels low by the high-backed chair,
And lo ! in the curls of her boy's fair hair
  The mother's fingers are twined to-night.

Is it a dream ? or can it be,
  This tall man, with the beard of gold,
That kneels so low by his mother's knee,
Is the blue-eyed boy that fled to sea
  That sunny morn in the day of old ?

Yes, it is he, for the joyful tears
  Drop from her eyes in a holy rain ;
" Our Father " anew from his lips she hears,
And the mother's blessing of bygone years
  Has brought her prodigal home again.

———◆———

ELSWITHA.

ELSWITHA knitteth the stocking blue
  In the flickering firelight's glow ;
Dyed are her hands in its ruddy hue,
And it glints on the shining needles too,
  And flushes her cap of snow.

Elswitha dreameth a waking dream,
  As busy her fingers ply ;
And it lights her eye with its olden gleam,
For the world seems now as it used to seem,
  And the things far off are nigh !

The things far off in the lapse of years,
  Dead faces and loves outgrown ;
Oh, many a form at her side appears,
And many a voice in her soul she hears,
  And many a long-hushed tone.

For Memory walks through her halls to-night,
  A torch in her lifted hand ;
And lo ! at the sound of her footsteps light
They shake them free from the dust and blight,
  And trooping around her stand.

Bright curls of auburn and braids of brown,
  With the sunlight sifted through,
And foreheads white as the hawthorn's crown,
And garlands fresh as when last thrown down,
  Ay, fresher in scent and hue!

They come from the aisles of the buried past,
  From the faded long ago,
From sepulchres old and dim and vast,
They come with their grave-clothes from them cast,
  To stand in the firelight glow.

And weird is the charm they weave, I trow —
  Elswitha is young and fair,
Gone are the furrows and tear-stains now,
Gone are the wrinkles from hand and brow,
  The silver from shining hair.

Gone are the years with their heavy weight
  (And heavy the years had grown),
For Love hath entered the lists with Fate,
And Memory needeth not name nor date,
  For Memory knoweth her own.

Now haste thee, Dame, for the fire is low,
  And the good man waits his tea;
Back to their tombs do the phantoms go,
And dark and deep do the shadows grow,
But Elswitha smileth — her dream to know,
  Not a dream — but a prophecy.

Maritime Monthly.   MARY BARRY.

TIRED.

WHEN the day with all its splendor, all its beauty, all its light,
Fades away, and leaves us standing in the shadow of the night,
And we turn with wistful longing to the purple fields that lie
Where the sunlight in departing leaves its glory in the sky;
Piling up the clouds like bastions full of fire along the west,
And the early star of evening gleams upon their fading crest, —
Then we feel that something brighter, fairer still lies out of sight,
Where the beauty and the glory will not fade away in night;
And that somewhere in the distance, in the beautiful beyond,
Our beloved and departed hold us still by some sweet bond;
And across the gold and crimson of the evening's changeful
      track
We can almost hear the music of their voices floating back.

Tell me, dreamers, say, what is it that we feel but cannot know?
Why these cravings, half of rapture, half of sorrow, haunt us so?
What these pictures half immortal, ne'er described by brush or
      word,
By which all the human spirit of a mortal soul is stirred?

Tell me, prophet, do they lead us to the looked-for " by-and-by,"
Where no mortal eye has parted back the shades of prophecy?
Oh, ye dreamers! oh, ye prophets! what your dreams and
    prophecies,
What to me the light and fading of the ever-changing skies,
What to me the glorious beauty in the cloud-land in the west,
While with every heart-beat moaning for the priceless boon of
    Rest!

THE LOST SHEEP.

De massa ob de sheepfol',
   Dat guard de sheepfol' bin,
Look out in de gloomerin' meadows
   Whar de long night rain begin —
So he call to de hirelin' shepa'd,
   " Is my sheep, is dey all come in?"
Oh, den says de hirelin' shepa'd,
   " Dey 's some, dey 's black and thin,
And some, dey 's po' ol' wedda's,
   But de res' dey 's all brung in, —
   But de res' dey 's all brung in."

Den de massa ob de sheepfol',
   Dat guard de sheepfol' bin,
Goes down in de gloomerin' meadows
   Whar de long night rain begin —
So he le' down de ba's ob de sheepfol',
   Callin' sof', " Come in, come in!"
   Callin' sof', " Come in, come in!"

Den up tro' de gloomerin' meadows,
   Tro' de col' night rain and win',
And up tro' de gloomerin' rain-paf,
   Whar de sleet fa' pie'cin' thin,
De po' los' sheep ob de sheepfol'
   Dey all comes gadderin' in.
De po' los' sheep ob de sheepfol'
   Dey all comes gadderin' in.

                Sally Pratt McLean.

WHEN THE COWS COME HOME.

I.

With klingle, klangle, klingle,
   Way down the dusty dingle,
   The cows are coming home;
Now sweet and clear, and faint and low,
The airy tinklings come and go,

Like chimings from some far-off tower,
Or patterings of an April shower
That makes the daisies grow —
    Ko-kling, ko-klang, koklinglelingle,
    Way down the darkening dingle
    The cows come slowly home.

II.

    With jingle, jangle, jingle,
    Soft sounds that sweetly mingle,
    The cows are coming home ;
Malime, and Pearl, and Florimel,
DeKamp, Redrose, and Gretchen Schell,
Queen Bess, and Sylph, and Spangled Sue —
Across the fields I hear loo-oo,
And clang her silver bell,
    Go-ling, go-lang, golinglelingle,
    With faint far sounds that mingle,
    The cows come slowly home ;
And mother-songs of long-gone years,
And baby joys, and childish fears,
And youthful hopes, and youthful fears,
    When the cows come home.

III.

    With ringle, rangle, ringle,
    By twos and threes and single,
    The cows are coming home.
Through the violet air we see the town,
And the summer sun a-slipping down ;
The maple in the hazel glade
Throws down the path a longer shade,
    And the hills are growing brown.
    To-ring, to-rang, toringleringle,
    By threes and fours and single,
    The cows come slowly home.
The same sweet sound of wordless psalm,
The same sweet June-day rest and calm,
The same sweet scent of bud and balm,
    When the cows come home.

IV.

    With a tinkle, tankle, tinkle,
    Through fern and periwinkle,
    The cows are coming home ;
A-loitering in the checkered stream,
Where the sun-rays glance and gleam,
Starine, Peachbloom, and Phœbe Phyllis
Stand knee deep in the creamy lilies,
In a drowsy dream,

To-link, to-lank, tolinklelinkle,
O'er banks with buttercups a-twinkle
The cows come slowly home;
And up through memory's deep ravine
Come the brook's old song and its old-time sheen,
And the crescent of the silver queen,
When the cows come home.

v.

With a klingle, klangle, klingle,
With a loo-oo, and moo-oo, and jingle,
The cows are coming home;
And over there on Merlin hill,
Hear the plaintive cry of the whippoorwill;
The dew-drops lie on the tangled vines,
And over the poplars Venus shines;
And over the silent mill,
Ko-ling, ko-lang, kolinglelingle,
With a ting-a-ling and jingle,
The cows come slowly home.
Let down the bars; let in the train
Of long-gone songs, and flowers, and rain;
For dear old times come back again
When the cows come home.

MRS. AGNES E. MITCHELL.

IF WE KNEW; OR, BLESSINGS OF TO-DAY.

IF we knew the woe and heart-ache
That await us on the road;
If our lips could taste the wormwood,
If our backs could feel the load;
Would we waste to-day in wishing
For a time that ne'er may be?
Would we wait in such impatience
For our ships to come from sea?

If we knew the baby fingers
Pressed against the window-pane
Would be cold and stiff to-morrow, —
Never trouble us again;
Would the bright eyes of our darling
Catch the frown upon our brow?
Would the print of baby fingers
Vex us then as they do now?

Ah! those little ice-cold fingers,
How they point our memories back
To the hasty words and actions
Strewn along the backward track!

How those little hands remind us,
    As in snowy grace they lie,
Not to scatter thorns, but roses,
    For the reaping by and by.

Strange, we never prize the music
    Till the sweet-voiced birds have flown ;
Strange, that we should slight the violets
    Till the lovely flowers are gone;
Strange, that summer skies and sunshine
    Never seem one half so fair
As when winter's snowy pinions
    Shake the white down in the air.

Lips from which the seal of silence
    None but God can roll away
Never blossomed in such beauty
    As adorns the mouth to-day ;
And sweet words that freight our memory
    With their beautiful perfume
Come to us in sweeter accents
    Through the portals of the tomb.

Let us gather up the sunbeams
    Lying all around our path ;
Let us keep the wheat and roses,
    Casting out the thorns and chaff ;
Let us find our sweetest comfort
    In the blessings of to-day,
With a patient hand removing
    All the briers from the way.

The Hearthstone.   Mrs. May Riley Smith.

GROWING OLD.

Is it parting with the roundness
    Of the smoothly moulded cheek ?
Is it losing from the dimples
    Half the flashing joy they speak?
Is it fading of the lustre
    From the wavy, golden hair ?
Is it finding on the forehead
    Graven lines of thought and care?

Is it dropping, as the rose-leaves
    Drop their sweetness overblown,
Household names that once were dearer,
    More familiar than our own?

Is it meeting on the pathway
  Faces strange and glances cold,
While the soul with moan and shiver
  Whispers sadly, " Growing old " ?

Is it frowning at the folly
  Of the ardent hopes of youth?
Is it cynic melancholy
  At the rarity of truth?
Is it disbelief in loving?
  Selfish hate, or miser's greed?
Then such blight of Nature's noblest
  Is a " growing old " indeed.

But the silver thread that shineth
  Whitely in the thinning tress,
And the pallor where the bloom was,
  Need not tell of bitterness :
And the brow's more earnest writing
  Where it once was marble fair,
May be but the spirit's tracing
  Of the peace of answered prayer.

If the smile has gone in deeper,
  And the tears more quickly start,
Both together meet in music
  Low and tender in the heart ;
And in others' joy and gladness,
  When the life can find its own,
Surely angels learn to listen
  To the sweetness of the tone.

Nothing lost of all we planted
  In the time of budding leaves ;
Only some things bound in bundles
  And set by — our precious sheaves ;
Only treasure kept in safety,
  Out of reach and out of rust,
Till we clasp it grown the richer
  Through the glory of our trust.

On the gradual sloping pathway,
  As the passing years decline,
Gleams a golden love-light falling
  Far from upper heights divine.
And the shadows from that brightness
  Wrap them softly in their fold,
Who unto celestial whiteness
  Walk, by way of growing old.

MARGARET E. SANGSTER.

14

A WOMAN'S COMPLAINT.

I KNOW that deep within your heart of hearts
  You hold me shrined apart from common things,
And that my step, my voice, can bring to you
  A gladness that no other presence brings.

And yet, dear love, through all the weary days
  You never speak one word of tenderness,
Nor stroke my hair, nor softly clasp my hand
  Within your own in loving, mute caress.

You think, perhaps, I should be all content
  To know so well the loving place I hold
Within your life, and so you do not dream
  How much I long to hear the story told.

You cannot know, when we two sit alone,
  And tranquil thoughts within your mind are stirred,
My heart is crying like a tired child
  For one fond look, one gentle, loving word.

It may be when your eyes look into mine
  You only say, " How dear she is to me ! "
Oh, could I read it in your softened glance,
  How radiant this plain old world would be !

Perhaps, sometimes, you breathe a secret prayer
  That choicest blessings unto me be given ;
But if you said aloud, " God bless thee, dear ! "
  I should not ask a greater boon from Heaven.

I weary sometimes of the rugged way ;
  But should you say, " Through thee my life is sweet,"
The dreariest desert that our path could cross
  Would suddenly grow green beneath my feet.

'T is not the boundless waters ocean holds
  That give refreshment to the thirsty flowers,
But just the drops that, rising to the skies,
  From thence descend in softly falling showers.

What matter that our granaries are filled
  With all the richest harvest's golden stores,
If we who own them cannot enter in,
  But famished stand before the close-barred doors ?

And so 't is sad that those who should be rich
  In that true love which crowns our earthly lot,
Go praying with white lips from day to day
  For love's sweet tokens, and receive them not.

The Advance.

SONGS IN SLEEP.

IF I could frame for you in cunning words
   The songs my heart in sleep is often singing,
You 'd fancy, love, an orchestra of birds
   Upon their quivering throats the dawn were bringing.

Now in some wild, weird flush of melody
   I 'd feign the skylark, with his music sifting
The final films of nightshade from the lea,
   And all the waking world to heaven uplifting.

Then, ere the lengthening liquid solo went —
   In skylark fashion — out of hearing o'er us,
I 'd mock with skill, as sweet as my intent,
   Thrustle and blackbird coming in for chorus.

There 's not a strain of joy the birds could sing,
   I could not set to words that I 've been dreaming;
But when I wake, alas! they all take wing,
   And leave of music but the empty seeming.

Believe me, love, I sing to you, in sleep,
   Songs that if voiced would waken you to pleasure;
Would you could hear them in your dreams, and keep
   Their inner meaning, though you missed the measure.
               REV. WM. C. RICHARDS.

FIFTY YEARS APART.

THEY sit in the winter gloaming,
   And the fire burns bright between;
One has passed seventy summers,
   And the other just seventeen.

They rest in a happy silence
   As the shadows deepen fast;
One lives in a coming future,
   And one in a long, long past.

Each dreams of a rush of music,
   And a question whispered low;
One will hear it this evening,
   One heard it long ago.

Each dreams of a loving husband
   Whose brave heart is hers alone;
For one the joy is coming,
   For one the joy has flown.

Each dreams of a life of gladness
  Spent under the sunny skies;
And both the hope and the memory
  Shine in the happy eyes.

Who knows which dream is the brightest?
  And who knows which is the best?
The sorrow and joy are mingled,
  But only the end is rest.

Parlor Magazine.

A WOMAN'S WISH.

WOULD I were lying in a field of clover,
  Of clover cool and soft, and soft and sweet,
With dusky clouds in deep skies hanging over,
  And scented silence at my head and feet.

Just for one hour to slip the leash of worry
  In eager haste from Thought's impatient neck,
And watch it coursing — in its heedless hurry
  Disdaining Wisdom's whistles, Duty's beck.

Ah, it were sweet where clover clumps are meeting,
  And daisies hiding, so to hide and rest;
No sound except my own heart's steady beating,
  Rocking itself to sleep within my breast, —

Just to lie there, filled with the deeper breathing
  That comes of listening to a free bird's song!
Our souls require at times this full unsheathing —
  All swords will rust if scabbard-kept too long.

And I am tired! — so tired of rigid duty,
  So tired of all my tired hands find to do!
I yearn, I faint, for some of life's free beauty,
  Its loose beads with no straight string running through.

Ay, laugh, if laugh you will, at my crude speech,
  But women sometimes die of such a greed, —
Die for the small joys held beyond their reach,
  And the assurance they have all they need.

MARY A. TOWNSEND.

AT THE PIANO.

PLAY on! play on! As softly glides
  The low refrain, I seem, I seem
To float, to float, on golden tides
  By sunlit isles, where life and dream

Are one, are one; and hope and bliss
Move hand in hand, and, thrilling, kiss
    'Neath bowery blooms
    In twilight glooms,
And love is life and life is love.

Play on! play on! As higher rise
The lifted strains, I seem, I seem
To mount, to mount, through roseate skies,
Through drifted clouds and golden gleam,
To realms, to realms of thought and fire,
Where angels walk and souls aspire,
And sorrows come but as the night
That brings a star for our delight.

Play on! play on! The spirit fails,
The star grows dim, the glory pales,
The depths are roused — the depths, and oh!
The heart that wakes, the hopes that glow!
The depths are roused, their billows call
The soul from heights to slip and fall;
To slip and fall and faint, and be
Made part of their immensity;
To slip from heaven; to fall and find
In love the only perfect mind.
To slip and fall and faint, and be
Lost, drowned within this melody,
As life is lost, and thought, in thee.

Ah, sweet, art thou the star, — the star
That draws my soul afar, afar?
The voice the silvery tide on which
I float to island rare and rich?
Thy love the ocean, deep and strong,
In which my hopes and being long
To sink and faint and fall away?
I cannot know; I cannot say.
    Play on! play on!

———◆———

A TWILIGHT REVERIE.

THE fire in the west burns low;
    A fading gleam of light
Only remains of the crimson glow
    That made half heaven so bright;
And the weary day, in her shroud of gray,
Sighs out her life on the breast of night.

The fire on my hearth burns low;
    Beside the glimmering light
I dream of that sunset long ago
    When all my heaven seemed bright.

But since that day, with each sunset ray
I 've longed to die in the gloom of night.

> The fire of my life burns low ;
>   And through the darkening night
> Strange, shadowy shapes flit to and fro,
>   Awaiting my spirit's flight.
> And these shadowy things show glistening wings
> To bear me away on the morning light.

———◆———

MY CIGARETTE.

My cigarette ! The amulet
  That charms afar unrest and sorrow ;
The magic wand that far beyond
  To-day can conjure up to-morrow.
Like love's desire, thy crown of fire
  So softly with the twilight blending,
And ah ! meseems, a poet's dreams
  Are in thy wreaths of smoke ascending.

My cigarette ! Can I forget
  How Kate and I, in sunny weather,
Sat in the shade the elm-tree made
  And rolled the fragrant weed together ?
I at her side beatified,
  To hold and guide her fingers willing ;
She rolling slow the paper's snow,
  Putting my heart in with the filling.

My cigarette ! I see her yet,
  The white smoke from her red lips curling,
Her dreaming eyes, her soft replies,
  Her gentle sighs, her laughter purling !
Ah, dainty roll, whose parting soul
  Ebbs out in many a snowy billow,
I, too, would burn if I might earn
  Upon her lips so soft a pillow !

Ah, cigarette ! The gay coquette
  Has long forgot the flames she lighted,
And you and I unthinking by
  Alike are thrown, alike are slighted.
The darkness gathers fast without,
  A rain-drop on my window plashes ;
My cigarette and heart are out,
  And nought is left me but the ashes.

Harvard Crimson, Jan. 9, 1880.   C. F. LUMMIS, '81.

PART VIII.

Home and Fireside.

But in his eyes a mist unwonted rises,
    And for a moment clear,
Some sweet home face his foolish thought surprises
    And passes in a tear.

Some boyish vision of his Eastern village,
    Of uneventful toil,
Where golden harvests followed quiet tillage
    Above a peaceful soil.

BRET HARTE.

PART VIII.

Home and Fireside.

———

AT HOME.

WHERE burns the fireside brightest,
  Cheering the social breast?
Where beats the fond heart lightest,
  Its humblest hopes possessed?
Where is the hour of sadness,
  With meek-eyed patience borne,
Worth more than those of gladness,
  Which mirth's gay cheeks adorn?
Pleasure is marked by fleetness,
  To those who ever roam;
While grief itself has sweetness
  At home — sweet home.

BERNARD BARTON

———

FORTUNE MY FOE.

"AIM not too high at things beyond thy reach,"
Nor give the rein to reckless thought or speech.
Is it not better all thy life to bide
Lord of thyself, than all the earth beside?

Thus if high Fortune far from thee take wing,
Why shouldst thou envy counsellor or king?
Purple or homespun, — wherefore make ado
What coat may cover, if the heart be true?

Then, if at last thou gather wealth at will,
Thou most shalt honor Him who grants it still;
Since he who best doth poverty endure,
Should prove, when rich, best brother to the poor.

The Spectator.   ALFRED PERCIVAL GRAVES.

HOME IS WHERE THE HEART IS.

'T is home where'er the heart is,
  Where'er its loved ones dwell,
In cities or in cottages,
  Thronged haunts or mossy dell.
The heart 's a rover ever,
  And thus, on wave and wild,
The maiden with her lover walks,
  The mother with her child.

'T is bright where'er the heart is;
  Its fairy spell can bring
Fresh fountains to the wilderness,
  And to the desert spring.
Green isles are in the ocean
  O'er which affection glides,
A haven on each sunny shore,
  When love 's the sun that guides.

'T is free where'er the heart is;
  Nor chains nor dungeons dim
May check the mind's aspiring thought,
  The spirit's pealing hymn.
The heart gives life its beauty,
  Its glory, and its powers;
'T is sunlight to its rippling stream,
  And soft dew to its flowers.

———◆———

HOME–COMING.

WHEN brothers leave the old hearthstone
  And go, each one, a separate way,
We think, as we go on alone
  Along our pathway, day by day,
Of olden scenes and faces dear,
  Of voices that we miss so much;
And memory brings the absent near,
  Until we almost feel the touch
Of loving hands, and hear once more
  The dear old voices ringing out,
As in that happy time of yore,
  Ere life had caught a shade of doubt.

If you should place against your ear
  The shell you plundered from the sea,
Down in its hidden heart you 'd hear
  A low and tender melody;

A murmur of the restless tide,
  A yearning born of memory;
And though its yearnings be denied,
  The shell keeps singing of the sea.
And sometimes when old memories throng
  Like ghosts the memories of our soul,
We feel the yearning, deep and strong,
  A longing we cannot control,
To lay our care and business by,
  And seek the old familiar ways,
And cross home's threshold, and sit down
  With comrades of our earlier days.

For though our paths are sundered wide,
  We feel that we are brothers yet,
And by and by we turn aside
  From hurrying care and worldly fret,
And each one wanders back to meet
  His brother by the hearth of home;
I think the meeting is more sweet
  Because so far and wide we roam.
We cross the lengthening bridge of years,
  Meet outstretched hands and faces true;
The silent eloquence of tears
  Speaks welcome that no words can do.

But ah, the meeting holds regret!
  The sad, sad story, often told,
Of hands that ours have often met,
  Close folded under churchyard mould;
Of eyes that smiled into our own,
  Closed in the dreamless sleep of God;
A sweeter rest was never known
  Than theirs, beneath the grave's white sod.
A tender thought for them to-night,
  A tribute tear from memory;
Beneath their covering of white
  Sweet may their dreamless slumber be.

A SONG FOR THE HOT WINDS.

  OH for a breath o' the moorlands,
    A whiff o' the caller air!
  For the smell o' the flowerin' heather
    My very heart is sair.

  Oh for the sound o' the burnies
    That whimple to the sea;
  For the sight o' the browning bracken
    On the hillside waving free!

Oh for the blue lochs cradled
    In the arms o' mountains gray,
That smile as they shadow the drifting clouds
    A' the bonny summer day !

Oh for the tops o' mountains
    White wi' eternal snaw ;
For the mists that drift across the lift ;
    For the strong east winds that blaw !

I am sick o' the blazing sunshine
    That burns through the weary hours,
O' the gaudy birds singing never a song,
    O' beautiful scentless flowers.

I wud gie a' the southern glory
    For a taste o' a good saut wind,
Wi' a road ower the bonny sea before,
    And a track o' foam behind.

Auld Scotland may be rugged,
    Her mountains stern and bare ;
But, oh for a breath o' her moorlands,
    A whiff o' her caller air !

HARRIET MILLER DAVIDSON.

Adelaide, Australia, Jan. 13, 1872.

THE SERMON IN A STOCKING.

THE supper is over, the hearth is swept,
    And in the wood-fire's glow
The children cluster to hear a tale
    Of that time so long ago,

When grandmamma's hair was golden brown,
    And the warm blood came and went
O'er the face that could scarce have been sweeter then
    Than now in its rich content.

The face is wrinkled and careworn now,
    And the golden hair is gray ;
But the light that shone in the young girl's eyes
    Has never gone away.

And her needles catch the fire's light
    As in and out they go,
With the clicking music that grandma loves,
    Shaping the stocking's toe.

And the waking children love it too,
  For they know the stocking song
Brings many a tale to grandma's mind
  Which they shall hear ere long.

But it brings no story of olden time
  To grandma's heart to-night, —
Only a ditty quaint and short
  Is sung by the needles bright.

" Life is a stocking," grandma says,
  " And yours is just begun ;
But I am knitting the toe of mine,
  And my work is almost done.

" With merry hearts we begin to knit,
  And the ribbing is almost play ;
Some are gay-colored, and some are white,
  And some are ashen gray.

" But most are made of many a hue,
  With many a stitch set wrong,
And many a row to be sadly ripped
  Ere the whole is fair and strong.

"There are long plain stretches without a break,
  That in youth are hard to bear ;
And many a weary tear is dropped
  As we fashion the heel with care.

" But the saddest, happiest time is that,
  We court and yet would shun,
When our Heavenly Father breaks the thread,
  And says our work is done."

And the children come to say good-night,
  With tears in their bright young eyes ;
While in grandma's lap, with broken thread,
  The finished stocking lies.

MY MOTHER'S HANDS.

SUCH beautiful, beautiful hands !
  They 're neither white nor small ;
And you, I know, would scarcely think
  That they were fair at all.
I 've looked on hands whose form and hue
  A sculptor's dream might be ;
Yet are those wrinkled, aged hands
  Most beautiful to me.

Such beautiful, beautiful hands!
  Though heart were weary and sad,
These patient hands kept toiling on,
  That the children might be glad;
I always weep, as looking back
  To childhood's distant day,
I think how those hands rested not,
  When mine were at their play.

Such beautiful, beautiful hands!
  They 're growing feeble now,
For time and pain have left their mark
  On hands, and heart, and brow.
Alas! alas! the nearing time,
  And the sad, sad day to me,
When 'neath the daisies, out of sight,
  These hands will folded be.

But oh, beyond this shadow land,
  Where all is bright and fair,
I know full well these dear old hands
  Will palms of victory bear;
Where crystal streams through endless years
  Flow over golden sands,
And where the old grow young again,
  I 'll clasp my mother's hands.

            ELLEN M. H. GATES.

THE EXILES.

THE sea at the crag's base brightens,
  And shivers in waves of gold;
And overhead, in its vastness,
  The fathomless blue is rolled.
There comes no wind from the water,
  There shines no sail on the main,
And not a cloudlet to shadow
  The earth with its fleecy grain.
Oh, give in return for this glory,
  So passionate, warm, and still,
The mist of a highland valley —
  The breeze from a Scottish hill!

Day after day glides slowly,
  Ever and ever the same, —
Seas of intensest splendor,
  Airs which smite hot as a flame;
Birds of imperial plumage,
  Palms straight as columns of fire,
Flutter and glitter around me,
  But not so my soul's desire.

I long for the song of the laverock,
  The cataract's leap and flash,
The sweep of the red deer's antlers,
  The gleam of the mountain ash.

Only when night 's quiescent,
  And peopled with alien stars,
Old faces come to the casement
  And peer through the vine-leaved bars.
No words, but I guess their fancies —
  Their dreamings are also mine —
Of the land of the cloud and heather,
  The region of " Auld Lang Syne."
Again we are treading the mountains,
  Below us broadens the firth,
And billows of light keep rolling
  Down leagues of empurpled heath.

Speed swift through the glowing tropics,
  Stout ship which shall bear me home ;
Oh, pass as a God-sent arrow
  Through tempest, darkness, and foam.
Bear up through the silent girdle
  That circles the flying earth,
Till there shall blaze on thy compass
  The loadstar over the north ;
That the winds of the hills may greet us,
  That our footsteps again may be
In the land of our hearts' traditions,
  And close to the storied sea.

Chambers's Journal.

———◆———

OUR OWN.

If I had known in the morning
How wearily all the day
  The words unkind
  Would trouble my mind
I said when you went away,
I had been more careful, darling,
  Nor given you needless pain ;
    But we vex our own
    With look and tone
  We might never take back again.

For though in the quiet evening
You may give me the kiss of peace,
  Yet it might be
  That never for me
The pain of the heart should cease.
How many go forth in the morning

That never come home at night;
  And hearts have broken
  For harsh words spoken
That sorrow can ne'er set right.

We have careful thoughts for the stranger,
And smiles for the sometime guest,
  But oft for "our own"
  The bitter tone,
Though we love "our own" the best.
Ah, lips with the curve impatient,
  Ah, brow with that look of scorn,
   'T were a cruel fate
   Were the night too late
To undo the work of morn!
                MARGARET E. SANGSTER.

DAN'S WIFE.

UP in early morning light,
Sweeping, dusting, "setting right,"
Oiling all the household springs,
Sewing buttons, tying strings,
Telling Bridget what to do,
Mending rips in Johnny's shoe,
Running up and down the stair,
Tying baby in her chair,
Cutting meat and spreading bread,
Dishing out so much per head,
Eating as she can by chance,
Giving husband kindly glance;
Toiling, working, busy life, —
    Smart woman,
    Dan's wife.

Dan comes home at fall of night,
Home so cheerful, neat, and bright;
Children meet him at the door,
Pull him in and look him o'er;
Wife asks how the work has gone.
"Busy times with us at home!"
Supper done, Dan reads with ease, —
Happy Dan, but one to please!
Children must be put to bed —
All the little prayers are said;
Little shoes are placed in rows,
Bedclothes tucked o'er little toes;
Busy, noisy, wearing life, —
    Tired woman,
    Dan's wife.

Dan reads on and falls asleep —
See the woman softly creep;
Baby rests at last, poor dear,
Not a word her heart to cheer;
Mending-basket full to top,
Stockings, shirt, and little frock;
Tired eyes and weary brain,
Side with darting, ugly pain;
"Never mind, 't will pass away,"
She must work, but never play;
Closed piano, unused books,
Done the walks to easy nooks,
Brightness faded out of life, —
    Saddened woman,
    Dan's wife.

Up stairs, tossing to and fro,
Fever holds the woman low;
Children wander free to play
When and where they will to-day;
Bridget loiters — dinner's cold,
Dan looks anxious, cross, and old;
Household screws are out of place,
Lacking one dear, patient face;
Steady hands, so weak but true,
Hands that knew just what to do,
Never knowing rest or play,
Folded now — and laid away;
Work of six in one short life, —
    Shattered woman,
    Dan's wife.

            MRS. KATE TANNATT WOODS.

TIRED MOTHERS.

A LITTLE elbow leans upon your knee,
   Your tired knee, that has so much to bear;
A child's dear eyes are looking lovingly
   From underneath a thatch of tangled hair.
Perhaps you do not heed the velvet touch
   Of warm, moist fingers, folding yours so tight; —
You do not prize this blessing overmuch;
   You almost are too tired to pray to-night.

But it *is* blessedness!   A year ago
   I did not see it as I do to-day, —
We are so dull and thankless; and too slow
   To catch the sunshine till it slips away.
And now it seems surpassing strange to me
   That, while I wore the badge of motherhood,
I did not kiss more oft and tenderly
   The little child that brought me only good.

15

And if, some night, when you sit down to rest,
    You miss this elbow from your tired knee,
This restless, curling head from off your breast,
    This lisping tongue that chatters constantly;
If from your own the dimpled hands had slipped,
    And ne'er would nestle in your palm again;
If the white feet into their grave had tripped,
    I could not blame you for your heartache then!

I wonder so that mothers ever fret
    At little children clinging to their gown,
Or that the footprints, when the days are wet,
    Are ever black enough to make them frown.
If I could find a little muddy boot,
    Or cap, or jacket, on my chamber floor;
If I could kiss a rosy, restless foot,
    And hear its patter in my home once more;

If I could mend a broken cart to-day,
    To-morrow make a kite to reach the sky, —
There is no woman in God's world could say
    She was more blissfully content than I.
But ah! the dainty pillow next my own
    Is never rumpled by a shining head;
My singing birdling from its nest has flown,
    The little boy I used to kiss is dead!

                    MRS. MAY RILEY SMITH.

---◆---

LITTLE STITCHES.

OH, thoughts that go in with the stitches
    That women quietly take,
While castles are built with the needle,
    And bubbles are rounded to break.

You see in your kerchief-hem, Freshman,
    A dotted line fairy and fine;
But see you the prayers low and tender
    Pricked in with the lengthening line?

Betrothed, as you bend o'er the trousseau,
    Absorbed in your rose-tinted dream,
Speak low as you censure the seamstress
    For waver and knot in the seam.

In 'broidery dainty and foreign,
    That falls at your waist, you can see
How trembled the hand of a novice,
    In spite of the vigil-taught knee.

For throbs of a woman heart smothered,
  And cries that no penance can still,
Are lifting the wreath and the roses,
  Are echoed from girdle and frill.

Oh, terrible, blood-reddened ladder
  Of loops hung on poverty's hands,
Up which goes the foot of Oppression
  To gather gold out of its strands!

Waits yonder no echoing thunder,
  No lightnings to smite from the cloud,
When falling tears rust the swift needle,
  And threads tie the neck of a shroud?

Ah, beautiful stitches so tiny,
  Where brooding love waits in the nest,
In shadow of motherhood coming,
  Half fearful, yet consciously blest!

What happy hopes lie in the gathers,
  Or lurk in the robes soft and fine!
What buds underneath the leaves silky,
  What day-dreams run with the vine!

No tale can you tell, little stitches, —
  Such tales as you might if you could!
From flounces that cover a ball dress,
  To seams in a holy monk's hood.

———◆———

LIKE HIS MOTHER USED TO MAKE.

"I was born in Indiany," says a stranger lank and slim,
As us fellers in the restaurant was kind o' guyin' him,
And Uncle Jake was slidin' him another pun'kin pie
And an extra cup o' coffee, with a twinkle in his eye —
"I was born in Indiany — more 'n forty year ago,
And I hain't been back in twenty — and I 'm workin' back'ards
        slow;
But I 've et in every restarunt 'twixt here and Santa Fee,
And I want to state, this coffee tastes like gittin' home to me!

"Pour us out another, daddy," says the feller, warmin' up,
A speakin' crost a saucerful, as uncle tuck his cup —
"When I seed your sign out yonder," he went on to Uncle
        Jake —
"'Come in and git some coffee like your mother used to make' —
I thought of my old mother and the Posey County farm,
And me a little kid ag'in, a hangin' in her arm
As she set the pot a bilin' — broke the eggs an' poured 'em in" —
And the feller kind o' halted, with a trimble in his chin.

And Uncle Jake he fetched the feller's coffee back, and stood
As solemn, fer a minute, as an undertaker would ;
Then he sort o' turned an' tiptoed to'rds the kitchen door, and
  next —
Here comes his old wife out with him a rubbin' of her specs —
And she rushes for the stranger, and she hollers out, " It 's him !
Thank God, we 've met him comin' ! Don't you know your
  mother, Jim ? "
And the feller as he grabbed her says : " You bet I hain't forgot "—
But, wipin' of his eyes, says he, " Your coffee 's mighty hot ! "

JAMES WHITCOMB RILEY.

ENCORE.

THE singer stood in a blaze of light,
 And fronted the flowery throng ;
Her lips apart with her greeting smile,
 Her soul soared out in her song.
Now hovering like an imprisoned bird
 With its plainings thrilling nigh,
Then faintly sweet, as the reapers hear
 A lark afar in the sky ;

And forth like thunder the praises broke,
 And the singer bowed and smiled,
And flowers fell fast in a scented storm —
 But she was not to be wiled.
" Shall I throw my gifts to this fickle throng ? "
 She thought with a bitter sigh.
" What do they care for my simple song ? "
 As she courtesied a glad good-by.

The singer sat in her lonely room,
 As the stars peeped out of the haze,
And her voice poured forth in its sweetest gush,
 Though none was beside to praise —
Till she saw a form to her window creep
 And crouch by its misty pane, —
An old dame wept at the wondrous song
 That gave back her youth again !

The singer stirred not, nor made a sign
 That she saw where the listener stood,
But once and again she raised her voice
 And poured out its golden flood,
And only ceased when the minster bells
 Shook out their evening clang —
Then one thanked God for the song she heard,
 And one for the song she sang.

ROCKING THE BABY.

I HEAR her rocking the baby —
  Her room is next to mine —
And I fancy I feel the dimpled arms
  That round her neck entwine,
As she rocks and rocks the baby,
  In the room just next to mine.

I hear her rocking the baby
  Each day when the twilight comes,
And I know there 's a world of blessing and love
  In the " baby-by " she hums.

I can see the restless fingers
  Playing with " mamma's rings,"
The sweet little smiling, pouting mouth
  That to hers in kissing clings,
As she rocks and sings to the baby,
  And dreams as she rocks and sings.

I hear her rocking the baby,
  Slower and slower now,
And I hear she is leaving her good-night kiss
  On its eyes, and cheek, and brow.

From her rocking, rocking, rocking,
  I wonder would she start
Could she know, through the wall between us,
  She is rocking on a heart?
While my empty arms are aching
  For a form they may not press, —
And my empty heart is breaking
  In its desolate loneliness.

I list to the rocking, rocking,
  In the room just next to mine,
And breathe a prayer in silence,
  At a mother's broken shrine,
For the woman who rocks the baby
  In the room just next to mine.

                                MADGE MORRIS.

PART IX.

Hope, Encouragement, and Contentment.

And as, in sparkling majesty, a star
  Gilds the bright summit of some gloomy cloud ;
Brightening the half-veiled face of heaven afar :
  So when dark thoughts my brooding spirit shroud,
Sweet Hope ! celestial influence round me shed,
Waving thy silver pinions round my head.

KEATS.

PART IX.

Hope, Encouragement, and Contentment.

———•◦•———

THE CHEERFUL HEART.

"THE world is ever as we take it,
And life, dear child, is what we make it."

Thus spoke a grandam, bent with care,
To little Mabel, flushed and fair.

But Mabel took no heed that day
Of what she heard her grandam say.

Years after, when no more a child,
Her path in life seemed dark and wild.

Back to her heart the memory came
Of a quaint utterance of the dame :

"The world, dear child, is as we take it,
And life, be sure, is what we make it."

She cleared her brow, and smiling thought,
"'T is even as the good soul taught!

"And half my woes thus quickly cured,
The other half may be endured."

No more her heart its shadows wore ;
She grew a little child once more.

A little child in love and trust,
She took the world (as we, too, must)

In happy mood; and lo! it grew
Brighter and brighter to her view.

She made of life (as we, too, should)
A joy; and lo! all things were good

And fair to her as in God's sight
When first he said, "Let there be light."

SOMETIME.

SOMETIME, when all life's lessons have been learned,
   And sun and stars forevermore have set,
The things which our weak judgments here have spurned,
   The things o'er which we grieved with lashes wet,
Will flash before us out of life's dark night,
   As stars shine most in deeper tints of blue;
And we shall see how all God's plans were right,
   And how what seemed reproof was love most true.

And we shall see how, while we frown and sigh,
   God's plans go on as best for you and me;
How, when we called, he heeded not our cry,
   Because his wisdom to the end could see.
And e'en as prudent parents disallow
   Too much of sweet to craving babyhood,
So God, perhaps, is keeping from us now
   Life's sweetest things because it seemeth good.

And if, sometimes, commingled with life's wine,
   We find the wormwood, and rebel and shrink,
Be sure a wiser hand than yours or mine
   Pours out the potion for our lips to drink.
And if some friend we love is lying low,
   Where human kisses cannot reach his face,
Oh, do not blame the loving Father so,
   But bear your sorrow with obedient grace!

And you shall shortly know that lengthened breath
   Is not the sweetest gift God sends his friends,
And that, sometimes, the sable pall of death
   Conceals the fairest boon his love can send.
If we could push ajar the gates of life,
   And stand within, and all God's working see,
We could interpret all this doubt and strife,
   And for each mystery could find a key.

But not to-day ; then be content, poor hearts;
　　God's plans like lilies pure and white unfold ;
We must not tear the close-shut leaves apart —
　　Time will reveal the calyxes of gold.
And if, through patient toil, we reach the land
　　Where tired feet, with sandals loosed, may rest,
When we shall know and clearly understand,
　　I think that we shall say that "God knows best."

MRS. MAY RILEY SMITH.

WHAT LIFE HATH.

LIFE hath its barren years,
When blossoms fall untimely down,
When ripened fruitage fails to crown
The summer toil, when Nature's frown
　　Looks only on our tears.

Life hath its faithless days —
The golden promise of the morn,
That seemed for light and gladness born,
Mean only noontide wreck and scorn,
　　Hushed harp instead of praise.

Life hath its valleys too,
Where we must walk with vain regret,
With mourning clothed, with wild rain wet —
Towards sunlit hopes that soon must set,
　　All quenched in pitying dew.

Life hath its harvest moons,
Its tasselled corn and purple-weighted vine,
Its gathered sheaves of grain, the blessed sign
Of plenteous ripening, bread, and pure, rich wine;
　　Full hearts for harvest tunes.

Life hath its hopes fulfilled,
Its glad fruitions, its blessed answered prayers,
Sweeter for waiting long whose holy air,
Indrawn to silent souls, breathes forth its rare,
　　Grand speech by joy distilled.

Life hath its Tabor heights,
Its lofty mounts of heavenly recognition,
Whose unveiled glories flash to earth, munition
Of love and truth and clear intuition.
　　Hail! mount of all delights.

SARAH DOUDNEY.

LOVE AND LABOR.

WE die not at all, for our deeds remain
To crown with honor or mar with stain;
Through endless sequence of years to come
Our lives shall speak when our lips are dumb.

What though we perish, unknown to fame,
Our tomb forgotten and lost our name,
Since nought is wasted in heaven or earth,
And nothing dies to which God gives birth!

Though life be joyless and death be cold,
And pleasures pall as the world grows old,
Yet God has granted our hearts relief,
For Love and Labor can conquer grief.

Love sheds a light on the gloomy way,
And Labor hurries the weary day;
Though death be fearful and life be hard,
Yet Love and Labor shall win reward.

If Love can dry up a single tear,
If life-long Labor avail to clear
A single web from before the true
Then Love and Labor have won their due.

What though we mourn, we can comfort pain;
What if we die, so the truth be plain!
A little spark from a high desire
Shall kindle others, and grow a fire.

We are not worthy to work the whole,
We have no strength which may have a soul;
Enough for us if our life begin
Successful struggles with grief and sin.

Labor is mortal and fades away,
But Love shall triumph in perfect day;
Labor may wither beneath the sod,
But Love lives ever, for Love is God.

———◆———

LIFE'S TRIUMPH.

EACH life has one grand day: the clouds may lie
　　Along the hills, and storm-winds fiercely blow —
　　The great red sun shine like a thing of woe,
And death's sad skeleton stalk grimly by.
Yet none of these, no matter how they try,
　　Can shroud the perfect triumph we shall know,
　　Or dim the glory that some star will show
Set far away in depths of purple sky.

Sweet love may bring to us this day supreme,
  Or it may thrill our souls through art or song,
  Or meet us where red battle-surges foam ;
Hope's stranded wrecks the barren coasts may gleam,
  And weeks and months rush by, a sombre throng,
  But sometime, somewhere, it will surely come.

THOMAS S. COLLIER.

WHEN MY SHIP COMES IN.

SOMEWHERE, out on the blue seas sailing,
  Where the winds dance and spin ;
Beyond the reach of my eager hailing,
  Over the breakers' din ;
Out where the dark storm-clouds are lifting,
Out where the blinding fog is drifting,
Out where the treacherous sand is shifting,
  My ship is coming in.

Oh, I have watched till my eyes were aching,
  Day after weary day ;
Oh, I have hoped till my heart was breaking,
  While the long nights ebbed away ;
Could I but know where the waves had tossed her,
Could I but know what storms had crossed her,
Could I but know where the winds had lost her,
  Out in the twilight gray !

But though the storms her course have altered,
  Surely the port she 'll win ;
Never my faith in my ship has faltered,
  I know she is coming in.
For through the restless ways of her roaming,
Through the mad rush of the wild waves foaming,
Through the white crest of the billows combing,
  My ship is coming in.

Breasting the tides where the gulls are flying,
  Swiftly she 's coming in ;
Shallows and deeps and rocks defying,
  Bravely she 's coming in ;
Precious the love she will bring to bless me,
Snowy the arms she will bring to caress me,
In the proud purple of kings she will dress me,
  My ship that is coming in.

White in the sunshine her sails will be gleaming,
  See, where my ship comes in ;
At mast-head and peak her colors streaming,
  Proudly she 's sailing in ;

Love, hope, and joy on her decks are cheering,
Music will welcome her glad appearing,
And my heart will sing at her stately nearing,
    When my ship comes in.

ROBERT J. BURDETTE.

SILENCE.

IN silence mighty things are wrought —
Silently builded, thought on thought,
   Truth's temple greets the sky;
And like a citadel with towers,
The soul with her subservient powers
   Is strengthened silently.

—— LYNCH.

OUTWARDS OR HOMEWARDS.

STILL are the ships that in haven ride,
Waiting fair winds or a turn of the tide;
Nothing they fret, though they do not get
Out on the glorious ocean wide.
Oh, wild hearts, that yearn to be free,
Look, and learn from the ships of the sea!

Bravely the ships, in the tempest tossed,
Buffet the waves till the sea be crossed;
Not in despair of the haven fair,
Though winds blow backward, and leagues be lost;
Oh, weary hearts, that yearn for sleep,
Look, and learn from the ships of the deep!

F. W. BOURDILLON

THE JOY OF INCOMPLETENESS.

IF all our life were one broad glare
   Of sunlight, clear, unclouded;
If all our path were smooth and fair,
   By no soft gloom enshrouded;
If all life's flowers were fully blown
   Without the sweet unfolding,
And happiness were rudely thrown
   On hands too weak for holding —
     Should we not miss the twilight hours,
      The gentle haze and sadness?
     Should we not long for storms and showers
      To break the constant gladness?

If none were sick and none were sad,
    What service could we render?
I think if we were always glad,
    We scarcely could be tender.
Did our beloved never need
    Our patient ministration,
Earth would grow cold and miss indeed
    Its sweetest consolation;
        If sorrow never claimed our heart,
           And every wish were granted,
        Patience would die, and hope depart —
           Life would be disenchanted.

And yet in heaven is no more night,
    In heaven is no more sorrow!
Such unimagined new delight
    Fresh grace from pain will borrow.
As the poor seed that underground
    Seeks its true life above it,
Not knowing what will there be found
    When sunbeams kiss and love it,
        So we in darkness upward grow,
           And look and long for heaven,
        But cannot picture it below
           Till more of light be given.

NOTE. — A more complete version of this anonymous poem than that found in Harper's *Encyclopædia of Poetry*, in which the last eight lines given here are missing.

A PLEA FOR "CASTLES IN THE AIR."

AMID the myriad troubles that meet us day by day,
Who would not from the conflict a moment turn away,
And in a far-off fairy-land, where men no burdens bear,
Forget awhile our tears and toil in "castles in the air"?

When many a bright-hued prospect fades fast beyond our view,
And hopes which neared fruition prove shadowy and untrue;
May we not in that dreamland, beyond all clouds and care,
Behold our Paradise restored in "castles in the air"?

Oh, there are lonely chambers in every home and heart —
And in life's song of sorrow each one must bear a part.
But hark! what mystic melodies soon hush the voice of care,
As parted hands are clasped once more in "castles in the air."

Then never grow discouraged though fortune favors not,
And we pursue life's pilgrimage unnoticed or forgot;
We have an hour of victory and lustrous laurels wear —
For all are kings and conquerors in "castles in the air."

                                  JACOB GOUGH

LEARN TO WAIT.

LEARN to wait — life's hardest lesson,
  Conned perchance, through blinding tears,
While the heart-throbs sadly echo
  To the tread of passing years.

Learn to wait — hope's slow fruition;
  Faint not, though the way seem long;
There is joy in each condition,
  Hearts, through suffering, may grow strong.

Constant sunshine, howe'er welcome,
  Ne'er would ripen fruit or flower;
Giant oaks owe half their greatness
  To the scathing tempest's power.

Thus a soul untouched by sorrow
  Aims not at a higher state;
Joy seeks not a brighter morrow,
  Only sad hearts learn to wait.

Human strength and human greatness
  Spring not from life's sunny side;
Heroes must be more than driftwood
  Floating on a waveless tide.

———◆———

BETTER TO CLIMB AND FALL.

GIVE me a man with an aim,
  Whatever that aim may be,
Whether it's wealth, or whether it's fame,
  It matters not to me.
Let him walk in the path of right,
  And keep his aim in sight,
And work and pray in faith alway,
  With his eye on the glittering height.

Give me a man who says, —
  " I will do something well,
And make the fleeting days
  A story of labor tell."
Though the aim he has be small,
  It is better than none at all;
With something to do the whole year through
  He will not stumble or fall.

But Satan weaves a snare
   For the feet of those who stray
With never a thought or care
   Where the path may lead away.
The man who has no aim,
   Not only leaves no name
When this life is done, but ten to one
   He leaves a record of shame.

Give me a man whose heart
   Is filled with ambition's fire ;
Who sets his mark in the start,
   And keeps moving it higher and higher.
Better to die in the strife,
   The hands with labor rife,
Than to glide with the stream in an idle dream,
   And lead a purposeless life.

Better to strive and climb,
   And never reach the goal,
Than to drift along with time,
   An aimless, worthless soul.
Ay, better to climb and fall,
   Or sow, though the yield be small,
Than to throw away day after day,
   And never to strive at all.

BY AND BY.

WAS the parting very bitter ?
   Was the hand clasped very tight ?
Is a storm of tear-drops falling
   From a face all sad and white ?
Think not of it, in the future,
   Calmer, fairer days are nigh —
Gaze not backward, but look onward
   For a sunny "by and by."

Was the priceless love you lavished,
   Sought for, played with, and then slain ?
Were its crushed and quivering remnants
   Calmly thrown you back again ?
Calmly, too, those remnants gather,
   Bring them home without a sigh ;
Sweet returns they yet shall bring you
   In the coming " by and by."

Are the eyelids very heavy ?
   Does the tired head long for rest ?
Are the temples hot and throbbing,
   And the hands together pressed ?
16

Hope shall lay you on her bosom,
  Cool the poor lips parched and dry,
And shall whisper, " Rest is coming —
  Rest forever, ' by and by.' "

And when calmed and cheered and freshened
  By her soul-inspiring voice,
Then look up, the heavens are brightening —
  Cease your wailing and rejoice.
Cry not for the days departed,
  None will hear you, none reply;
But look up where light is breaking
  O'er a brighter " by and by."

FAILURE.

THE Lord, who fashioned my hands for working,
  Set me a task and it is not done;
I have tried and tried since the early morning,
  And now to the westward sinketh the sun.

Noble the task that was kindly given
  To one so little and weak as I, —
Somehow my strength would never grasp it,
  Never as days and years flew by.

Others found me cheerfully toiling,
  Showed me their work as they passed away;
Filled were their hands to overflowing,
  Proud were their hearts, and glad and gay.

Laden with harvest spoils they entered
  In at the golden gate of their rest;
Laid their sheaves at the feet of the Master,
  Found their places among the blest.

Happy are those who strove to help me —
  Failing ever in spite of their aid;
Fain would their love have borne me with them,
  But I was unready and sore afraid.

Now I know my task will never be finished,
  And when the Master calleth my name,
His voice will find me still at my labor,
  Weeping beside it in weary shame.

With empty hands I shall rise to meet him,
  And when he looks for the fruit of years,
Nothing have I to lay before him
  But broken efforts and bitter tears.

Yet when he calls I fain would hasten —
 Mine eyes are dim and their light is gone ;
And I am weary as though I carried
 A burden of beautiful work well done.

I will fold my empty hands on my bosom —
 Meekly thus, in the shape of a cross;
And the Lord, who made me so frail and feeble,
 Maybe will pity their strife and loss.

————◆————

NEAR THE DAWN.

WHEN life's troubles gather darkly
 Round the way we follow here,
When no hope the sad heart lightens,
 No voice speaks a word of cheer;
Then the thought the shadow scatters,
 Giving us a cheering ray, —
When the night appears the darkest,
 Morning is not far away.

When adversity surrounds us,
 And our sunshine friends pass by,
And the dreams so fondly cherished
 With our shattered treasures lie ;
Then amid such gloomy seasons
 This sweet thought can yet be drawn, —
When the darkest hour is present,
 It is always near the dawn.

When the spirit fluttering lingers
 On the confines of this life,
Parting from all joyful memories,
 And from every scene of strife,
Though the scene is sad and gloomy,
 And the body shrinks in fear,
These dark hours will soon be vanished,
 And the glorious morn be here.

Pain cannot affect us always,
 Brighter days will soon be here ;
Sorrow may oppress us often,
 Yet a happier time is near;
All along our earthly journey
 This reflection lights the way, —
Nature's darkest hour is always
 Just before the break of day.

MAGDALENA.

MAGDALENA'S robes are trailing through the highway's soiling
    dust,
Spotless hem and seam are glazing over with apparent rust;
Hooded cloak conceals the contour of her drooping head and
    face,
Hiding outline and proportion of her form whose step is grace.
Small her feet and arched her instep gliding onward travel-
    stained —
Feet whose wealth and pride of birthright have the common
    earth disdained.
Who can prove that Magdalena walks alone in strange dis-
    guise?
Who unclasp the hooded mantle hiding face and veiling eyes?

Magdalena lives in grandeur, and the nobles round her wait,
And her chariot on the highway bears armorial gauds of state;
Fair and proud is Magdalena, pride of birth and pride of
    scorn;
Fairer, earth ne'er gave existence since the day that Eve was
    born.
Form as stately, mould as perfect, eyes of blue and forehead
    fair,
Crowned with woman's crown of glory — wondrous waves of
    golden hair.

Magdalena loves in secret, loves the lowliest fisher's son; —
She can never wed the Gentile who her faith and soul has
    won;
He is brave and tall and graceful, fair as any son of earth,
But his grace is all of nature, not from gentle blood and birth.
Yesterday the highest ruler in the land of Judah came,
Kneeling at her feet in splendor, offering her his hand and
    name;
But he tarried not till evening, whispering love vows 'neath
    the moon,
Rode away in crimson anger, anger o'er his slighted boon.

Magdalena, pale with passion, struggling in her bonds of love,
Envying every meaner thing from mated man to mated dove,
Spurns the laws of men and birthright, spurns the laws of
    maiden shame,
Scorns the ruler and his greatness, scorns alike her wealth and
    fame;
Heeding but the charm which draws her towards the fisher's
    manly grace,
Parting with the hopes of woman for his ardent love embrace.

Magdalena's cheeks are glowing with her lover's kisses warm,
And his manly arms close folding round her lithe and yielding
form;
Nature owns no paltry barrier, love has conquered pride of
birth,
And their wedded souls in spirit know no other bonds on
earth.
Wrapt in bliss of love's elysium, answering pulse and beating
heart,—
Fame and name and life forgotten, e'en the law that bids them
part.

Magdalena's fame is sullied, like her robes with highway dust;
Scribes and Pharisees proclaim her sin and shame before the
just;
Fair and high-born Magdalena, drooping form and head low-
bowed,
Guilty captive at the mercy of a coarse, vindictive crowd
Clamoring for the law of Moses, so to stone her till she dies,
Waiting judgment from the Master, life or death as he replies.
Spies have proved that Magdalena walks alone in strange
disguise,
Torn away the hooded mantle hiding face and veiling eyes.

Magdalena scorned the ruler; he it was who hired the spies,
Into all her secrets prying, forcing off her strange disguise,
Tearing from the fond embraces of her lover's folding arms,
Forcing her from love's protection, rudely railing at her
charms,
Bringing her within the temple with her head and bosom bare,
No disguise to hide her blushes, save her veil of golden hair.

Magdalena stands in terror, with her small hands tightly pressed,
Hiding with those waves of glory half the beauty of her breast;
Torn her robes and lost her sandals, vain she hides her gleam-
ing feet,
Guilt ne'er brought so fair a captive pleading at a mercy·seat;
He who never knew the passion of the sinner's throbbing soul,
Bows his spotless head in pity as her tears of anguish roll.

Magdalena's eyes are heavy with their penitential tears,
As she gazes on the Master and his words of mercy hears;
See the hideous crowd before her, dropping each his vengeful
stone,
Gliding out with guilty faces, leaving her with him alone.
Jesus, when the last had left her, gazed in pity on her face,
Gave assurance of his pardon by his looks and words of grace,
Gave his strength to Magdalena, strength to walk without
disguise;
His large soul of purest love-light dried her penitential eyes.

Magdalena's robes are floating in the pathway of the just,
Spotless seam and hem protected from the earth's corrosive
    rust ;
Pride of wealth and pride of nature made subservient to the
    good,
Thousands bless the unknown giver for the boon of daily food ;
And the manly fisher, leaving tent, and net, and fisher's rod,
Follows as a meek disciple worshipping the Son of God ;
In his strength walks Magdalena evermore without disguise,
Faithful to the hand that saved her and his love-light in her
    eyes.

WAITING.

LISTENING, yearning,
While the lingering, lengthening shadows
    Link the twilight to the day,
While the dewy breath of evening,
    Sweet with balm from far away,
      Sways the drooping passion-flower
      Clinging to my lonely bower,
      Where I sit, heart-sore and weary,
      Facing the sad sight so dreary ;
        Listening, yearning
      For a step that 's ne'er returning.

Listening, yearning —
Oh, sad heart, be stilled thy moaning, —
    Suns may wane and months may roll,
Years may glide in silent sorrow
    O'er the hope that mocks my soul.
      Hush thy wail — let no sharp crying
      Strike upon the dumb hours, flying,
      While I sit, 'mid shadows falling,
      Hoping, heark'ning, watching, calling,
        Listening, yearning
      For a wanderer's step returning.

Listening, yearning —
Oh, the night grows cold and dreary,
    Loud the chill wind moans and sighs —
Ghostly faces, wan and eerie,
    Haunt me with their pitying eyes ;
      Ghosts of dead hopes yet remaining —
      With their sad eyes still complaining
      Though their mute lips make no wailing,
      Ah, lone watch so unavailing !
        Listening, yearning
      For a dear one's step returning.

Listening, yearning —
Bleak the night, and storm-clouds gather,
   Light grows dim, and hope grows cold;
Closer press the pitying spectres —
   Ah! they clasp me in their fold.
      Life was mournful — death is sweeter —
      Memory maketh love completer.
      Dear, through evening shadows falling,
      Nevermore I wait thee, calling,
         Listening, yearning
      For thy step too late returning.

Listening, yearning —
O'er the battlements celestial,
   See the pure-browed seraphs lean
Earthward, keeping calms of silence,
   Waves of pulsing songs between.
      Oh, by Love Divine once yearning
      O'er a world, Love's call proud spurning,
      Love for loss full compensating, —
      I adjure thee, seek me, waiting,
         Listening, yearning,
      Down from heaven for thy returning.

————◆————

HEADS, HEARTS, AND HANDS.

HEADS that think and hearts that feel,
Hands that turn the busy wheel,
   Make our life worth living here,
   In this mundane hemisphere:
Heads to plan what hearts shall do,
Hearts to bear us bravely through —
   Thinking head and toiling hand
   Are the masters of the land.

When a thought becomes a thing,
Busy hands make hammers ring
   Until honest work has wrought
   Into shape the thinker's thought;
Which will aid to civilize,
And make nations great and wise,
   Lifting to a lofty height
   In this age of thought and light.

Miracles of science show
With their light the way to go;
   Touch a tube of gas, and light
   Blossoms like the stars of night;

Touch another tube, and lo !
Streams of crystal waters flow;
   Touch a telegraphic wire,
   And your thought has wings of fire.

Hail to honest hearts and hands,
And to the head that understands ;
   Hands that dare to truth subscribe,
   Hands that never touched a bribe;
Hearts that hate a deed unjust,
Hearts that other hearts can trust ;
   Heads that plan for others' weal,
   Heads poised over hearts that feel.

GEORGE W. BUNGAY.

THROUGH TOIL.

I HOLD it better far that one should rule
Imperious tempers with a sinewy will,
Than, amiable and passionless of soul,
With folded hands amid life's din sit still.
Since, though ofttimes the battle goeth hard,
Strength comes with struggle, and wild olive leaves
Twined round a brow begrimed and battle-scarred
Mean more to noble men and nobler gods
Than costliest purples of inglorious ease.

Though tired men through toil-encumbered years
Seek restful havens, lotus-lands of dreams,
Who that hath seen doth evermore forget
What glory o'er his burnished armor gleams
Who fights with grosser self, or crushes down
With stalwart blows the vices of his age,
Thridding the austere heights of chaste renown ?
The victor's joy Fate nevermore reveals
To sluggish souls, — nor his transcendent peace.

A. L. HINDS

"TIME TO ME."

TIME to me this truth hath taught,
   'T is a truth that 's worth revealing :
More offend from want of thought
   Than from want of feeling.

If advice we would convey,
   There 's a time we should convey it;
If we 've but a word to say,
   There 's a time in which to say it.

Many a beauteous flower decays,
    Though we tend it e'er so much;
Something secret on it preys,
    Which no human aid can touch.

So in many a loving breast
    Lies some canker-grief concealed,
That, if touched, is more oppressed,
    Left unto itself — is healed!

Oft, unknowingly, the tongue
    Touches on a chord so aching
That a word or accent wrong
    Pains the heart almost to breaking.

Many a tear of wounded pride,
    Many a fault of human blindness,
Has been soothed or turned aside
    By a quiet voice of kindness.

Time to me this truth hath taught,
    'T is a truth that's worth revealing:
More offend from want of thought
    Than from want of feeling.

SOMEHOW OR OTHER.

LIFE is a burden to every one's shoulder;
    None may escape from its troubles and care;
Miss it in youth and 't will come when we 're older,
    And fit us as close as the garments we wear.
Sorrow comes into our home uninvited,
    Robbing our heart of its treasures of song;
Lovers grow cold and our friendships are slighted,
    Yet somehow or other we worry along.

Midst the sweet blossoms that smile on our faces
    Grow the rank weeds that would poison and blight;
And e'en in the midst of earth's beautiful places
    There 's always a something that is n't just right.
Yet oft from the rock we may pick a gay flower,
    And drink from a spring in a desolate waste;
They come to the heart as a heavenly dower,
    And nought is so sweet to the eye or the taste.

Every-day toil is an every-day blessing,
    Though poverty's cottage and crust we may share;
Weak is the back on which burdens are pressing,
    But stout is the heart which is strengthened by prayer.

Somehow or other the pathway grows brighter
    Just when we mourned there was none to befriend;
Hope in the heart makes the burden seem lighter,
    And somehow or other we get to the end.

——◆——

FALLEN.

HERE is my hand,
    O weary one —
A smile for love defiled,
A tear for hope reviled,
A brother's faith for her whom men are taught to shun.

What men may do or say
    I care not now;
To me thou art a ray
Of sunlight — borne away
By too sweet dreams of earth, whose shadows haunt thy brow.

The visions I recall —
    Thy girlish face,
Thy voice like music's fall,
Thy tender glances, all
Thy nature like the heart of life's impassioned grace.

And now thine eyes are filled
    With tears of shame!
Where passion burned and thrilled,
Death's angels have instilled
The anguish and remorse that lips with horror frame.

The world's taunts hotly burn
    Upon thy cheek;
Thy pitiless sisters turn
From thy sad eyes, and spurn
Thy prayers — like cries of sin unworthy to bespeak.

Yet art thou lost indeed?
    O stricken soul!
Must life forever bleed
For one embittered deed?
Shall all the golden days be useless to console?

Is charity then dead,
    And pity blind?
O child! but few have read
Thy heart.   Yet I have shed
Tears scorching as thine own for Christ's love undivined.

GEO. EDGAR MONTGOMERY.

PESSIMISM.

"Is life worth living? — Well, to tell you true,
It scarcely is, if all men were like you."

BRIGHT-FACED maiden, bright-souled maiden,
    What is this that I must hear?
Is thy heart with sorrow laden,
    Is thine eye dimmed with a tear?
Can it be that lips so sweetly
    Rounded to be kindly kissed
Could be twisted indiscreetly
    To the vile word *Pessimist?*
Not for thine own ills thou weepest;
    Softly feathered is thy nest;
When thou wakest, when thou sleepest,
    Thou art fortuned with the best.
But thy sisters and thy brothers
    Pierced with many a woful smart,
Dying children, wailing mothers,
    Fret thy nerve and stab thy heart.
In the country, in the city,
    Godless deeds, a loveless list,
Stir thy blood and move thy pity,
    And thou art a PESSIMIST.
Storms and wars and tribulations,
    Fevered passions' reinless tide,
With insane hallucinations
    Mingled, travel far and wide.
Can there be an Eye inspecting
    Things so tumbling in pell-mell,
With a cool control directing
    Such a hotbed, such a hell?
Nay, sweet maid, but think more slowly;
    Though this thing and that be sad,
'T is a logic most unholy
    That the gross of things is bad;
'T is a trick of melancholy,
    Tainting life with death's alloy;
Or in wisdom, or in folly,
    Nature still delights in joy.
Dost thou hear of starving sinners, —
    Nine and ten, or ninety-nine?
Many thousands eat good dinners,
    Many hundreds quaff good wine.
Hast thou seen a score of cripples?
    Equal legs are not uncommon;
If you know one fool that tipples,
    Thousands drink not — man and woman;

Tell me if you know how many
    Murders happen in the town?
One a year, perhaps, if any;
    Should that weigh your heart quite down?
No doubt, if you read the papers,
    You will find a strange hotch-potch —
Doting dreams, delirious capers,
    Many a blunder, blot, and blotch;
Bags of windy speculation,
    Babblement of small and great,
Cheating, swindling, peculation,
    Squabblement of Church and State;
Miners blown up, humbugs shown up,
    Beaten wives, insulted brides,
Raving preachers, witless teachers,
    Lunatics and suicides;
Drains and cesspools, faintings, fevers,
    Poisoned cats and stolen collies,
Simple women, gay deceivers,
    Every sort and size of follies;
Wandering M. P.'s brainless babble,
    Deputations, meetings, dinners,
Riots of the lawless rabble,
    Purple sins of West End sinners;
Driving, dicing, drinking, dancing,
    Spirit rapping, ghostly stuff;
Bubble schemes and deft financing,
    When the shares are blown enough.
All this is true; when men cut capers
    That make the people talk or stare,
To-morrow when you ope the papers
    You're sure to find their antics there.
But you and I and all our neighbors
    Meanwhile, in pure and peaceful ways,
With link on link of fruitful labors,
    Draw out our chain of happy days.
See things as they are; be sober;
    Balance well life's loss and gain;
If to-day be chill October,
    Summer suns will come again.
Are bleak winds forever sighing?
    Do dark clouds forever lower?
Are your friends all dead and dying?
    All your sweetness turned to sour?
Great men, no doubt, have sometimes small ways,
    But a horse is not an ass,
And a black snake is not always
    Lurking in the soft green grass.
Don't be hasty, gentle lady,
    In this whirl of diverse things
Keep your footing, and with steady
    Poise control your equal wings.

All things can't to all be pleasant;
  I love bitter, you love sweet;
Some faint when a cut is present;
  Rats find babies' cheeks a treat.
If all tiny things were tall things,
  If all petty things were grand,
Where would greatness be, when all things
  On one common level stand?
Do you think the wingèd breezes,
  Fraught with healthy ventilation,
When a tender infant sneezes
  Should retreat with trepidation?
When dry Earth to Heaven is calling
  For soft rain and freshening dew,
Shall the rain refrain from falling
  Lest my lady wet her shoe?
Fools still rush to rash conclusions,
  And the mole-eyed minion, man,
Talks of troubles and confusions,
  When he sees not half the plan.
Spare to blame and fear to cavil,
  With short leave dismiss your pain,
Let no fretful fancies revel
  In the sanctum of your brain.
Use no magnifying-glasses
  To change molehills into mountains,
Nor on every ill that passes
  Pour hot tears from bitter fountains.
Trust in God and know your duty;
  Some good things are in your power;
Every day will bring its booty
  From the labor of the hour.
Never reck what fools are prating,
  Work and wait, let sorrow lie;
" Live and love; have done with hating,"
  Goethe says — and so say I.

Blackwood.

DO SOMETHING.

IF the world seems cool to you,
  Kindle fires to warm it!
Let their comfort hide from you
  Winters that deform it.
Hearts as frozen as your own
  To that radiance gather;
You will soon forget to moan,
  " Ah! the cheerless weather!"

If the world 's a " vale of tears,"
  Smile till rainbows span it ;
Breathe the love that life endears —
  Clear from clouds to fan it.
Of your gladness lend a gleam
  Unto souls that shiver ;
Show them how dark sorrow's stream
  Blends with hope's bright river.

                    LUCY LARCOM.

THE GOLDEN SIDE.

THERE 's many a rest on the road of life,
  If we only would stop to take it ;
And many a tone from the better land,
  If the querulous heart would wake it.
To the sunny soul that is full of hope,
  And whose beautiful trust ne'er faileth,
The grass is green and the flowers are bright,
  Though the wintry storm prevaileth.

Better to hope though the clouds hang low,
  And to keep the eyes still lifted ;
For the sweet blue sky will soon peep through,
  When the ominous clouds are rifted.
There was never a night without a day,
  Nor an evening without a morning ;
And the darkest hour, the proverb goes,
  Is the hour before the dawning.

There is many a gem in the path of life,
  Which we pass in our idle pleasure,
That is richer far than the jewelled crown
  Or the miser's hoarded treasure ;
It may be the love of a little child,
  Or the mother's prayer to Heaven,
Or only a beggar's grateful thanks
  For a cup of water given.

Better to weave in the web of life
  A bright and golden filling,
And to do God's will with a ready heart,
  And hands that are swift and willing,
Than to snap the delicate silver threads
  Of our curious lives asunder,
And then Heav'n blame for the tangled ends,
  And sit and grieve and wonder.

WAITING.

SERENE I fold my hands and wait,
  Nor care for wind, nor tide, nor sea ;
I rave no more 'gainst time or fate,
  For lo ! my own shall come to me.

I stay my haste, I make delays ;
  For what avails this eager pace ?
I stand amid the eternal ways,
  And what is mine shall know my face.

Asleep, awake, by night or day,
  The friends I seek are seeking me ;
No wind can drive my bark astray,
  Nor change the tide of destiny.

What matter if I stand alone ?
  I wait with joy the coming years ;
My heart shall reap where it has sown,
  And garner up its fruit of tears.

The waters know their own, and draw
  The brook that springs in yonder heights ;
So flows the good with equal law
  Unto the soul of pure delights.

Yon floweret nodding in the wind
  Is ready plighted to the bee ;
And, maiden, why that look unkind ?
  For lo ! thy lover seeketh thee.

The stars come nightly to the sky,
  The tidal wave unto the sea ;
Nor time, nor space, nor deep, nor high,
  Can keep my own away from me.

JOHN BURROUGHS.

THE GREEN GRASS UNDER THE SNOW.

THE work of the sun is slow,
But as sure as heaven, we know ;
    So we 'll not forget,
    When the skies are wet,
There 's green grass under the snow.

When the winds of winter blow,
Wailing like voices of woe,
    There are April showers,
    And buds and flowers,
And green grass under the snow.

We find that it 's ever so
In this life's uneven flow;
    We 've only to wait,
    In the face of fate,
For the green grass under the snow.

ANNIE A. PRESTON.

RAIN IN THE HEART.

" Into each life some rain must fall."

IF this were all — oh! if this were all,
That into each life *some* rain must fall,
There were fewer sobs in the poet's rhyme,
There were fewer wrecks on the shores of time.

But tempests of woe dash over the soul —
Since winds of anguish we cannot control;
And shock after shock are we called to bear,
Till the lips are white with the heart's despair.

The shores of time with wrecks are strewn,
Unto the ear comes ever a moan —
Wrecks of hope that set sail with glee,
Wrecks of love sinking silently.

Many are hid from the human eye;
Only God knoweth how deep they lie;
Only God heard when arose the prayer,
" Help me to bear — oh! help me to bear."

" Into each life some rain must fall."
If this were all — oh! if this were all;
Yet there 's a refuge from storm and blast —
Gloria Patri — we 'll reach at last.

Be strong, be strong, to my heart I cry,
The pearl in the wounded shell doth lie;
Days of sunshine are given to all,
Though " into each life some rain must fall."

"GIVE THANKS FOR WHAT?"

" LET earth give thanks," the deacon said,
And then the Proclamation read.

" Give thanks fer what, an' what about ? "
Asked Simon Soggs when church was out; —
" Give thanks fer what ?   I don't see why,
The rust got in an' spiled my rye,

And hay wa'n't half a crop, and corn
All wilted down and looked forlorn.
The bugs just gobbled my pertaters
The what you call 'em — lineaters,
And gracious! when you come to wheat,
There 's more than all the world can eat;
Onless a war should interfere,
Crops won't bring half a price this year;
I 'll hev to give 'em away, I reckon!"

"Good for the poor!" exclaimed the deacon.

"Give thanks fer what?" asked Simon Soggs;
"Fer th' freshet carryin' off my logs?
Fer Dobbin goin' blind? Fer five
Uv my best cows, that was alive
Afore the smashin' railroad come
And made it awful troublesome?
Fer that haystack the lightnin' struck
And burnt to ashes? — thunderin' luck! —
Fer ten dead sheep?" sighed Simon Soggs.

The deacon said, "You 've got yer hogs!"

"Give thanks? And Jane and baby sick?
I e'enmost wonder if Ole Nick
Ain't running things!"
                        The deacon said,
"Simon, your people might be dead!"

"Give thanks!" said Simon Soggs again.
"Jest look at what a fix we 're in!
The country 's rushin' to the dogs
At race-horse speed!" said Simon Soggs.
"Rotten all through, in every State;
Why, ef we don't repudiate,
We 'll have to build, for big and small,
A poorhouse that 'll hold us all!
Down South the crooked whiskey-still
Is running like the Devil's mill.
The nigger skulks in night's disguise,
And hooks a chicken as he flies.
Up North there 's murder everywhere,
And awful doings, I declare.
Give thanks? How mad it makes me feel
To think how office-holders steal!
The taxes paid by you and me
Is four times bigger 'n they should be.
The Fed'ral Gover'ment 's all askew;
The ballot 's sech a mockery, too!
Some votes too little, some too much,
Some not at all — it beats the Dutch!

And now no man knows what to do,
Or how is how or who is who.
Deacon, corruption 's sure to kill!
This ' glorious Union ' never will,
I 'll bet a Continental cent,
Elect another President!
Give thanks fer what, I 'd like to know!"

The deacon answered, sad and low,
"Simon, it fills me with surprise
Ye don't see where yer duty lies;
Kneel right straight down in all the muss,
And thank God that it ain't no wuss!"

The American Queen.

------◆------

COMPENSATION.

SHE folded up the worn and mended frock,
    And smoothed it tenderly upon her knee,
Then through the soft web of a wee red sock
    She wove the bright wool, musing thoughtfully:
" Can this be all?   The outside world so fair,
    I hunger for its green and pleasant ways;
A cripple prisoned in her restless chair
    Looks from her window with a wistful gaze.

" The fruits I cannot reach are red and sweet,
    The paths forbidden are both green and wide;
O God! there is no boon to helpless feet
    So altogether sweet as paths denied.
Home is most fair; bright all my household fires,
    And children are a gift without alloy;
But who would bound the field of their desires
    By the prim hedges of mere fireside joy?

" I can but weave a faint thread to and fro,
    Making a frail woof in my baby's sock;
Into the world's sweet tumult I would go,
    At its strong gates my trembling hand would knock."
Just then the children came, the father too;
    Their eager faces lit the twilight gloom;
" Dear heart," he whispered, as he nearer drew,
    " How sweet it is within this little room!

" God puts my strongest comfort here to draw
    When thirst is great and common wells are dry.
Your pure desire is my unerring law,
    Tell me, dear one, who is so safe as I?
Home is the pasture where my soul may feed,
    This room a paradise has grown to be;
And only where these patient feet shall lead
    Can it be home to these dear ones and me."

He touched with reverent hand the helpless feet,
   The children crowded close and kissed her hair.
"Our mother is so good, and kind, and sweet,
   There's not another like her anywhere!"
The baby in her low bed opened wide
   The soft blue flowers of her timid eyes,
And viewed the group about the cradle-side
   With smiles of glad and innocent surprise.

The mother drew the baby to her knee
   And, smiling, said: "The stars shine soft to-night;
My world is fair; its edges sweet to me,
   And whatsoever is, dear Lord, is right."

THE SADDEST FATE.

To touch a broken lute,
   To strike a jangled string,
To strive with tones forever mute
   The dear old tunes to sing —
What sadder fate could any heart befall?
Alas! dear child, never to sing at all.

To sigh for pleasures flown,
   To weep for withered flowers,
To count the blessings we have known,
   Lost with the vanished hours —
What sadder fate could any heart befall?
Alas! dear child, ne'er to have known them all.

To dream of love and rest,
   To know the dream has past,
To bear within an aching breast
   Only a void at last —
What sadder fate could any heart befall?
Alas! dear child, ne'er to have loved at all.

To trust an unknown good,
   To hope, but all in vain,
Over a far-off bliss to brood,
   Only to find it pain —
What sadder fate could any soul befall?
Alas! dear child, never to hope at all.

RIGHT AND WRONG.

ALAS! how hardly things go right!
'T is hard to watch on a summer's night,
For the sigh will come, and the kiss will stay,
And the summer's night is a winter's day.

Alas! how easily things go wrong!
A sigh too much or a kiss too long,
And there comes a mist and a weeping rain,
And life is never the same again.

And yet how easily things go right,
If the sigh and the kiss of the summer's night
Come deep from the soul in the stronger ray
That is born in the light of the winter's day.

And things can never go badly wrong
If the heart be true and the love be strong;
For the mist, if it comes, and the weeping rain,
Will be changed by the love into sunshine again.

WHAT OF THAT?

TIRED! Well, what of that?
Didst fancy life was spent on beds of ease,
Fluttering the rose leaves scattered by the breeze?
Come, rouse thee! work while it is called to-day!
Coward, arise! go forth upon thy way!

Lonely! And what of that?
Some must be lonely! 't is not given to all
To feel a heart responsive rise and fall,
To blend another life into its own.
Work may be done in loneliness. Work on.

Dark! Well, and what of that?
Didst fondly dream the sun would never set?
Dost fear to lose thy way? Take courage yet!
Learn thou to walk by faith and not by sight;
Thy steps will guided be, and guided right.

Hard! Well, and what of that?
Didst fancy life one summer holiday,
With lessons none to learn, and nought but play?
Go, get thee to thy task! Conquer or die!
It must be learned! Learn it then patiently.

No help! Nay, it 's not so!
Though human help be far, thy God is nigh,
Who feeds the ravens, hears his children's cry.
He 's near thee, wheresoe'er thy footsteps roam,
And he will guide thee, light thee, help. thee home.

"BIDE A WEE, AND DINNA FRET."

Is the road very dreary?
Patience yet!
Rest will be sweeter if thou art aweary,
And after the night cometh the morning cheery;
Then bide a wee, and dinna fret.

The clouds have silver lining,
Don't forget;
And though he 's hidden, still the sun is shining.
Courage! instead of tears in vain repining,
Just bide a wee, and dinna fret.

With toil and cares unending
Art beset?
Bethink thee how the storms from heaven descending
Snap the stiff oak, but spare the willow bending,
And bide a wee, and dinna fret.

Grief sharper sting doth borrow
From regret:
But yesterday is gone, and shall its sorrow
Unfit us for the present and to-morrow?
Nay; bide a wee, and dinna fret.

An over-anxious brooding
Doth beget
A host of fears and fantasies deluding;
Then, brother, lest the torments be intruding,
Just bide a wee, and dinna fret.

Leisure Hour.   S. E. G.

WORK.

IF some great angel spoke to me to-night,
In awful language of the unknown land,
Bidding me choose from treasure infinite,
From goodly gifts and glories in his hand,

The thing I coveted, what should I take?
    Fame's wreath of bays?   The fickle world's esteem?
Nay, greenest bays may wave on brows that ache,
    And world's applauding passeth as a dream.
Should I choose love to fill my empty heart
    With soft, strong sweetness, as in days of old?
Nay, for love's rapture hath an after smart,
    And on love's rose the thorns are manifold.
Should I choose life with long succeeding years?
    Nay, earth's long life is longer time for tears.
I would choose work, and never-failing power,
    To work without weak hindrance by the way,
Without recurrence of the weary hour
    When tired tyrant Nature holds its sway
Over the busy brain and toiling hand.
    Ah! if an angel came to me to-night,
Speaking in language of the unknown land,
    So would I choose from treasures infinite.
But well I know the blessed gift I crave,
    The tireless strength for never-ending task,
Is not for this life.   But beyond the grave
    It may be I shall find the thing I ask;
For I believe there is a better land,
    Where will and work and strength go hand in hand.

All the Year Round.

THE HARDEST TIME OF ALL.

THERE are days of silent sorrow
    In the seasons of our life;
There are wild, despairing moments,
    There are hours of mental strife;
There are times of stony anguish,
    When the tears refuse to fall;
But the waiting time, my brothers,
    Is the hardest time of all.

Youth and love are oft impatient,
    Seeking things beyond their reach;
But the heart grows sick of hoping
    Ere it learns what life can teach;
For before the fruit be gathered
    We must see the blossoms fall;
And the waiting time, my brothers,
    Is the hardest time of all.

We can bear the heat of conflict,
    Though the sudden, crushing blow,
Beating back our gathered forces,
    For a moment lay us low;

We may rise again beneath it
　None the weaker for the fall ;
But the waiting time, my brothers,
　Is the hardest time of all.

For it wears the eager spirit,
　As the salt waves wear the stone,
And the garb of hope grows threadbare
　Till the brightest tints are flown ;
Then amid youth's radiant tresses
　Silent snows begin to fall ;
Oh ! the waiting time, my brothers,
　Is the hardest time of all.

But at last we learn the lesson
　That God knoweth what is best;
For with wisdom cometh patience,
　And with patience cometh rest.
Yea, a golden thread is shining
　Through the tangled woof of fate ;
And our hearts shall thank him meekly,
　That he taught us how to wait.

　　　　　　　　　　　SARAH DOUDNEY.

AS PEBBLES IN THE SEA.

WHO shall judge man from his manner,
　Who shall know him by his dress ?
Paupers may be fit for palaces,
　Princes fit for nothing else.
Crumpled shirt and dirty jacket
　May beclothe the golden ore
Of the deepest thoughts and feelings —
　Satin vest can do no more.

There are streams of crystal nectar
　Ever flowing out of stone;
There are purple beds and golden
　Hidden, crushed, and overthrown ;
God, who counts by souls, not dresses,
　Loves and prospers you and me,
While he values thrones the highest
　But as pebbles in the sea.

Man upraised above his fellows
　Oft forgets his fellows then ;
Masters — rulers — lords, remember
　That your meanest kind are men !
Men of labor, men of feeling,
　Men of thought and men of fame,
Claiming equal rights to sunshine
　In a man's ennobling name.

There are foam-embroidered oceans,
   There are little wood-clad rills;
There are feeble inch-high saplings,
   There are cedars on the hills.
God, who counts by souls, not stations,
   Loves and prospers you and me;
For to him all vague distinctions
   Are as pebbles in the sea.

Toiling hands alone are builders
   Of a nation's wealth and fame;
Titled laziness is pensioned,
   Fed and fattened on the same;
By the sweat of others' foreheads,
   Living only to rejoice,
While the poor man's outraged freedom
   Vainly lifts its feeble voice.

Truth and justice are eternal,
   Born with loveliness and light;
Secret wrongs shall never prosper
   While there is a sunny right!
God, whose world-wide voice is singing
   Boundless love to you and me,
Sinks oppression, with its titles,
   But as pebbles in the sea.

FALSE AND TRUE.

WE grasp a hand, we think it true and strong,
   We look in eyes where love-light seems to play;
The hand we hold clings but to guide us wrong,
   The light within the eyes gleams to betray.

We feel a heart beat near our own, close pressed,
   We think it echoes back love's secret lore,
But find 't is but a *tool* — within the breast —
   Of curious mechanism, nothing more.

We listen to soft tones from lips which seem
   Too regal even a foe's name to belie;
We drink their freshness, and we fondly dream
   That nought can mar our soul's sweet harmony.

E'en as we dream — forth from the heart's fair gate
   Issue barbed words which pierce us through and through,
Whilst we, bewildered, find, even though so late,
   This seal of royalty is earthly too.

We place our heart's best treasure, trustingly,
  In the safe keeping of a thing of clay;
The trust is broken. Though we do not die,
  Our faith in human love shows slow decay.

We tread the earth to find, where'er we roam,
  Lips fair but subtle, heart-beats quick but cold;
Lightnings in eyes which only seem love's home,
  And treachery even in the hand we hold.

But is this all of friendship, love? Ah, no!
  These well-wrought counterfeits from Satan's hand
To me conclusive evidence do show
  That the pure coin is still in good demand.

And if we seal our hearts, rolling the stone
  Of cold distrust firmly against the door,
The whitest angel near love's pearly throne
  Can roll that stone away, ah! nevermore.

So, after all, 't is better that we err
  In loving overmuch, though oft deceived,
Than make our heart a sealèd sepulchre
  From which the angel turns away aggrieved.

PATIENT.

I was not patient in that olden time
  When my unchastened heart began to long
For bliss that lay beyond its reach; my prime
  Was wild, impulsive, passionate, and strong.
I could not wait for happiness and love,
  Heaven-sent, to come and nestle in my breast;
I could not realize that time might prove
  That patient waiting would avail me best.
"Let me be happy now," my heart cried out,
  "In mine own way, and with my chosen lot;
The future is too dark and full of doubt
  For me to tarry, and I trust it not.
Take all my blessings, all I am and have,
But give that glimpse of heaven before the grave."

"Ah me!" God heard my wayward, selfish cry,
  And, taking pity on my blinded heart,
He bade the angel of strong grief draw nigh,
  Who pierced my bosom in its tenderest part.
I drank wrath's wine-cup to the bitter lees,
  With strong amazement and a broken will;
Then, humbled, straightway fell upon my knees,
  And God doth know my heart is kneeling still;

I have grown patient, seeking not to choose
    Mine own blind lot, but take that God shall send,
In which, if what I long for I should lose,
    I know the loss will work some blessed end, —
Some better fate for mine and me than I
Could ever compass underneath the sky.

———◆———

CONTENTMENT.

HE that holds fast the golden mean,
And lives contentedly between
    The little and the great,
Feels not the wants that pinch the poor,
Nor plagues that haunt the rich man's door,
    Embittering all his state.

———◆———

BEYOND THE HAZE.

A WINTER RAMBLE REVERIE.

THE road was straight, the afternoon was gray,
    The frost hung listening in the silent air;
    On either hand the rimy fields were bare;
Beneath my feet rolled out the long white way,
Drear as my heart, and brightened by no ray
    From the wide winter sun, whose disk reclined
    In distant, copper sullenness, behind
The broken network of the western hedge —
A crimson blot upon the fading day.

Three travellers went before me, — one alone,
    Then two together, who their fingers nursed
    Deep in their pockets, and I watched the first
Lapse in the curtain the slow haze had thrown
Across the vista which had been my own;
    Next vanished the chill comrades, blotted out
    Like him they followed; but I did not doubt
That there beyond the haze the travellers
Walked in the fashion that my sight had known.

Only "beyond the haze;" oh, sweet belief!
    That this is also death; that those we 've kissed
    Between our sobs are just "beyond the mist;"
An easy thought to juggle with to grief!
The gulf seems measureless, and Death a thief.
    Can we, who were so high and are so low,
    So clothed in love, who now in tatters go,
Echo serenely, "Just beyond the haze,"
And of a sudden find a trite relief?

Cornhill Magazine.

CONTENT.

My heart and I but lately were at strife.
   She fell a-longing for a certain thing
The which I could not give her, and my life
   Grew sick and weary with her clamoring.
God knows I would have given my youth's wide scope
   To buy my heart but one brief, blessed day
Of the blind bliss she coveted ; but hope,
   When I appealed to it, turned, dumb, away.
Until hope failed, I did not chide my heart,
   But was full tender to her misery, —
I knew how hard and bitter was her part ;
   But when I saw that good was not for me,
I felt that time and tears were vainly spent ;
"Heart," said I, "hope is silent ; be content."

Poor heart ! She listened, earnest, humble-wise,
   While my good angel gave her counsel strong,
Then from the dust and ashes did arise,
   And through her trembling lips broke forth a song ;
A soothing song, that grew into a strain
   Of praise for bliss denied as well as given :
She sang it then to charm a lingering pain,
   She sings it now for gladness, morn and even.
She sings it, seeing on life's garden wall
   Love's deep red roses in the sunshine stir,
And singing, passes, envying not at all,
   Content to feel that love is not for her.
The roses are another's, bloom and scent,
My heart and I have "heart's-ease" — and content.

CONTENTMENT.

The banks are all a bustin', Nance, an' things is goin' to smash ;
The people sold fur credit whar they 'd oughter sell fur cash,
An' winter 's bringin' poverty to everybody's door ;
The rich can stand it pretty well — hit 's orful on the poor.

The workin' man 's the sufferer, Nance, he 's got no work to do
An' folks are goin' to suffer what sufferin' never knew ;
An' them that 's always "showin' off " to poor folks what they 've
   got,
You 'll find, perhaps, that they 'll turn out the poorest of the lot.

I 've just been thinkin', Nancy Jane, about the awful muss,
How folks had better live an' raise thar children jist like us ;
For as I told old Deacon Smith, he seed it all was true ;
He never in his life had seed two folks like me an' you.

Our home's an old log cabin, Nance, half hidden in the woods;
Our family's rich in life an' health, but poor in this "world's
    goods."
We hain't no fine lace curtains, or no carpet on the floor,
But the sun is always shinin' through the window an' the door.

Our farm is small — we've got a spring, an' horses, hogs, an' cows;
We've gals to milk, an' cook, an' sew, an' boys to tend the
    ploughs,
We've got no gold in banks that bust, nor owe no man a cent;
I tell you, Nance, the Lord is good, an' we should feel content.

We're plain an' honest country folks, an' know no "city airs;"
We read the Bible every night before we kneel in prayers;
We go to church on Sunday, Nance, an' walk jist like the rest,
An' live like Christian people ought — we try to do what's best.

Our boys are not like city boys, who from their duty shirk,
Whose parents raise 'em up to think 't is a disgrace to work;
Our gals ain't like them city gals you will so otten meet,
Who ought to help their mothers more, an' run less on the street.

You don't see Thomas Henry pushin' billiards every night,
Or loafin' 'bout the tavern gittin' treated till he's tight;
You don't find him a runnin' round to catch some damsel's eye,
Or courtin' of some gal that's rich, whose daddy's about to die.

Ah, Nance, the time has come at last when pride must have a fall,
The folks will find the workin'man's the life an' prop of all;
The farmer's independent, Nance, his trade will never spoil
So long as he is able with his sons to till the soil.

The proud aristocratic folks, who sot in fortune's door,
Who thought they'd never come to want, are busted up an' poor;
Their servants gone, their horses sold, their houses an' their
    lands,
An' everything, except their lives, is in the sheriff's hands.

Old woman, put your knittin' up; it's gittin' purty late,
I'll read about two chapters in the Bible if you'll wait;
We'll pray to God before we sleep, as every Christian ought;
An' thank him not for what we want, but what we've had an' got.

                       WILL S. HAYES.

THE WORLD AND I.

WHETHER my heart be glad or no,
   The summers come, the summers go,
The lanes grow dark with dying leaves,
Icicles hang beneath the eaves,
The asters wither to the snow;
      Thus doth the summer end and go,
      Whether my life be glad or no.

Whether my life be sad or no,
  The winters come, the winters go,
The sunshine plays with baby leaves,
Swallows build about the eaves,
The lovely wild flowers bend and blow ;
    Thus doth the winter end and go,
    Whether my life be sad or no.

Yet Mother Nature gives to me
A fond and patient sympathy ;
In my own heart I find the charm
To make her tender, near, and warm ;
Through summer sunshine, winter snow,
She clasps me, sad or glad or no.

NELLY M. HUTCHINSON.

SATISFIED.

WHERE moss-made beds are brightest by the river,
  And curtained round with wondrous-woven vines,
I lie and watch the water-lilies quiver
  In the soft shadow of the haunted pines, —
Lie, as in dreams, amidst the languid laughter
  Of waves at play upon the harbor bar,
And hear the sound of wings that follow after
  The wind who knoweth where the bird-nests are.

So sweet the hour, I cannot well remember
  If care has been, or wearying toil or pain,
Or life low leaning to a drear December,
  Or vision tortured by a teary rain ;
The eyes of sorrow have been kissed to sleeping
  By lips where many a tender mystery hides,
Like music in the merry waters, keeping
  My feet from climbing up the mountain sides.

Upon my book unread a bee sits sipping
  Wild honey from the fragrant wild-rose mark,
And, listening, I can hear the dipping, dipping
  Of light oars piloting a home-bound bark.
A new life flows through all the aisles of being ;
  I seem a pulsing portion of the haze
That floats and floats where saints sing softlier, seeing
  The dawn of heaven's own Indian summer days.

And once again, oh, once again is lying
  Upon my heart a dainty, dimpled cheek,
For whose young bloom my lips were ever crying
  In the old time of which I cannot speak.

One little word — the first that babies mangle —
  I hear, and flush with mother-love and pride,
Feeling my fingers in a golden tangle
  Of locks long longed for — and am satisfied.

Home Journal.   HESTER A. BENEDICT.

———◆———

RETROSPECTION.

I NOTE this morning how the sunshine falleth,
  Just as it fell one morning long ago;
A white dove walks the window-ledge, soft cooing;
  The waters murmur in their ebb and flow.

The aspen whispers to the autumn breezes,
  I see the golden-rod on sloping hills;
I catch the odors of the brown leaves dying,
  And hear the babble of the shrunken rills.

I listen to some notes of children's laughter,
  Smiling to think how late I was a child —
A happy elf with cheeks of sun-kissed crimson,
  And curls of tawny gold, wind-tossed and wild.

The very winds stir memories with their wailing,
  The very clouds that dot the azure sky,
The heliotrope within my window blooming,
  Even the swallows swiftly skimming by.

On a dead oak that lifts its leafless branches
  A raven sits, and croaks with fretful tone,
Like some old prophet who with mystic lore foresees
  The evil that he sees with sob and moan.

A sense of pain, half hidden, half definèd,
  Stirs in my heart an unborn babe of sorrow
Whose birth, unwelcome and unasked, with wail
  Shall usher in a darker, sadder morrow.

And I shall meet it as I met the day departed,
  With pride unbending and an iron will,
That holds me steadfast in the path I chose, but hated,
  Yet hating, love, and loving, loathe it still.

I see and hear; I know I am not dreaming;
  And still somehow I cannot make it seem
But that I sleep, and hear and see things dimly,
  As one does often in a troubled dream.

Ah, well! what matter, since so soon for all
    Our struggles and our dreams will have an ending,
And our tired hearts and brains shall rest for aye
    In that blest land to which our feet are tending?

GARNET B. FREEMAN.

GOING SOFTLY.

SHE makes no moan above her faded flowers,
    She will not vainly strive against her lot,
Patient she wears away the slow, sad hours,
    As if the ray they had were quite forgot;
While stronger fingers snatch away the sword,
    And lighter footsteps pass her on the ways,
Yielding submissive to the stern award
    That said she must go softly all her days.

She knows the pulse is beating quickly yet,
    She knows the dream is sweet and subtle still,
That, struggling from the cloud of past regret,
    Ready for conflict, live Hope, Joy, and Will;
So soon, so soon to veil the eager eyes,
    To dull the throbbing ear to blame or praise,
So soon to crush re-awakening sympathies,
    And teach them she goes softly all her days.

She will not speak or move beneath the doom,
    She knows she had her day and flung her cast,
The loser scarce the laurel may assume,
    Nor evening think the noonday glow can last.
Only, oh youth and love, as in your pride,
    Of joyous triumph your gay notes you raise,
Throw one kind glance and word, where, at your side,
    She creeps, who must go softly all her days.

"EN VOYAGE."

WHICHEVER way the wind doth blow,
Some heart is glad to have it so;
Then, blow it east, or blow it west,
The wind that blows, that wind is best.

My little craft sails not alone;
A thousand fleets from every zone
Are out upon a thousand seas;
What blows for one a favoring breeze
Might dash another with the shock
Of doom upon some hidden rock.

And so I do not dare to pray
For winds to waft me on my way,
But leave it to a higher Will
To stay or speed me, trusting still
That all is well, and sure that He
Who launched my bark will sail with me
Through storm and calm, and will not fail,
Whatever breezes may prevail,
To land me, every peril past,
Within the sheltered haven at last.

Then, whatsoever wind doth blow,
My heart is glad to have it so ;
And, blow it east, or blow it west,
The wind that blows, that wind is best.

CAROLINE A. MASON.

WHAT HOUSE TO LIKE.

SOME love the glow of outward show,
  Some love mere wealth and try to win it ;
The house to me may lowly be,
  If I but like the people in it.
What's all the gold that glitters cold,
  When linked to hard or haughty feeling ?
Whate'er we're told, the noble gold
  Is truth of heart and manly dealing.
Then let them seek, whose minds are weak,
  Mere fashion's smile and try to win it ;
The house to me may lowly be,
  If I but like the people in it.

A lowly roof may give us proof
  That lowly flowers are often fairest ;
And trees whose bark is hard and dark
  May yield us fruit and bloom the rarest.
There 's worth as sure 'neath garments poor
  As e'er adorned a loftier station ;
And minds as just as those, we trust,
  Whose claim is but of wealth's creation.
Then let them seek, whose minds are weak,
  Mere fashion's smile, and try to win it :
The house to me may lowly be,
  If I but like the people in it.

TIRED OUT.

HE does well who does his best ;
Is he weary ? let him rest.
Brothers ! I have done my best,
I am weary — let me rest.

After toiling oft in vain,
Baffled, yet to struggle fain,
After toiling long, to gain
Little good with mickle pain,
Let me rest.   But lay me low
Where the hedge-side roses blow,
Where the little daisies grow,
Where the winds a-maying go,
Where the footpath rustics plod,
Where the breeze-bowed poplars nod,
Where the old woods worship God,
Where his pencil paints the sod,
Where the wedded throstle sings,
Where the young bird tries his wings,
Where the wailing plover swings,
Near the runlet's rushing springs !
Where, at times, the tempests roar,
Shaking distant sea and shore,
Still will rave old Barnesdale o'er,
To be heard by me no more !
There, beneath the breezy west,
Tired and thankful, let me rest,
Like a child that sleepeth best
On its mother's gentle breast.

PART X.

Life, Religion, and Death's Mystery.

Resembles life what once was held of light,
Too ample in itself for human sight?
An absolute self? an element ungrounded?
All that we see, all colors of all shade
  By encroach of darkness made?
Is very life, my consciousness, unbounded?
And all the thoughts, pains, joys of mortal breath
A war-embrace of wrestling life and death?

COLERIDGE.

PART X.

Life, Religion, and Death's Mystery.

———◦◦◦———

MY AIM.

I LIVE for those who love me, whose hearts are kind and true,
For the heaven that smiles above me, and awaits my spirit
    too ;
For all human ties that bind me, for the task by God assigned
    me ;
For the bright hopes yet to find me, and the good that I can
    do.

I live to learn their story who suffered for my sake ;
To emulate their glory and follow in their wake :
Bards, patriots, martyrs, sages, the heroic of all ages,
Whose deeds crowd History's pages, and Time's great volume
    make.

I live to hold communion with all that is divine,
To feel there is a union 'twixt Nature's heart and mine ;
To profit by affliction, reap truth from fields of fiction,
Grow wiser from conviction, and fulfil God's grand design.

I live to hail the season, by gifted ones foretold,
When man shall live by reason, and not alone by gold ;
When man to man united, and every wrong thing righted,
The whole world shall be lighted, as Eden was of old.

I live for those who love me, for those who know me true ;
For the heaven that smiles above me, and awaits my spirit
    too ;
For the cause that lacks assistance, for the wrong that needs
    resistance,
For the future in the distance, and the good that I can do.

                                        G. LINNÆUS BANKS.

———◆———

THE BRIDGE OF LIFE.

ACROSS the rapid stream of seventy years
    The slender bridge of human life is thrown ;
The past and future form its mouldering piers,
    The present moment is its frail keystone.

From " dust thou art " the arch begins to rise,
  " To dust " the fashion of its form descends,
" Shalt thou return," the higher curve implies,
  In which the first to the last lowness bends.

Seen by youth's magic light upon that arch,
  How lovely does each far-off scene appear !
But ah ! how changed when on the onward march
  Our weary footsteps bring the vision near !

'T was fabled that beneath the rainbow's foot
  A treasure lay, the dreamer to bewitch ;
And many wasted in the vain pursuit
  The golden years that would have made them rich.

So where life's arch of many colors leads,
  The heart expects rich wealth of joy to find ;
But in the distance the bright hope recedes,
  And leaves a cold, gray waste of care behind.

A sunlit stream upon its bosom takes
  The inverted shadow of a bridge on high,
And thus the arch in air and water makes
  One perfect circle to the gazer's eye.

So 't is with life ; the things that do appear
  Are fleeting shadows on time's passing tide,
Cast by the sunshine of a larger sphere
  From viewless things that changelessly abide.

The real is but the half of life ; it needs
  The ideal to make a perfect whole ;
The sphere of sense is incomplete, and pleads
  For closer union with the sphere of soul.

All things of use are bridges that conduct
  To things of faith, which give them truest worth ;
And Christ's own parables do us instruct
  That heaven is but a counterpart of earth.

The pier that rests upon this shore 's the same
  As that which stands upon the farther bank ;
And fitness for our duties here will frame
  A fitness for the joys of higher rank.

Oh ! dark were life without heaven's sun to show
  The likeness of the other world in this ;
And bare and poor would be our lot below
  Without the shadow of a world of bliss.

Then let us, passing o'er life's fragile arch,
  Regard it as a means, and not an end ;
As but the path of faith on which we march
  To where all glories of our being tend.

LIFE.

A BUSY dream, forgotten ere it fades;
  A vapor, melting into air away;
Vain hopes, vain fears, a mesh of lights and shades,
  A checkered labyrinth of night and day —
This is our life; a rapid, surging flood,
  Where each wave haunts its fellow; on they press;
To-day is yesterday; and Hope's young bud
  Has fruited a to-morrow's nothingness;
Still on they press, and we are borne along,
  Forgetting and forgotten; trampling down
The living and the dead in that fierce throng,
  With little heed of Heaven's smile or frown,
And little care for others, right or wrong,
  So we in iron selfishness stand strong.

---◆---

LIFE.

(FROM THE SPANISH.)

OH! let the soul its slumber break,
Arouse its senses and awake,
    To see how soon
Life, with its glory, glides away,
And the stern footsteps of decay
    Come rolling on.

And while we eye the rolling tide
Down which our flowing minutes glide
    Away so fast,
Let us the present hour employ,
And dream each future dream of joy
    Already past.

Let no vain hope deceive the mind;
No happier let us hope to find
    To-morrow than to-day.
Our golden dreams of yore were bright:
Like them, the present shall delight;
    Like them, decay.

Our lives like hasting streams must be,
That into one engulfing sea
    Are doomed to fall, —
The sea of death, whose waves roll on
O'er king and kingdom, crown and throne,
    And swallow all.

Alike the river's lordly tide,
Alike the humble rivulet's glide,
 To that sad wave;
Death levels poverty and pride,
And rich and poor sleep side by side
 Within the grave.

Our birth is but the starting-place,
Life is the running of the race,
 And death the goal;
There all those glittering toys are brought:
The path alone of all unsought
 Is found of all.

Say, then, how poor and little worth
Are all those glittering toys of earth
 That lure us here!
Dreams of a sleep that death must break:
Alas! before it bids us wake,
 Ye disappear!

Edinburgh Review.

NOTE. — Compare with Longfellow's translation of "Coplas de Manrique" by Don Jorge Manrique.

THROUGH LIFE.

WE slight the gifts that every season bears,
 And let them fall unheeded from our grasp,
 In our great eagerness to reach and clasp
The promised treasure of the coming years;

Or else we mourn some great good passed away,
 And, in the shadow of our grief shut in,
 Refuse the lesser good we yet might win,
The offered peace and gladness of to-day.

So through the chambers of our life we pass,
 And leave them one by one and never stay,
Not knowing how much pleasantness there was
In each, until the closing of the door
 Has sounded through the house and died away,
And in our hearts we sigh, "Forevermore!"

Chambers's Journal.

A CHARACTER AND A QUESTION.

A DUBIOUS, strange, uncomprehended life,
 A roll of riddles with no answer found;
 A sea-like soul which plummet cannot sound,
Torn with belligerent winds at mutual strife.

The god in him hath taken unto wife
  A daughter of the pit, and, strongly bound
  In coils of snake-like hair about him wound,
Dies, straining hard to raise the severing knife.

For such a sunken soul, what room in heaven?
For such a soaring soul, what place in hell?
Can those desires be damned, those doings shriven,
Or in some lone mid-region must he dwell
Forever?   Lo! God sitteth with the seven
Stars in his hand, and shall not he judge well?

The Spectator.

WITH THE TIDE.

WAVE by wave o'er the sandy bar,
  Up to the coast lights, glimmering wan,
Out of the darkness deep and far,
  Slowly the tide came creeping on.
Through the clamor of billowy strife
  Another voice went wailing thin;
The first faint cry of a new-born life
  Broke on the night — and the tide was in.

Wave by wave o'er the sandy bar,
  Back again from the sleeping town,
Back to the darkness deep and far,
  Slowly the tide went dropping down.
Silence lay on the chamber of death;
  Silence lay on the land about;
The last low flutter of weary breath
  Fell on the night — and the tide was out.

TWO PICTURES.

SOMEBODY'S heart is gay,
  And somebody's heart is sad;
For lights shine out across the way,
  And a door with crape is clad.
Sadness and gladness alike
  Are dwelling side by side.
Perhaps the death of an early one,
  And the crowning of a bride.

Bright eyes are filled with mirth,
  Pale faces bend in prayer,
And hearts beside the household hearth
  Are crushed by stout despair;

Ah, sorrow and hope and joy
　Are parted by thinnest walls ;
But on the hearts of the thoughtless ones
　No shadow of sorrow falls !

No thoughts of the funeral train
　Come to the festive throng ;
No hopes that the past will come again
　To the anguished hearts belong ;
The future 's a sunny sea
　To the lovers of joy and mirth ;
But the past alone to those who weep
　For the sundered ties of earth.

Somebody's heart is gay,
　And somebody's heart is sad ;
For the lights are bright across the way,
　And a door with crape is clad.
Sadness and gladness alike
　Confront us on every side ;
A wealth of smiles and a flood of tears,
　With hope and sorrow allied !

———◆———

WHY IS IT SO?

SOME find work where some find rest,
　And so the weary world goes on ;
I sometimes wonder which is best :
　The answer comes when life is gone.

Some eyes sleep where some eyes wake,
　And so the dreary night hours go ;
Some hearts beat where some hearts break :
　I often wonder why 't is so.

Some wills faint where some wills fight —
　Some love the tent and some the field ;
I often wonder who are right,
　The ones who strive or the ones who yield.

Some hands fold where other hands
　Are lifted bravely in the strife ;
And so through ages and through lands
　Move on the two extremes of life.

Some feet halt where some feet tread
　In tireless march a thorny way ;
Some struggle on where some have fled ;
　Some seek where others shun the fray.

Some swords rust where others clash,
  Some fall back where others move on,
Some flags furl where others flash,
  Until the battle has been won.

Some sleep on while others keep
  The vigils of the true and brave;
They will not rest till roses creep
  Around their names above a grave.

WHAT HAVE I DONE?

I LAY my finger on Time's wrist to score
  The forward-surging moments as they roll;
Each pulse seems quicker than the one before;
  And lo! my days pile up against my soul
As clouds pile up against the golden sun;
Alas! What have I done? What have I done?

I never steep the rosy hours in sleep,
  Or hide my soul, as in a gloomy crypt;
No idle hands into my bosom creep;
  And yet, as water-drops from house-eaves drip,
So, viewless, melt my days, and from me run;
Alas! What have I done? What have I done?

I have not missed the fragrance of the flowers,
  Or scorned the music of the flowing rills,
Whose numerous liquid tongues sing to the hours;
  Yet rise my days behind me, like the hills,
Unstarred by light of mighty triumphs won;
Alas! What have I done? What have I done?

Be still, my soul; restrain thy lips from woe!
  Cease thy lament! for life is but the flower;
The fruit comes after death; how canst thou know
  The roundness of its form, its depth of power?
Death is life's morning. When thy work 's begun,
Then ask thyself— What yet is to be done?

LILLIAN BLANCHE FEARING.

LIFE.

(A LITERARY CURIOSITY.)

WHY all this toil for triumphs of an hour? [*Young.*
Life 's a short summer — man is but a flower. [*Dr. Johnson.*
By turns we catch the fatal breath and die; [*Pope.*
The cradle and the tomb, alas! how nigh. [*Prior.*

To be better far than not to be,   [*Sewell.*
Though all man's life may seem a tragedy ;   [*Spencer.*
But light cares speak when mighty griefs are dumb — [*Daniel.*
The bottom is but shallow whence they come.
                              [*Sir Walter Raleigh.*
Thy fate is the common fate of all ;   [*Longfellow.*
Unmingled joys here no man befall ;   [*Southwell.*
Nature to each allots his proper sphere,   [*Congreve.*
Fortune makes folly her peculiar care.   [*Churchill.*
Custom does often reason overrule,   [*Rochester.*
And throw a cruel sunshine on a fool.   [*Armstrong.*
Live well ; how long or short permit to Heaven.   [*Milton.*
They who forgive most shall be most forgiven.   [*Bailey.*
Sin may be clasped so close we cannot see its face — [*French.*
Vile intercourse where virtue has no place ;   [*Somerville.*
Then keep each passion down, however dear,   [*Thompson.*
Thou pendulum betwixt a smile and tear.   [*Byron.*
Her sensual snares let faithless pleasure lay,   [*Smollett.*
With craft and skill to ruin and betray :   [*Crabbe.*
Soar not too high to fall, but stoop to rise ;   [*Massinger.*
We masters grow of all that we despise.   [*Crowley.*
Oh, then, renounce that impious self-esteem,   [*Beattie.*
Riches have wings and grandeur is a dream.   [*Cowper.*
Think not ambition wise because 't is brave,
                              [*Sir William Davenant.*
The paths of glory lead but to the grave ;   [*Gray.*
What is ambition ?   'T is a glorious cheat,   [*Willis.*
Only destructive to the brave and great.   [*Addison.*
What 's all the gaudy glitter of a crown ?   [*Dryden.*
The way to bliss lies not on beds of down.   [*Francis Quarles.*
How long we live, not years, but actions tell ;   [*Watkins.*
That man lives twice who lives the first life well.   [*Herrick.*
Make, then, while yet ye may, your God your friend,
                              [*William Mason.*
Whom Christians worship, yet not comprehend.   [*Hill.*
The trust that 's given guard, and to yourself be just, [*Dana.*
For live we how we may, yet die we must.   [*Shakspeare.*

                                   MRS. H. A. DEMING.

NOTE. — Accompanying this is a statement that a year was occupied in
searching for and fitting the lines in this remarkable mosaic from English
and American poets.

SHADOWS.

SOMETIMES I smile, sometimes I sigh,
    But mostly sorrow fills my heart ;
The present and the future lie,
    Like two grim shadows, just apart.
I change as often as the clouds,
    That on a gusty morning run
In cold and sad and solemn crowds
    To bar and blind the faithful sun.

Why come these thoughts in baleful forms
  To darken life's too fleeting hours,
E'en as the summer's sullen storms
  That sob their gloom away in showers?
I cannot smile as others smile,
  Nor yet be merry half so long;
For sorrow fills me even while
  I yearn to sing a joyous song.

The knowledge that my youth is gone
  Broods ever darkly on the mind;
I look, as some poor hapless one,
  For what he needs but cannot find.
I long in vain for peace or rest,
  And mourn each lost and faded scene,
Like some poor bird that finds its nest
  All vacant where its young had been.

Pain waits on pleasure evermore,
  To blanch its blush, to dim its light;
To mock it when its dreams are o'er,
  When all its charms have taken flight.
And thus it is we cannot sing,
  Or long be joyous, when we're old;
When summer hours have taken wing,
  The flowers must perish in the cold!

AT THE LOOM.

She stood at the clumsy loom,
  And wove with a careless song;
For her task would soon be done,
  And the day was bright and long;
So she worked at her pattern, roses red
And trailing vines; but she thought instead
Where the sweetbrier grew in the distant wood,
And of pleasant shade where the old oak stood.

She stood at the stately loom,
  And wove with a girlish grace;
And her eyes grew tender and sweet
  As she wrought in the web apace.
Strong men mounted with lance and spear,
Then a chase with hounds and a frightened deer;
But she thought the while of her lover knight,
And whispered softly, " He comes to-night."

She stood at the tireless loom,
  And wove with a steady hand;
And a watchful eye on the twain
  Without, at play in the sand.

Stripes of warm, dark colors she wrought,
And every thread with a hope was fraught;
Some day, she thought, my lad will be great,
And my bonnie lass a nobleman's mate.

She stood at the dusty loom,
　　Bent, and wrinkled, and old,
But the shuttle she feebly plied
　　Dropped from her nerveless hold.
"Ah, well! whom have I to work for now?"
The old dame said, with shaded brow.
"But I've seen the time when I worked with the best;"
And she dropped her chin on her wrinkled breast.

At a silent, invisible loom,
　　Always, morning and night,
With tender care wrought one
　　Who was hidden from human sight.
Tangled and broken threads wrought he,
And his finished web was fair to see;
For he gathered the hopes that were broken in twain,
And wrought them into his web again.

Public Opinion.

———◆———

?

THIS mortal body that I wear
　　Will soon return to whence it came,
Resolved into the earth and air
　　By foul decay or purer flame.
The elements again will take
　　The atoms that they have bestowed,
And give them in their turn to make
　　Some other thinking soul's abode.

To die — is it another birth?
　　Or is it but an endless swoon?
Will we still roam the plains of earth,
　　Or climb the mountains of the moon?
Will memory still retain its hold
　　Upon the sad and sunny past,
Or in the eternal future's mould
　　Are all the precious metals cast?

Will love and truth and honor live,
　　And hate and wrong and falsehood die?
Will only grace and beauty give
　　Their glory to the by and by?

Or will the fruits and flowers and weeds
  Still rankly flourish side by side, —
The laurels of heroic deeds
  Twined with the poisonous vine of pride?

The child I danced upon my knee,
  The sunlit hair and heaven-hued eyes,
Whose laughter filled my heart with glee,
  My sweetest joy, my dearest prize, —
The years of grief have reached a score,
  Yet still her soft embrace I miss, —
Will she upon the other shore
  Welcome me with a spirit-kiss?

My boy grown near to man's estate,
  My wife whose smile had blest the years,
Victims of a relentless fate —
  I yielded to the grave with tears.
And like a seared and blasted tree,
  Alone I stand where tempests lower;
The joys of earth have fled from me,
  But yet I fear the parting hour.

Great Lord of Life, Creative Power,
  If thou canst hear thy creatures' call,
Before that dark impending hour
  Disclose to me the mighty *All.*
Unlock the volume sealed so long,
  The mystery of death and pain,
The cause and final doom of wrong,
  That all the race have sought in vain.

Yet stay; I would not read the book;
  Too awful might its secret be
For mortal eyes to rashly look
  Upon the dreadful mystery.
Let me grope on through life's dark maze,
  And blindly bow before thy will,
That o'er my few remaining days
  The light of hope may linger still.

New York Commercial Advertiser.   F. A. LE H

--◆--

A QUERY.

OH the wonder of our life,
Pain and pleasure, rest and strife,
Mystery of mysteries,
Set twixt two eternities!

Lo, the moments come and go,
E'en as sparks, and vanish so;
Flash from darkness into light,
Quick as thought are quenched in night.

With an import grand and strange
Are they fraught in ceaseless change
As they post away; each one
Stands eternally alone.

The scene more fair than words can say,
I gaze upon and go my way;
I turn, another glance to claim —
Something is changed, 't is not the same.

The purple flush on yonder fell,
The tinkle of that cattle-bell,
Came, and have never come before,
Go, and are gone forevermore.

Our life is held as with a vice,
We cannot do the same thing twice;
Once we may, but not again;
Only memories remain.

What if memories vanish too,
And the past be lost to view;
Is it all for nought that I
Heard and saw and hurried by?

Where are childhood's merry hours,
Bright with sunshine, crossed with showers?
Are they dead, and can they never
Come again to life forever?

No — 't is false, I surely trow;
Though awhile they vanish now;
Every passion, deed, and thought
Was not born to come to nought!

Will the past then come again,
Rest and pleasure, strife and pain,
All the heaven and all the hell?
Ah, we know not: God can tell.

Good Words.

———◆———

LIFE AND DEATH.

WHAT is the life of man? A passing shade
  Upon the changeful mirror of old Time;
A sear leaf, long ere autumn comes decayed;
  A plant or tree that scantly reaches prime;

A dew-drop of the morning gone ere noon;
  A meteor expiring in its fall;
A blade of grass that springs to wither soon;
  A dying taper on a darksome pall;
The foam upon the torrent's whirling wave;
  A bird that flutters on a drooping wing;
A shadowy spectre o'er an open grave;
  A morning-glory's moments in the spring;
A breaking bubble on a rushing stream;
A sunset after storm, an erring angel's dream.

What is this death we fear? The peaceful close
  Of stormy life — of reckless passion's sway;
The veil that mantles all our cares and woes;
  The heavenly ending of an earthly day;
The crown of time well spent; the portal fair
  Which opes the way to never-ending joy;
It sets the captive spirit free as air,
  From all the fetters which on earth annoy.
What is this death? The sleep the pilgrim takes
  After much weary travail he has known,
And whence with renovated power he wakes,
  His soul more mighty for its slumber grown;
The glorious conquest over human ill;
A spirit's joy which death can never kill.

LIVING.

WE can only live once; and death's terrors
  With life's bowers and roses entwine,
And our lives would be darkened by errors
  Did we even, like cats, possess nine!
They would be, perhaps, all of them wasted,
  And recklessly squandered away,
And not half of the joys would be tasted
  That one life can embrace in a day.

Let the lives that we live be worth living;
  Let the days that we spend be well spent;
Let us save for the pleasure of giving,
  And not borrow at fifty per cent;
Let us never cease loving and learning,
  And use life for its noblest of ends;
Then when dust to its dust is returning,
  We shall live in the hearts of our friends.

London Fun.

MIDGES IN THE SUNSHINE.

IF I could see with a midge's eye,
   Or think with a midge's brain,
I wonder what I 'd say of the world,
   With all its joy and pain.
Would my seven brief hours of mortal life
   Seem long as seventy years,
As I danced in the flickering sunshine
   Amid my tiny peers?
Should I feel the slightest hope or care
   For the midges yet to be;
Or think I died before my time,
   If I died at half-past three
Instead of living till set of sun
   On the breath of the summer wind;
Or deem that the world was made for me
   And all my little kind?
Perhaps if I did I 'd know as much
   Of Nature's mighty plan,
And what it meant for good or ill,
   As that larger midge, a man!

———◆———

WHO GATHER GOLD.

THEY soon grow old who grope for gold
In marts where all is bought and sold:
Who live for self and on some shelf
In darkened vaults hoard up their pelf;
Cankered and crusted o'er with mould —
For them their youth itself is old.

They ne'er grow old who gather gold
Where spring awakes and flowers unfold;
Where suns arise in joyous skies,
And fill the soul within their eyes.
For them the immortal bards have sung;
For them old age itself is young.

Scribner's Magazine.   ANDREW B. SAXTON.

———◆———

FLOTSAM AND JETSAM.

THE sea crashed over the grim gray rocks,
It thundered beneath the height,
It swept by reef and sandy dune,
It glittered beneath the harvest moon
That bathed it in yellow light.

Shell and seaweed and sparkling stone
It flung on the golden sand.
Strange relics torn from its deepest caves —
Sad trophies of wild victorious waves —
It scattered upon the strand.

Spars that had looked so strong and true
When the gallant ship was launched,
Shattered and broken, flung to the shore,
While the tide in its deep, triumphant roar,
Rang the dirge for old wounds long stanched.

Pretty trifles that love had brought
From many a foreign clime,
Snatched by the storm from the clinging clasp
Of hands that the lonely will never grasp,
While the world yet counteth time.

Back, back to its depths went the ebbing tide,
Leaving its stores to rest
Unsought and unseen in the silent bay,
To be gathered again, ere close of day,
To the ocean's mighty breast.

Kinder than man art thou, O sea ;
Frankly we give our best, —
Truth, and hope, and love, and faith,
Devotion that challenges time and death, —
Its sterling worth to test.

We fling them down at our darling's feet,
Indifference leaves them there ;
The careless footstep turns aside,
Weariness, changefulness, scorn, or pride,
Brings little of thought or care.

No tide of human feeling turns ;
Once ebbed, love never flows ;
The pitiful wreckage of time and strife,
The flotsam and jetsam of human life,
No saving reflux knows.

All the Year Round.

BY THE SEA.

Slowly, steadily, under the moon,
  Swings the tide in its old-time way ;
Never too late and never too soon,
  And the evening and morning make up the day.

Slowly, steadily, over the sands,
   And over the rocks they fall and flow;
And this wave has touched a dead man's hands,
   And that one has seen a face we know.

They have borne the good ship on her way,
   Or buried her deep from love and light;
And yet, as they sink at our feet to-day,
   Ah, who shall interpret their message aright?

For their separate voices of grief and cheer
   Are blended at last in one solemn tone;
And only this song of the waves I hear, —
   " Forever and ever His will be done!"

Slowly, steadily, to and fro,
   Swings our life in its weary way;
Now at its ebb and now at its flow,
   And the evening and morning make up the day.

Sorrow and happiness, peace and strife,
   Fear and rejoicing, its moments know;
How from the discords of such a life
   Can the clear music of heaven flow?

Yet to the ear of God it swells,
   And to the blessed round the throne,
Sweeter than chime of silver bells, —
   " Forever and ever His will be done!"

———◆———

ELIAB ELIEZER.

The Reverend Eliab Eliezer
   Sat toasting his shins by the grate;
His ponderous brain busy musing
   On man's most pitiable state.

Abroad the storm-king was raging,
   And the snow was fast whitening the ground;
But its fury disturbed not Eliab,
   In his reverie so deep and profound.

For he thought how wicked and sinful
   Was poor fallen man at the best;
And even Eliab Eliezer
   Was almost as bad as the rest!

And he piously groaned in the spirit,
   At the flesh which so leads us astray;
" There 's nothing that 's good," saith Eliab,
   " In these weak, worthless vessels of clay.

"Yea; man is a poor, sinful creature
  Even when he tries to do right;
But when he does not, and to ruin
  Willing rushes, how dreadful the sight!

"Now, there's swearing Meg, at the corner,
  Her case shows plainly, I think,
How wicked our natural hearts are —
  How much lower than brutes we can sink.

"I will preach to my people a sermon,
  And take old Meg for my text;
And show them how narrow the safe road
  That leads from this world to the next."

So he sat himself down at the table,
  And began with "Original Sin;"
And by and by Meg and her swearing
  Were deftly dovetailed therein.

With "thirdly" and "fourthly" he finished;
  Then turned to his grate nice and warm,
When he thought of Widow Mory, and wondered
  If she was prepared for the storm.

"I 'll call around soon in the morning,
  And be sure that all is quite right."
He did; and found food in abundance,
  And the grate with a fire glowing bright.

And the widow, with joy fairly weeping,
  Told how she was caught by the storm;
Not a morsel of food for her children —
  Not a coal her poor hovel to warm!

And that they would surely have perished, —
  Too cold to go out and beg, —
When pitying Heaven sent succor
  By such a strange angel — Old Meg!

Then a light slowly dawned on Eliab —
  I can't say what conclusion he reached;
But I know, stowed away 'mong his sermons,
  Lies *one* that never was preached!

JAMES ROANN REED.

JUDGE NOT.

How do we know what hearts have vilest sin?
    How do we know?
Many, like sepulchres, are foul within,
  Whose outward garb is spotless as the snow,
  And many may be pure we think not so.
How near to God the souls of such have been,
What mercy secret penitence may win —
    How do we know?

How can we tell who sinnèd more than we?
    How can we tell?
We think our brother walkèd guiltily,
  Judging him in self-righteousness.   Ah, well!
  Perhaps had we been driven through the hell
Of his untold temptations, we might be
Less upright in our daily walk than he —
    How can we tell?

Dare we condemn the ills that others do?
    Dare we condemn?
Their strength is small, their trials not a few,
  The tide of wrong is difficult to stem.
  And if to us more clearly than to them
Is given knowledge of the great and true,
More do they need our help and pity too —
    Dare we condemn?

God help us all, and lead us day by day, —
    God help us all!
We cannot walk alone the perfect way.
  Evil allures us, tempts us, and we fall.
  We are but human, and our power is small;
Not one of us may boast, and not a day
Rolls o'er our heads but each hath need to say,
    God bless us all!

THE CHIMES OF OLD ENGLAND.

THE chimes, the chimes of Motherland,
  Of England green and old,
That out from fane and ivied tower
  A thousand years have tolled:
How glorious sounds their music,
  As breaks the hallowed day,
And calleth with a seraph's voice
  A nation up to pray!

Those chimes that tell a thousand tales,
　　Sweet tales of olden time,
And ring a thousand memories
　　At vesper and at prime !
At bridal and at burial,
　　For cottager and king,
Those chimes, those glorious Christian chimes,
　　How blessedly they ring !

Those chimes, those chimes of Motherland,
　　Upon a Christmas morn,
Outbreaking as the angels,
　　For a Redeemer born !
How merrily they call afar,
　　To cot and baron's hall,
With holly decked and mistletoe,
　　To keep the festival !

Those chimes of England, how they peal
　　From tower and Gothic piles,
Where hymn and swelling anthem fill
　　The dim cathedral aisles ;
Where windows bathe the holy light
　　On priestly heads that falls,
And stain the florid tracery
　　Of banner-lighted walls !

And then, those Easter bells in spring,
　　Those glorious Easter chimes,
How loyally they hail thee round,
　　Old Queen of holy times !
From hill to hill, like sentinels,
　　Responsively they cry,
And sing the rising of the Lord
　　From vale to mountain high.

I love ye, chimes of Motherland,
　　With all this soul of mine,
And bless the Lord that I am sprung
　　Of good old English line :
And like a son I sing the lay
　　That England's glory tells ;
For she is lovely to the Lord,
　　For you, ye Christian bells.

And, heir of her ancestral fame,
　　Though far away my birth,
Thee, too, I love, my Forest home,
　　The joy of all the earth ;
For thine thy mother's voice shall be,
　　And here, where God is King,
With English chimes, from Christian spires,
　　The wilderness shall ring.

　　　　　　　　　　　　BISHOP COXE.

THE SABBATH BELLS.

THE old man sits in his easy-chair,
  And his ear has caught the ringing
Of many a church-bell far and near,
  Their own sweet music singing.
And his head sinks low on the aged breast,
  While his thoughts far back are reaching
To the Sabbath morns of his boyish days
  And a mother's sacred teaching.

A few years later, and lo! the bells
  A merrier strain were pealing,
And heavenward bore the marriage vows
  Which his manhood's joys were sealing.
But the old man's eyes are dimming now,
  As memory holds before him
The sad, sad picture of later years,
  When the tide of grief rolled o'er him;

When the bells were tolling for loved ones gone, —
  For the wife, the sons and daughters,
Who, one by one, from his home went out,
  And down into death's dark waters.
But the aged heart has still one joy
  Which his old life daily blesses,
And his eyes grow bright and his pulses warm
  'Neath a grandchild's sweet caresses.

But the old man wakes from his reverie,
  And his dear old face is smiling,
While the child with her serious eyes reads on,
  The Sabbath hours beguiling.
Ah! bells, once more ye will ring for him,
  When the heavenly hand shall sever
The cord of life, and his freed soul flies
  To dwell with his own forever.

NO SECT IN HEAVEN.

TALKING of sects till late one eve,
Of the various doctrines the saints believe,
That night I stood in a troubled dream
By the side of a darkly flowing stream;

And a Churchman down to the river came,
When I heard a strange voice call his name;
"Good father, stop; when you cross this tide,
You must leave your robes on the other side."

But the aged father did not mind,
And his long gown floated out behind,
As down to the stream his way he took,
His pale hands clasping a gilt-edged book.

" I am bound for heaven, and when I 'm there
I shall want my Book of Common Prayer ;
And though I put on a starry crown,
I should feel quite lost without my gown."

Then he fixed his eye on the shining track,
But his gown was heavy and held him back ;
And the poor old father tried in vain
A single step in the flood to gain.

I saw him again on the other side,
But his silk gown floated on the tide,
And no one asked, in that blissful spot,
Whether he belonged to " The Church " or not.

Then down to the river a Quaker strayed ;
His dress of a sombre hue was made.
" My coat and hat must all be of gray,
I cannot go any other way."

Then he buttoned his coat straight up to his chin,
And slowly, solemnly waded in ;
And his broad-brimmed hat he pulled down tight
Over his forehead so cold and white.

But a strong wind carried away his hat ;
A moment he silently sighed over that,
And then, as he gazed to the farther shore,
His coat slipped off and was seen no more.

As he entered heaven his suit of gray
Went quietly sailing away, away ;
And none of the angels questioned him
About the width of his beaver's brim.

Next came Dr. Watts with a bundle of psalms
Tied nicely up in his aged arms,
And hymns as many, a very nice thing,
That the people in heaven, all round, might sing.

But I thought that he heaved an anxious sigh
As he saw that the river ran broad and high,
And looked rather surprised as, one by one,
The psalms and the hymns in the waves went down.

After him, with his MSS.,
Came Wesley, the pattern of godliness ;
But he cried, " Dear me, what shall I do,
The water has soaked them through and through ? "

And there on the river far and wide
Away they went down the swollen tide,
While the saint astonished passed through alone,
Without his manuscript, up to the throne.

Then, gravely walking, two saints by name
Down to the stream together came ;
But as they stopped at the river's brink,
I saw one saint from the other shrink.

" Sprinkled or plunged, may I ask you, friend,
How you attained to life's great end ? "
" Thus, with a few drops on my brow "—
" But I 've been dipped, as you 'll see now,

" And I really think it will hardly do,
As I 'm ' close communion,' to cross with you.
You 're bound, I know, to the realms of bliss,
But you must go that way, and I 'll go this."

Then straightway plunging with all his might,
Away to the left, his friend to the right,
Apart they went from this world of sin,
But at last together they entered in.

And now, when the river was rolling on,
A Presbyterian Church went down ;
Of women there seemed an innumerable throng,
But the *men* I could count as they passed along.

And concerning the road they could never agree,
The old or the new way, which it could be,
Nor ever for a moment paused to think
That both would lead to the river's brink.

And a constant murmuring, long and loud,
Came ever up from the moving crowd :
" You 're in the old way, and I 'm in the new,
That is the false and this is the true."

Or, " I 'm in the old way, and you 're in the new,
That is the false and this is the true."
But the brethren only seemed to speak ;
Modest the sisters walked, and meek.

But if ever one of them chanced to say
What troubles she met with on the way,
How she longed to be on the other side,
Nor feared to cross o'er the swollen tide,

A voice arose from the brethren then :
" Let no one speak but the holy men ;
For have ye not heard the words of Paul,
Oh ! let the women keep silence all ? "

I watched them long in my curious dream,
Till they stood by the borders of the stream;
Then, just as I thought, the two ways met,
And all the brethren were talking yet,

And would talk on till the heaving tide
Carried them over side by side —
Side by side, for the way was one;
The toilsome journey of life was done.

And priest and Quaker and all who died
Came out alike on the other side —
No forms or crosses or books had they;
No gowns of silk or suits of gray;
No creeds to guide them, nor MSS.,
For all had put on Christ's righteousness.

MRS. CECELIA JOCELYN CLEVELAND.

THE MODEL CHURCH.

WELL, wife, I've found the model church! I worshipped there
    to-day!
It made me think of good old times before my hairs were gray;
The meetin'-house was fixed up more than they were years ago,
But then I felt when I went in it was n't but for show.

The sexton did n't seat me away back by the door;
He knew that I was old and deaf as well as old and poor;
He must have been a Christian, for he led me boldly through
The long aisle of the crowded church to find a pleasant pew.

I wish you'd heard the singin'; it had the old-time ring;
The preacher said with trumpet voice, "Let all the people
    sing!"
The tune was "Coronation," and the music upward rolled,
Till I thought I heard the angels playing on their harps of
    gold.

My deafness seemed to melt away; my spirit caught the fire;
I joined my feeble, trembling voice with that melodious choir,
And sang as in my youthful days, "Let angels prostrate fall;
Bring forth the royal diadem and crown him Lord of all."

I tell you, wife, it did me good to sing that hymn once more;
I felt like some wrecked mariner who gets a glimpse of shore;
I almost wanted to lay down this weather-beaten form,
And anchor in the blessed port, forever from the storm.

The preachin'? Well, I can't just tell all that the preacher
    said;
I know it was n't written, I know it was n't read;
He had n't time to read it, for the lightnin' of his eye
Went flashing 'long from pew to pew, nor passed a sinner by.

The sermon was n't flowery; 't was simple gospel truth;
It fitted poor old men like me, it fitted hopeful youth;
'T was full of consolation for weary hearts that bleed,
And bade us copy Him in thought and word and deed.

The preacher made sin hideous in Gentiles and in Jews;
He shot the golden sentences down into the finest pews;
And — though I can't see very well — I saw the falling tear
That told me hell was some ways off and heaven very near.

How swift the golden moments fled within that holy place;
How brightly beamed the light of heaven from every happy
    face!
Again I longed for that sweet time when friend shall meet with
    friend,
" When congregations ne'er break up and Sabbaths have no
    end."

I hope to meet that minister — that congregation too —
In the dear home beyond the stars that shine from heaven's
    blue;
I doubt not I 'll remember, beyond life's evening gray,
The happy hours of worship in that model church to-day.

Dear wife, the fight will soon be fought, the victory be won;
The shinin' goal is just ahead, the race is nearly run;
O'er the river we are nearin' they are throngin' to the shore,
To shout our safe arrival where the weary weep no more.

                                        JOHN H. YATES.

THE FOOL'S PRAYER.

THE royal feast was done; the king
    Sought some new sport to banish care,
And to his jester cried, " Sir Fool,
    Kneel now for us and make a prayer! "

The jester doffed his cap and bells,
    And stood the mocking court before;
They could not see the bitter smile
    Behind the painted grin he wore.

He bowed his head, and bent his knee
 Upon the monarch's silken stool;
His pleading voice arose: "O Lord,
 Be merciful to me, a fool!

"No pity, Lord, could change the heart
 From red with wrong to white as wool;
The rod must heal the sin; but, Lord,
 Be merciful to me, a fool!

"'Tis by our guilt the onward sweep
 Of truth and light, O Lord, we stay;
'T is by our follies that so long
 We hold the earth from heaven away.

"These clumsy feet, still in the mire,
 Go crushing blossoms without end;
These hard, well-meaning hands we thrust
 Among the heart-strings of a friend.

"The ill-time truth that we have kept —
 We know how sharp it pierced and stung!
The word we had not sense to say —
 Who knows how grandly it had rung?

"Our faults no tenderness should ask,
 The chastening stripes must cleanse them all;
But for our blunders — oh, in shame
 Before the eyes of Heaven we fall.

"Earth bears no balsam for mistakes;
 Men crown the knave, and scourge the tool
That did his will; but thou, O Lord,
 Be merciful to me, a fool!"

The room was hushed. In silence rose
 The king, and sought his garden cool,
And walked apart, and murmured low,
 "Be merciful to me, a fool!"

E. R. SILL.

WHAT IS HIS CREED?

He left a load of anthracite
 In front of a poor widow's door
When the deep snow, frozen and white,
 Wrapped street and square, mountain and moor.
   That was his deed!
   He did it well!
   "What was his creed?"
   I cannot tell!

Blessed " in his basket and his store,"
In sitting down and rising up ;
When more he got, he gave the more —
    Withholding not the crust and cup.
        He took the lead
        In each good task.
        " What was his creed ? "
        I did not ask.

His charity was like the snow —
    Soft, white, and silent in its fall ;
Not like the noisy winds that blow
    From shivering trees the leaves — a pall
        For flower and weed,
        Dropping below !
        " What was his creed ? "
        The poor may know.

He had great faith in loaves of bread
    For hungry people, young and old ;
And hope-inspired, kind words he said
    To those he sheltered from the cold.
        For we must feed
        As well as pray.
        " What was his creed ? "
        I cannot say.

In works he did not put his trust ;
    His faith in words he never writ ;
He loved to share his cup and crust
    With all mankind who needed it.
        In time of need
        A friend was he.
        " What was his creed ? "
        He told not me.

He put his trust in Heaven, and he
    Worked well with hand and head ;
And what he gave in charity
    Sweetened his sleep and daily bread.
        Let us take heed,
        For life is brief ;
        " What was his creed,
        What his belief ? "

———◆———

TO THINE OWN SELF BE TRUE.

BY thine own soul's law learn to live,
And if men thwart thee take no heed,
And if men hate thee have no care ;
Sing thou thy song and do thy deed.

Hope thou thy hope and pray thy prayer,
And claim no crown they will not give,
Nor bays they grudge thee for thy hair.

Keep thou thy soul-sworn steadfast oath,
And to thy heart be true thy heart;
What thy soul teaches learn to know,
And play out thine appointed part;
And thou shalt reap as thou shalt sow,
Nor helped nor hindered in thy growth,
To thy full stature thou shalt grow.

Fix on the future's goal thy face,
And let thy feet be lured to stray
Nowhither, but be swift to run,
And nowhere tarry by the way,
Until at last the end is won,
And thou mayst look back from thy place
And see thy long day's journey done.

The Spectator.   PAKENHAM BEATTY.

THE HINDOO SCEPTIC.

I THINK till I weary with thinking,
    Said the sad-eyed Hindoo king,
And I see but shadows around me,
    Illusion in everything.

How knowest thou aught of God,
    Of his favor or his wrath?
Can the little fish tell what the lion thinks,
    Or map out the eagle's path?

Can the finite the Infinite search?
    Did the blind discover the stars?
Is the thought that I think a thought,
    Or a throb of the brain in its bars?

For aught that my eye can discern,
    Your God is what you think good, —
Yourself flashed back from the glass,
    When the light pours on it in flood.

You preach to me to be just,
    And this is his realm, you say;
And the good are dying of hunger,
    And the bad gorge every day.

You say that he loveth mercy,
    And the famine is not yet gone;
That he hateth the shedder of blood,
    And he slayeth us every one.

You say that my soul shall live,
　That the spirit can never die —
If he were content when I was not,
　Why not when I have passed by?

You say I must have a meaning,
　So must dung, and its meaning is flowers;
What if our souls are but nurture
　For lives that are greater than ours?

When the fish swims out of the water,
　When the birds soar out of the blue,
Man's thought may transcend man's knowledge,
　And your God be no reflex of you.

The Spectator.

———◆———

SOME SWEET DAY.

INTO all lives some rain must fall,
　Into all eyes some tear-drops start,
Whether they fall as gentle shower,
　Or fall like fire from an aching heart.
Into all hearts some sorrow must creep,
　Into all souls some doubtings come,
Lashing the waves of life's great deep
　From dimpling waters to seething foam.

Over all paths some clouds must lower,
　Under all feet some sharp thorns spring,
Tearing the flesh to bitter wounds,
　Or entering the heart with their bitter sting.
Upon all brows rough winds must blow,
　Over all shoulders a cross be lain,
Bowing the form in its lofty height
　Down to the dust in bitter pain.

Into all hands some duty 's thrust;
　Unto all arms some burden 's given,
Crushing the heart with its weary weight,
　Or lifting the soul from earth to heaven.
Into all hearts and homes and lives
　God's dear sunlight comes streaming down,
Gilding the ruins of life's great plain —
　Weaving for all a golden crown.

The Presbyterian.　　　　　　　　　　LEWIS J. BATES.

THE LITTLE CHURCH ROUND THE CORNER.

"Bring him not here, where our sainted feet
  Are treading the path to glory;
Bring him not here, where our Saviour sweet
  Repeats for *us* his story.
Go, take him where such things are done
  (For he sat in the seat of the scorner),
To where they have room, for we have none, —
  To the little church round the corner."

So spake the holy man of God,
  Of another man, his brother,
Whose cold remains, ere they sought the sod,
Had only asked that a Christian rite
Might be read above them by one whose light
  Was, "Brethren, love one another;"
Had only asked that a prayer be read
Ere his flesh went down to join the dead,
While his spirit looked with suppliant eyes,
Searching for God throughout the skies.
But the priest frowned "No," and his brow was bare
  Of love in the sight of the mourner,
And they looked for Christ and found him — where?
  In that little church round the corner.

Ah! well, God grant when, with aching feet,
  We tread life's last few paces,
That we may hear some accents sweet,
  And kiss, to the end, fond faces.
God grant that this tired flesh may rest
  ('Mid many a musing mourner),
While the sermon is preached and the rites are read
In no church where the heart of love is dead.
And the pastor's a pious prig at best,
But in some small nook where God's confessed, —
  Some little church round the corner.
                                        A. E. Lancaster.

———◆———

ROCK OF AGES.

"Rock of Ages, cleft for me,"
  Thoughtlessly the maiden sung,
Fell the words unconsciously
  From her girlish, gleeful tongue;
Sang as little children sing;
  Sang as sing the birds in June;
Fell the words like light leaves down
  On the current of the tune, —
"Rock of Ages, cleft for me,
Let me hide myself in thee."

20

"Let me hide myself in thee," —
    Felt her soul no need to hide ;
Sweet the song as song could be,
    And she had no thought beside ;
All the words unheedingly
    Fell from lips untouched by care,
Dreaming not they each might be
    On some other lips a prayer —
"Rock of Ages, cleft for me,
Let me hide myself in thee."

"Rock of Ages, cleft for me" —
    'T was a woman sung them now,
Pleadingly and prayerfully ;
    Every word her heart did know.
Rose the song as storm-tossed bird
    Beats with weary wing the air ;
Every note with sorrow stirred —
    Every syllable a prayer, —
"Rock of Ages, cleft for me,
Let me hide myself in thee."

"Rock of Ages, cleft for me," —
    Lips grown aged sung the hymn
Trustingly and tenderly —
    Voice grown weak and eyes grown dim.
"Let me hide myself in thee" —
    Trembling though the voice and low,
Ran the sweet strain peacefully,
    Like a river in its flow.
Sung as only they can sing
    Who life's thorny paths have pressed;
Sung as only they can sing
    Who behold the promised rest, —
"Rock of Ages, cleft for me,
Let me hide myself in thee."

"Rock of Ages, cleft for me,"
    Sung above a coffin-lid ;
Underneath all restfully
    All life's joys and sorrows hid.
Nevermore, O storm-tossed soul,
    Nevermore from wind or tide,
Nevermore from billow's roll,
    Wilt thou need thyself to hide.
Could the sightless, sunken eyes,
    Closed beneath the soft gray hair,
Could the mute and stiffened lips
    Move again in pleading prayer ;
Still, aye still the words would be,
"Let me hide myself in thee."

ELLA MAUD MOORE.

NIGHT AND MORNING.

Was it a lie that they told me,
  Was it a pitiless hoax?
A sop for my soul and its longing
  Only to cozen and coax?
And a voice came down through the night and rain:
" They lied; thou hast trusted in vain."

Must I vanish off-hand into darkness,
  Blown out with a breath like a lamp?
Have I nought in the future to look to
  Save rotting in darkness and damp?
And the answer came with a mocking hiss:
" Thou hast nothing to look to save this."

What of the grave and its conquest,
  Of death and the loss of its sting?
Was it only the brag of a madman
  Who believed an impossible thing?
And the voice returned, as the voice of a ghost:
" It was but a madman's boast."

Am I the serf of my senses?
  Is my soul a slave without rights?
Are feeding and breeding and sleeping
  My first and truest delights?
And the cruel answer cut me afresh:
" Thou art but the serf of thy flesh."

Is it all for nought that I travail,
  That I long for leisure from sin,
That I thirst for the pure and the perfect,
  And feel like a god within?
The voice replied to my passionate thought:
" Thy longing and travail is nought."

Then I bowed my head in my anguish,
  Folding my face in my hands,
And I shuddered as one that sinketh
  In the clutch of quaking sands.
And I stared, as I clinched my fingers tight,
Out through the black, black night.

For life was shorn of its meaning,
  And I cried: " O God, is it so?
Utter the truth though it slay me,
  Utter it, yes or no!"
But I heard no answer to heal my pain,
Save the bluster of wind and rain.

And behold, as I sat in my sorrow,
   A quick ray shot from the east,
Another and then another,
   And I knew that the night had ceased.
And the dark clouds rolled away to the west
As the great sun rose from his rest.

And now, as the fair dawn broadened,
   Strong and joyous and bright,
My whole soul swept to meet it,
   Rapt with a deep delight;
And a new voice rang down the radiant skies:
" Rejoice; I have heard thee.   Arise."

Good Words.

THE PRINCE OF PEACE.

DEATH sent his messengers before.
   " Our master comes apace," they cried;
" Ere night he will be at the door
   To claim thy darling from thy side."
I drove them forth with curses fell;
   I drove them forth with jeer and scoff;
Not all the powers of heaven or hell
   Combined should bear my darling off.

I armed me madly for the fight;
   My gates I bolted, barred, and locked;
At sunset came a sable knight,
   Dismounted at my doors, and knocked.
I answered not; he knocked again;
   I braved him sole, I braved his band;
He knocked once more — in vain, in vain;
   My barriers crumbled 'neath his hand.

I rushed into the breach; I stood
   Dazed with the flood of ebbing light;
" A victory over senseless wood
   Adds scanty glory to thy might!
A stronger champion guards these walls —
   A human love, a living heart;
And while each earthly bulwark falls,
   It stays thee, awful as thou art!"

My sabre shivered on his mail,
   My lance dropped headless at his feet;
I saw my darling's cheek grow pale,
   I saw her turn, my foe to meet.
He passed, — my lips alone could move;
   Mad words of passion forth I hurled:
" They lied who said that God was love,
   Who lets a tyrant rule the world."

He gathered her to his embrace,
  While yet I raved in my despair;
He raised his visor from his face,
  I looked, and saw an angel there.
Such conquering love, such mercy rare,
  Such heavenly pity in his eyes,
As surely Love Divine might wear
  When He assumed our mortal guise.

He bent above her dear, dumb lips —
  Mine own, whom I had loved too well —
And, struggling from life's last eclipse,
  They smiled in peace ineffable.
Awe-struck I watched; he raised his head,
  And then in tones like summer's breath,
" Am I a thing so vile," he said,
  " I, whom ye men call shuddering Death ? "

And sword and targe aside I flung,
  Forgotten wrath, and loss, and pride ;
To his departing feet I clung,
  " And me too, take me too," I cried ;
" Without her all is blank and black,
  With her and thee so fair — me too; "
The solemn voice came ringing back,
  " Not yet, for thee is work to do."

The sunset sank from rose to gray ;
  His accents died away with it,
And from my soul, as from the day,
  The glow and glory seemed to flit ;
And 'mid my stronghold's shattered strength
  I knelt alone, yet not alone ;
Death's angel left me hope at length
  Through tasks fulfilled to reach my own.

———◆———

IF I SHOULD DIE TO–NIGHT.

              IF I should die to-night,
My friends would look upon my quiet face
Before they laid it in its resting-place,
And deem that death had left it almost fair ;
And, laying snow-white flowers against my hair,
Would smooth it down with tearful tenderness,
And fold my hands with lingering caress, —
Poor hands, so empty and so cold to-night !

If I should die to-night,
My friends would call to mind, with loving thought,
Some kindly deed the icy hands had wrought;
Some gentle word the frozen lips had said;
Errands on which the willing feet had sped;
The memory of my selfishness and pride,
My hasty words, would all be put aside,
And so I should be loved and mourned to-night.

If I should die to-night,
Even hearts estranged would turn once more to me,
Recalling other days remorsefully;
The eyes that chill me with averted glance
Would look upon me as of yore, perchance,
And soften, in the old familiar way;
For who could war with dumb, unconscious clay!
So I might rest, forgiven of all, to-night.

Oh, friends, I pray to-night,
Keep not your kisses for my dead, cold brow —
The way is lonely, let me feel them now.
Think gently of me; I am travel-worn;
My faltering feet are pierced with many a thorn.
Forgive, oh, hearts estranged, forgive, I plead!
When dreamless rest is mine I shall not need
The tenderness for which I long to-night.

ARABELLA E. SMITH.

———◆———

THE BURIAL OF MOSES.

By Nebo's lonely mountain,
    On this side Jordan's wave,
In a vale in the land of Moab
    There lies a lonely grave;
And no man dug that sepulchre,
    And no man saw it e'er;
For the " Sons of God " upturned the sod
    And laid the dead man there.

That was the grandest funeral
    That ever passed on earth;
But no man heard the trampling,
    Or saw the train go forth.
Noiselessly as the daylight
    Comes when the night is done,
And the crimson streak on ocean's cheek
    Grows into the great sun;

Noiselessly as the springtime
    Her crown of verdure weaves,
And all the trees on all the hills
    Put forth their thousand leaves:

So, without sound of music,
　Or voice of them that wept,
Silently down from the mountain's crown
　The great procession swept.

Perchance the bald old eagle,
　On gray Beth-peor's height,
Out of his rocky eyrie
　Looked on the wondrous sight;
Perchance the lion stalking
　Still shuns that hallowed spot;
For beast and bird have seen and heard
　That which man knoweth not.

But when the warrior dieth,
　His comrades in the war,
With arms reversed and muffled drums,
　Follow the funeral car;
They show the banners taken,
　They tell his victories won,
And after him lead his masterless steed,
　While peals the minute-gun.

Amid the noblest of the land
　Men lay the sage to rest,
And give the bard an honored place,
　With costly marble drest.
In the great minster transept,
　Where lights like glories fall,
And the sweet choir sings, and the organ rings
　Along the emblazoned wall.

This was the bravest warrior
　That ever buckled sword;
This the most gifted poet
　That ever breathed a word;
And never earth's philosopher
　Traced with his golden pen,
On the deathless page, truths half so sage
　As he wrote down for men.

And had he not high honor? —
　The hillside for his pall,
To lie in state while angels wait,
　The stars for tapers tall;
And the great rock-pines, like tossing plumes,
　Over his bier to wave,
And God's own hand, in that lonely land,
　To lay him in his grave, —

In that deep grave without a name,
　Whence his uncoffined clay
Shall break again (most wondrous thought!)
　Before the judgment-day,

And stand, with glory wrapped around,
  On the hills he never trod,
And speak of the strife that won our life
  With the Incarnate God.

O lonely tomb in Moab's land !
  O dark Beth-peor's hill !
Speak to these anxious hearts of ours,
  And teach them to be still.
God hath his mysteries of grace,
  Ways that we cannot tell ;
He hides them deep, like the secret sleep
  Of him he loved so well.

MRS. C. F. ALEXANDER.

REST AT EVENTIDE.

" The night cometh, when no man can work."

FOLD ye the ice-cold hands
  Calm on the pulseless breast ;
The toil of the summer day is o'er,
  Now cometh the evening rest ;
And the folded hands have nobly wrought
  Through noontide's din and strife,
And the dauntless heart hath bravely fought
  In the ceaseless war of life.

Smooth ye the time-thinned hair
  Still on the marble brow ;
No earthly cloud doth linger there
  To mar its beauty now.
But brow and lip and darkened eye
  Bear a shade of deep repose,
As twilight shadows softly lie
  On the wide-spread winter snows.

No voice of discord wakes
  The silence still and deep,
And the far-off sounds of worldly strife
  Cannot break the dreamless sleep.
Oh, welcome rest to a heart long tossed
  On the tide of hopes and fears, —
To the feet that have wandered far and wide
  O'er the weary waste of years.

From the gorgeous glare of day,
  Welcome the gentle night,
Fading the tranquil lines away,
  Solemn and calm and bright.

Then tenderly, tenderly fold the hands
  In peace on the pulseless breast,
For the evening shadows come quickly on,
  And sweet is the Christian's rest.

THOMAS D'ARCY MCGEE.

TWO ROBBERS.

WHEN Death from some fair face
  Is stealing life away,
All weep, save she, the grace
  That earth shall lose to-day.

When Time from some fair face
  Steals beauty year by year,
For her slow-fading grace
  Who sheds, save she, a tear?

And Death not often dares
  To wake the world's distress;
While Time, the cunning, mars
  Surely all loveliness.

Yet though by breath and breath
  Fades all thy fairest prime,
Men shrink from cruel Death,
  But honor crafty Time.

The Spectator.   F. W. BOURDILLON.

LAY ME LOW.

LAY me low, my work is done;
  I am weary. Lay me low,
Where the wild flowers woo the sun,
  Where the balmy breezes blow
Where the butterfly takes wing,
  Where the aspens drooping grow,
Where the young birds chirp and sing;
  I am weary, let me go.

I have striven hard and long,
  In the world's unequal fight,
Always to resist the wrong,
  Always to maintain the right;
Always with a stubborn heart,
  Taking, giving blow for blow.
Brother, I have played my part,
  And am weary, let me go.

Stern the world, and bitter cold,
  Irksome, painful to endure;
Everywhere a love of gold,
  Nowhere pity for the poor.
Everywhere mistrust, disguise,
  Pride, hypocrisy, and show;
Draw the curtain, close mine eyes,
  I am weary, let me go.

Others, 'chance, when I am gone,
  May restore the battle call;
Bravely lead a good cause on,
  Fighting in the which I fall.
God may quicken some true soul
  Here to take my place below
In the hero's muster-roll;
  I am weary, let me go.

Shield and buckler, hang them up,
  Drape the standard on the wall,
I have drained the mortal cup
  To the finish, dregs and all.
When our work is done, 't is best,
  Brother, best that we should go.
I am weary, let me rest;
  I am weary, lay me low.

LIFE OR DEATH.

DOTH Life survive the touch of Death?
  Death's hand alone the secret holds,
  Which, as to each one he unfolds,
We press to know with bated breath.

A whisper there, a whisper here,
  Confirms the hope to which we cling;
  But still we grasp at anything,
And sometimes hope and sometimes fear.

Some whisper that the dead we knew
  Hover around us while we pray,
  Anxious to speak.   We cannot say;
We only wish it may be true.

I know a Stoic, who has thought,
  As healthy blood flows through his veins,
  And joy his present life sustains,
And all this good has come unsought,

For more he cannot rightly pray ;
  Life may extend, or life may cease, —
  He bides the issue, sure of peace,
Sure of the best in God's own way.

Perfection waits the race of man ;
  If, working out this great design,
  God cuts us off, we must resign
To be the refuse of his plan.

But I, for one, feel no such peace ;
  I dare to think I have in me
  That which had better never be,
If lost before it can increase.

And oh ! the ruined piles of mind,
  Daily discovered everywhere,
  Built but to crumble in despair !
I dare not think him so unkind.

The rudest workman would not fling
  The fragments of his work away,
  If every useless bit of clay
He trod on were a sentient thing.

And does the Wisest Worker take
  Quick human hearts, instead of stone,
  And hew and carve them, one by one,
Nor heed the pangs with which they break ?

And more : if but creation's waste,
  Would he have given us sense to yearn
  For the perfection none can earn,
And hope the fuller life to taste ?

I think, if we must cease to be,
  It is a cruelty refined
  To make the instincts of our mind
Stretch out toward eternity.

Wherefore I welcome Nature's cry
  As earnest of a life again,
  Where thought shall never be in vain,
And doubt before the light shall fly.

Macmillan's Magazine.   E. B

REST IN THE GRAVE.

Rest in the grave ! but rest is for the weary,
  And her slight limbs were hardly girt for toil ;
Rest for lives worn out, deserted, dreary,
  Which have no brightness left for death to spoil.

We yearn for rest when power and passion wasted
    Have left to memory nothing but regret ;
She sleeps, while life's best pleasures, all untasted,
    Had scarce approached her rosy lips as yet.

Her childlike eyes still lacked their crowning sweetness,
    Her form was ripening to more perfect grace ;
She died with the pathetic incompleteness
    Of beauty's promise on her pallid face.

What undeveloped gifts, what powers untested,
    Perchance with her have passed away from earth ;
What germs of thought in that young brain arrested
    May never grow and quicken and have birth !

She knew not love, who might have loved so truly,
    Though love-dreams stirred her fancy, faint and fleet ;
Her soul's ethereal wings were budding newly,
    Her woman's heart had scarce begun to beat.

We drink the sweets of life, and drink the bitter,
    And death to us would almost seem a boon ;
But why to her, for whom glad life were fitter,
    Should darkness come ere day had reached its noon ?

No answer, — save the echo of our weeping
    Which from the woodland and the moor is heard,
Where, in the springtime, ruthless storm-winds, sweeping,
    Have slain the unborn flower and new-fledged bird.

Temple Bar.

———◆———

THE NARROW HOUSE.

A NARROW home, but very still it seemeth ;
    A silent home, no stir of tumult here ;
Who wins that pillow of no sorrow dreameth,
    No whirling echoes jar his sealèd ear.
The tired hands lie very calm and quiet,
    The weary feet no more hard paths will tread ;
The great world may revolve in clash and riot,
    To its loud summons leaps nor heart nor head.

The violets bloom above the tranquil sleeper,
    The morning dews fall gently on the grass ;
Amid the daisies kneels the only weeper,
    He knows not where her lingering footsteps pass.
The autumn winds sigh softly o'er his slumber,
    The winter piles the snow-drifts o'er his rest ;
He does not care the flying years to number —
    The narrow home contents its silent guest.

No baffled hopes can haunt, no doubt perplexes,
　　No parted love the deep repose can chafe,
No petty care can irk, no trouble vexes,
　　From misconstruction his hushed heart is safe.
Freed from the weariness of worldly fretting,
　　From pain and failure, bootless toil and strife,
From the dull wretchedness of vain regretting,
　　He lies, whose course has passed away from life.

A narrow home; and far beyond it lieth
　　The land whereof no mortal lips can tell.
We strain our sad eyes as the spirit flieth;
　　Our fancy loves on heaven's bright hills to dwell.
God shuts the door no angel lip uncloses,
　　They whom Christ raised no word of guidance said;
Only the cross speaks where our dust reposes:
　　"Trust Him who calls unto His rest our dead."

---◆---

AN IDEAL FUTURE.

I SELDOM ponder the "future life,"
　　I hold it a waste of thought, you see,
For the most that a man may know is this:
　　That which is coming will surely be.
To those who find comfort in baseless faith
　　I leave the old myth in its newest dress,
For I can't cry *credo* the while the creed
　　Is at most but a clumsy guess.

Yet I've often thought, if one had his choice
　　Of all the heavens that man has made,
Which would he choose for his dwelling-place
　　When his soul (myth again) from his body strayed?
I've thought them over from first to last, —
　　Scarce one, I'm sure, did my fancy miss, —
And I found that while all contained much good,
　　Still not one offered perfect bliss.

There's Nirvana, the region of "blowing out,"
　　Where the Buddhist's soul in a stupor lies;
Pain enters not on that endless rest,
　　Yet who could such an existence prize?
Better have done with it, once for all, —
　　Be utterly nothing when death is past, —
Than pester one's self to redeem one's soul,
　　And then come to this end at last.

There were light and life in the Blessed Isles;
　　Still nobody seemed to exactly know
How he might merit those Happy Fields,
　　Or in which direction his soul might go.

It was n't a question of good and bad;
   Only the pets of the gods went there,
And Pluto's realm might receive a man
   Of virtue and valor rare.

Valhalla offered a " lively time,"
   Enough of excitement was there, at least;
It was guzzle and swill, then fight and kill,
   Then come to life for another feast.
But, mercy on us! a foeman's skull
   A very suggestive wine-cup makes,
And it can't be pleasant to lose one's head
   Just after each meal one takes.

In the Indian's Happy Hunting-grounds
   A sporting spirit were fitly placed;
But eternal camping-out won't suit
   A soul possessed of more varied taste.
Though a squaw has charms for her russet beau,
   She has passing few for you and me,
And Eden devoid of a pretty face
   Would a cheerless Eden be.

" Then turn to Mahomet's Paradise,"
   I think I hear you in triumph say;
" Bathed in the light of the houris' eyes
   Your taste for beauty can have full play."
Softly, O friend! thou hast heard it said
   Enough of a thing is good as a feast;
My ideas of " enough " of such company
   Don't agree with those of the East.

And thus in each heaven I find a flaw;
   From first to last there is none complete;
Not one where a dreaming epicure
   Can paint existence as nought but sweet.
He has to take an idea from each
   To build an Eden of perfect bliss;
Tastes differ — but mine would assume a shape
   Nearly, or quite, like this:

Elysium's glory at break of day,
   The Hunting-grounds in the cool of morn,
Valhalla's banquet at glowing eve,
   And the houris' soft embrace till dawn;
Nirvana's rest when the day is done,
   For a blessing not to be lost is sleep,
And weariness is a pleasant boon,
   That maketh the slumber deep.

The Argonaut.   T. A. HARCOURT.

IN A GRAVEYARD.

(FROM THE GERMAN.)

"HERE rests in God." 'T is all we read;
    The mouldering stone reveals no more.
"In God." Of other words what need?
    These span the broad eternal shore.

O'erladen with its starry blooms,
    A jasmine bush conceals the mound,
Neglected in the place of tombs,
    With spicy, golden sweetness crowned.

And deep within its leafy breast
    Some tuneful bird has sought a home,
The tiny brood within the nest
    Fearless and free to go and come.

A holy quietude is here,
    Save where the happy birdling's song
Breaks through the stillness pure and clear,
    And echoes the dark firs among.

Sleep on, sleep on, thou pulseless heart,
    Where jasmine stars drop golden rain,
From every troubled thought apart,
    Forgotten every earthly pain.

Sleep on; thy long repose is sweet,
    Tender and cool thy grassy sod.
O traveller! stay thy hurrying feet;
    Step softly here — "he rests in God."

The Catholic World.

REST.

WHEN thou art weary of the world, and leaning
        Upon my breast,
My soul will show to thine its hidden meaning,
        And thou shalt rest.
When thou art eagerly but vainly aiming
        At some far end,
Thou knowest not thy pining and complaining
        Have pierced thy Friend.
My presence is around thee and about thee —
        Thou dost not know —
But if thou knewest, thou wouldst not doubt me,
        I love thee so.

Thou art a very child, and needest guiding, —
    Thee I will lead ;
Another guide might be too quick in chiding,
    Nor know thy need.

Lean on me, child — nor faint beneath thy sighing,
    With help so near ;
I took upon me all thy grief and dying,
    To heal thy fear.
When thou art resting in my secret dwelling,
    Shadowed by me,
Thou shalt not tire of listening — I of telling
    My love for thee.
Thine eyes are bent upon each loving token
    Sent by my hand ;
With these alone thy spirit would be broken
    In thy fair land.
Thou art a lover of all things of beauty
    In earth and space ;
Then, surely, 't were thy pleasure and thy duty
    Their source to trace.

Track the bright river of each much-prized blessing
    Back to its source ;
See all the blooming growth thy foot is pressing
    Along its course.
See, gathered in the storehouse of sweet dreaming,
    Each glowing thought
Which daylight, starlight, or the moon's sweet gleaming
    To thee have brought.
All real beauty which thy heart is greeting
    In this fair earth,
All music which thy charmed ear is meeting,
    From me had birth.
But this will be revealed when thou art leaning
    Upon my breast ;
Thy soul shall comprehend my hidden meaning —
    And thou shalt rest.

Chambers's Journal.

———◆———

THE CHURCH STEPS.

Two centuries of steps and then
    A field of graves !
With many a sculptured tale of men
    Lost in the waves.

You climb and climb, with here and there
  A seat for breath,
To find amid the loftier air
  A realm of death.

And thus it is with human life —
  Men toil to rise,
And lo ! above the strain and strife
  A graveyard lies.

Two centuries of steps, and then
  Amid the graves
A holy house that tells to men
  Of Him that saves.

O weary men, and women worn,
  That there have found
And find bright hints of heavenly morn
  On earthly ground !

And so atop the steps of time,
  If climbed aright,
Heaven's glad and everlasting clime,
  And home of light.

GEORGE T. FOSTER.

NEARING PORT.

THE noble river widens as we drift,
And the deep waters more than brackish grow ;
We note the sea-birds flying to and fro,
And feel the ocean-currents plainly lift
Our bark, and yet our course we would not shift:
These are but signs by which the boatmen know
They 're drawing near the port to which they go
To land their cargo or to bring their gift.
So may our lives reach out on either hand,
Broader and broader, as the end draws near ;
So may we seek God's truths to understand,
As the sea-birds shelter seek when storms appear ;
So may the currents from the heavenly sea
Lift us and bear us to eternity.

Jackson, Mich.   C. P. R.

GIVE ME REST.

ONLY one moment unfettered by care,
Hushed as the temple devoted to prayer,
 When heaven is painting the west,
Flooding the sky through its portals ajar,
Looping the curtains of night with a star —
  Give me rest.

Spirit of power, forever you 'll reign,
Tyrant, enslaving the heart and the brain,
 With every endeavor oppressed.
Sick of the lessons that Nature has taught,
Weary with burdens of infinite thought —
  Give me rest.

Grant me a potion lethean, a draught
Sparkling with tranquil repose never quaffed
 By mortals at pleasure's behest.
Give me a peace the world cannot give —
Respite from action; to act is to live —
  Give me rest.

Ceaseless the toil of the spirit distraught,
Boundless the realm of invisible thought,
 Where imagery lingers caressed.
Waves of oblivion over me roll,
Welcome forgetfulness bring to my soul —
  Give me rest.

———◆———

THE KING'S SHIPS.

GOD hath so many ships upon the sea;
 His are the merchantmen that carry treasure,
The men-of-war, all bannered gallantly,
 The little other boats, and barks of pleasure.
On all this sea of time there is not one
That sailed without the glorious name thereon.

The winds go up and down upon the sea,
 And some they lightly clasp, entreating kindly,
And waft them to the port where they would be,
 And other ships they buffet long and blindly.
The cloud comes down on the great sinking deep,
And on the shore the watchers stand and weep.

And God hath many wrecks within the sea;
  Oh, it is deep! I look in fear and wonder;
The Wisdom throned above is dark to me,
  Yet it is sweet to think his care is under;
That yet the sunken treasure may be drawn
Into his storehouse — when the sea is gone.

So I, that sail in peril on the sea
  With my beloved, whom the waves may cover,
Say, God hath more than angel's care of me,
  And larger share than I in friend and lover.
Why weep ye so, ye watchers on the land?
This deep is but the hollow of his hand.

CAROLINE SPENCER.

THE PARSON'S COMFORTER.

THE parson goes about his daily ways,
  With all the parish troubles on his head,
And takes his Bible out, and reads and prays
  Beside the sufferer's chair, the dying bed.

Whate'er the secret skeleton may be —
  Doubt, drink, or debt — that keeps within his lair,
When parson comes, the owner turns the key,
  And lets him out to "squeak and gibber" there.

seems a possibility unguessed —
  r little borne in mind, if haply known —
  t he who cheers in trouble all the rest
  ay, now and then, have troubles of his own.

! God knows he has his foes to fight,
  is closet-atomy, severe and grim ;
  others claim his comfort as of right,
  ut, hapless parson! who shall comfort him?

friend he has to whom he may repair
  Besides that One who carries all our grief),
  nd when his load is more than he can bear,
  He seeks his comforter, and finds relief.

He finds a cottage, very poor and small,
  The meanest tenement where all are mean ;
Yet decency and order mark it all, —
  The panes are bright, the steps severely clean.

He lifts the latch ; his comforter is there,
  Propt in the bed, where now for weeks she stays,
Or, haply, seated, knitting, in her chair,
  If this be one of those rare "better days."

A tiny woman, stunted, bent, and thin;
  Her features sharp with pain that always wakes;
The nimble hand she holds the needles in
  Is warped and wrenched by dire rheumatic aches.

Sometimes she gets a grateful change of pain,
  Sometimes for half a day she quits her bed;
And — lying, sitting, crawled to bed again —
  Always she knits; her needles win her bread.

Too well she knows what 't is a meal to miss,
  Often the grate has not a coal of fire:
She has no hope of better things than this;
  The future darkens, suffering grows more dire.

Where will they take her, if betide it should
  Her stiffened hands the needles cannot ply?
Not to the workhouse, — God is very good;
  He knows her weakness — he will let her die.

Sometimes, but seldom, neighbors hear her moan,
  Wrung by some sudden stress of fiercer pain;
Often they hear her pray, but none has known,
  No single soul has heard her lips complain.

The parson enters, and a gracious smile
  Over the poor, pinched features brightly grows;
She lets the needles rest a little while;
  " You 're kindly welcome, sir ! "   Ah, that he kn

He takes the Book, and opens at the place —
  No need to ask her which her favorite psalm:
And, as he reads, upon her tortured face
  There comes a holy rapture, deep and calm.

She murmurs softly with him as he reads
  (She can repeat the Psalter through at will):
" He feeds me in green pastures, and he leads, —
  He leads me forth beside the waters still.

" Yea, through death's shadowy valley though I tread,
  I will not fear, for Thou dost show the way;
Thy holy oil is poured upon my head,
  Thy loving-kindness follows me for aye."

The reading 's done, and now the prayer is said;
  He bids farewell, and leaves her to her pain:
But grace and blessing on his soul are shed, —
  He goes forth comforted and strong again.

He takes his way, on divers errands bound,
  Abler to plead, and warn, and comfort woes;
That is the darkest house on all his round,
  And yet, be sure, the happiest house he knows.

Will it not ease, poor soul, thy restless bed,
  And make thee more content, if that can be,
To know that from thy suffering balm is shed,
  That comforts him who comes to comfort thee?

FREDERICK LANGBRIDGE.

WE SHALL BE SATISFIED.

THE course of the weariest river
  Ends in the great, gray sea;
The acorn forever and ever
  Strives upward to the tree;
The rainbow, the sky adorning,
  Shines promise through the storm;
The glimmer of coming morning
  Through midnight gloom will form.
By time all knots are riven,
  Complex although they be,
And peace will at last be given,
  Dear, both to you and me.

Then, though the path be dreary,
  Look forward to the goal;
Though the heart and the head be weary,
  Let faith inspire the soul;
Seek the right, though the wrong be tempting;
  Speak the truth at any cost;
Vain is all weak exempting
  When once that gem is lost;
Let strong hand and keen eye be ready
  For plain or ambushed foes;
Thought earnest and fancy steady
  Bear best unto the close.

The heavy clouds may be raining,
  But with evening comes the light;
Through the dark, low winds complaining,
  Yet the sunrise gilds the height;
And Love has his hidden treasure
  For the patient and the pure;
And Time gives his fullest measure
  To the workers who endure;
And the word that no lore has shaken
  Has the future pledge supplied;
For we know that when we "awaken"
  We shall be "satisfied."

S. K. PHILLIPS.

"ACROSS THE LOT."

Do you remember, when we came from school
  (You leading me, although not much the older),
How I would skip across the meadow cool,
  Saucily calling backward, o'er my shoulder,
" Do as you please, — come on with me or not,
But I am going home across the lot "?

Away I danced, and you, though left alone,
  Pursued the way, with face serene and smiling,
Singing beside the road with low, sweet tone,
  And still one thought your tender heart beguiling;
Wild though I was, you knew that I would wait
To meet and greet you at the garden-gate.

There with a bunch of flowers would I stand,
  Or fresh-plucked apples, with their ripeness blushing,
Or with a glass of water in my hand,
  Just brought from where the hillside spring was gushing,
Saying, as you bent down to quench your thirst,
" Now, are n't you glad that I am home the first?"

I am dying, sister — start not! Well I know
  That day by day my little strength is failing;
Strive not to hold me back, for I must go ; —
  God's mighty love o'er my weak will prevailing
Frees you from care and me from pain accurst :
'T is only that I shall be home the first.

And as of old, sweet sister, I will stand,
  Until you come, beside the heavenly portal,
Keeping the fadeless wreath within my hand
  With which to crown you for your life immortal.
Others will call me dead : believe them not —
I only have gone home " across the lot."

                                        C. S.

PART XI.

With a Story to Tell.

It may be glorious to write
Thoughts that shall glad the two or three
High souls, like those far stars that come in sight
Once in a century; —

But better far it is to speak
One simple word, which now and then
Shall waken their free nature in the weak
And friendless sons of men;

To write some earnest verse or line,
Which, seeking not the praise of art,
Shall make clear faith and manhood shine
In the untutored heart.

He who doth this, in verse or prose,
May be forgotten in his day,
But surely shall be crowned at last with those
Who live and speak for aye.

LOWELL.

With a Story to Tell.

—◆—

LITTLE PHIL.

"MAKE me a headboard, mister, smooth and painted. You see,
Our ma she died last winter, and sister and Jack and me
Last Sunday could hardly find her, so many new graves about,
And Bud cried out, ' We 've lost her,' when Jack gave a little
       shout.
We have worked and saved all winter — been hungry, sometimes
       I own —
But we hid this much from father, under the old door-stone:
He never goes there to see her ; he hated her ; scolded Jack
When he heard us talking about her and wishing that she 'd
       come back.
But up in the garret we whisper, and have a good time to cry,
For our beautiful mother who kissed us, and was n't afraid to die.
Put on that she was forty, in November she went away,
That she was the best of mothers, and we have n't forgot to pray ;
And we mean to do as she taught us — be loving and true and
       square,
To work and read — to love her, till we go to her up there.
Let the board be white, like mothe (the small chin quivered
       here,
And the lad coughed something under and conquered a rebel
       tear).
Here is all we could keep from father, a dollar and thirty cents ,
The rest he 's got for coal and flour, and partly to pay the rents."
Blushing the while all over, and dropping the honest eyes :
" What is the price of headboards, with writing, and handsome
       size ? "
" Three dollars ! " — A young roe wounded just falls with a
       moan ; and he,
With a face like the ghost of his mother, sank down on his
       tattered knee.
" Three dollars ! and we shall lose her ; next winter the rain and
       the snow —"
But the boss had his arms about him, and cuddled the head of
       tow

Close up to the great heart's shelter, and womanly tears fell
    fast —
"Dear boy, you shall never lose her; oh, cling to your sacred past!
Come to-morrow, and bring your sister and Jack, and the board
    shall be
The best that this shop can furnish; then come here and live
    with me."

    .   .   .   .

When the orphans loaded their treasure on the rugged old cart
    next day, —
The surprise of a footboard varnish, with all that their love
    could say;
And "Edith St. John, Our Mother," — Baby Jack gave his little
    shout,
And Bud, like a mountain daisy, went dancing her doll about;
But Phil grew white, and trembled, and close to the boss he crept;
Kissing him like a woman, shivered, and laughed, and wept.
"Do you think, my benefactor, in heaven that she'll be glad?"
"Not as glad as you are, Philip — but finish this job, my lad."

MRS. HELEN RICH.

——◆——

BILLY'S ROSE.

BILLY's dead and gone to glory — so is Billy's sister Nell;
There's a tale I know about them were I poet I would tell;
Soft it comes, with perfume laden, like a breath of country air
Wafted down the filthy alley, bringing fragrant odors there.

In that vile and filthy alley, long ago, one winter's day,
Dying quick of want and fever, hapless, patient Billy lay;
While beside him sat his sister, in the garret's dismal gloom,
Cheering with her gentle presence Billy's pathway to the tomb.

Many a tale of elf and fairy did she tell the dying child,
Till his eyes lost half their anguish, and her worn, wan features
    smiled, —
Tales herself had heard haphazard, caught amid the Babel roar,
Lisped about by tiny gossips playing at their mothers' door.

Then she felt his wasted fingers tighten feebly as she told
How beyond this dismal alley lay a land of shining gold,
Where, when all the pain was over, where, when all the tears
    were shed,
He would be a white-frocked angel, with a gold thing on his head.

Then she told some garbled story of a kind-eyed Saviour's love;
How he'd built for little children great big playgrounds up
    above,
Where they sang, and played at hop-scotch and at horses all
    the day,
And where beadles and policemen never frightened them away.

This was Nell's idea of heaven,—just a bit of what she'd heard,
With a little bit invented, and a little bit inferred;
But her brother lay and listened, and he seemed to understand,
For he closed his eyes, and murmured he could see the Promised
    Land.

"Yes," he whispered, "I can see it — I can see it, sister Nell,
Oh, the children look so happy, and they're all so strong and
    well;
I can see them there with Jesus,—he is playing with them too;
Let us run away and join them, if there's room for me and you."

She was eight, this little maiden, and her life had all been spent
In the alley and the garret, where they starved to pay the rent;
Where a drunken father's curses and a drunken mother's blows
Drove her forth into the gutter from the day's dawn to its close.

But she knew enough, this outcast, just to tell the sinking boy,
"You must die before you're able all these blessings to enjoy.
You must die," she whispered, "Billy, and *I* am not even ill,
But I'll come to you, dear brother, yes, I promise you I will.

"You are dying, little brother,—you are dying, oh, so fast!
I heard father say to mother that he knew you could n't last.
They will put you in a coffin, then you'll wake and be up there,
While I'm left alone to suffer in this garret bleak and bare."

"Yes, I know it," answered Billy. "Ah, but, sister, I don't mind;
Gentle Jesus will not beat me — he's not cruel or unkind;
But I can't help thinking, Nelly, I would like to take away
Something, sister, that you gave me, I might look at every day.

"In the summer, you remember how the Mission took us out
To the great, green, lovely meadow, where we played and ran
    about;
And the van that took us halted by a sweet white patch of land,
Where the fine red blossoms grew, dear, half as big as mother's
    hand.

"Nell, I asked the kind, good teacher, what they called such
    flowers as those,
And he told me, I remember, that the pretty name was 'rose.'
I have never seen them since, dear, — how I wish that I had one!
Just to keep, and think of you, Nell, when I'm up beyond the
    sun."

Not a word said little Nelly; but at night, when Billy slept,
On she flung her scanty garments, down the creaking stairs she
    crept;
Through the silent streets of London she ran nimbly as a fawn,
Running on and running ever, till the night had changed to dawn.

When the foggy sun had risen, and the mist had cleared away,
All around her, wrapped in snow-drift, there the open country
    lay;
She was tired, her limbs were frozen, and the roads had cut her
    feet,
But there came no flowery gardens her keen, hungry eyes to meet.

She had traced the road by asking; she had learnt the way to go;
She had found the famous meadow — it was wrapped in cruel
    snow;
Not a buttercup or daisy, not a single verdant blade,
Showed its head above its prison. Then she knelt her down
    and prayed.

With her eyes upcast to heaven, down she sank upon the ground,
And she prayed to God to tell her where the roses might be
    found.
Then the cold blast numbed her senses, and her sight grew
    strangely dim,
And a sudden, awful tremor seemed to rack her every limb.

"Oh, a rose!" she moaned, "good Jesus, just a rose to take to
    Bill!"
Even as she prayed, a chariot came thundering down the hill;
And a lady sat there toying with a red rose, rare and sweet;
As she passed she flung it from her, and it fell at Nelly's feet.

Just a word her lord had spoken caused her ladyship to fret,
And the rose had been his present, so she flung it in a pet;
But the poor, half-blinded Nelly thought it fallen from the skies,
And she murmured, "Thank you, Saviour," as she clasped the
    dainty prize.

Lo! that night from out the alley did a child's soul pass away
From dirt and sin and misery, to where God's children play.
Lo! that night a wild, fierce snow-storm burst in fury o'er the
    land,
And at morn they found Nell, frozen, with the red rose in her
    hand.

Billy's dead and gone to glory — so is Billy's sister Nell;
Am I bold, to say this happened in the land where angels dwell:
That the children met in heaven, after all their earthly woes,
And that Nelly kissed her brother, saying, "Billy, here's your
    rose"?

———◆———

TOLD AT THE TAVERN.

I CAN see *you're* a gentleman; time has been —
    Though you would n't think it to look at me, dressed
In these beggarly rags, and bloated with gin —
    I held my head as high as the best.

Reduced? I should say so! Stand a treat —
   I'm shaky, you see, and dead for a drink —
And then, if you've time, I'll tell you, complete,
   A tale that'll quicken your blood, as I think.

I was a countryman born, brought up on a farm
   (It fell to my share when the old man died),
Got married at twenty, and little of harm
   Was prophesied then of me and my bride.

Things ran along smooth, and money came in,
   And my acres increased as the years went by,
And nothing of sorrow, or care, or sin,
   Came thither to trouble my wife and I.

We'd been married, I guess, a dozen of years,
   When our only child, a girl, was born.
A husband yourself? You'll pardon my tears,
   For the birth at night there was death at morn.

The girl grew up — was the village queen,
   Reigning by right of her violet eyes,
Of her cheek's rich bloom, and marvellous sheen
   Of the goldenest ringlets under the skies.

Poetical? Ay; but she was a saint,
   And her pure, pale brow forever appears
When I tell the tale; and the old-time plaint
   Stirs itself to a language of tears.

What gold could buy she had only to ask;
   She was all I had, and should I be mean?
To humor her whims was an envious task;
   I'd have sold my soul for my golden-haired queen.

The love I lavished she paid tenfold;
   I was all to her as she all to me;
No angel in heaven of gentler mould,
   Or tenderer, lovinger heart than she.

But — your pardon again — her girlhood's prime —
   Well, the child had no mother, knew nought of sin.
This bunch in my throat! — please spare me a dime
   To wash it down with a tumbler of gin.

In her beautiful prime the tempter came;
   Through such as he the angels fell;
He had wealth of words, and mien, and a name —
   Ah, he bore the title of "Gentleman" well!

He made long prayers, to be seen of men;
   Sinners he urged from the wrath to come:
He met my innocent girl — and then —
   Let's mix that gin with a trifle of rum!

You know it all ?　Yes, the tale is old,
　And worn to shreds by poets and priests ;
But it 's little you know of the heart I hold —
　Of its bitter, blasted, Dead Sea feasts.

Did she die?　Of course !　To fall was death ;
　Could *she* live dishonored, forsaken, betrayed ?
He ?　Somewhere, I suppose, his scented breath
　Lifts eloquent prayers to Him who made.

Remorse ?　Ay, ay ; to the utmost stretch !
　Repentance ?　Don't pray, sir, trifle with me ;
I could curse whoever would plead for a wretch
　So lost to honor and manhood as he !

And so, as you see, I took to drink ;
　Can you stand another ?　I 'm in your debt:
A pitiful tale ?　I should rather think !
　And true as God's own gospel, you bet.

THEO F HAYES.

RETRIBUTION.

Here, you, policeman, just step inside ;
　See this young woman here —
Only just died.
　Facts in the case look to be
　　Somewhat peculiar ;
　Cause of death as you see,
Stabbed in the side.

Me and Maud Myrtle was standing right here,
　Takin' a drink ;
In come a loafer, chock full o' beer,
　Leading a little child sweet as a pink ;
Not more 'n three years old, pretty and bright,
Such little chaps as him 's good for the sight.
First thing we knowed the villain was rarin',
An' cursin', and swearin',
　To make the child drink.

Maud was the nearest by,
Sprung at him with a cry,
　Dashed the glass down !
Glared the brute's evil eye,
　Wicked his frown.
Quick as the lightning's gleam
　Flashed out the villain's knife ;
Maud gave one gurgling scream
　As the steel reached her life—
Tore through her tender side.
So the girl died !

Policeman — there she lies,
　　Resting at last!
Trouble was twins with her;
　　That is all past!
Her life was hard enough,
Bore on her rather rough;
　　But to see that peaceful face,
Pale and sweet beneath the light,
　　Goes to argue that the place
Where she's travelled to to-night,
　　Whatso sort of world it is,
　　Can't be worse for her than this.

The murderer? Yes!
　　Yonder he lies;
Dead in the dirt,
　　Like a dog he dies.
Some says its doubtful if hanging's played out,
It don't suit me to admit of a doubt.
　　Think I'm wanted! Do you, though?
　　Well, let's go.

DAVID L. PROUDFIT.
(Peleg Arkwright.)

Daily Graphic.

ONLY JOE.

THIS grave were ye meanin', stranger? Oh, there's nobody
　　much lies here;
It's only poor Joe, a dazed lad — been dead now better 'n a year.
He was nobody's child, this Joe, sir — orphaned the hour of his
　　birth,
And simple and dazed all his life, yet the harmlessest cretur
　　on earth.

Some say that he died broken-hearted; but that is all nonsense,
　　you know,
For a body could never do that as were simple and dazed like
　　Joe.
But I 'll tell you the story, stranger, an' then you can readily see
How easy for some folks to fancy a thing that never could be.

Do you see that grave over yonder? Well, the minister's
　　daughter lies there;
She were a regular beauty, an' as good as she were fair.
She 'd a nod an' a kind word for Joe, sir, whenever she passed
　　him by;
But bless ye, that were nothin' — she could n't hurt even a fly.

It wern't very often, I reckon, that people a kind word would
    say,
For Joe was simple an' stupid, an' allus in somebody's way;
So I s'pose he kind o' loved her; but then that were nothin',
    you know,
For there was n't a soul in the village but loved her better'n Joe.

An' when Milly took down with consumption, or some such
    weakness as that,
Joe took on kind o' foolish — there was nothin' for him to cry at;
An' he'd range the woods over for hours for flowers to place
    by her bed,
An' Milly, somehow or other, kind o' liked his dazed ways,
    they said.

But when winter was come, she died, sir, an' I well remember
    the day
When we carried the little coffin to the old churchyard away;
It were so bitter cold, we were glad when the grave were made,
An' when we were done an' went home, I suppose poor Joe
    must have stayed;

They found him here the next mornin', lyin' close to the grave,
    they said,
An' a looking like he was asleep; but then, of course, he were
    dead.
I suppose he got chilled and sleepy — an' how could a body know
How dangerous that kind o' sleep is, as never knowed nothin',
    like Joe?

So they say that he died broken-hearted; but that only shows,
    do you see,
How easy for some folks to fancy a thing that never could be;
For now you have heard the story, you'll agree with me,
    stranger, I know,
That a body could never do that, as were simple and dazed,
    like Joe!

San Francisco, 1874.   JAMES ROANN REED.

THE OUTCAST'S DREAM.

FROM morn till noon the golden glow
    Of bright September sunlight falls
On dewy glades, where fall flowers hide
    Behind the dull, dark lichen walls.
From noon till night the slanting rays
    Creep through the tangled winter vine,
Where berries fringe the bending sprays,
    Like crimson drops of rare old wine.

From morn till noon, from noon till night,
  O'erspreads the earth with jewelled robes,
And fire-flies light the purplish dusk
  With countless golden glowing globes;
A woman stalks through dust and heat,
  Until the fleece-like mists of night
Enfold her thin and ill-clad form
  In trailing robes of bridal white.

Her feet are bruised with jagged stones, —
  Her tender feet that years ago
Her mother's hands had fondly wrapped
  In infant robes of downy snow;
Her pallid brow, that mother's lips
  Had kissed with mother's kisses pure,
Is racked with pain that only they
  Who homeless roam the world endure.

The clear, rich notes of wild birds break
  The slumberous calm like Sabbath bells,
And from the brakes the thrush's song
  In sad, pathetic sweetness swells.
The cool night-air is fragrant with
  The scents that rise from dewy flowers,
As by the new moon's waning light
  She counts the twilight's fleeting hours.

Her wild, sad eyes with wistful glare
  Count all the landmarks, one by one,
Until she stands beyond the ridge
  Where blossoms catch the morning sun;
And where the plover builds her nest
  In meadow grasses lush and long,
And where in girlhood's happy years
  She raked the hay, with mirthful song.

The old white stone beside the spring
  Is there, as white and smooth as when
She filled her pail and mocked the caw
  Of blackbirds in the reedy glen.
And when the gates of morn unfold,
  She knows the sunbeams drifting down
Will steal through casements quaint and old,
  And snow-white locks with glory crown.

She wanders on to where the spring
  Is lost in countless silvery rills,
Then drops asleep, her silvery head
  On pillows fringed with daffodils;
While in her dream her mother comes
  And strokes her brow with soothing palms
That wash away the marks of shame,
  And fill her soul with restful calms.

22

She feels warm, quivering kisses on her face
  (The dews that heaven kindly sends),
And hears again the dear, brave voice
  That gently censures or commends.
The vesper hymns they sang at eve,
  The Sabbath chants of humble praise,
Float through her dreams, sweet memories from
  The deathless bliss of childhood's days.

Ah! once again she 's young and pure;
  Ah! once again her sinless brow
Is bound with roses rich and red,
  Whose hearts with crimson beauty glow;
She hears again the subtle voice
  That taught her love's most bitter pain.
On cheek and lips and wrinkled brow
  His kisses fall like summer rain.

She cries aloud, her yearning hands
  Outstretched to meet each fond caress,
Then sinks in shame to hide her face
  In dripping clumps of watercress.
For what has life for such as her
  But tortured thought, undying pain;
And what are dreams but stray chords from
  Some old home song or old love strain?

Pittsburgh, 1874.   OLIVE BELL.

———◆———

FISHERMAN JOB.

WELL, young 'un, you 're mighty smooth spoken, an' it all may
    be as you say,
That God never interferes with us, but lets each one go on his
    own way;
But when heaven has silvered your locks with the snows of
    some eighty odd year —
As it has mine, an' always in marcy — you 'll regret this wild
    fancy, I fear.

Just let me spin ye a yarn, sir, as happened a long time agone
To me, an' if such is all luck, why, I hope it 'll always hold on;
It 's now nearly threescore summers since this incident happened
    to me, —
Just after I 'd married my wife, an' settled down here by the sea.

For I was a fisherman born, sir, lovin' always the wild waves
    to ride;
They 're the type of my life, an' I 'm thinkin' that it 's now
    near the ebb o' the tide.
There were three of us then as were partners in the trimmest
    an' snug little boat
As ever was true to her colors, just a bright little " Sunbeam "
    afloat.

We had had a long run o' good luck, sir; wi' the weather as
    fair as could be,
An' the morrow were goin' again, when the gray light first
    dawned on the sea.
But before I was fairly turned out, it seemed as I heard some-
    thing say,
"There's breakers ahead o' ye, Job; don't go on the sea, lad,
    to-day!"

At first I felt kind o' scared like, but I thought 't was all fancy,
    you see,
So I took a good look at the sky; 't was as clear and as bright
    as could be.
But it still seemed to whisper, "Beware!" an' the breeze crept
    by soughin' an' slow,
An' a voice, like a wail for the dead, with each gust seemed
    to murmur, "Don't go!"

Then I got kind o' nettled to think that my narves should
    sarve me that way;
An' I says to myself, "You're an ass, Job, but you'll go for
    all that, lad, this day!"
So I kissed wife a hasty good-by, an' set off a-hummin' a song,
Till the path took a turn by that cliff at whose foot the sand
    stretches along.

Then what happened I never could tell; but the first I remem-
    ber, I know,
The cliff were a frownin' above me, an' I, stunned and bruised,
    down below,
An' my wife kneelin' there by my side, an' lookin' as frightened
    as if
I were dead. Says she, "Job, were ye crazy? *Ye walked right
    straight off of the cliff!*"

I didn't say much; an', of course, my partners went that day
    alone;
An' I lay on my bed kind o' happy to find, after all, I'd not
    gone.
But the strangest of all is yet comin'; for that mornin', as fair
    as could be,
Was followed ere noon by a storm as was fairly terrific to see.

We waited in agony, knowin' such a sea the boat could not
    outride;
An' were thankful when even the bodies were laid at our feet
    by the tide.
It's no use in askin' my fate, if that mornin' I only had gone;
An' if such things all happen by luck, why, I hope it'll always
    hold on.

JAMES ROANN REED.

POOR LITTLE JOE.

Prop yer eyes wide open, Joey,
　　Fur I 've brought you sumpin' great.
Apples?　No, but something better!
　　Don't you take no int'rest?　Wait!
Flowers, Joe, — I knowed you 'd like 'em —
　　Ain't them scrumptious?　Ain't them high?
Tears, my boy?　Wot 's them fur, Joey?
　　There — poor little Joe! — don't cry.

I was skippin' past a winder
　　Where a bang-up lady sot
All amongst a lot of bushes,
　　Each one climbin' from a pot;
Every bush had flowers on it —
　　Pretty?　Mebbe!　Oh, no!
Wish you could a seen 'em growin',
　　It was sich a stunnin' show.

Well, I thought of you, poor feller,
　　Lyin' here so sick and weak,
Never knowin' any comfort,
　　And I puts on lots o' cheek.
"Missus," says I, "if you please, mum,
　　Could I ax you for a rose?
For my little brother, missus,
　　Never seed one, I suppose."

Then I told her all about you, —
　　How I bringed yer up, poor Joe!
(Lackin' women-folks to do it)
　　Such a' imp you was, you know, —
Till yer got that awful tumble,
　　Just as I had broke yer in
(Hard work too) to earn your livin'
　　Blackin' boots for honest tin.

How that tumble crippled of you,
　　So 's you could n't hyper much, —
Joe, it hurted when I seen you
　　Fur the first time with yer crutch.
"But," I says, "he 's laid up now, mum,
　　'Pears to weaken every day."
Joe, she up and went to cuttin', —
　　That 's the how of this bokay.

Say, it seems to me, ole feller,
　　You is quite yourself to-night;
Kind o' chirk; it 's been a fortnight
　　Since yer eyes has been so bright.

Better? Well, I 'm glad to hear it.
   Yes, they 're mighty pretty, Joe.
Smellin' of 'em 's made you happy!
   Well, I thought it would, you know.

Never seed the country, did you?
   Flowers growin' everywhere!
Sometime, when you 're better, Joey,
   Mebbe I kin take you there.
Flowers in heaven? 'M — I s'pose so;
   Don't know much about it, though;
Ain't as fly as what I might be
   On them topics, little Joe.

But I 've heard it hinted, somewheres,
   That in heaven's golden gates
Things is everlastin' cheerful, —
   B'lieve that 's wot the Bible states.
Likewise, there folks don't get hungry;
   So good people when they dies
Finds themselves well fixed forever —
   Joe, my boy, wot ails yer eyes?

Thought they looked a little sing'ler.
   Oh, no! Don't you have no fear;
Heaven was made for such as you is —
   Joe, what makes you look so queer?
Here — wake up! Oh, don't look that way!
   Joe! My boy! Hold up your head!
Here 's your flowers — you dropped 'em, Joey —
   Oh, my God! can Joe be dead?

THE CURTAIN FALLS.

CLOWNS are capering in motley, drums are beating, trumpets
   blown,
Laughing crowds block up the gangway — husky is the show-
   man's tone.
Rapidly the booth is filling, and the rustics wait to hear
A cadaverous strolling player who will presently appear.

Once his voice in tones of thunder shook the crazy caravan;
Now he entered pale and gasping, and no sentence glibly ran;
Sad and vacant were his glances, and his memory seemed to
   fail,
While with feeble effort striving to recall Othello's tale.

O'er his wasted form the spangles glittered in the lamp's dull
      ray;
Ebon tresses, long and curling, covered scanty locks of gray;
Rouge and powder hid the traces of the stern, relentless years,
As gay flowers hide a ruin, tottering ere it disappears.

Not with age, serenely ebbing to the everlasting sea,
Calmly dreaming of past pleasures, or of mysteries to be;
Nay, the melancholy stroller kept his onward pilgrimage,
Until Death, the pallid prompter, called him from life's dusky
      stage.

Lofty hopes and aspirations all had faded with his youth,
And for daily bread he acted now in yonder canvas booth;
Yet there flashed a fire heroic from his visage worn and grave;
Deeper, fuller came his accents — Man was master, Time was
      slave.

And again with force and feeling he portrayed the loving Moor;
Told the story to the Senate — told the pangs which they endure
Who are torn with jealous passion, — while delightedly the
      crowd
Watched the stroller's changing aspect, and applauded him
      aloud.

Was it but a trick of acting to depict a frenzied mood,
That there came a sudden silence, and Othello voiceless stood?
Ah, 't was all Othello's story Nature left the power to tell —
'T was his own sad drama ending as the dark-green curtain fell.

While they shouted for the stroller, and the hero's fate would
      see,
He had made his final exit — joined a higher company.
With no loving kiss at parting, with no friend to press his hand,
The invisible scene-shifter had unveiled the spirit-land.

Huskier still became the showman as he forward came and
      bowed,
Vaguely muttering excuses to appease the gaping crowd;
Then he knelt beside the stroller, but his words were lost on
      air —
Nevermore uprose the curtain on the figure lying there.

One brief hour their cares forgetting, his old comrades of the
      show
Stood around his grave in silence, and some honest tears did
      flow.
Then the booth again was opened, crammed with many a rustic
      boor,
And another strolling player told the story of the Moor.

Tinsley's Magazine.   JOSEPH VEREY.

IN BAY CHALEUR.

THE birds no more in dooryard trees are singing,
　The purple swallows all have left the eaves,
And 'thwart the sky the broken clouds are winging,
　Shading the land-slopes, bright with harvest-sheaves.
Old Hannah waits her sailor-boy returning,
　His fair young brow to-day she hopes to bless;
But sees the red sun on the hill-tops burning,
　The flying cloud, the wild, cold gloominess
　　　　Of Bay Chaleur.

The silver crown has touched her forehead lightly
　Since last his hand was laid upon her hair;
The golden crown will touch her brow more brightly
　Ere he again shall print his kisses there.
The night comes on, the village sinks in slumber,
　The rounded moon illumes the water's rim;
Each evening hour she hears the old clock number,
　But brings the evening no return of him
　　　　To Bay Chaleur.

She heard low murmurs in the sandy reaches,
　And knew the sea no longer was at rest;
The black clouds scudded o'er the level beaches,
　And barred the moonlight on the ocean's breast.
The night wore on, and grew the shadows longer;
　Far in the distance of the silvered seas
Tides lapped the rocks, and blew the night-wind stronger,
　Bending the pines and stripping bare the trees
　　　　Round Bay Chaleur.

Then Alice came; on Hannah's breast reclining,
　She heard the leaves swift whistling in the breeze,
And, through the lattice, saw the moon declining
　In the deep shadows of the rainy seas.
The fire burned warm, — upon the hearth was sleeping
　The faithful dog that used his steps to follow.
"'T is almost midnight," whispered Alice, weeping,
　While blew the winds more drearily and hollow
　　　　O'er Bay Chaleur.

No organ stands beneath a bust of Pallas,
　No painted Marius to the ruin clings,
No Ganymede, borne up from airy Hellas,
　Looks through the darkness 'neath the eagle's wings.
But the sweet pictures from the shadowed ceiling
　Reflect the firelight near old Hannah's chair, —
One a fair girl, with features full of feeling,
　And one a boy, a fisher, young and fair,
　　　　Of Bay Chaleur.

The boy returns with humble presents laden,
  For on the morrow is his wedding morn ;
To the old church he hopes to lead the maiden
  Whose head now rests his mother's breast upon.
Now Hannah droops her cheek, the maiden presses, —
  " He will return when come the morning hours,
And he will greet thee with his fond caresses,
  And thou shalt meet him diademed with flowers."
      Sweet Bay Chaleur !

Gray was the morning, but a light more tender
  Parted at last the storm-cloud's lingering glooms ;
The sun looked forth in mellowness and splendor,
  Drying the leaves amid the gentian blooms.
And wrecks came drifting to the sandy reaches,
  As inward rolled the tide with sullen roar ;
The fishers wandered o'er the sea-washed beaches,
  And gathered fragments as they reached the shore
      Of Bay Chaleur.

Then Alice, with the village maidens roaming
  Upon the beaches where the breakers swirl,
Espied a fragment 'mid the waters foaming,
  And found a casket overlaid with pearl.
It was a treasure.   " Happy he who claimed it,"
  A maiden said, " 't is worthy of a bride."
Another maid " the ocean's dowry " named it ;
  But gently Alice, weeping, turned aside, —
      Sad Bay Chaleur ! —

And went to Hannah with the new-found treasure,
  And stood again beside the old arm-chair ;
The maids stood round her, radiant with pleasure,
  And playful wove the gentians in her hair.
Then Hannah said, her feelings ill dissembling,
  " Some sailor-lad this treasure once possessed ;
And now, perhaps," she added, pale and trembling,
  " His form lies sleeping 'neath the ocean's breast,
      In Bay Chaleur."

Now on her knee the opened box she places, —
  Her trembling hand falls helpless on her breast ;
Into her face look up two pictured faces,
  The faces that her sailor-boy loved best.
One picture bears the written words, " My mother," —
  Old Hannah drops her wrinkled cheek in pain ;
" Alice," sweet name, is writ beneath the other —
  Old Hannah's tears fall over it like rain.
      Dark Bay Chaleur !

The spring will come, the purple swallows bringing,
  The green leaves glitter where the gold leaves fell ;
But nevermore the time of flowers and singing
  Will hope revive in her poor heart to dwell.

Life ne'er had brought to her so dark a chalice,
  But from her lips escaped no bitter moan;
They, 'mid the gentians, made the grave of Alice,
  And Hannah lives in her old cot alone,
        By Bay Chaleur.
                HEZEKIAH BUTTERWORTH.

------◇------

THE NEW MAGDALEN.

The *Memphis Appeal*, a short time ago, told the story of a fallen woman
of that place, Mollie Cooke by name, who, owning a gilded palace of sin,
turned it into a hospital for the yellow-fever sufferers, and with her hands
nursed the sick and dying back to life again, until at last, wearied and ex-
hausted with the long watching, she too fell a prey to the fever. I am told
that a marble shaft, the gift of the city, marks her last resting-place in the
cemetery there ; and it seems but a fitting tribute to one who gave all she
had — her life — to redeem the errors of the past.

THE yellow death came stealing
    Up from the river's edge ;
Up from the dark, dark morass,
    With its tangled fringe of sedge ;
Up from the misty bayous,
    On the south wind's tainted breath, —
Till the skies grew dark at Memphis
    With the shadowy wings of death.

The air grew dense and silent,
    The wild bird ceased its song,
And strong men cried in anguish,
    "How long, O God, how long ? "
But the skies gave back no answer,
    Death's pitiless scythe still swung,
And the harvest the reaper gathered
    Was a harvest of old and young.

The babe in the cradle sleeping,
    In the flush of morning light,
With a smile of dimpled features,
    In a coffin slept at night ;
And the man who knelt at evening,
    Thanking God for the strength he gave,
Lay down to sleep at dawning
    In the cold and narrow grave.

The pavements only echoed
    To the wheels of the passing hearse,
As it bore to the silent city
    The victims of the curse ;
And the voice of the stricken mourners,
    Who heard not the rustling wing,
But saw on the sleeper's forehead
    The seal of the saffron king.

Then out from the gilded palace
  Of sorrow, and sin, and shame,
Clad in the robes of scarlet,
  A fallen woman came;
And the song of the noisy revel
  Gave place in its stately hall
To a prayer for the sick and dying,
  And a woman's soft footfall.

Back from death's dark portal,
  From the verge of an unseen land,
Came many a wandering mortal
  At the touch of that woman's hand;
Till the fever, wrathful, sullen,
  Touched her with his tainted breath,
And asleep, in snowy garment,
  She lay in the arms of death.

Oh, girl with the jewelled fingers,
  Oh, maid with the laces rare,
Will that woman's grand action
  Count less than thy studied prayer?
Have the angels, looking earthward,
  A love more tender seen
Than that of this fallen woman, —
  The true new Magdalen?

                              R. L. CARY, JR.

FOR LIFE AND DEATH.

"NOUGHT to be done," — eh?   It was that he said, —
  The doctor, as you stopped him at the door?
Nay, never try to smile and shake thy head,
  I could ha' told thee just as well afore.
I have n't lived these thirty year to want
  Parsons or women telling what is nigh
When the pulse hovers, and the breath is scant,
  And all grows dim before the glazing eye.

I felt that something gave, here, at my heart,
  In that last tussle down there on the Scar;
Nay, never cry, fond lassie as thou art,
  Thou wilt do fine without me — better far.
Thou 'st been a good and patient wife to me
  Sin' that spring day, last year, when we were wed;
I never meant so cold and strange to be;
  Come, and I 'll tell thee.   Sit here by my bed.

So, where the sunshine rests upon thy hair,
  It shows almost as smooth and bright as hers
The girl I wooed in Dunkerque, over there —
  Fie, how the thought the slackening life-blood stirs!

Oh, wild black eyes, so quick to flash and fill !
    Oh, rich red lips, so ripe for kiss and vow !
Did not your spell work me enow of ill,
    That ye must haunt and vex me even now ?

I swore, as we drove out into the gale,
    And staggering down mid-channel went the boat,
Never at Dunkerque pier to furl my sail,
    While I and the old " Lion " kept afloat, —
The pier where she and her French lover laughed
    At the poor, trusting fool, who had his due ;
Quick though his hand flew to his keen knife's haft,
    The English fist was yet more quick and true.

She and her beaten sweetheart, do they prate
    Yet of her triumph ?   Let them, an they please.
I shall know nought about it, lying straight
    Up on the headland, 'neath the tall fir-trees.
I wish I could ha' been content, my lass,
    With thee, and thy blue eyes and quiet ways :
Thou hast thy bairn, and as the calm years pass
    Thou wilt forget thy stormy April days.

Thou 'rt young and bonnie still, my wench.   Thou 'lt make
    A happy wife yet.   Choose some quiet chap,
Who 'll love the little 'un for thy sweet sake,
    And bear thee to some inland home, mayhap.
We 're rough and stern, we on the seaboard bred,
    And can't forget, or smooth a rankling wound.
Come close ; there 's just one thing left to be said,
    Before I 'm dumb forever, and under ground.

Last night they watched the life-boat driven back,
    The rocket battling vainly with the blast,
While the good bark, amid the roar and wrack,
    Drove headlong — struck, and lay there, hard and fast.
They neither saw nor heeded, as the flash
    Of cold blue fire lit all, above, below,
The French flag flying o'er the whirl and crash,
    " Louise, Dunkerque," the letters on her prow.

I saw, plunged, fought, and reached the sinking bark,
    The old, hot poison fierce in every vein,
Seized on two sailors, shrieking in the dark,
    Bore them to land, and turned to swim again.
Clasping the rigging yet one man I found ;
    I caught him, struggled on ; the beach was near, —
" Louise," he gasped, and, 'mid the roar around,
    I knew the voice last heard on Dunkerque pier.

The murderer's lust surged to the throbbing heart,
    The murderer's cunning loosed the saving hand ;
'T was but to let him go ; I 'd done my part —
    Praised and avenged !   Why, thus 't were well to land.

But she —   No cloud on her bright life should rest
    An I could ward it ; love and hate at strife
A moment, then, snatched from the breaker's crest,
    I dragged him, stunned and bleeding, back to life.

Somehow I hurt myself, and so it 's over,
    And better so for all.   Thou 'lt rear the lad
To make some Yorkshire lass an honest lover,
    Nor tell him all the wrong his mother had ;
And sometimes, — for thou 'rt kind, — when stars are out,
    In the green country, where no tempests blow,
Thou 'lt say, " Thy father had his faults, no doubt,
    But still he died to save his bitterest foe."

———◆———

TO-MORROW.

THE setting sun, with dying beams,
    Had waked the purple hill to fire,
    And citadel and dome and spire
Were gilded by the far-off gleams ;
And in and out dark pine-trees crept
    Full many a slender thread of gold ;
Gold shafts athwart the river swept,
    And kissed it as it onward rolled :
And sunlight lingered, loath to go ;
Ah, well ! it causeth sorrow
To part from those we love below ;
And yet the sun as bright shall glow
        To-morrow.

Two hearts have met to say farewell
    At even when the sun went down ;
    Each life-sound from the busy town
Smote sadly as a passing bell.
One whispered, " Parting is sweet pain —
    At morn and eve returns the tide ; "
" Nay, parting rends the heart in twain."
    And still they linger side by side ;
And still they linger, loath to go ;
Ah, well ! it causeth sorrow
To part from those we love below —
For shall we ever meet or no,
        To-morrow?

———◆———

DRIFTED OUT TO SEA.

Two little ones, grown tired of play,
Roamed by the sea, one summer day,
Watching the great waves come and go,
Prattling, as children will, you know,
Of dolls and marbles, kites and strings ;
Sometimes hinting at graver things.

At last they spied within their reach
An old boat cast upon the beach ;
Helter-skelter, with merry din,
Over its sides they scrambled in, —
Ben, with his tangled, nut-brown hair,
Bess, with her sweet face flushed and fair.

Rolling in from the briny deep,
Nearer, nearer, the great waves creep,
Higher, higher, upon the sands,
Reaching out with their giant hands,
Grasping the boat in boisterous glee,
Tossing it up and out to sea.

The sun went down, 'mid clouds of gold ;
Night came, with footsteps damp and cold ;
Day dawned ; the hours crept slowly by ;
And now across the sunny sky
A black cloud stretches far away,
And shuts the golden gates of day.

A storm comes on, with flash and roar,
While all the sky is shrouded o'er ;
The great waves, rolling from the west,
Bring night and darkness on their breast.
Still floats the boat through driving storm,
Protected by God's powerful arm.

The home-bound vessel, " Sea-bird," lies
In ready trim, 'twixt sea and skies :
Her captain paces, restless now,
A troubled look upon his brow,
While all his nerves with terror thrill, —
The shadow of some coming ill.

The mate comes up to where he stands,
And grasps his arm with eager hands.
" A boat has just swept past," says he,
" Bearing two children out to sea ;
'T is dangerous now to put about,
Yet they cannot be saved without."

" Nought but their safety will suffice !
They must be saved ! " the captain cries.
" By every thought that 's just and right,
By lips I hoped to kiss to-night,
I 'll peril vessel, life, and men,
And God will not forsake us then."

With anxious faces, one and all,
Each man responded to the call ;

And when at last, through driving storm,
They lifted up each little form,
The captain started, with a groan :
" My God is good, they are my own ! "

ROSA HARTWICK THORPE
(*Author of " Curfew Shall Not Ring To-night "*).

TWO.

WE two will stand in the shadow here,
    To see the bride as she passes by;
Ring soft and low, ring loud and clear,
    Ye chiming bells that swing on high !
Look ! look ! she comes ! The air grows sweet
    With the fragrant breath of the orange-blooms,
And the flowers she treads beneath her feet
    Die in a flood of rare perfumes !

She comes ! she comes ! The happy bells
    With their joyous clamor fill the air,
While the great organ dies and swells,
    Soaring to trembling heights of prayer !
Oh ! rare are her robes of silken sheen,
    And the pearls that gleam on her bosom's snow ;
But rarer the grace of her royal mien,
    Her hair's fine gold, and her cheek's young glow.

Dainty and fair as a folded rose,
    Fresh as a violet dewy sweet,
Chaste as a lily, she hardly knows
    That there are rough paths for other feet.
For Love hath shielded her ; Honor kept
    Watch beside her night and day ;
And Evil out from her sight hath crept,
    Trailing its slow length far away.

Now in her perfect womanhood,
    In all the wealth of her matchless charms,
Lovely and beautiful, pure and good,
    She yields herself to her lover's arms.
Hark ! how the jubilant voices ring !
    Lo ! as we stand in the shadow here,
While far above us the gay bells swing,
    I catch the gleam of a happy tear !

The pageant is over. Come with me
    To the other side of the town, I pray,
Ere the sun goes down in the darkening sea,
    And night falls around us, chill and gray.

In the dim church porch an hour ago
  We waited the bride's fair face to see;
Now life has a sadder sight to show,
  A darker picture for you and me.

No need to seek for the shadow here,
  There are shadows lurking everywhere;
These streets in the brightest days are drear,
  And black as the blackness of despair.
But this is the house. Take heed, my friend,
  The stairs are rotten, the way is dim;
And up the flights, as we still ascend,
  Creep, stealthily, phantoms dark and grim.

Enter this chamber. Day by day,
  Alone in this chill and ghostly room,
A child — a woman — which is it, pray? —
  Despairingly waits for the hour of doom!
Ah! as she wrings her hands so pale,
  No gleam of a wedding-ring you see;
There 's nothing to tell. You know the tale —
  God help her now in her misery!

I dare not judge her. I only know
  That love was to her a sin and a snare,
While to the bride of an hour ago
  It brought all blessings its hands could bear!
I only know that to one it came
  Laden with honor and joy and peace;
Its gifts to the other were woe and shame,
  And a burning pain that shall never cease.

I only know that the soul of one
  Has been a pearl in a golden case;
That of the other a pebble thrown
  Idly down in a wayside place,
Where all day long strange footsteps trod,
  And the bold, bright sun drank up the dew!
Yet both were women. O righteous God,
  Thou only canst judge between the two!

THE COURT OF BERLIN.

King Frederick, of Prussia, grew nervous and ill
  When pacing his chamber one day,
Because of the sound of a crazy old mill
  That clattered so over the way.

"Ho, miller!" cried he, "what sum shall you take
    In lieu of that wretched old shell?
It angers my brain and it keeps me awake."
    Said the miller, "I want not to sell."

"But you must," said the king, in a passion for once.
    "But I won't," said the man, in a heat.
"Gods! this to my face?   Ye are daft, or a dunce—
    We can raze your old mill with the street."

"Ay, true, my good sire, if such be your mood,"
    Then answered the man with a grin;
"But never you'll move it the tenth of a rood
    As long as a court's in Berlin."

"Good, good," said the king,—for the answer was grand,
    As opposing the Law to the Crown,—
"We bow to the court, and the mill shall stand,
    Though even the palace come down."

Frankfort Yeoman.

PART XII.

Parting and Absence.

23

Why, why repine, my friend,
  At pleasures slipt away?
Some the stern Fates will never lend,
  And all refuse to stay.

I see the rainbow in the sky,
  The dew upon the grass, —
I see them, and I ask not why
  They glimmer or they pass.

With folded arms I linger not
  To call them back ; 't were vain ;
In this or in some other spot
  I know they'll shine again.

WALTER S. LANDOR.

PART XII.

Parting and Absence.

———◦◦———

"GOOD–BY."

WE say it for an hour or for years;
We say it smiling, say it choked with tears;
We say it coldly, say it with a kiss;
And yet we have no other word than this, —
　　　　　　" Good-by."

We have no dearer word for our heart's friend,
For him who journeys to the world's far end,
And scars our soul with going; thus we say,
As unto him who steps but o'er the way, —
　　　　　　" Good-by."

Alike to those we love and those we hate,
We say no more in parting.　At life's gate,
To him who passes out beyond earth's sight,
We cry, as to the wanderer for a night, —
　　　　　　" Good-by."

GRACE DENIO LITCHFIELD.

———◆———

PARTING.

IF thou dost bid thy friend farewell,
But for one night though that farewell may be,
Press thou his hand in thine.
How canst thou tell how far from thee
Fate or caprice may lead his steps ere that to-morrow comes?
Men have been known to lightly turn the corner of a street,
And days have grown to months, and months to lagging years,
Ere they have looked in loving eyes again.
Parting, at best, is underlaid
With tears and pain.

Therefore, lest sudden death should come between,
Or time, or distance, clasp with pressure firm
The hand of him who goeth forth;
Unseen, Fate goeth too.
Yes, find thou always time to say some earnest word
Between the idle talk,
Lest with thee henceforth,
Night and day, regret should walk.

CShare COVENTRY PATMORE

MY DAUGHTER LOUISE.

IN the light of the moon, by the side of the water,
  My seat on the sand and her seat on my knees,
We watch the bright billows, do I and my daughter,
  My sweet little daughter Louise.
We wonder what city the pathway of glory
  That broadens away to the limitless west
Leads up to — she minds me of some pretty story
  And says — "To the city that mortals love best."
Then I say, "It must lead to the far-away city,
  The beautiful city of rest."

In the light of the moon, by the side of the water,
  Stand two in the shadow of whispering trees,
And one loves my daughter, my beautiful daughter,
  My womanly daughter Louise.
She steps to the boat with a touch of his fingers,
  And out on the diamonded pathway they move.
The shallop is lost in the distance; it lingers,
  It waits, but I know that its coming will prove
That it went to the walls of the beautiful city
  The magical city of love.

In the light of the moon, by the side of the water,
  I wait for her coming from over the seas;
I wait but to welcome the dust of my daughter,
  To weep for my daughter Louise.
The path, as of old, reaching out in its splendor,
  Gleams bright, like a way that an angel has trod;
I kiss the cold burden its billows surrender,
  Sweet clay to lie under the pitiful sod;
But she rests, at the end of the path, in the city,
  "Whose builder and maker is God."

HOMER GREENE.

ONLY.

AND this is the end of it all! it rounds the year's completeness;
Only a walk to the stile, through fields afoam with sweetness;
Only the sunset light, purple and red on the river,
And a lingering, low good-night, that means good-by forever.

So be it! and God be with you!   It had been perhaps more
    kind,
Had you sooner (pardon the word) been sure of knowing your
    mind.
We can bear so much in youth — who cares for a swift, sharp
    pain?
And the two-edged sword of truth cuts deep, but it leaves no
    stain.

I shall just go back to my work — my little household cares,
That never make any show.   By time, perhaps in my prayers,
I may think of you!   For the rest, on this way we 've trodden
    together
My foot shall fall as lightly as if my heart were a feather,

And not a woman's heart, strong to have and to keep,
Patient when children cry, soft to lull them to sleep,
Hiding its secrets close, glad when another's hand
Finds for itself a gem where hers found only sand.

Good-by!   The year has been bright.   As oft as the blossoms
    come,
The peach with its waxen pink, the waving snow of the plum,
I shall think how I used to watch, so happy to see you pass,
I could almost kiss the print of your foot on the dewy grass.

I am not ashamed of my love!   Yet I would not have yours
    now,
Though you laid it down at my feet; I could not stoop so low.
A love is but half a love that contents itself with less
Than love's utmost faith and truth and unwavering tenderness.

Only this walk to the stile; this parting word by the river,
That flows so quiet and cold, ebbing and flowing forever.
"Good-by!"   Let me wait to hear the last, last sound of his
    feet!
Ah me! but I think in this life of ours the bitter outweighs the
    sweet.
The Argosy.

BEFORE SAILING.

LEAN closer, darling, let thy tender heart
    Beat against mine that aches with heavy woe;
Drop thy quick woman's tears to soothe thy smart.
    Ah me! that I could ease my sorrow so!
But man must work, sweetheart, and women weep,
    So says the song, so runs the world's behest;
Yet time will pass, and tender comfort creep
    With hope in company unto thy breast.
Now, ere we part, while yet on lip and cheek
    Close kisses linger, clinging, passionate,

There is a farewell word love fain would speak,
  A tender thought love labors to translate
In earnest words, whose memory through the years
Shall calm thy soul and dry thy dropping tears.

If in thy garden, when the roses blow,
  Or by the shelter of thine evening fire,
In any winter gloom or summer glow,
  Thy soul floats seaward with a fond desire
(Fonder and stronger than thy tender use),
  Think thou, " One longs for me across the foam ; "
And if, sweet-falling like the evening dews,
  A special peace enfolds that heart and home,
Then say thou, dear, with softly bated breath,
  " In some lone wilderness beyond the sea,
Whether in light of life, or gloom of death,
  My lover's spirit speaks to God for me ! "
Kiss me, beloved, without doubt or dread ;
We are not sundered, though farewell be said.

All the Year Round.

GOOD-NIGHT.

GOOD-NIGHT, dear friend ! I say good-night to thee
  Across the moonbeams, tremulous and white,
Bridging all space between us, it may be.
  Lean low, sweet friend ; it is the last good-night.

For, lying low upon my couch, and still,
  The fever flush evanished from my face,
I heard them whisper softly, " 'T is His will ;
  Angels will give her happier resting-place ! "

And so from sight of tears that fell like rain,
  And sounds of sobbing smothered close and low,
I turned my white face to the window-pane,
  To say *good-night* to thee before I go.

Good-night ! good-night ! I do not fear the end,
  The conflict with the billows dark and high ;
And yet, if I could touch thy hand, my friend,
  I think it would be easier to die ;

If I could feel through all the quiet waves
  Of my deep hair thy tender breath athrill,
I could go downward to the place of graves
  With eyes ashine and pale lips smiling still ;

Or it may be that, if through all the strife
  And pain of parting I should hear thy call,
I would come singing back to sweet, sweet life,
  And know no mystery of death at all.

It may not be.   Good-night, dear friend, good-night !
    And when you see the violets again,
And hear, through boughs with swollen buds awhite,
    The gentle falling of the April rain,

Remember her whose young life held thy name
    With all things holy, in its outward flight,
And turn sometimes from busy haunts of men
    To hear again her low good-night ! good-night !

HESTER A. BENEDICT.

SAD VENTURES.

I stood and watched my ships go out,
    Each, one by one, unmooring, free,
What time the quiet harbor filled
    With flood-tide from the sea.

The first that sailed, her name was Joy;
    She spread a smooth, white, shining sail,
And eastward drove with bending spars
    Before the sighing gale.

Another sailed, her name was Hope ;
    No cargo in her hold she bore;
Thinking to find in western lands
    Of merchandise a store.

The next that sailed, her name was Love ;
    She showed a red flag at her mast, —
A flag as red as blood she showed,
    And she sped south right fast.

The last that sailed, her name was Faith ;
    Slowly she took her passage forth,
Tacked and lay to ; at last she steered
    A straight course for the north.

My gallant ships, they sailed away
    Over the shimmering summer sea ;
I stood at watch for many a day —
    But one came back to me.

For Joy was caught by pirate Pain ;
    Hope ran upon a hidden reef,
And Love took fire and foundered fast
    In whelming seas of grief.

Faith came at last, storm-beat and torn —
  She recompensed me all my loss ;
For, as a cargo safe, she brought
  A crown linked to a cross.

Boston Cultivator.

HOPE DEFERRED.

His hand at last !   By his own fingers writ,
  I catch my name upon the wayworn sheet :
His hand — oh, reach it to me quick !   And yet,
  Scarce can I hold, so fast my pulses beat.

O feast of soul !   O banquet richly spread !
  O passion-lettered scroll from o'er the sea !
Like a fresh burst of life to one long dead,
  Joy, strength, and bright content come back with thee,

Long prayed and waited for through months so drear ;
  Each day methought my waiting heart must break ;
Why is it that our loved ones grow more dear
  The more we suffer for their sweetest sake ?

His hand at last ! each simple word aglow
  With truthful tenderness and promise sweet.
Now to my daily tasks I 'll singing go,
  Fed by the music of this wayworn sheet.

FATE.

As two proud ships upon the pathless main
Meet once and never hope to meet again, —
Meet once with merry signallings, and part,
Each homeward bound to swell the crowded mart,
So we two met, one golden summer day,
Within the shelter of life's dreaming bay,
And rested, calmly anchored from the world,
For one brief hour, with snowy pinions furled ;
But when the sun sank low along the west,
We left our harbor, with its peaceful rest,
And floated outward in life's tangled sea
With foam-kissed waves between us, wild and free.
As two ships part upon the trackless main,
So we two parted.   Shall we meet again ?

THOUGH LOST TO SIGHT, TO MEM'RY DEAR.

SWEETHEART, good-by! The fluttering sail
    Is spread to waft me far from thee,
And soon before the fav'ring gale
    My ship shall bound upon the sea.
Perchance, all desolate and forlorn,
    These eyes shall miss thee many a year,
But unforgotten every charm, —
    Though lost to sight, to mem'ry dear.

Sweetheart, good-by! one last embrace!
    O cruel Fate, true souls to sever!
Yet in this heart's most sacred place
    Thou, thou alone shalt dwell forever!
And still shall recollection trace,
    In Fancy's mirror, ever near,
Each smile, each tear, that form, that face, —
    Though lost to sight, to mem'ry dear.

        (Verses written in an old memorandum-book.
                The author unknown.)

HIS MESSENGER.

MARJORIE, with the waiting face,
    Marjorie, with the pale brown hair,
She sits and sews in the silent place,
    She counts the steps on the outer stair.
Two, three, four — they pass her door,
    The patient face droops low again,
Still it is as it was before —
Oh! will he come indeed no more,
    And are her prayers all prayed in vain?

Through the warm and the winter night,
    Marjorie, with the wistful eyes,
She keeps her lonely lamp alight
    Until the stars are dim in the skies.
Through the gray and the shining day
    Her pallid fingers, swift and slim,
Set their stitches, nor one astray,
Though her heart it is far away,
    Over the summer seas with him.

Over the distant summer seas
    Marjorie's yearning fancies fly;
She feels the kiss of the island breeze,
    She sees the blue of the tropic sky.

Does she know, as they come and go,
  Those waves that lap the island shore,
That under their ceaseless ebb and flow
Golden locks float to and fro, —
  Tangled locks she will comb no more?

Many a hopeless hope she keeps,
  Marjorie with the aching heart;
Sometimes she smiles, and sometimes she weeps,
  At thoughts that all unbidden start.
I can see what the end will be:
  Some day when the Master sends for her,
A voice she knows will say joyfully,
" God is waiting for Marjorie,"
  And her lover will be his messenger.

PART XIII.

Tragedy and Sorrow.

Such is my name, and such my tale.
    Confessor! to thy secret ear
I breathe the sorrows I bewail,
    And thank thee for the generous tear
This glazing eye could never shed.
Then lay me with the humblest dead,
And, save the cross above my head,
Be neither name nor emblem spread.

BYRON.

PART XIII.

Tragedy and Sorrow.

—◆◇◆—

THE ASH POOL.

The wet wind sobs o'er the sodden leas,
And wails through the branches of leafless trees,
As mourning the seeds in the fallows lost,
And the pale buds peeping to die in the frost,
When Winter asserts his lingering reign,
And his sceptre glitters on hill and plain.
Drearily meadows and uplands lie
'Neath the low long sweep of sullen sky,
And, sad and still as the hushed green Yule,
'Neath the straggling boughs lies the Great Ash Pool.

Black and cold, and stagnant and deep,
No silvery fins from its waters leap;
No brown wings flutter, no pattering feet,
Tell that life in its banks finds safe retreat;
No lily-buds to its surface cling,
But docken and nightshade around it spring;
The very trees that about it stand
Are twisted and gnarled as by witches' hand,
And the ghost of a story of sin and dule
Like a mist hangs over the Great Ash Pool.

When June's soft magic is on the earth,
And the rose and the violet spring to birth,
When the bright becks dance 'neath the bright leaves' shade,
And the wild birds carol from glen and glade,
Not a sunbeam glints on its breast to play,
Not a murmur welcomes the golden day,
No children loiter beside its brink,
No shy fawn lingers its wave to drink;
The old tree's shadow is deep and cool,
Yet no lovers keep tryst at the Great Ash Pool.

Yet once by its waters wild vows were spoken,
In passion heard and in falsehood broken,
Two bright heads over its margin bent,
When the moon to its depths soft radiance lent;
A little while and one face lay there,
With its blue eyes glazed in their last despair, —
Eyes that stared upward through weed and slime,
With their story of sorrow, and shame, and crime;
So, in glory of summer, or gladness of Yule,
A curse hangs over the Great Ash Pool.

———◆———

ACCURSED.

PALLID white the moonlight gloweth
  Through the shadows weird and dim;
Mournfully the river floweth
  Past the cedars gaunt and grim.
    Soft across the twilight bar,
    In the rosy light afar,
    Like a gem of antique splendor,
      Gleams the mystic Eastern star.

Once o'er Judah's hill of purple
  Shone the star like living flame;
Through her valleys, green and fertile,
  Came the echo of His name.
    In those years so long agone —
    In religion's blessed dawn,
    On my head the black curse falleth —
      "Ever — evermore move on."

Eighteen hundred years I 've wandered, —
  And my eyes are dimmed with tears, —
Seeking death where storms have thundered,
  With a heart unknown to fears.
    Years may come and years may go
    In their vast eternal flow,
    But upon my vague, wild wanderings
      Still my weary feet must go.

Shiveringly the night wind waileth
  Sibilant dirges of my doom,
And the gold of evening paleth —
  Fadeth into deeper gloom.
    'Neath the star I kneel and cry,
    " Mercy, mercy, Thou on high!
    Thou whose heart is filled with pity,
      List to my despairing cry!"

Sacramento Union, 1874.

SLANDER.

'T WAS but a breath —
And yet the fair, good name was wilted;
And friends once fond grew cold and stilted,
And life was worse than death.

One venomed word,
That struck its coward, poisoned blow,
In craven whispers, hushed and low —
And yet the wide world heard.

'T was but one whisper — one,
That muttered low, for very shame,
The thing the slanderer dare not name —
And yet its work was done.

A hint so slight,
And yet so mighty in its power,
A human soul in one short hour
Lies crushed beneath its blight.

———◆———

CALUMNY.

A WHISPER woke the air,
A soft, light tone and low,
Yet barbed with shame and woe.
Ah! might it only perish there,
Nor farther go.

But no, a quick and eager ear
Caught up the little, meaning sound;
Another voice has breathed it clear,
And so it wandered round
From ear to lip, from lip to ear,
Until it reached a gentle heart
That throbbed from all the world apart,
And that — it broke.

MRS. FRANCES OSGOOD.

———◆———

THE OUTCAST.

BLEAK winds of the winter, sobbing and moaning,
Pluck not my rags with your pitiless hand;
Here in the darkness, cold and despairing,
Homeless, and friendless, and starving I stand.

Scourged by the white, icy whips of the tempest,
  I wander forlorn on my desolate way,
Forgotten of earth and forsaken of Heaven,
  Too frozen to kneel and too hungry to pray.

I look at the stately and palace-like dwellings
  That line with their grandeur the pathway I tread;
I fancy the brightness and warmth of the hearthstone,
  The plenteous board with the wine and the bread;
I see the heads bowed with a reverent meaning,
  A blessing is breathed o'er the sumptuous fare;
Will it rise to the ear of the pitiful Father,
  Or die of the cold, like the vagabond's prayer?

Hark! Midnight. The chime from the church-tower above me
  Drops solemnly down through the whirl of the storm;
If one could pass through the gate to the portal,
  Could sleep there, and dream it was lighted and warm!
Give away, cruel bars! let me through to a refuge!
  Give away! But I rave, and the fierce winds reply:
"No room in his house for his vagabond children,
  No room in his porch for an outcast to die."

No room in his dwelling — no room in the churches,
  No room in the prison — for hunger's no crime;
Is there room in the bed of the river, I wonder,
  Deep down by the pier in the ooze and the slime?
Mock on, taunting wind! I can laugh back an answer,
  An hour, and your bitterest breath I defy;
Since bars shut me out of God's house among mortals,
  I will knock at the gate of his home in the sky!

                                    MARY L. RITTER.

DESERTED.

COLD! so cold! and the night looks down
On a shivering form in a tattered gown,
On a lone, lone heart, and a pair of eyes
Abrim with life's keen miseries.
      Kiss on kiss
      By the flakes are told,
      Kiss on kiss —
      But oh! so cold.
Even the touch that ought to bless
Mocketh the wanderer's wretchedness.

How can the loved in the land of light
Peer through the dismal deeps of night,
With never a star to break the gloom,
Or sweep one cloud from the path of doom?

Flake on flake
O'er vale and hill,
Flake on flake
With touch so chill,—
With touch that sinks like the shaft of hate
Deep in the heart so desolate.

"Cold! so cold!" and the ruddy glare
Of lights that glint in the frosty air
Reddens each flake that falls upon
A hapless, homeless, friendless one;
Drop by drop
Of the blood-red snow,
Drop by drop
In the cup of woe—
A chalice filled for Want's pale bride,
A pauper's feast for a Christmas-tide.

Joy sails out on the winter's wings,
And tuned for self is the lay she sings;
Its echoes drift with the icy air,
And mock the sufferer's piteous prayer;
Wave on wave
With the night wind strong,
Wave on wave
Of the bitter song
That floats where the sails of hope are furled,
And crowns the wounds of a heartless world.

"Cold! *so* cold!" Not the cutting blast,
Nor the frosty cloak of the night-cloud cast,
But the cramped, unpitying hearts that beat
The rhyme of life in the thronging street.
Throb on throb
With the chime of pelf,
Throb on throb
To the song of self,
But not one pulse to the measure sweet,
That times the love at the mercy-seat.

The night wears on, and the moon sails out,
And the clouds sweep back to the realms of doubt,
And the stars look down for the shivering form
That braved the thrusts of the cruel storm.
Fold on fold
Is the mantle white,
Fold on fold
'Neath the eyes of night;
The drifts are still on the winter's breath,
And the spotless robe is the wing of death.

ONLY A WOMAN.

ONLY a woman, shrivelled and old!
The play of the winds and the prey of the cold!
    Cheeks that are shrunken,
    Eyes that are sunken,
    Lips that were never o'erbold;
Only a woman, forsaken and poor,
Asking an alms at the bronze church-door.

Hark to the organ! roll upon roll
The waves of its music go over the soul!
    Silks rustle past her
    Thicker and faster;
    The great bell ceases its toll.
Fain would she enter, but not for the poor
Swingeth wide open the bronze church-door.

Only a woman — waiting alone,
Icily cold on an ice-cold throne.
    What do they care for her?
    Mumbling a prayer for her,
    Giving not bread but a stone.
Under old laces their haughty hearts beat,
Mocking the woes of their kin in the street!

Only a woman! In the old days
Hope carolled to her, her happiest lays;
    Somebody missed her,
    Somebody kissed her,
    Somebody crowned her with praise;
Somebody faced up the battles of life,
Strong *for her sake* who was mother or wife.

Somebody lies with a tress of her hair
Light on his heart where the death-shadows are;
    Somebody waits for her,
    Opening the gates for her,
    Giving delight for despair.
Only a woman — nevermore poor —
Dead in the snow at the bronze church-door!

        HESTER A. BENEDICT.

BEAUTIFUL SNOW.

(AS ORIGINALLY WRITTEN, DECEMBER, 1852.)

BEAUTIFUL snow! Beautiful snow!
    Falling so lightly,
    Daily and nightly,
Alike round the dwellings of lofty and low.
    Horses are prancing,
    Cheerily dancing,
Stirred by the spirit that comes from the snow.

Beautiful snow! Beautiful snow!
    Up at the dawning,
    In the cold morning,
Children exult, though the winds fiercely blow;
    Hailing the snowflakes
    Falling as day breaks —
Joyful they welcome the beautiful snow.

Beautiful snow! Beautiful snow!
    Childhood's quick glances
    See the bright fancies
Decking the window-panes softly and slow;
    Forest and city,
    Figure so pretty,
Left by the magical fingers of snow.

Beautiful snow! Beautiful snow!
    Atmosphere chilling,
    Carriage-wheels stilling,
Warming the cold earth, and kindling the glow
    Of Christian pity
    For the great city
Of wretched creatures who starve 'mid the snow.

Beautiful snow! Beautiful snow!
    Fierce winds blowing,
    Thickly 't is snowing;
Night gathers round us — how warm then the glow
    Of the fire so bright,
    On the cold winter night,
As we draw in the curtains to shut out the snow.

Beautiful snow! Beautiful snow!
    Round the bright fireside,
    In the long eventide,
Closely we gather though keen the winds blow;
    Safely defended,
    Kindly befriended,
Pity the homeless exposed to the cold, icy snow.

                        Major Sigourney

BEAUTIFUL SNOW.

Oh the snow, the beautiful snow,
Filling the sky and the earth below!
Over the house-tops, over the street,
Over the heads of the people you meet,
      Dancing,
        Flirting,
          Skimming along.
Beautiful snow! it can do no wrong.

Flying to kiss a fair lady's cheek;
Clinging to lips in a frolicsome freak.
Beautiful snow, from the heavens above,
Pure as an angel and fickle as love.

Oh the snow, the beautiful snow!
How the flakes gather and laugh as they go!
Whirling about in its maddening fun,
It plays in its glee with every one.
                    Chasing,
                         Laughing,
                              Hurrying by,
It lights up the face and it sparkles the eye;
And even the dogs with a bark and a bound
Snap at the crystals that eddy around.
The town is alive and its heart in a glow,
To welcome the coming of beautiful snow.

How the wild crowd goes swaying along,
Hailing each other with humor and song!
How the gay sledges like meteors flash by, —
Bright for a moment, then lost to the eye!
                    Ringing,
                         Swinging,
                              Dashing, they go
Over the crest of the beautiful snow;
Snow so pure when it falls from the sky,
To be trampled in mud by the crowd rushing by;
To be trampled and tracked by the thousands of feet,
Till it blends with the horrible filth of the street.

Once I was pure as the snow, — but I fell;
Fell, like the snow-flakes, from heaven — to hell;
Fell to be tramped as the filth of the street;
Fell to be scoffed, to be spit on, and beat.
                    Pleading,
                         Cursing,
                              Dreading to die,
Selling my soul to whoever would buy,
Dealing in shame for a morsel of bread,
Hating the living and fearing the dead.
Merciful God! have I fallen so low?
And yet I was once like the beautiful snow!

Once I was fair as the beautiful snow,
With an eye like its crystals, a heart like its glow;
Once I was loved for my innocent grace, —
Flattered and sought for the charm of my face.
                    Father,
                         Mother,
                              Sisters all,
God, and myself, I have lost by my fall.

The veriest wretch that goes shivering by
Will take a wide sweep, lest I wander too nigh ;
For of all that is on or about me, I know,
There is nothing that's pure but the beautiful snow.

How strange it should be that this beautiful snow
Should fall on a sinner with nowhere to go !
How strange it would be, when the night comes again,
If the snow and the ice struck my desperate brain !
            Fainting,
                Freezing,
                    Dying alone,
Too wicked for prayer, too weak for my moan
To be heard in the crash of the crazy town,
Gone mad in its joy at the snow's coming down ;
To lie and to die in my terrible woe,
With a bed and a shroud of beautiful snow !

Helpless and frail as the trampled-on snow,
Sinner, despair not — Christ stoopeth low
To rescue the soul that is lost in its sin,
And raise it to life and enjoyment again.
            Groaning,
                Bleeding,
                    Dying for thee,
The Crucified hung on the accursed tree.
His accents of mercy fall soft on my ear ;
Is there mercy for me, will he heed my weak prayer ?
O God, in the stream that for sinners doth flow,
Wash me, and I shall be whiter than snow.

                                JAMES W. WATSON.

———◆———

SISTER MADELEINE.

THE blessed hush of eventide
    Over the weary city fell,
    And softly pealed the vesper-bell
Across the waters dim and wide,
    Breathing a sacred spell.

Across the waters wide and dim,
    And through the dusty, murky street,
    The chimes passed on, with silver feet :
Chords of the never-silent hymn
    With which the air doth beat.

They pulsed across the silent space
    Which closed the old cathedral in,
    And rang remotely through the din
That still was in the market-place,
    With echo faint and thin.

One of the bustling, careless throng
  Listened apart, with low-bowed head;
  A toiler, he, for daily bread, —
What time had such to heed the song?
  Why works he not instead?

A far-off look is in his eyes,
  He seeth nothing that is near,
  He only doth those bell-tones hear,
Soft ringing through the purple skies,
  Distant, but ever dear.

Oh, happy magic of their chime!
  The dreams of youth again enfold
  That time-worn spirit, growing old
Too early in this alien clime,
  Where hearts as snow are cold.

But fairest of the treasures sweet
  By memory brought from their dim place,
  Shineth the vision of a face
For angel habitations meet
  In its transcendent grace.

He saw her as she used to stand,
  With parted lips and lifted eyes,
  Watching the wondrous sunset skies,
And pointing, with her slender hand,
  Towards their changeful dyes.

Ah, what can give the world release
  From under thraldom of this pain,
  That life can never know again
The rapturous joy, the trust and peace
  Of youth's departed train?

But not of this he thought to-night:
  The happy days of long ago
  Were round him, with unfaded glow;
The flowers as fresh, the skies as bright,
  As those he used to know.

More deep and dark the shadows grew,
  The bell's last echoes died away
  Within the heavens still and gray.
The peace of night seemed sweet and new
  After the toilful day.

But lo! a sudden, blinding glare
  Shot upward in the northern sky;
  And loud and sharp rang out a cry
That human seemed in its despair, —
  The bells of Trinity,

Which but a few short hours ago
　　Breathed their good-night so tenderly
　　Over the quiet earth and sea,
And faded with the sunset glow
　　Peaceful exceedingly.

But now across the night they ring
　　With a wild terror and despair
　　That thrills through all the fearful air,
Till the wide heavens seem shuddering
　　With the impassioned prayer.

And human hearts have heard the call :
　　Thousands are thronging up the steep
　　Whereon the gray old tower doth keep
Its steadfast vigil over all
　　Within its shade asleep.

Too late, too late the help had come,
　　The flames were curling everywhere,
　　And, fainting in the scorching air,
The very bells at last were dumb
　　In uttermost despair.

But in the silence that succeeds
　　The sudden hushing of the bells,
　　One awful human cry upswells,
And not a listening heart but bleeds
　　For her whose fate it tells.

" Alas, 't is Sister Madeleine ! "
　　The nuns cry out, with faces pale,
　　And then they wring their hands, and wail ;
For sweeter sister ne'er was seen
　　Beneath a convent veil.

But while the thousands held their breath,
　　One listener sprang with footstep light,
　　Pushing the crowd to left and right,
Forcing his way to fiery death,
　　While every cheek grew white.

He vanished through the smoke-veiled door,
　　And higher yet, with fearful glee,
　　The red flames clambered merrily,
Wrapping the lofty tower o'er
　　With splendor sad to see.

The abbess knelt, with ashen face —
　　" For those two souls we cry to Thee,
　　Through Him who died upon the tree,
That Thou wilt grant to them thy grace
　　In their extremity."

A thousand voices cried, "Amen,"—
  And as in answer to the prayer
  Out from the blinding, stifling glare,
Like life that wakens from the dead,
  Forth came the fated pair.

Scorched, blinded, deafened, on they pressed, —
  The dreamer of the market-place,
  Close holding in a last embrace,
Close holding 'gainst a dying breast,
  That dreamed-of angel face.

Parting and pain for both were done;
  Together from the stranger's strand
  Peacefully passed they, hand in hand,
Before the rising of the sun,
  Into the " Silent Land."

CLARE EVEREST.

LAST AND WORST.

UPON life's highway I was hastening, when
  I met a trouble grim,
Whom I had often seen with other men,
  But I was far from him.

He seized my arm, and with a sneering lip
  Looked o'er my happy past;
With sinking heart I felt his bony grip
  Clutch tight and hold me fast.

" You look," said he, " so happy and bright,
  That I have come to see
Why other troubles miss you in their flight,
  And what you 'll do with me."

"And have you come to stay with me?" I cried,
  Hoping respite to win.
" Yes, I have come to stay.   Your world is wide;
  I 'm crowded where I have been."

I would not look him in the face, but turned
  To take him home with me
To all my other troubles, who had spurned
  His hateful company.

So he was "crowded," and with me would roam?
  I laughed with sullen glee;
At arm's length took him up the steps of home
  Under my own roof-tree.

And there I clutched his scrawny neck and thin,
  To thrust him in the room
Where, locked and barred, I kept my troubles, in
  Seclusion's friendly gloom.

Grimly he looked at me with eyes that burned:
  "You nothing know of me;
The key on other troubles may be turned,
  But I — am Poverty."

Ah! soon I knew it was in vain, in vain,
  No locks avail for him;
Nor double doors, nor thickly curtained pane
  Could make his presence dim.

He wrote his name on all my threadbare ways,
  And in my shrinking air;
He told the tale of useless shifts and stays
  I made against despair;

He brushed the smile from off my sweet wife's face,
  And left an anxious frown;
The fresh young joys that should my children grace
  His heavy foot trod down;

He took my other troubles out, and walked
  With them the public street;
Clad in my sacred sorrows, cheaply talked
  With all he chanced to meet.

The hours he stretched upon the rack of days,
  The days to weeks of fears;
The weeks were months, whose weary toilsome ways
  Stretched out through hopeless years.

To-day I stooped to fan with eager strife
  A single hope which glowed,
And 'mid the fading embers of my life
  A fitful warmth bestowed.

Cheered by a spark, I turned with trembling limb
  Once more the strife to wage;
But as I turned I saw my trouble grim
  Linking his arm with Age.

Old age and poverty, — here end the strife!
  And ye, remorseless pair,
Drape on the last, dim milestone of my life
  Your banner of despair.

FRANCES EKIN ALLISON

A LOST LETTER.

JUST read this letter, old friend of mine;
　　I picked it up upon Margate Pier,
In a whirling world of women and wine;
　　'T was blotted and blurred with a fallen tear.
Come, think one minute of years ago,
　　When the chance was with us — a soul to save,
The whim was in us to love, you know,
　　But the woman, she fell to a fool or knave.

" 'T is easy to picture the tortured heart
　　That faced despair and a grief like this."
She saw her lover unloved depart
　　And turn again to a hateful kiss.
" Had I been loved by a man like you " —
　　O weary woman ! O fearful fate !
'T is a passionate cry ; but it strikes me through,
　　Who sigh too soon, but who love too late.

" Who was the woman ? "   I seem to trace
　　Her footprints here in Vanity Fair :
A mother, perchance, with an earnest face ;
　　A wife with a glory of Titian hair ;
A soul perplexed, and a faith at stake,
　　A life nigh lost — there are thousands such
Who face the world, when their heart-strings break
　　For the one kind word and the tender touch !

Who was the man ?   What matter at all ?
　　'T is man who ruins and sows the tears ;
'T is men who tempt, but women who fall,
　　And are never absolved in the deathless years.
The least we can do, O brothers, is this ;
　　Whilst love is with us, and life seems down,
We can soothe the sad with a gentle kiss,
　　And dry the eyes that our sins can drown !

Go back, lost letter of wild despair,
　　I will cast you forth on the infinite sea ;
But the day glides on, and the Margate air
　　Is piercing sweet to the world and me.
But still I can never forget — can you ? —
　　That cry that nothing can soothe or cease ;
" Had I been loved by a man like you,
　　I had lived far better and died in peace ! "

CLEMENT SCOTT.

NOTE. — Extract from a letter picked up on Margate Pier : " I am so sorry
you are obliged to go away to-day. You do not know how much I care to
be with you. You are so different to other men, — so kind to me. If I had
known a man like you years ago, I might have been a better woman."

PART XIV.

Every-day Lights and Shadows.

The thoughtless world to majesty may bow,
* Exalt the brave, and idolize success;*
But more to innocence their safety owe
* Than power or genius e'er conspired to bless.*

And thou who, mindful of the unhonored Dead,
* Dost in these notes their artless tales relate,*
By night and lonely contemplation led
* To wander in the gloomy walks of fate:*

Hark! how the sacred calm, that breathes around,
* Bids every fierce, tumultuous passion cease;*
In still small accents whispering from the ground,
* A grateful earnest of eternal peace.*

Lines rejected from the "Elegy."   GRAY.

PART XIV.

Every-day Lights and Shadows.

NOTHING AT ALL IN THE PAPER TO-DAY.

NOTHING at all in the paper to-day !
　　Only a murder somewhere or other ;
A girl who has put her child away,
　　Not being a wife as well as a mother ;
Or a drunken husband beating a wife,
　　With the neighbors lying awake to listen,
Scarce aware he has taken a life,
　　Till in at the window the dawn rays glisten.
But that is all in the regular way —
There 's nothing at all in the paper to-day.

Nothing at all in the paper to-day !
　　To be sure, there 's a woman died of starvation,
Fell down in the street, as so many may
　　In this very prosperous Christian nation ;
Or two young girls, with some inward grief
　　Maddened, have plunged in the inky waters ;
Or father has learnt that his son 's a thief,
　　Or mother been robbed of one of her daughters.
Things that occur in their regular way —
There 's nothing at all in the paper to-day.

There 's nothing at all in the paper to-day,
　　Unless you care about things in the city —
How great rich rogues for their crimes must pay
　　(Though all gentility cries out, " Pity ! ")
Like the meanest shop-boy that robs a till.
　　There 's a case to-day, if I 'm not forgetting,
The lad only " borrowed " — as such lads will —
　　To pay some money he lost in betting ;
But there 's nothing in this that 's out of the way —
There 's nothing at all in the paper to-day.

Nothing at all in the paper to-day
  But the births and bankruptcies, deaths and marriages,
But life's events in the old survey,
  With Virtue begging, and Vice in carriages;
And kindly hearts under ermine gowns,
  And wicked breasts under hodden gray;
For goodness belongs not only to clowns,
  And o'er others than lords does sin bear sway.
But what do I read? "Drowned! wrecked!"   Did I say
There was nothing at all in the paper to-day?

CITY CONTRASTS.

A BAREFOOTED child on the crossing,
  Sweeping the mud away,
A lady in silks and diamonds,
  Proud of the vain display;
A beggar blind on the curbstone,
  A rich man passing along;
A tiny child with a tambourine
  Wailing out her life in song.

A pauper in lone hearse passing,
  Hurried away to the tomb;
A train of carriages, music grand,
  And the flutter of waving plume.
For the one there is never a mourner,
  He cumbered the earth alway;
For the other the flags at half-mast droop,
  And the city wears black to-day.

A soldier with one sleeve empty,
  That sadly hangs by his side,
Another shuffling along the walk
  In the flush of health and pride;
A cripple-girl slowly toiling
  Through the vexed and crowded street,
And tearfully gazing at those who pass
  With hearts as light as their feet.

A wreck of a woman flaunting,
  As if proud of her very shame,
A purer sister whose modest cheeks
  Would crimson e'en at the name;
A petty thief stealing in terror,
  Afraid in your face to gaze,
And one who has robbed by thousands,
  Courting the sun's broad blaze.

The millionnaire in his carriage,
  The workman plodding along,
The humble follower of the right,
  And the slave of the giant wrong;
The murderer seeking a refuge,
  Looking ever wearily back,
And the sleuth-hounds of the broken law
  Following silently in his track.

The judge, freed now of the ermine,
  Pompous of place and power,
And the shivering wretch his word will doom
  To prison within an hour;
The miser clutching his pennies,
  The spendthrift squandering gold,
The meek-eyed Sister of Mercy,
  And the woman brazen and bold.

The widow, in weeds of blackness,
  Meets the bride at the church door —
The future for one holds nothing but tears,
  But joy for the other in store.
A cradle jostles a coffin —
  Orange-flowers, with honeyed breath,
Are wove by the self-same fingers
  That but now made a cross for death.

Dives and Lazarus elbow
  Each other whene'er they meet,
And the crumbs from the rich man's table
  Feed the beggar upon the street.
And penury crowdeth plenty,
  And sin stalks boldly abroad,
And the infidel holds his head proudly
  As the child of the living God.

The bee in its ceaseless searching
  Finds sweets in each flower fair,
And the noisome spider, creeping up,
  Finds nothing but poison there.
And so life is made up of contrasts —
  Rich and poor, coward and brave,
Virtue and vice, and all will find
  Equality in the grave.

THE HUMMING OF THE WIRES.

OVER the telegraph wires
  The wild winds sweep to-day,
And I catch a musical humming
  As of harpers at their play, —
As of distant bells slow ringing
  At the dying of the day.

Many the messages shooting
  Along the slender line,
And it seems as if every message
  Must have left some voice behind, —
Must have set the bells to swinging,
  That I hear in silvery chime.

Tidings of death are they sending ?
  So hushed the sad refrain !
Now it quickens, merrily quickens,
  And it peals a blither strain !
Of its joy some heart is telling,
  Ring, O bells, glad bells, again !

Here by the track I am asking,
  These varying sounds so blend,
Whether God, who wills for his children
  All events toward good shall tend,
May not hear our joys and sorrows
  In like harmony ascend.

Over the marsh by the railroad
  The wild winds sweep to-day,
And they touch the telegraph wires,
  And a strange, weird tune they play,
Till the air is sweet with harpings,
  And with church-bells far away.

Boston Journal.   EDWARD A. RAND.

THE TELEGRAPH CLERK.

SITTING here by my desk all day,
  Hearing the constant click
As the messages speed on their way,
  And the call comes sharp and quick —
Oh, what a varied tale they tell
  Of joy and hope and fear !
The funeral knell and the marriage bell
  In their steady tick I hear.

" *Mother is dying ; come at once.*"
   And the tears will almost start,
For tender daughters and loving sons —
   God pity each aching heart !
Ah ! how the haunting memories press
   Back to the mind once more,
Of the mother's unfailing tenderness,
   That is now forever o'er.

" *I am well ; will come to-night.*"
   How bright some eyes will glow
All day long with a happy light
   As they watch the moments go.
" *Have had no letters ; is something wrong ?* "
   Some heart is sad to-day,
Counting the hours that seem so long
   For the sake of one away.

" *Arthur Ross, by accident killed ;
   Tell his mother, am coming home.*"
Alas for the home with such sorrow filled,
   When the bitter tidings come !
" *Alice is better ; gaining fast.*"
   And hearts that have been bowed
Under their weight of fear, at last
   Shall lose their weary load.

So over the wires the tidings speed,
   Bitter and grave and gay;
Some hearts shall beat, and some shall bleed,
   For the tale they have to say.
As I sit all day by my desk alone
   I hear the stream go by,
And catch the wires' changeful tone,
   With a smile and then a sigh.

GOING HOME IN THE MORNING.

A POOR little bird trilled a song in the west, —
A poor little bird with a stain on its breast.
Beaten down by the rain and too weak for flight,
It fell in the city unseen in the night.
As it trilled its sad song, other birds of the air,
The respectable ones, wondered who could be there.
Out in the darkness, while passing, I heard
The wail of the poor little vagabond bird.
Being homeless myself, I hunted and found
The weak little vagrant stretched out on the ground.
I raised it, and gave it of all I possessed,
A warm cosey shelter close up to my breast;

And I whispered : " Don't worry, rather whistle and sing,
You poor little innocent vagabond thing.
Very soon now the storm will have passed from the sky,
Very soon, too, the sun will be shining on high,
    And you shall go home in the morning."

A broken-down man then was walking the street;
As I passed him I stayed for a moment my feet.
Cried the man : " It is hard !   So many have health
And beauty and youth and pleasure and wealth,
Whilst we are unnoticed by God or by man,
Accursed and degraded, and under the ban ! "
" My brother," said I, " I am seeking, like you,
For a something to eat, for a something to do;
Let us keep on our way, let us keep it together,
Through the cold and the mire and the pitiless weather,
Hoping still for the best ; soon the night will be gone,
And after the night always cometh the dawn,
    And we can go home in the morning."

We paused as we passed an old rickety shed ;
We glanced well within — then we glanced overhead ;
The sky with the darkness was all overcast,
The snowflakes whirled down and clung to us fast ;
How I fondled my bird — it had no one to love it.
Said the man : " This is bad — grows worse and more of it ; "
But we entered the shed, and out under the lamp
Slowly drifted anigh us the form of a tramp.
To be out in the storm-blast ! Ah, me ! 't was a sin !
So I stepped from the shelter, invited her in,
And took the poor babe, without wasting of words,
And then, you 'll perceive, I had two little birds !
And we all stood there hungry, haggard, and wan,
Awaiting in silence the coming of dawn,
    So we could go home in the morning.

An hour ere dawn, being cold and a-shiver,
We moved all together a-down to the river.
Thus passing, the poor little bird from the west
Trilled a poor little song.   It was doing its best
To help us along, and it tried hard to sing ;
But being a famished and pitiful thing,
It skipped now and then a few bars, and a note
Died out now and then in its weak little throat.
The babe on my arm lay and listened awhile,
Then looked in my face with a wondering smile,
As out through my vest, that was ragged and torn,
Peeped the poor little bird, who thought it was morn,
And twittered, and looked at the child and its mother ;
And the child and the bird grieved the one for the other,

And thought it was strange in a city of priests
Two such innocent things should be out on the streets.
Well, we passed on our way — a vagabond crew,
Yet I think in our hearts every one of us knew
    That we should go home in the morning.

We came to the ferry-house, stately and tall,
And crowded for warmth in the shade of the wall.
Then I saw, 'mid the dirt and the filth at my feet,
A crust of nice bread lying out on the street;
I grasped it and gave to the woman; she smiled
And said, " It don't matter now, me and the child,
    We are going home in the morning."

It was very near daybreak, I noticed at last
A streak like the dawn afar off in the east.
Then we moved all together — they loosened the bar —
We passed through the gates that were standing ajar;
Moved down the incline where, toward us afloat,
From over the river was drifting the boat.
We had nothing to pay — no passage — no fares —
For the houseless and homeless there 's nobody cares;
With the bird and the child and the vagabond crew
I sailed from the shore, and I very well knew
    Where we all should rejoice in the morning.

                WAYNE DOUGLAS.

DEAD IN HIS BED.

ONLY a man dead in his bed — that is all !
Stark, stiff, and rigid — white face to the wall.

Come out of yesterday somewhere, to here —
Well, no : don't think he had friends anywheres near.

Wanted employment — that 's what he said ;
No work to give him — next thing, he 's dead.

What did he die of, sir ?   Can any one tell ?
A fit, did they think it was ?   Last night he was well.

Heart-disease ?   May be.   What was his name ?
Don't know; did n't register, sir, when he came.

Laud'num, they say it was, there on the stand —
No, stranger ; don't reckon he held a fair hand.

Suicide ?   Yes, that 's what the coroner said —
Scooped out, was what put the thing into his head

Money? Guess not, sir. Why, he had n't enough
To pay for this hole in the sod, of the stuff.

Friends, did you ask? Oh, yes! Sometime or other —
Reckon, of course, the boy *once* had a mother.

Rather rough on him, pard; but where 's it to end,
When you 're panned out of cash and can't count on a friend?

Down to the calaboose — that 's where they took him;
Good enough place, when a man's money 's forsook him!

Funeral? Just you see that express at the coroner's!
County can't pay for no hearse, nor no mourners.

Well, stranger, you 've got me! Can pray if you will —
Rather late in the day, when a man 's dead and still.

Strikes me, it don't count, to this, under my spade;
And as for the rest of him — stranger, that 's played.

No offence, sir; beg pardon, but strikes me as fair,
And a pretty sure way to get answer to prayer,

Better give a poor devil a lift while he 's here,
Than wait till he 's passed in his checks over there!

A. L. BALLOU.

GUILTY, OR NOT GUILTY?

SHE stood at the bar of justice,
  A creature wan and wild,
In form too small for a woman,
  In feature too old for a child.
For a look so worn and pathetic
  Was stamped on her pale young face,
It seemed long years of suffering
  Must have left that silent trace.

" Your name," said the judge, as he eyed her
  With kindly look, yet keen,
" Is — ? " " Mary McGuire, if you please, sir."
  " And your age? " " I am turned fifteen."
" Well, Mary — " And then from a paper
  He slowly and gravely read,
" You are charged here — I am sorry to say it —
  With stealing three loaves of bread.

" You look not like an offender,
　And I hope that you can show
The charge to be false.   Now, tell me,
　Are you guilty of this, or no ? "
A passionate burst of weeping
　Was at first her sole reply ;
But she dried her tears in a moment,
　And looked in the judge's eye.

" I will tell you just how it was, sir ;
　My father and mother are dead,
And my little brothers and sisters
　Were hungry, and asked me for bread.
At first I earned it for them
　By working hard all day,
But somehow the times were hard, sir,
　And the work all fell away.

" I could get no more employment ;
　The weather was bitter cold ;
The young ones cried and shivered
　(Little Johnnie 's but four years old).
So what was I to do, sir ?
　I am guilty, but do not condemn ;
I *took* — oh, was it *stealing ?* —
　The bread to give to them."

Every man in the court-room —
　Graybeard and thoughtless youth —
Knew, as he looked upon her,
　That the prisoner spake the truth.
Out from their pockets came kerchiefs,
　Out from their eyes sprung tears,
And out from old faded wallets
　Treasures hoarded for years.

The judge's face was a study,
　The strangest you ever saw,
As he cleared his throat and murmured
　Something about the *law.*
For one so learned in such matters,
　So wise in dealing with men,
He seemed on a simple question
　Sorely puzzled just then.

But no one blamed him, or wondered,
　When at last these words they heard,
" The sentence of this young prisoner
　Is for the present deferred."
And no one blamed him, or wondered,
　When he went to her and smiled,
And tenderly led from the court-room,
　Himself, the " guilty " child.

SCANDAL-MONGERS.

Do you hear the scandal-mongers
          Passing by,
Breathing poison in a whisper,
          In a sigh?
Moving cautiously and slow,
Smiling sweetly as they go,
Never noisy — gliding smoothly as a snake,
     Supping here and sliding there
     Through the meadows fresh and fair,
Leaving subtle slime and poison in their wake.

Saw you not the scandal-monger
          As she sat
Beaming brightly 'neath the roses
          On her hat?
In her dainty gloves and dress
Angel-like, and nothing less,
Seemed she — casting smiles and pleasing words about.
     Once she shrugged and shook her head,
     Raised her eyes and nothing said,
When you spoke of friends, and yet it left a doubt.

Did you watch the scandal-monger
          At the ball?
Through the music, rhythm, beauty,
          Light, and all,
Moving here and moving there,
With a whisper light as air,
Casting shadows on a sister woman's fame —
     Just a whispered word or glance —
     As she floated through the dance,
And a doubt forever hangs upon a name.

You will find the scandal-mongers
          Everywhere;
Sometimes men, but often women,
          Young and fair;
Yet their tongues drip foulest slime,
And they spend their leisure time
Casting mud on those who climb by work and worth!
     Shun them, shun them as you go —
     Shun them, whether high or low;
They are but the cursed serpents of the earth.

THE CHURNING SONG.

APRON on and dash in hand,
O'er the old churn here I stand, —
    Cachug!
How the thick cream spurts and flies,
Now on shoes and now in eyes! —
    Cachug! Cachug!

Ah! how soon I tired get!
But the butter lingers yet;
    Cachug!
Aching back and weary arm
Quite rob churning of its charm! —
    Cachug! Cachug!

See the golden specks appear!
And the churn rings sharp and clear, —
    Cachink!
Arms, that have to flag begun,
Work on, you will soon be done, —
    Cachink! Cachink!

Rich flakes cling to lid and dash;
Hear the thin milk's watery splash! —
    Calink!
Sweetest music to the ear,
For it says the butter's here! —
    Calink! Calink!

St. Nicholas.
                 SILAS DINSMORE.

TURNED OUT FOR RENT.

OUT, out in the night, in the chill wintry air,
Turned out on the pave with its stones cold and bare;
Shut out from her home with its sad dearth of bread,
Alone with her God and the stars overhead!
Cast out with her babe still asleep on her breast,
Asleep to the sorrow that mars not his rest;
Asleep to the new pearls bedecking his hair,
Bright gems from the sea of his mother's despair.
Out, out like her Lord, "with no place for her head,"
All friendless, and houseless, and starving for bread;
Thus brought face to face with her life's direst woe,
And yet 't is unfelt 'neath a bitterer blow;
For this is the wail, voiceless, deep in her heart,
"Cast out like a thief, put to shame, set apart!"
But what hath she done, with her wild startled eyes,
And what with her tremulous, short, gasping sighs?

Ah, what, with her weary and faltering feet,
Now dragging like lead through the fast darkening street?
What! Is one so weak found a dangerous thing,
Concealing 'mid softness a treacherous sting,
That ye to expel her have borrowed a need
Of two brawny knights of the star and the reed;
This, this is her crime — O ye winds, whisper low!
Nor give to the echoes her sad tale of woe,
Lest they tell the hills, and the beasts cry, "For shame!"
— Gaunt poverty fills all her measure of blame.

M. L. S. Burke.

AT THE COURT-HOUSE DOOR.

No! no! I don't defend him —
   You need n't, sir, be afraid!
Of course he 's bad, and he 's broke the laws,
   And they 've got to be obeyed;
But I can't help kind of thinking —
   I beg your pardon, squire ! —
If we had had a start like him
   We might n't got much higher.

"So poor?" 'T wan't that ! — 't wan't that, sir!
   A home may be awful bare,
And keep some kind of quiet
   And show of comfort there;
But when it 's all dirt and disorder —
   I never saw such a place ! —
And you see folks said 't would always be,
   Because it was in the race;

And it had been so — that 's true, sir;
   His father was very bad;
And the poor boy looked some like him —
   And 't was all against the lad;
Folks would n't allow that anything good
   Could come of such a stock —
Kind folks they were, too, in everything else,
   But here as set as a rock.
They would n't employ him to labor —
   They did n't want him around;
There were plenty of nice young fellows,
   That needed work, to be found.

And his mother — she was a drunkard;
   And that was against him, too!
And so, no home, no comfort,
   And nothing to get to do.

Oh, well ! folks always expected —
　　His poor old father, you see —
'T is curious how their figures
　　And the way he went agree !
But I 've thought a good deal about it,
　　And I 've kind of made it out,
That the way to bring up a fellow
　　Is n't just to kick him about !

I don't think much of talking,
　　And I have n't much to say ;
But the better you use a creature,
　　The more you will get to pay.
And we who have had our chances,
　　And friends to give us a lift,
Won't be too hard on this one,
　　That the town has set adrift ;
For if the neighbors had took to him,
　　And tried to help him along,
You see — it may be, brother,
　　He had n't gone quite so wrong !

———◆———

TRUST.

SEARCHING for strawberries ready to eat,
Finding them crimson, and large, and sweet,
What do you think I found at my feet,
　　Deep in the green hillside ?
Four brown sparrows, the cunning things
Feathered on back and breast and wings,
Proud with the dignity plumage brings,
　　Opening their four mouths wide.

Stooping low to scan my prize,
Watching the motions with curious eyes,
Dropping my berries in glad surprise,
　　A plaintive sound I heard.
And looking up at the mournful call,
I spied on a beech near the old stone wall,
Trembling and twittering, ready to fall,
　　The poor little mother-bird.

With grief and terror her heart was wrung,
And while to the slender bough she clung,
She felt that the lives of her birdlings hung
　　On a still more slender thread.
"Ah, birdie ! " I said, " if you only knew
My heart was tender and warm and true ! "
But the thought that I loved the birdlings too
　　Never entered her small brown head.

And so through this world of ours we go,
Bearing our burdens of needless woe;
Many a heart beating heavy and slow
    Under its load of care.
But oh, if we only, only knew
That God was tender, warm, and true,
And that he loved us through and through,
    Our hearts would be lighter than air.

———◆———

WABASH VIOLETS.

WHAT? Sho'! You don't! Do you mean it, though?
    Are you really goin' with me
To meetin' in all that bandbox rig?
    I'm so awkward, don't you see?
A reg'lar Hoosier. Yes, I know
    We're cousins, as you say;
But I growed wild on the Wabash here,
    And you like a sweet nosegay

Sprung sprightly-like to life in the air
    Miles away, in Boston town.
Why, 't would be like a schoolma'am, college bred,
    A-walking with a clown.
No, I don't guess that's just what I'd say;
    But — what? what's that? As we stroll
We'll gather some violets by the way,
    To put in my buttonhole?

Do you know, I don't exactly see
    What you find in them little things
To make you go as crazy as though
    They was like an angel's wings?
If they was bright and handsome, now,
    Like a poppy or a marigold,
I'd work like a man, and gather for you
    All that your arms could hold.

It's culture that makes one like such flowers?
    Yes, I reckon that's 'bout so;
But that's a yarb that grows more peart
    In Boston than here, you know.
But some here, too, thinks a right smart chance
    Of violets, cousin Kate —
Like schoolma'ams, you know, and notional gals,
    As takes their poetry straight.

Don't know but I might have liked 'em too,
    But for memories of a thing
That happened a dozen years ago,
    In the days of early spring.

It seems like a dream.   Jim Brown and I
　　We used to spend whole hours,
When we could n't find anything else to do,
　　A-battlin' with them flowers.

We called them "roosters."   Don't you see
　　How their necks lap over, so?
And then, when we pull, the strongest one
　　Jerks the other's head off.   Oh,
The fun we had !   We 'd gather piles,
　　And hunt for the largest ones,
And then sit down on a rotten log
　　And fight like bloody Huns.

The violets' heads would drop in a pile,
　　Till I sometimes think a peck
Or more would be scraped up side of the log,
　　Where the war was neck and neck.
A joke ? Well, I reckon. . . . But that 's why
　　I can't give myself away
O'er the little posies, just as though
　　They was pinies or poppies gay.

Well, yes, I reckon there 's a lesson here,
　　If you 're bound to look for one ;
There 's many a page of poetry sp'iled
　　From a-draggin' it down to fun.
If the fountain-head of youth is foul,
　　Its stream through life will be riled ;
Because these flowers were "roosters" then,
　　My love for them now is sp'iled.

EARL MARBLE.

THE WATER-MILL.

LISTEN to the water-mill
　　Through the livelong day ;
How the clanking of the wheels
　　Wears the hours away !
Languidly the autumn wind
　　Stirs the greenwood leaves ;
From the fields the reapers sing,
　　Binding up the sheaves ;
And a proverb haunts my mind,
　　As a spell is cast :
"The mill will never grind
　　With the water that has passed."

Take the lesson to thyself,
　　Living heart and true ;
Golden years are floating by,
　　Youth is passing too ;

Learn to make the most of life,
  Lose no happy day;
Time will never bring thee back
  Chances swept away.
Leave no tender word unsaid;
  Love while life shall last, —
"The mill will never grind
  With the water that has passed."

Work while yet the daylight shines,
  Man of strength and will;
Never does the streamlet glide
  Useless by the mill.
Wait not till to-morrow's sun
  Beams upon the way;
All that thou canst call thine own
  Lies in thy to-day.
Power, intellect, and health
  May not, cannot last;
"The mill will never grind
  With the water that has passed."

Oh, the wasted hours of life
  That have drifted by;
Oh, the good we might have done,
  Lost without a sigh;
Love that we might once have saved
  By a single word;
Thoughts conceived, but never penned,
  Perishing unheard.
Take the proverb to thine heart,
  Take! oh, hold it fast! —
"The mill will never grind
  With the water that has passed."

                              Sarah Doudney.

Note. — The authorship of this poem has been credited with singular
persistency to Gen. Daniel C. McCallum, but without justification.

STONE THE WOMAN, LET THE MAN GO FREE.

Yes, stone the woman, let the man go free!
Draw back your skirts, lest they perchance may touch
Her garment as she passes; but to him
Put forth a willing hand to clasp with his
That led her to destruction and disgrace.
Shut up from her the sacred ways of toil,
That she no more may win an honest meal;
But ope to him all honorable paths

Where he may win distinction ; give to him
Fair, pressed-down measures of life's sweetest joys.
Pass her, O maiden, with a pure, proud face,
If she puts out a poor, polluted palm ;
But lay thy hand in his on bridal day,
And swear to cling to him with wifely love
And tender reverence. Trust him who led
A sister woman to a fearful fate.

Yes, stone the woman, let the man go free !
Let one soul suffer for the guilt of two —
It is the doctrine of a hurried world,
Too out of breath for holding balances
Where nice distinctions and injustices
Are calmly weighed.   But ah, how will it be
On that strange day of final fire and flame,
When men shall wither with a mystic fear,
And all shall stand before the one true Judge ?
Shall sex make *then* a difference in sin ?
Shall he, the searcher of the hidden heart,
In his eternal and divine decree
Condemn the woman and forgive the man ?

THE BAR-TENDER'S STORY.

WHEN I knowed him at first there was suthin',
   A sort of a general air,
That was wery particular pleasin',
   And what you might call — debonair.
I 'm aware that expression is Frenchy,
   And highfalutin, perhaps,
Which accounts that I have the acquaintance
   Of several quality chaps,

And such is the way they converses.
   But, speakin' of this here young man, —
Apparently natur' had shaped him
   On a sort of a liberal plan ;
Had give him good looks and good language,
   And manners expressin' with vim
His belief in hisself, and that others
   Was just as good fellers as him.

Well, this chap was n't stuck up, by no means,
   Nor inclined to be easy put down ;
And was thought to be jolly agreeable
   Wherever he went around town.
He used to come in for his beverage
   Quite regular every night ;
And I took a consid'able interest
   In mixing the thing about right.

A judicious indulgence in liquids
    It is nat'ral for me to admire ;
But I 'm free to admit that for some folks
    They is pison complete and entire ;
For rum, though a cheerful companion,
    As a boss is the Devil's own chum ;
And this chap, I am sorry to state it,
    Was floored in a wrastle with rum.

For he got to increasin' his doses,
    And took 'em more often, he did, —
And it growed on him faster and faster,
    Till inter a bummer he slid.
I was grieved to observe this here feller
    A shovin' hisself down the grade,
And I lectured him onto it sometimes,
    At the risk of its injurin' trade.

At last he got thunderin' seedy,
    And lost his respect for hisself,
And all his high notions of honor
    Was bundled away on the shelf.
But at times he was dreadful remorseful,
    Whenever he 'd stop for to think,
And he 'd swear to reform hisself frequent,
    And end it by takin' a drink.

What saved that young feller ?   A woman !
    She done it the singlerest way, —
He come into the bar-room one evenin'
    (He had n't been drinkin' that day),
And sot hisself down to a table,
    With a terrible sorrowful face,
And he sot there a groanin' repeated,
    And callin' hisself a gone case.

He was thinkin', and thinkin', and thinkin',
    And cussin' hisself and his fate,
And ended his thinkin', as usual,
    By orderin' a Bourbon straight.
He was holdin' the glass in his fingers,
    When into the place, from the street,
There come a young gal like a spirit,
    With a face that was wonderful sweet ;

And she glided right up to the table,
    And took the glass gently away,
And she says to him, " George, it is over ;
    I am only a woman to-day !
I rejected you once in my anger,
    But I come to you, lowly and meek ;
For I can't live without you, my darling ;
    I thought I was strong, but I 'm weak.

" You are bound in a terrible bondage,
 And I come, love, to share it with you ;
Is there shame in the deed ?   I can bear it,
 For, at last, to my love I am true ;
I have turned from the home of my childhood,
 And I come to you, lover and friend,
Leaving comfort, contentment, and honor;
 And I'll stay till the terrible end.

" Is there hunger and want in the future ?
 I will share them with you, and not shrink !
And together we'll join in the pleasures,
 The woes, and the dangers of drink ! "
Then she raised up the glass, firm and steady,
 But her face was as pale as the dead, —
" Here's to wine, and the joys of carousals,
 The songs and the laughter," she said.

Then he riz up, his face like a tempest,
 And took the glass out of her hand,
And slung it away, stern and savage, —
 And, I tell you, his manner was grand !
And he says, " I have done with it, Nellie,
 And I'll turn from the ways I have trod,
And I'll live to be worthy of you, dear,
 So help me, a merciful God ! "

What more was remarked, it is needless
 For me to attempt to relate ;
It was some time ago since it happened,
 But the sequel is easy to state :
I seen that same feller last Monday,
 Lookin' nobby and han'some and game ;
He was wheeling a vehicle, gen'lemen,
 And a baby was into the same.

DAVID L. PROUDFIT.

———◆———

DUTY'S REWARD.

IT was an English summer day,
 Some six or seven years ago,
That a pointsman before his cabin paced,
 With a listless step, and slow.
He lit his pipe — there was plenty of time —
 In his work there was nothing new ;
Just to watch the signals and shift the points
 When the next train came in view.

He leant 'gainst his cabin and smoked away,
 He was used to lounge and wait ;
Twelve hours at a stretch he must mind those points,
 And down-trains were mostly late !

A rumble, a roar, — " She 's coming now —
  She 's truer to time to-day ! "
He turns, and not far between the rails
  Sees his youngest boy at play.

Not far, *but too far !* The train is at hand,
  And the child is crawling there,
And patting the ground with crows of delight —
  And not a moment to spare !
His face was dead white, but his purpose firm,
  As straight to his post he trod,
And shifted the points and saved the down-train,
  And trusted his child to God.

There 's a rush in his ears, though the train has passed ;
  He gropes, for he cannot see,
To the place where the laughing baby crawled,
  Where the mangled limbs must be.
But he hears a cry that is only of fear,
  His joy seems too great to bear ;
For his duty done, God saw to his son —
  The train had not touched a hair.

———◆———

GENTLEMAN JIM.

In the Diamond Shaft worked Gentleman Jim,
Handsome of face and stout of limb,
Coarse in dress ; but something in him,
Whether down in the coal mine, soiled and grim,
Or wandering alone in holiday time,
Won the love and respect of all in that clime.

He had no sweetheart, he had no wife,
Some mighty sorrow had dimmed his life —
His earnings hardly won, and small,
Were aye at the orphans' and widows' call —
Of those who had perished in shaft or winze,
He was the friend of all living things,
And moving along in those toilsome ways,
He wore the demeanor of gentler days.

In April last, when the mine fell in,
Beneath the timbers stood Gentleman Jim ;
With a giant grasp he flung two of the boys
Clear of the danger — with deafening noise
The shaft gave way on every side ;
The boys were safe, but Jim — he died ;
Died as men die, and will die again,
Giving their lives for their fellow-men.

When rocks and timbers were cleared away,
And Jim borne up to the light of day,
They took from his bosom, stained with blood,
Two withered leaves and a withered bud
Pinned on a card. " Toute à toi — Marie,"
Was written beneath them; beneath it he,
On this relic his heart for years had worn,
Had written, " All withered — except the thorn."

What life romance, what story of wrong,
This man had locked up in his soul so long,
None who loved him may ever know ;
But the tale of his glorious chivalric deed
Shall not perish as long as men hold this creed, —
That the hero whose blood for his kind is shed
Wins a deathless fame and an honored bed ;
A monument grander than sculptor ere gave,
In the glory that hallows the martyr's grave.

San Francisco Mail.   DANIEL O'CONNELL.

---◆---

FATHER JOHN.

HE preached but little; argued less;
But if a girl was in distress,
Or if a kinchen came to grief,
Or trouble tackled rogue or thief,
There Father John was sure to be,
To blunt the edge of misery ;
And somehow managed every time
To ease despair or lessen crime.

That corner house was allus known
Around these parts as Podger's Own,
Till two pals in a drunken fight
Set the whole thing afire one night ;
And where it stood they hypered round,
And blasted rocks and shovelled ground
To build the factory over there —
The one you see ; and that is where
Poor Father John — God give him rest ! —
Preached his last sermon and his best.

One summer's day the thing was done ;
The workmen set a blast and run ;
They ain't so keerful here, I guess,
Where lives ain't worth a cent apiece,
As in the wards where things are dear,
And nothink ain't so cheap as here ;
Leastwise, the first they seed or knowed,
A little chick had crossed the road ;

26

He seemed to be just out of bed —
Bare-legged, with nothink on his head;
Chubby and cunnin', with his hair
Blown criss-cross by the mornin' air;
Draggin' a tin horse by a string,
Without much care for anything;
A talkin' to hisself for joy, —
A toddlin', keerless, baby boy.

Right for the crawlin' fuse he went,
As though to find out what it meant;
Trudgin' toward the fatal spot
Till less 'n three feet off he got
From where the murderin' thing lay still,
Just waitin' for to spring and kill —
Marching along toward his grave,
And not a soul dared go to save!

They hollered — all they durst to do;
He turned and laughed, and then bent low
To set the horsey on his feet,
And went right on a crowin' sweet!
And then a death-like silence grew
On all the tremblin', coward crew,
As each swift second seemed the last
Before the roaring of the blast.

Just then some chance or purpose brought
The priest.   He saw, and quick as thought
He ran and caught the child and turned
Just as the slumberin' powder burned,
And shot the shattered rocks around,
And with its thunder shook the ground.

The child was sheltered!   Father John
Was hurt to death.   Without a groan,
He set the baby down, then went
A step or two; but life was spent.
He tottered, looked up to the skies
With ashen face, but strange, glad eyes.
" My love, I come ! " was all he said,
Sank slowly down, and so was dead!

Stranger, he left a memory here
That will be felt for many a year:
And since that day this ward has been
More human in its dens of sin.

PART XV.

War and Peace.

But *three feet* good of that old wood,
  So scarred in war, and rotten,
Was thrown aside, unknown its pride,
  Its honors all forgotten:

When, as in shade the block was laid,
  Two robins, perching on it,
Thought that place best to build a nest, —
  They planned it, and have done it:

The splintered spot which lodged a shot
  Is lined with moss and feather,
And, chirping loud, a callow brood
  Are nestling up together.

How full of bliss, — how peaceful is
  That spot the soft nest caging,
Where war's alarms and blood-stained arms
  Were once around it raging.

                              TUPPER.

PART XV.

War and Peace.

———◆◆◆———

DRIVING HOME THE COWS.

Out of the clover and blue-eyed grass
  He turned them into the river-lane;
One after another he let them pass,
  And fastened the meadow bars again.

Under the willows and over the hill
  He patiently followed their sober pace;
The merry whistle for once was still,
  And something shadowed the sunny face.

Only a boy! and his father had said
  He never would let his youngest go;
Two already were lying dead
  Under the feet of the trampling foe.

But after the evening work was done,
  And the frogs were loud in the meadow-swamp,
Over his shoulder he slung his gun
  And stealthily followed the foot-path damp,

Across the clover and through the wheat,
  With resolute heart and purpose grim,
Though cold was the dew to the hurrying feet,
  And the blind bat's flitting startled him.

Thrice since then had the lane been white,
  And the orchards sweet with apple-bloom;
And now, when the cows came back at night,
  The feeble father drove them home.

For news had come to the lonely farm
  That three were lying where two had lain;
And the old man's tremulous, palsied arm
  Could never lean on a son's again.

The summer days grew cold and late,
  He went for the cows, when the work was done;
But down the lane, as he opened the gate,
  He saw them coming, one by one, —

Brindle, Ebony, Speckle, and Bess,
  Shaking their horns in the evening wind;
Cropping the buttercups out of the grass —
  But who was it following close behind?

Loosely swung in the idle air
  The empty sleeve of army blue;
And worn and pale, from the crisping hair
  Looked out a face that the father knew.

For Southern prisons will sometimes yawn,
  And yield their dead unto life again;
And the day that comes with a cloudy dawn
  In golden glory at last may wane.

The great tears sprang to their meeting eyes;
  For the heart must speak when the lips are dumb,
And under the silent evening skies
  Together they followed the cattle home.

KATE PUTNAM OSGOOD.

ROLL-CALL.

"CORPORAL GREEN!" the orderly cried;
  "Here!" was the answer, loud and clear,
  From the lips of the soldier who stood near;
And "Here" was the word the next replied.

"Cyrus Drew!" — then a silence fell —
  This time no answer followed the call;
  Only his rear man had seen him fall,
Killed or wounded; he could not tell.

There they stood in the falling light,
  These men of battle with grave, dark looks,
  As plain to be read as open books,
While slowly gathered the shades of night.

The fern on the hillsides was splashed with blood,
 And down in the corn where the poppies grew
 Were redder stains than the poppies knew,
And crimson dyed was the river's flood.

For the foe had crossed from the other side
 That day, in the face of a murderous fire,
 That swept them down in its terrible ire,
And their life-blood went to color the tide.

"Herbert Kline!" At the call there came
 Two stalwart soldiers into the line,
 Bearing between them this Herbert Kline,
Wounded and bleeding, to answer his name.

"Ezra Kerr!"—and a voice answered, "Here!"
 "Hiram Kerr!"—but no man replied.
 They were brothers, these two; the sad winds sighed,
And a shudder crept through the cornfield near.

"Ephraim Deane!"—then a soldier spoke;
 "Deane carried our regiment's colors," he said;
 "Where our ensign was shot, I left him dead,
Just after the enemy wavered and broke.

"Close to the roadside his body lies;
 I paused a moment and gave him drink;
 He murmured his mother's name, I think,
And death came with it and closed his eyes."

'T was a victory, yes, but it cost us dear—
 For that company's roll, when called at night,
 Of a hundred men who went into the fight,
Numbered but twenty that answered "Here!"

San Francisco Argonaut.   N. G. SHEPARD.

THE COUNTERSIGN WAS MARY.

'T WAS near the break of day, but still
 The moon was shining brightly;
The west wind as it passed the flowers
 Set each one swaying lightly;
The sentry slow paced to and fro,
 A faithful night-watch keeping,
While in the tents behind him stretched
 His comrades,—all were sleeping.

Slow to and fro the sentry paced,
 His musket on his shoulder;
But not a thought of death or war
 Was with the brave young soldier.

Ah, no! his heart was far away
  Where, on a Western prairie,
A rose-twined cottage stood.   That night
  The countersign was " Mary."

And there his own true love he saw,
  Her blue eyes kindly beaming,
Above them, on her sun-kissed brow,
  Her curls like sunshine gleaming : —
He heard her singing, as she churned
  The butter in the dairy,
The song he loved the best.   That night
  The countersign was " Mary."

" Oh, for one kiss from her ! " he sighed,
  When, up the lone road glancing,
He spied a form, a little form,
  With faltering steps advancing ;
And as it neared him, silently
  He gazed at it in wonder ;
Then dropped his musket to his hand,
  And challenged, — " Who goes yonder ? "

Still on it came.   " Not one step more,
  Be you man, child, or fairy,
Unless you give the countersign ;
  Halt ! who goes there ! " — " 'T is Mary,"
A sweet voice cried, and in his arms
  The girl he 'd left behind him
Half fainting fell.   O'er many miles
  She 'd bravely toiled to find him.

"I heard that you were wounded, dear,"
  She sobbed.   " My heart was breaking;
I could not stay a moment, but,
  All other ties forsaking,
I travelled, by my grief made strong,
  Kind Heaven watching o'er me,
Until — unhurt and well ? "   " Yes, love —
  At last you stood before me."

" They told me that I could not pass
  The lines to seek my lover
Before day fairly came ; but I
  Pressed on ere night was over,
And, as I told my name, I found
  The way free as our prairie."
"Because, thank God ! to-night," he said,
  " The countersign is ' Mary.' "

                MARGARET EYTINGE.

OUR LAST TOAST.

We meet 'neath the sounding rafter,
   And the walls around are bare;
As they shout to our peals of laughter,
   It seems that the dead are there.
But stand to your glasses, steady!
   We drink to our comrades' eyes,
Quaff a cup to the dead already,
   And hurrah for the next that dies!

Not here are the goblets glowing —
   Not here is the vintage sweet;
'T is cold as our hearts are growing,
   And dark as the doom we meet.
But stand to your glasses, steady!
   And soon shall our pulses rise, —
A cup to the dead already,
   Hurrah for the next that dies!

Not a sigh for the lot that darkles,
   Not a tear for the friends that sink;
We 'll fall 'neath the wine-cup's sparkles
   As mute as the wine we drink.
So, stand to your glasses, steady!
   'T is this that respite buys,
One cup to the dead already,
   Hurrah for the next that dies!

Time was when we frowned at others —
   We thought we were wiser then;
Ha, ha! let them think of their mothers,
   Who hope to see them again.
No, stand to your glasses, steady!
   The thoughtless here are wise;
A cup to the dead already,
   Hurrah for the next that dies!

Here 's many a hand that 's shaking;
   Here 's many a cheek that 's sunk,
But soon, though our hearts are breaking,
   They 'll burn with the wine we 've drunk.
So, stand to your glasses, steady!
   'T is here the revival lies;
A cup to the dead already,
   Hurrah for the next that dies!

There 's a mist on the glass congealing —
   'T is the hurricane's fiery breath;
And thus doth the warmth of feeling
   Turn to ice in the grasp of death.

Ho, stand to your glasses, steady!
  For a moment the vapor flies;
A cup to the dead already,
  Hurrah for the next that dies!

Who dreads to the dust returning,
  Who shrinks from the sable shore,
Where the high and haughty yearning
  Of the soul shall sing no more ?
Ho, stand to your glasses, steady!
  The world is a world of lies;
A cup to the dead already,
  Hurrah for the next that dies!

Cut off from the land that bore us,
  Betrayed by the land we find,
Where the brightest have gone before us,
  And the dullest remain behind.
Stand — stand to your glasses, steady!
  'T is all we 've got to prize;
A cup to the dead already,
  And hurrah for the next that dies!

BARTHOLOMEW DOWLING.

AT LAST.

O'ER the sunlit hills of Berkshire drooped the drowsy summer
    calm,
Filling all the glens and valleys with the silence like a psalm;
Like an angel-chanted anthem thrilling toward a poet's ear,
Till he dreams the mystic rhythm God alone can live and hear.

By a little spring that bubbled from beneath a towering pine,
Hidden half and overshaded by the sprays of blackberry vine,
Stood a man and maiden, waiting till the parting hour should
    come,
When their clasping hands must sever at the rattle of the drum,

He to offer life for duty on the swart Virginian plain,
She to watch and hope his coming through the sunshine and the
    rain.
Very few the words they uttered as they waited hand in hand,
But the silence throbbed with voices that their hearts could
    understand.

Tender voices of the past time, and the days forever done, —
Days divinely sweet and holy, when their love had just begun;
Hopeful voices of the future whispering of the joys to be,
When the clanging calls of battle hushed to hymns of victory.

Sank the day into the sunset, and there came the tread of feet,
Marching to the sound of music, up the length of level street;
Then he drew her to his bosom, parting backward from her face
The long golden hair, whose halo made a glory in the place;

Almost calm above his passion, as he whispered, " I must go,
You will send me letters often? kiss them where you sign them
— so!
And if I no more come homeward," trembling grew his lips and
white,
" All these happy days together, you will not forget them quite?"

Answer none of word or gesture for a moment did she deign,
Save the mute, pathetic promise of her eyes' remonstrant pain.
Then, because her love sat higher than his doubts could lift their
fronts,
She drew down his lips and kissed them, as a woman kisses once.

"Would to God," she said, " my lover, that my life for thine
might be!
But where'er his voice shall call thee, in his time I'll follow
thee."
That was all. The soldiers' tramping passed and slowly died
away,
And she knelt beside the pine-tree all alone to weep and pray.

Came the solemn twilight gemming sky and stream with starry
spheres,
Came the tender twilight dropping over all its dewy tears;
And she sought once more her duties and the dull routine of life,
Tenfold harder in the bearing than the battle's frenzied strife.

Days of forced and weary marches and of combat fierce and
red,
Nights of bivouac round the camp-fire with the star alone
o'erhead,
Months of hopeless, hungry torture in the Southern prison-pen,
And a dumb, dead face that never love should wake to life again.

On the frozen hills of Berkshire white the snows of winter lie,
Scarlet red against the sunset where their summits pierce the sky.
In a little country churchyard climbing up the side of one,
Where the first arbutus blossoms, and the grass greens first
i' the sun,

Side by side two graves are sleeping. Over one the flowers have
grown
Ten long years, and bloomed and withered, and the autumn
leaves have blown.
On the headstone of the other the first wreaths have hardly dried,
Where at last the soldier's sweetheart slumbers by her lover's
side.

THE BLUE AND THE GRAY.

EACH thin hand resting on a grave,
   Her lips apart in prayer,
A mother knelt, and left her tears
   Upon the violets there.
O'er many a rood of vale and lawn,
   Of hill and forest gloom,
The reaper Death had revelled in
   His fearful harvest home.
The last unquiet summer shone
   Upon a fruitless fray ;
From yonder forest charged the blue —
   Down yonder slope the gray.

The hush of death was on the scene,
   And sunset o'er the dead,
In that oppressive stillness,
   A pall of glory spread.
I know not, dare not question how
   I met the ghastly glare
Of each upturned and stirless face
   That shrunk and whitened there.
I knew my noble boys had stood
   Through all that withering day,
I knew that Willie wore the blue,
   That Harry wore the gray.

I thought of Willie's clear blue eye,
   His wavy hair of gold,
That clustered on a fearless brow
   Of purest Saxon mould ;
Of Harry, with his raven locks
   And eagle glance of pride ;
Of how they clasped each other's hand
   And left their mother's side ;
How hand in hand they bore my prayers
   And blessings on the way —
A noble heart beneath the blue,
   Another 'neath the gray.

The dead, with white and folded hands,
   That hushed our village homes,
I 've seen laid calmly, tenderly,
   Within their darkened rooms ;
But there I saw distorted limbs,
   And many an eye aglare,
In the soft purple twilight of
   The thunder-smitten air.

Along the slope and on the sward
    In ghastly ranks they lay,
And there was blood upon the blue
    And blood upon the gray.

I looked and saw his blood, and his ;
    A swift and vivid dream
Of blended years flashed o'er me, when,
    Like some cold shadow, came
A blindness of the eye and brain —
    The same that seizes one
When men are smitten suddenly
    Who overstare the sun ;
And while, blurred with the sudden stroke
    That swept my soul, I lay,
They buried Willie in his blue,
    And Harry in his gray.

The shadows fall upon their graves ;
    They fall upon my heart ;
And through the twilight of this soul
    Like dews the tears will start ;
The starlight comes so silently
    And lingers where they rest ;
So hope's revealing starlight sinks
    And shines within my breast.
They ask not there, where yonder heaven
    Smiles with eternal day,
Why Willie wore the loyal blue,
    Why Harry wore the gray.

THE BLUE AND THE GRAY.

By the flow of the inland river,
    Whence the fleets of iron have fled,
Where the blades of the grave-grass quiver,
    Asleep are the ranks of the dead.
Under the sod and the dew,
    Waiting the judgment day, —
Under the one, the Blue,
    Under the other, the Gray.

Those in the robings of glory,
    These in the gloom of defeat,
All with the battle-blood gory,
    In the dusk of eternity meet.
Under the sod and the dew,
    Waiting the judgment day, —
Under the laurel, the Blue,
    Under the willow, the Gray.

From the silence of sorrowful hours
  The desolate mourners go,
Lovingly laden with flowers
  Alike for the friend and the foe.
Under the sod and the dew,
  Waiting the judgment day, —
Under the roses, the Blue,
  Under the lilies, the Gray.

So with an equal splendor
  The morning sun-rays fall,
With a touch, impartially tender,
  On the blossoms blooming for all.
Under the sod and the dew,
  Waiting the judgment day, —
Broidered with gold, the Blue,
  Mellowed with gold, the Gray.

So when the summer calleth
  On forest and field of grain,
With an equal murmur falleth
  The cooling drip of the rain.
Under the sod and the dew,
  Waiting the judgment day, —
Wet with the rain, the Blue,
  Wet with the rain, the Gray.

Sadly, but not upbraiding,
  The generous deed was done;
In the storm of the years that are fading
  No braver battle was won.
Under the sod and the dew,
  Waiting the judgment day, —
Under the blossoms, the Blue,
  Under the garlands, the Gray.

No more shall the war-cry sever,
  Nor the winding river be red;
They banish our anger forever,
  When they laurel the graves of our dead.
Under the sod and the dew,
  Waiting the judgment day, —
Love and tears for the Blue,
  Tears and love for the Gray.

FRANCIS MILES FINCH.

VANQUISHED.

ON THE DEATH OF GENERAL GRANT.

NOT by ball or brand
Sped by mortal hand,
Not by lightning stroke
When fiery tempests broke, —
Not 'mid ranks of war
Fell the great Conqueror.

Unmoved, undismayed,
In the crash and carnage of the cannonade —
Eye that dimmed not, hand that failed not,
Brain that swerved not, heart that quailed not,
Steel nerve, iron form —
The dauntless spirit that o'erruled the storm.

While the Hero peaceful slept
A foeman to his chamber crept,
Lightly to the slumberer came,
Touched his brow and breathed his name:
O'er the stricken form there passed
Suddenly an icy blast.

The Hero woke ; rose undismayed ;
Saluted Death — and sheathed his blade.

The Conqueror of a hundred fields
To a mightier Conqueror yields ;
No mortal foeman's blow
Laid the great soldier low ;
Victor in his latest breath —
Vanquished, but by Death.

FRANCIS F. BROWNE.

THE MESSAGE OF VICTORY.

" NEWS to the king, good news for all ! "
The corn is trodden, the river runs red.
" News of the battle," the heralds call,
" We have won the field ; we have taken the town,
We have beaten the rebels and crushed them down."
And the dying lie with the dead.

" Who was my bravest ? " quoth the king.
The corn is trodden, the river runs red.
" Whom shall I honor for this great thing ? "
" Threescore were best, where none was worst ;
But Walter Wendulph was aye the first."
And the dying lie with the dead.

"What of my husband?" quoth the bride.
  The corn is trodden, the river is red.
"Comes he to-morrow? how long will he bide?"
"Put off thy bride-gear, busk thee in black;
Walter Wendulph will never come back."
  And the dying lie with the dead.

                                    AUGUSTA WEBSTER.

——◆——

CONQUERED AT LAST.

Shortly after the last yellow-fever scourge swept up the Mississippi Valley
the *Mobile News* offered a prize for the poem by a Southern writer which
should best express the gratitude of the Southern heart towards the people of
the North for the philanthropy and magnanimity so nobly and freely displayed
during the pestilence. This offer called forth seventy-seven compositions from
various parts of the South, and the prize was finally awarded to Miss Maria
L. Eve, of Augusta, Ga., the author of *Conquered at Last.*

YOU came to us once, O brothers, in wrath,
And rude desolation followed your path.

You conquered us then, but only in part,
For a stubborn thing is the human heart.

So the mad wind blows in his might and main,
And the forests bend to his breath like grain,

Their heads in the dust and their branches broke;
But how shall he soften their hearts of oak?

You swept o'er our land like the whirlwind's wing,
But the human heart is a stubborn thing.

We laid down our arms, we yielded our will,
But our heart of heart was unconquered still.

"We are vanquished," we said, "but our wounds must heal;"
We gave you our swords, but our hearts were steel.

"We are conquered," we said, but our hearts were sore,
And "woe to the conquered" on every door.

But the spoiler came and he would not spare,
And the angel that walketh in darkness was there:—

He walked through the valley, walked through the street,
And he left the print of his fiery feet

In the dead, dead, dead, that were everywhere,
And buried away with never a prayer.

From the desolate land, from its very heart,
There went forth a cry to the uttermost part :—

You heard it, O brothers ! — With never a measure
You opened your hearts, and poured out your treasure.

O Sisters of Mercy, you gave above these !
For you helped, we know, on your bended knees.

Your pity was human, but oh ! it was more,
When you shared our cross and our burden bore.

Your lives in your hands you stood by our side ;
Your lives for our lives — you lay down and died.

And no greater love hath a man to give,
Than to lay down his life that his friends may live.

You poured in our wounds the oil and the wine
That you brought to us from a Hand Divine.

You conquered us once, and our swords we gave ;
We yield now our hearts — they are all we have.

Our last trench was there, and it held out long ;
It is yours, O friends ! and you 'll find it strong.

Your love had a magic diviner than art,
And " Conquered by Kindness " we 'll write on our heart.

                                        MARIA L. EVE.

PART XVI.

Comedy, Burlesque, Parody, and Epitaph.

Jog on, jog on, the foot-path way,
* And merrily hent the stile-a:*
A merry heart goes all the day,
* Your sad tires in a mile-a.*

SHAKSPEARE.

PART XVI.

Comedy, Burlesque, Parody, and Epitaph.

———◦◦◦———

"————————"

In the smoke of my dear cigarito
  Cloud castles rise gorgeous and tall,
And Eros, divine muchachito,
  With smiles hovers over it all.

But dreaming, forgetting to cherish
  The fire at my lips, as it dies,
The dream and the rapture must perish,
  And Eros descend from the skies.

O wicked and false muchachito,
  Your rapture I yet may recall;
But like my re-lit cigarito,
  A bitterness tinges it all.

Camilla K. von K.

———◆———

IN PRAISE OF WINE.

Diogenes, surly and proud,
  Who snarled at the Macedon youth,
Delighted in wine that was good,
  Because in good wine there was truth;
But, growing as poor as Job,
  Unable to purchase a flask,
He chose for his mansion a tub,
  And lived by the scent of the cask.

Heraclitus ne'er would deny
  To tipple and cherish his heart,
And when he was maudlin he 'd cry
  Because he had emptied his quart;

Though some are so foolish to think
　　He wept at men's folly and vice,
'T was only his fashion to drink
　　Till the liquor flowed out of his eyes.

Democritus always was glad
　　Of a bumper to cheer up his soul,
And would laugh like a man that was mad,
　　When over a good flowing bowl.
As long as his cellar was stored,
　　The liquor he 'd merrily quaff;
And when he was drunk as a lord,
　　At those who were sober he 'd laugh.

Copernicus, too, like the rest,
　　Believed there was wisdom in wine,
And thought that a cup of the best
　　Made reason the better to shine.
With wine he 'd replenish his veins
　　And make his philosophy reel ;
Then fancied the world, like his brain,
　　Turned round like a chariot wheel.

Aristotle, that master of arts,
　　Had been but a dunce without wine ;
And what we ascribe to his parts,
　　Is due to the juice of the vine ;
His belly, most writers agree,
　　Was as big as a watering-trough ;
He therefore leaped into the sea,
　　Because he 'd have liquor enough.

Old Plato, the learned divine,
　　He fondly to wisdom was prone ;
But had it not been for good wine,
　　His merits had never been known.
By wine we are generous made,
　　It furnishes fancy with wings;
Without it, we ne'er should have had
　　Philosophers, poets, or kings.

———◆———

WHY TRUTH GOES NAKED.

List to a tale well worth the ear
　　Of all who wit and sense admire ;
Invented, it is very clear,
　　Some ages prior to Matthew Prior.

Falsehood and Truth " upon a time,"
  One day in June's delicious weather
('T was in a distant age and clime),
  Like sisters, took a walk together.
On, on their pretty way they took
  Through fragrant wood and verdant meadow,
To where a beech beside a brook
  Invited rest beneath its shadow.
There, sitting in the pleasant shade
  Upon the margin's grassy matting
(A velvet cushion ready made),
  The young companions fell to chatting.
Now, while in voluble discourse
  On this and that their tongues were running,
As habit bids each speak — perforce,
  The one is frank, the other cunning ;
Falsehood, at length, impatient grown
  With scandals of her own creation,
Said, " Since we two are quite alone,
  And nicely screened from observation,
Suppose in this delightful rill,
  While all around is so propitious,
We take a bath ? " Said Truth, " I will —
  A bath, I 'm sure, will be delicious ! "
At this her robe she cast aside,
  And in the stream that ran before her
She plunged — like Ocean's happy bride —
  As naked as her mother bore her !
Falsehood now undressed,
  Put off the robes her limbs that hamper,
And having donned Truth's snow-white vest,
  Ran off as fast as she could scamper.
Since then the subtle maid, in sooth,
  Expert in lies and shrewd evasions,
Has borne the honest name of Truth,
  And wears her clothes on all occasions.
While Truth, disdaining to appear
  In Falsehood's petticoat and bodice,
Still braves all eyes from year to year
  As naked as a marble goddess.

IF YOU WANT A KISS, WHY, TAKE IT.

THERE 's a jolly Saxon proverb
  That is pretty much like this, —
That a man is half in heaven
  If he has a woman's kiss.
There is danger in delaying,
  For the sweetness may forsake it ;
So I tell you, bashful lover,
  If you want a kiss, why, take it.

Never let another fellow
   Steal a march on you in this;
Never let a laughing maiden
   See you spoiling for a kiss.
There 's a royal way to kissing,
   And the jolly ones who make it
Have a motto that is winning, —
   If you want a kiss, why, take it.

Any fool may face a cannon,
   Anybody wear a crown,
But a man must win a woman
   If he 'd have her for his own.
Would you have the golden apple,
   You must find the tree and shake it ;
If the thing is worth the having,
   And you want a kiss, why, take it.

Who would burn upon a desert
   With a forest smiling by ?
Who would change his sunny summer
   For a bleak and wintry sky ?
Oh, I tell you there is magic,
   And you cannot, cannot break it ;
For the sweetest part of loving
   Is to want a kiss, and take it.

TWO MEN I KNOW.

I KNOW a duke; well, let him pass —
I may not call his grace an ass ;
Though if I did I 'd do no wrong,
Save to the asses and my song.

The duke is neither wise nor good;
He gambles, drinks, scorns womanhood,
And at the age of twenty-four
Was worn and battered as threescore.

I know a waiter in Pall Mall
Who works, and waits, and reasons well ;
Is gentle, courteous, and refined,
And has a magnet in his mind.

What is it makes his graceless grace
So like a jockey out of place ?
What makes the waiter — tell who can —
So very like a gentleman ?

Perhaps their mothers — God is great ! —
Perhaps 't is accident, or fate !
Perhaps because — hold not my pen —
We can breed horses but not men.

English Newspaper.

———◇———

DARWINISM IN THE KITCHEN.

I WAS takin' off my bonnet
  One arternoon at three,
When a hinseck jumped upon it
  As proved to be a flea.

Then I takes it to the grate,
  Between the bars to stick it,
But I had n't long to wait
  Ere it changed into a cricket.

Says I, " Surelie my senses
  Is a-gettin' in a fog ! "
So to drown it I commences,
  When it halters to a frog.

Here my heart began to thump,
  And no wonder I felt funky ;
For the frog, with one big jump,
  Leaped hisself into a monkey.

Then I opened wide my eyes,
  His features for to scan,
And observed, with great surprise,
  That that monkey was a man.

But he vanished from my sight,
  And I sunk upon the floor,
Just as missus with a light
  Come inside the kitching door.

Then, beginnin' to abuse me,
  She says, " Sarah, you 've been drinkin' ! "
I says, " No, mum, you 'll excuse me,
  But I 've merely been a-thinkin'.

" But as sure as I 'm a cinder,
  That party what you see
A-gettin' out the winder
  Have developed from a flea ! "

NINETY-NINE IN THE SHADE.

OH for a lodge in a garden of cucumbers !
  Oh for an iceberg or two at control !
Oh for a vale that at mid-day the dew cumbers !
  Oh for a pleasure-trip up to the pole !

Oh for a little one-story thermometer
  With nothing but zeroes all ranged in a row !
Oh for a big double-barrelled hygrometer,
  To measure the moisture that rolls from my brow !

Oh that this cold world were twenty times colder !
  (That 's irony red hot, it seemeth to me.)
Oh for a turn of its dreaded cold shoulder !
  Oh what a comfort an ague would be !

Oh for a grotto frost-lined and rill-riven,
  Scooped in the rock under cataract vast !
Oh for a winter of discontent even !
  Oh for wet blankets judiciously cast !

Oh for a soda-fount spouting up boldly
  From every hot lamp-post against the hot sky !
Oh for a maiden to look on me coldly,
  Freezing my soul with a glance from her eye !

Then oh for a draught from the cup of cold pizen,
  And oh, for a through ticket *via* Coldgrave
To the baths of the Styx where a thick shadow lies on,
  And deepens the chill of its dark running wave !

ROSSITER JOHNSON.

A COCKNEY WAIL.

THE great Pacific journey I have done,
  In many a town and tent I 've found a lodgment,
I think I 've travelled to the setting sun,
  And very nearly reached the day of judgment.
Like Launcelot in quest of Holy Grail,
  From western Beersheba to Yankee Dan
I 've been a seeker, yet I sadly fail
  To find the genuine type American.

Where is this object of my youthful wonder,
  Who met me in the pages of Sam Slick, —
Who opened every sentence with " By thunder ! "
  And whittled always on a bit of stick ?

The more the crowd of friends around me thickens,
  The less my chance to meet him seems to be ;
Why did he freely show himself to Dickens,
  To Dixon, Sala, Trollope, not to me ?

No one accosts me with the words, " Wa'al, stranger ! "
  Greets me as " Festive cuss," or shouts "Old hoss ! "
No grim six-shooter threatens me with danger,
  If I don't " quickly pass the butter, boss."
Round friendly boards no " cocktail " ever passes,
  No "brandy smash " my morning hour besets ;
And petticoats are worn by all the lasses,
  And the pianos don't wear pantalettes.

The ladies, when you offer chicken salad,
  Don't say, " I'm pretty crowded now, I guess ; "
They don't sing Mrs. Barney Williams' ballad
  Of " Bobbing Round," nor add "sir-ee" to yes.
I, too, have sat, like every other fellow,
  In many a railway, omnibus, street car ;
No girl has spiked ME with a fierce umbrella,
  And said, " You git, I mean to sit right thar."

Gone are the Yankees of my early reading !
  Faded the Yankee land of eager quest !
I meet with culture, courtesy, good-breeding,
  Art, letters, men and women of the best.
Oh, fellow Britons, all my hopes are undone !
  Take counsel of a disappointed man :
Don't come out here, but stay at home in London,
  And seek in books the true American.

I WUD KNOT DYE IN WINTUR.

I WUD knot dye in wintur,
  When whiski punchez flo ;
When pooty galls air skatin'
  O'er fealds ov ice an' sno ;
When sassidge-meet is phrying,
  And hickrie knuts is thick ;
Owe ! who kud think of dighing,
  Or even gettin' sick ?

I wud knot dye in springtime,
  And miss the turnup greens,
And the pooty song ov the leetle fraugs,
  And the ski-lark's airly screams.
When burds begin thare wobbling,
  And taters 'gin to sprout,
When turkies go a-gobblering,
  I wud knot then peg out.

I wud knot dye in summer,
  And leave the gard'n sass,
The roasted lam, and buttermilk,
  The kool plase in the grass ;
I wud knot dye in summer,
  When everything 's so hot,
And leave the whiski jew-lips —
  Owe know ! Ide ruther knott.

I wud knot dye in ortum,
  With peeches fitt fur eating,
When the wavy corn is gettin' wripe,
  An' Kandidates is treating;
Phor these and other wreasons
  Ide knot dye in the fall,
And — sinse I 've thort it over —
  I wud knot dye at all.

THE LITTLE PEACH.

A LITTLE peach in the orchard grew —
A little peach of emerald hue ;
Warmed by the sun and wet by the dew,
    It grew.

One day, passing the orchard through,
That little peach dawned on the view
Of Johnnie Jones and his sister Sue —
    Those two.

Up at the peach a club he threw —
Down from the tree on which it grew
Fell the little peach of emerald hue —
    Mon dieu !

She took a bite and he a chew,
And then the trouble began to brew —
Trouble the doctor could n't subdue —
    Too true !

Under the turf where the daisies grew
They planted John and his sister Sue,
And their little souls to the angels flew —
    Boo-hoo !

But what of the peach of emerald hue,
Warmed by the sun and wet by the dew ?
Ah, well, its mission on earth was through —
    Adieu !

                              EUGENE FIELD.

PAT'S LETTER.

WELL, Mary, me darlint, I'm landed at last,
And troth, though they tell me the stamer was fast,
It seems as if years upon years had gone by
Since Paddy looked intil your beautiful eye.
For Amerikay, darlint, — ye'll think it is quare, —
Is twenty times furder than Cork from Kildare;
And the say is that broad, and the waves are that high,
Ye're tossed like a futball 'twixt wather and shky;
And ye fale like a pratie burstin' the shkin,
And all ye can do is to howld yersilf in.
Ochone! but me jewel, the say may be grand,
But when you come over, dear, thravel by land!

It's a wonderful country, this — so I am towld —
They'll not look at guineas so chape is the gowld;
And the three that poor mother sewed into me coat
I sowld for a thrifle on lavin' the boat.
And the quarest of fashions ye iver have seen!
They pay ye wid picters all painted in green.
And the crowds that are rushing here morning and night
Would make the Lord Lieutenant shake with the fright.
The strates are that full that no one can pass,
And the only law is, "Do not thread on the grass."
Their grass is the quarest of shows, by me vow,
For it would n't be munched by a Candlemas cow.

Tell father I wint, as he bid me, to see
His friend Tim O'Shannon, from Killycaughee.
It's rowlin' in riches O'Shannon is now,
With a wife and tin babies, six pigs and a cow,
In a nate little house standing down from the strate,
With two beautiful rooms and a pigsty complate.
I thought of ye, darlint, and dramed such a drame!
That mebbe some day we'd be the same;
Though troth, Tim O'Shannon's wife never could dare
(Poor yaller-skinned crayther!) with you to compare.
And as for the pigs, sure, 't is aisy to see
The bastes were not meant for this land of the free.

I think of ye, darlint, from morning till night,
And when I'm not thinkin' ye're still in my sight!
I see your blue eyes with the sun in their glance —
Your smile in the meadow, your feet in the dance.
I'll love ye and trust ye, both livin' and dead!
I'm workin', acushla, for you — only you,
And I'll make you a lady yit, if ye'll be true;

Though troth, ye can't climb Fortune's laddher so quick
Whin both of your shoulders are loaded with brick;
But I 'll do it — I swear it — by this and by that;
Which manes what I dare n't say — from your own Pat.

QUEERQUILL.

NOTE. — Fifth line of fourth stanza evidently lost.

TOO GREAT A SACRIFICE.

THE maid, as by the papers doth appear,
Whom fifty thousand dollars made so dear,
To test Lothario's passion, simply said:
"Forego the weed before we go to wed.
For smoke take flame; I 'll be that flame's bright fanner ;
To have your Anna, give up your Havana."
But he, when thus she brought him to the scratch,
Lit his cigar and threw away his match.

"OWED" TO MY POCKET-BOOK.

How fair thou art, O little book
  Of scented Russia leather !
With stitches fanciful and fine
  To hold you well together;
But stitches strong are useless all,
  There is no strain upon thee;
The great brogan of poverty
  Is very heavy on thee.

What endless room is here for bills
  Of large denominations,
With checks and bonds a goodly store —
  Ah, vain imaginations !
The hungriest pocket-book thou art
  That ever in a highway
Was picked up by a well-fooled man
  And cast into a by-way.

Consumption settled on thy form
  Till you cannot grow thinner;
In vain you plead with open mouth
  Of me a greenback dinner.
'T is very sad thou couldst not stand
  The drain upon thy system;
I never knew what dollars were
  Until I wholly missed them.

I 'm safe to say that there 's more cash
  Outside of thee than in thee;
I 'd stake thee on some risky bet,
  Nor care much who would win thee.
I look at thee and nothing see, —
  They say you can't see nothing;
Yet here it 's very palpable —
  In sooth, not very soothing.

Should some highwayman thee demand,
  I 'd gladly give thee to him;
'T would lead him into suicide,
  Or monstrously undo him.
Sad pocket-book ! I feel for thee,
  But not as in days sunny;
Henceforth the pocket of my vest
  Will carry all my money.

SUCH A DUCK.

ONCE Venus, deeming Love too fat,
  Stopped all his rich, ambrosial dishes,
Dooming the boy to live on chat, —
  To sup on songs and dine on wishes.
Love, lean and lank, flew off to prowl, —
  The starveling now no beauty boasted, —
He could have munched Minerva's owl,
  Or Juno's peacock, boiled or roasted.

At last, half famished, almost dead,
  He shot his mother's doves for dinner;
Young Lilla, passing, shook her head, —
  Cried Love, " A shot at you, young sinner ! "
" Oh, not at me ! " she urged her flight —
  " I 'm neither dove, nor lark, nor starling ! "
" No," fainting Cupid cried, " not quite ;
  But then — you 're such a duck, my darling ! "

ANY ONE WILL DO.

A MAIDEN once, of certain age,
To catch a husband did engage ;
But, having passed the prime of life
In striving to become a wife
Without success, she thought it time
To mend the follies of her prime.

Departing from the usual course
Of paint and such like for resource,
With all her might, this ancient maid
Beneath an oak-tree knelt, and prayed ;
Unconscious that a grave old owl
Was perched above — the mousing fowl !

"Oh, give ! a husband give ! " she cried,
" While yet I may become a bride ;
Soon will my day of grace be o'er,
And then, like many maids before,
I 'll die without an early love,
And none to meet me there above !

"Oh, 't is a fate too hard to bear !
Then answer this my humble prayer,
And oh, a husband give to me ! "
Just then the owl from out the tree,
In deep base tones cried, " Who–who–who ! "
" Who, Lord ?   And dost thou ask me who ?
Why, any one, good Lord, will do."

———◆———

THE RABBI'S PRESENT.

A Rabbi once, by all admired,
  Received, of high esteem the sign
From those his goodness thus inspired,
  A present of a cask of wine.
But lo ! when soon he came to draw,
  A miracle in mode as rapid
But quite unlike what Cana saw,
  Had turned his wine to water vapid.
The Rabbi never knew the cause,
  For miracles are things of mystery ;
Though some like this have had their laws
  Explained from facts of private history.
His friends, whom love did aptly teach,
  Wished all to share the gracious task,
So planned to bring a bottle each,
  And pour their wine in one great cask.
Now one by chance thought, " None will know,
  And with the wine of all my brothers
One pint of water well may go ; "
  And so by chance thought all the others.

'SPÄCIALLY JIM.

I wus mighty good-lookin' when I wus young,
  Peert an' black-eyed an' slim,
With fellers a-courtin' me Sunday nights,
  'Späcially Jim.

The likeliest one of 'em all wus he,
  Chipper an' han'som' an' trim ;
But I tossed up my head an' made fun o' the crowd,
  'Späcially Jim.

I said I had n't no 'pinion o' men,
  An' I would n't take stock in *him !*
But they kep' on a-comin' in spite o' my talk,
  'Späcially Jim.

I got so tired o' havin' 'em roun'
  ('Späcially Jim !)
I made up my mind I 'd settle down
  An' take up with him.

So we wus married one Sunday in church,
  'T was crowded full to the brim ;
'T was the only way to git rid of 'em all,
  'Späcially Jim.

Century.   B. M.

————◆————

A PULL–BACK.

A little Pull-Back sought one day
  The gates of Paradise ;
Saint Peter wiped his spectacles
  And rubbed his ancient eyes.

And throngs of female angels came
  With curious gaze the while,
Intent, as ladies always are,
  To see the latest style.

The saint put on his glasses then —
  An observation took ;
"What ! what !" he said, "this traverses
  The laws of 'must n't look.'

"Tied up in front ! Piled up behind !
  'T will never do, I fear !
The thing is too ridiculous —
  You cannot enter here."

What did she do? My curious friend,
   She got behind a tree;
And in a jiffy she was dressed
   As angels ought to be.

Saint Peter kissed her then, and said:
   "Pass in, my little dear;
But mind, you must n't introduce
   Such naughty fashions here."

—◆—

A LESSON IN MYTHOLOGY.

I READ to her, one summer day,
   A little mythologic story
About the maid who laughed at love,
   And ran a race for love and glory.

I closed the book. She raised her eyes
   And hushed the song she had been humming;
Glancing across the shady lawn,
   I saw my wealthy rival coming.

"These ancient tales," I gravely said,
   "With meaning wise are often laden;
And Atalanta well may stand
   As type of many a modern maiden.

"Minus, of course, the classic scandal,
   But with no less of nimble grace,
How many dainty slippered feet
   Are running now that self-same race!

"And when Hippomenes casts down
   His golden apples, is there ever
A chance for Love to reach the goal?"
   With saucy smile, she answered, "Never!"

I rose to go — she took my hand
   (O Fate, you ne'er that clasp can sever!).
And, "Stay," she said, with sudden blush, —
   "You *know* that I meant —' *hardly* ever.'"

                     ELIZA C. HALL.

ZOÖLOGY.

OH! merry is the Madrepore that sits beside the sea;
The cheery little Coralline hath many charms for me;
I love the fine Echinoderms, of azure, green, and gray,
That handled roughly fling their arms impulsively away;
Then bring me here the microscope and let me see the cells
Wherein the little Zoöphite like garden floweret dwells.

We 'll take the fair Anemone from off its rocky seat,
Since Rondeletius has said when fried 't is good to eat.
Dyspeptics from Sea-Cucumbers a lesson well may win,
They blithely take their organs out and then put fresh ones in.
The Rotifer in whirling round may surely bear the bell,
With Oceanic Hydrozoids that Huxley knows so well.

You 've heard of the Octopus, 't is a pleasant thing to know
He has a ganglion makes him blush, not red, but white as snow;
And why the strange Cercaria, to go a long way back,
Wears ever, as some ladies do, a fashionable "sac;"
And how the Pawn has parasites that on his head make holes;
Ask Dr. Cobbold, and he 'll say they 're just like tiny soles.

Then study well zoölogy, and add unto your store
The tales of Biogenesis and Protoplasmic lore;
As Paley neatly has observed, when into life they burst,
The frog and the philosopher are just the same at first;
But what 's the origin of life remains a puzzle still,
Let Tyndall, Haeckel, Bastian, go wrangle as they will.

Punch.

OLD FIDDLING JOSEY.

GIT yo' pardners, fust kwattilion!
   Stomp yo' feet an' raise 'em high;
Tune is, "Oh, dat watermillion!
   Gwine to git home bime-bye."
S'lute yo' pardners! scrape perlitely —
   Don't be bumpin' 'gin de res' —
Balance all! now step out rightly;
   Alluz dance yo' lebbel bes'.
Fo'wa'd foah! — whoop up, niggers!
   Back ag'in! don't be so slow —
Swing cornah's! min' de figgers,
   When I hollers den yo' go.
Top ladies cross ober,
   Hold on till I takes a dram —
Gemmen solo! yes, I 's sober —
   Kaint say how de fiddle am.

Hands around! hol' up yo' faces;
  Don't be lookin' at yo' feet!
Swing yo' pardners! to yo' places!
  Dat 's de way — dat 's hard to beat.
Sides fo'w'd — when yo 's ready —
  Make a bow as low 's you kin.
Swing acrost wid opp'site lady,
  Now we 'll let you swop ag'in;
Ladies change — shut up dat talkin';
  Do yo' talkin' arter while —
Right an' lef' ! don't want no walkin';
  Make yo' steps an' show yo' style.

                              Irwin Russell.

—————◆—————

A SEASIDE INCIDENT.

"Why, Bob, you dear old fellow,
  Where have you been these years?
In Egypt, India, Khiva,
  With the Khan's own volunteers?
Have you scaled the Alps or Andes,
  Sailed to Isles of Amazons?
What climate, Bob, has wrought the change
  Your face from brown to bronze?"

She placed a dimpled hand in mine,
  In the same frank, friendly way;
We stood once more on the dear old beach,
  And it seemed but yesterday
Since, standing on this same white shore,
  She said, with eyelids wet,
"Good-by. You may remember, Bob,
  But I shall not forget."

I held her hand and whispered low,
  "Madge, darling, what of the years —
The ten long years that have intervened
  Since, through the mist of tears,
We looked good-by on this same white beach
  Here by the murmuring sea?
You, Madge, were then just twenty,
  And I was twenty-three."

A crimson blush came to her cheek,
  "Hush, Bob," she quickly said;
"Let 's look at the bathers in the surf —
  There 's Nellie and Cousin Ned."
"And who 's that portly gentleman
  On the shady side of life?"
"Oh, he belongs to our party, too —
  In fact, Bob, I 'm his wife!

" And I tell you, Bob, it 's an awful thing,
  The way he does behave ;
Flirts with that girl in steel-gray silk —
  Bob, why do you look so grave ? "
" The fact is, Madge — I — well, ahem !
  Oh, nothing at all, my dear —
Except that she of the steel-gray silk
  Is the one I married last year."

New York Clipper.   MARC COOK.
                                                 (*Vandyke Brown.*)

LINES BY AN OLD FOGY.

I 'M thankful that the sun and moon
  Are both hung up so high,
That no presumptuous hand can stretch
  And pull them from the sky.
If they were not, I have no doubt
  But some reforming ass
Would recommend to take them down
  And light the world with gas.

ASTRONOMICAL.

" COUSIN Edward, what do these scientists mean,
  With all their big words and new fangles ?
This morning at breakfast they talked a whole hour
  Of parallactical angles."

" Well, Lu, we will demonstrate here on the beach,
  In a manner strikingly practical ;
You 're the moon, I the earth, and Simpkins a star ;
  The angle is styled parallactical.

" The farther we get from our star, you perceive,
  The shorter this line, which the base is,
Till he melts in the infinite azure, and then,
  There 's no space at all between faces."

"Oh, Edward, how could you ! and Simpkins right there,
  With his handkerchief over his lips ;
What will the man think ? "   " Oh, never mind, Lu,
  He 'll think it a lunar eclipse."

Daily Graphic.

LINES ON A GRASSHOPPER.

(By a Granger Naturalist.)

I 've got him, at last, in the focus
    Of a powerful telescope glass,
But he, magnified, looks like a slow cuss,
    And his ears much like those of an ass.

His eyes are like two peeled potatoes;
    His wings like the sails of a ship;
And his beard, which unshaven that way grows,
    Seems to cover an acre of lip.

His stomach is large and capacious,
    It always is hungry, no doubt;
And, much like a hog, his rapacious
    Desires may be gauged by his snout.

His legs are not merely for creeping,
    They are muscular, angular, high;
Just fitted for gallantly leaping,
    When he chooses, plumb into the sky!

From his brawny bull neck, saffron-tinted,
    Suspended by weather-stained rope,
Hangs a medal with Sanscrit imprinted:
    " With this monster no mortal can cope!

" He 's descended through long generations,
    With a pedigree perfect and straight,
From the locust that scooped ancient nations
    Whenever he lit at their gate."

———◆———

CONVERSATIONAL.

" How 's your father?" came the whisper,
    Bashful Ned the silence breaking;
" Oh, he 's nicely," Annie murmured,
    Smilingly the question taking.

Conversation flagged a moment,
    Hopeless, Ned essayed another:
" Annie, I — I," then a coughing,
    And the question, " How 's your mother?"

" Mother? Oh, she 's doing finely! "
    Fleeting fast was all forbearance,
When in low, despairing accents,
    Came the climax, " How 's your parents?"

A SADDENED TRAMP.

"Now unto yonder wood-pile go,
    Where toil till I return;
And feel how proud a thing it is
    A livelihood to earn."
A saddened look came o'er the tramp;
    He seemed like one bereft.
He stowed away the victuals cold,
    He — saw the wood, and left.

DELIGHTS OF CAMP LIFE.

COME to the home of the friendly mosquito,
    List to his cheerful inspiriting hum;
With his exuberant spirits he 'll greet, O,
    All who will deign to his marshes to come.

Come where the bullfrogs are croaking around us,
    Croaking our choruses back in our teeth;
Come, for the black flies above do surround us;
    Come where the centipedes crawl underneath.

A ROMANCE.

A CALM, delightful autumn night;
A moon's mysterious, misty light;
A maiden at her window height,
In proper robe of fleecy white.

The little wicket gate ajar;
A lover tripping from afar,
With tuneful voice and light guitar,
To woo his radiant guiding star.

The lute gave forth a plaintive twang —
Oh, how that doting lover sang!
A bull-dog with invidious fang —
A nip, a grip, and then a pang!

A maiden swooning in affright,
A lover in a piteous plight,
A canine quivering with delight —
A wild, delirious autumn night!

                    EUGENE FIELD.

OLD TIME AND I.

OLD Time and I the other night
  Had a carouse together;
The wine was golden warm and bright —
  Ay! just like summer weather.
Quoth I, "There's Christmas come again,
  And I no farthing richer."
Time answered, "Ah! the old, old strain, —
  I prithee pass the pitcher.

"Why measure all your good in gold?
  No rope of sand is weaker;
'T is hard to get, 't is hard to hold —
  Come, lad, fill up your beaker.
Hast thou not found true friends more true,
  And loving ones more loving?"
I could but say, "A few — a few;
  So keep the liquor moving."

"Hast thou not seen the prosperous knave
  Come down a precious thumper,
His cheats disclosed?" "I have — I have!"
  "Well, surely that's a bumper."
"Nay, hold awhile; I've seen the just
  Find all their hopes grow dimmer."
"They will hope on, and strive, and trust,
  And conquer!" "That's a brimmer."

"'T is not because to-day is dark,
  No brighter day's before 'em;
There's rest for every storm-tossed bark."
  "So be it! Pass the jorum!
Yet I must own I would not mind
  To be a little richer."
"Labor and wait, and you may find —
  Hallo! an empty pitcher."

                                   MARK LEMON.

THE HIGHWAY COW.

THE hue of her hide was dusky brown,
  Her body was lean and her neck was slim,
One horn was turned up and the other turned down,
  She was keen of vision and long of limb;
With a Roman nose and a short stump tail,
And ribs like the hoops on a home-made pail.

Many a mark did her body bear;
   She had been a target for all things known;
On many a scar the dusky hair
    Would grow no more where it once had grown;
Many a passionate, parting shot
Had left upon her a lasting spot.

Many and many a well-aimed stone,
   Many a brickbat of goodly size,
And many a cudgel swiftly thrown
    Had brought the tears to her loving eyes,
Or had bounded off from her bony back
With a noise like the sound of a rifle-crack.

Many a day had she passed in the pound
   For helping herself to her neighbor's corn;
Many a cowardly cur and hound
    Had been transfixed on her crumpled horn;
Many a teapot and old tin pail
Had the farmer-boys tied to her time-worn tail.

Old Deacon Gray was a pious man,
   Though sometimes tempted to be profane,
When many a weary mile he ran
    To drive her out of his growing grain.
Sharp were the pranks she used to play
To get her fill and to get away.

She knew when the deacon went to town.
   She wisely watched when he went by;
He never passed her without a frown,
    And an evil gleam in each angry eye;
He would crack his whip in a surly way,
And drive along in his " one-horse shay."

Then at his homestead she loved to call,
   Lifting his bars with crumpled horn;
Nimbly scaling his garden wall,
    Helping herself to his standing corn;
Eating his cabbages, one by one,
Hurrying home when her work was done.

His human passions were quick to rise,
   And striding forth with a savage cry,
With fury blazing from both his eyes
    As lightnings flash in a summer sky,
Redder and redder his face would grow,
And after the creature he would go.

Over the garden, round and round,
   Breaking his pear and apple trees;
Tramping his melons into the ground,
    Overturning his hives of bees,
Leaving him angry and badly stung,
Wishing the old cow's neck was wrung.

The mosses grew on the garden wall,
    The years went by with their work and play,
The boys of the village grew strong and tall,
    And the gray-haired farmers passed away
One by one, as the red leaves fall ;
But the highway cow outlived them all.

Countryside.   EUGENE J. HALL.

———◆———

THE HINDOO'S DEATH.

A HINDOO died ; a happy thing to do,
When fifty years united to a shrew.
Released, he hopefully for entrance cries
Before the gates of Brahma's paradise.
"Hast been through purgatory ? " Brahma said.
"I have been married ! " and he hung his head.
"Come in ! come in ! and welcome to my son !
Marriage and purgatory are as one."
In bliss extreme he entered heaven's door,
And knew the bliss he ne'er had known before.

He scarce had entered in the gardens fair,
Another Hindoo asked admission there.
The self-same question Brahma asked again :
"Hast been through purgatory ? " " No ; what then ?
"Thou canst not enter ! " did the god reply.
"He who went in was there no more than I."
"All that is true, but he has married been,
And so on earth has suffered for all his sin."
"Married ?   'T is well, for I 've been married twice."
"Begone !   We 'll have no fools in paradise."

GEORGE BIRDSEYE.

———◆———

WHY DRINK WINE.

SI bene commemini causæ sunt quinque bibere—
Hospitis adventus, præsens sitis, atque futura,
Aut vini bonitas, aut quælibet altera causa.

"If I the reasons well divine,
There are just five for drinking wine —
Good wine, a friend, or being dry,
Or lest you should be by and by,
Or — any other reason why."

NOTE. — Ascribed by *Notes and Queries* to Dr. Henry Aldrich, Dean of
Christ Church, Oxford, A. D. 1689-1711.

IMPROVED "ENOCH ARDEN."

PHILIP RAY and Enoch Arden
    Both were "spoons" on Annie Lee.
Phil did not fulfil her notion —
    She preferred to wed with E.

Him she married and she bore him
    Pretty little children three;
But becoming short of "rhino,"
    Enoch started off for sea,

Leaving Mrs. Arden mistress
    Of a well-stocked village shop,
Selling butter, soap, and treacle,
    Beeswax, whipcord, lollipop.

Ten long years she waited for him,
    But he neither came nor wrote;
Therefore she concluded Enoch
    Could no longer be afloat.

So when Philip came to ask her
    If she would be Mrs. Ray,
She, believing herself widowed,
    Could not say her suitor nay.

So a second time she married,
    Gave up selling bread and cheese —
And in due time Philip nursèd
    A little Ray upon his knees.

But, alas! the long-lost Enoch
    Turn'd up unexpectedly,
And was vastly disconcerted
    At this act of bigamy.

But on thinking o'er the matter,
    He determined to atone
For his lengthen'd absence from her
    By just leaving well alone.

So he took to bed and dwindled
    Down to something like a shade;
Settled with his good landlady,
    Then the debt of nature paid.

And when both the Rays discovered
   How poor Enoch's life had ended,
They came down in handsome manner,
   And gave his corpse a fun'ral splendid.

This is all I know about it.
   If it's not sufficient, write
By next mail to Alfred Tenny
   son, M. P., Isle of Wight.

———◆———

MARCH.

A SODDEN gray in the chilly dawn,
   A burst of the red gold sun at noon;
A windy lea for the dying day,
   And a wail at dusk like the distant loon;
   A ghost at night in the leafless larch,
      A sigh and a moan,
         And this is March.

A frown in the morning black and dim;
   A smile when the day is half-way run;
A moan when the wind comes up from the sea,
   And tosses the larch when the day is done.
   A penitent, changeful, grewsome thing,
      Is this fierce love child
         Of winter and spring.

It is mad with the love of an unloved one,
   It is chill with the winters that long have set;
It is sad at times and anon it laughs,
   And is warm with the summer that is not yet.
   And its voice laughs loud in the leafless larch,
      But to sigh again,
         And this is March.

A dose of quinine when the sun comes up
   From its tossed-up bed in the eastern sea;
Some castor-oil when the moon has sped,
   A blue pill dark and catnip tea;
   A decoction made from the leafless larch,
      And another blue pill,
         And this is March.

THE MAD, MAD MUSE.

(After Swinburne.)

Out on the margin of moonshine land,
  Tickle me, love, in these lonesome ribs,
Out where the whing-whang loves to stand,
Writing his name with his tail on the sand,
And wipes it out with his oogerish hand;
  Tickle me, love, in these lonesome ribs.

Is it the gibber of gungs and keeks?
  Tickle me, love, in these lonesome ribs,
Or what is the sound the whing-whang seeks,
Crouching low by winding creeks,
And holding his breath for weeks and weeks?
  Tickle me, love, in these lonesome ribs.

Anoint him the wealthiest of wraithy things!
  Tickle me, love, in these lonesome ribs.
'T is a fair whing-whangess with phosphor rings,
And bridal jewels of fangs and stings,
And she sits and as sadly and softly sings,
As the mildewed whir of her own dead wings;
  Tickle me, dear; tickle me here;
  Tickle me, love, in these lonesome ribs.

                    James Whitcomb Riley.

A GIRL'S A GIRL FOR A' THAT.

Is there a lady in the land
  That boasts her rank and a' that?
With scornful eye we pass her by,
  And little care for a' that:
For Nature's charm shall bear the palm, —
  A girl 's a girl for a' that.

What though her neck with gems she deck,
  With folly's gear and a' that,
And gayly ride in pomp and pride?
  We can dispense with a' that:
An honest heart acts no such part, —
  A girl 's a girl for a' that.

The nobly born may proudly scorn
   A lowly lass and a' that;
A pretty face has far more grace
   Than haughty looks and a' that;
A bonnie maid needs no such aid, —
   A girl's a girl for a' that.

Then let us trust that come it must,
   And sure it will for a' that,
When faith and love, all arts above,
   Shall reign supreme and a' that ;
And every youth confess the truth, —
   A girl's a girl for a' that.

————◆————

OUT WEST.

I HEAR thee speak of a Western land,
Thou callest its children a wide-awake band —
Father, oh, where is that favored spot?
Shall we not seek it and build us a cot?
Is it where the hills of Berkshire stand,
Whence the honey comes already canned?
      Not there, not there, my child !

Is it far away in the Empire State,
Where Horace Greeley feels first-rate,
Where the people are ruled by Tammany ring,
And Mr. Fisk is a railway king,
With two thousand men at his command,
Besides a boat with a big brass band?
      Not there, not there, my child !

Is it where the little pigs grow great
In the fertile vales of the Buckeye State,
And get so fat on acorns and meal
That they sell every bit of them, all but the squeal,
Where the butchers have such a plenty of hogs
That they don't make sausages out of dogs?
      Not there, not there, my child !

Or is it where they fortunes make,
Where they've got a tunnel under the lake,
Where the stores are full of wheat and corn,
And divorces are plenty, as sure as you're born,
Where Long John Wentworth is right on hand, —
Is it there, dear father, that Western land?
      Not there, not there, my child !

Is it in the dominions of Brigham Young,
The most married man that is left unhung,
Where every man that likes can go,
And get forty wives or more, you know,
Where "saints" are plenty with "cheeks" sublime, —
Can that be the gay and festive clime?
    Not there, not there, my child!

Is it where Nevada's mountains rise
From the alkali plains which we all despise,
Where a man may beg, or borrow, or steal,
Yet he often will fail to get a square meal,
Where the rocks are full of silver ore, —
Is it there we 'll find that Western shore?
    Not there, not there, my child!

Eye hath not seen it, my verdant youth,
Tongue cannot name it and speak the truth;
For though you go to the farthest State,
And stand on the rocks by the Golden Gate,
They 'll point you across the western sea,
To the land whence cometh the "heathen Chinee,"
    Saying — " 'T is there, my child."

———◆———

BRANDY AND SODA.

(AFTER SWINBURNE.)

MINE eyes to mine eyelids cling thickly,
    My tongue feels a mouthful and more,
My senses are sluggish and sickly,
    To live and to breathe is a bore.
My head weighs a ton and a quarter
    By pains and by pangs ever split,
Which manifold washings with water
    Relieve not a bit.

My longings of thirst are unlawful,
    And vain to console or control,
The aroma of coffee is awful,
    Repulsive the sight of the roll.
I take my matutinal journal,
    And strive my dull wits to engage,
But cannot endure the infernal
    Sharp crack of its page.

What bad luck my soul had bedevilled,
    What demon of spleen and of spite,
That I rashly went forth and I revelled
    In riotous living last night?

Had the fumes of the goblet no odor
  That well might repulse or restrain?
O insidious brandy and soda,
  Our Lady of Pain!

Thou art golden of gleam as the summer
  That smiled o'er a tropical sod,
O daughter of Bacchus, the bummer,
  A foamer, a volatile tod!
But thy froth is a serpent that hisses,
  And thy gold as a balefire doth shine,
And the lovers who rise from thy kisses
  Can't walk a straight line.

I recall with a flush and a flutter
  That orgy whose end is unknown;
Did they bear me to bed on a shutter,
  Or did I reel home all alone?
Was I frequent in screams and in screeches?
  Did I swear with a forcèd affright?
Did I perpetrate numerous speeches?
  Did I get in a fight?

Of the secrets I treasure and prize most
  Did I empty my bacchanal breast?
Did I buttonhole men I despise most,
  And frown upon those I like best?
Did I play the low farmer and flunky
  With people I always ignore?
Did I caracole round like a monkey?
  Did I sit on the floor?

O longing no research may satiate —
  No aim to exhume what is hid!
For falsehood were vain to expatiate
  On deeds more depraved than I did;
And though friendly faith I would flout not,
  On this it were rash to rely,
Since the friends who beheld me, I doubt not,
  Were drunker than I.

Thou hast lured me to passionate pastime,
  Dread goddess, whose smile is a snare!
Yet I swear thou hast tempted me the last time —
  I swear it; I mean what I swear!
And thy beaker shall always forebode a
  Disgust 't were not wise to disdain,
O luxurious brandy and soda,
  Our Lady of Pain!

                                    HUGH HOWARD.

THAT AMATEUR FLUTE.

(AFTER POE.)

HEAR the fluter with his flute —
        Silver flute,
Oh, what a world of wailing is awakened by its toot !
        How it demi-semi quavers
            On the maddened air of night !
        And defieth all endeavors
            To escape the sound or sight
        Of the flute, flute, flute,
            With its tootle, tootle, toot —
With reiterated tooings of exasperating toots,
The long protracted tootelings of agonizing toots
        Of the flute, flute, flute, flute,
            Flute, flute, flute,
And the wheezings and the spittings of its toot.

        Should he get that other flute —
            Golden flute —
What a deep anguish will its presence institoot !
        How his eyes to heaven he 'll raise
            As he plays, all the days !
        How he 'll stop us on our ways
            With its praise !
        And the people, oh, the people
        That don't live up in the steeple,
        But inhabit Christian parlors
        Where he visiteth and plays —
            Where he plays, plays, plays,
            In the cruelest of ways,
        And thinks we ought to listen,
            And expects us to be mute
        Who would rather have an ear-ache
            Than the music of his flute —
        Of his flute, flute, flute,
            And the tooings of its toot —
Of the toos wherewith he tooteleth the agonizing toot,
        Of the flute, flewt, fluit, floot,
            Phlute, phlewt, phlewght,
And the tootle-tootle-tootle-tooing of its toot.

POKER.

To draw, or not to draw, that is the question.
Whether it is safer in the player to take
The awful risk of skinning for a straight,
Or, standing pat, to raise 'em all the limit.

And thus, by bluffing, get it.   To draw — to skin;
No more — and by that skin to get a full,
Or two pairs, or the fattest bouncing kings
That luck is heir to — 't is a consummation
Devoutly to be wished.   To draw — to skin;
To skin! perchance to burst — ay, there's the rub!
For in the draw of three what cards may come,
When we have shuffled off the uncertain pack,
Must give us pause.   There's the respect
That makes calamity of a bobtail flush;
For who would bear the overwhelming blind,
The reckless straddle, the wait on the edge,
The insolence of pat hands, and the lifts
That patient merit of the bluffer takes,
When he himself might be much better off
By simply passing?   Who would trays uphold,
And go out on a small progressive raise,
But that the dread of something after call,
The undiscovered ace-full, to whose strength
Such hands must bow, puzzles the will,
And makes us rather keep the chips we have
Than be curious about the hands we know not of.
Thus bluffing does make cowards of us all,
And thus the native hue of a four-heart flush
Is sicklied with some dark and cussed club,
And speculators in a jack-pot's wealth
With this regard their interest turn awry
And lose the right to open.

———◆———

ALL THE SAME IN THE END.

(Epitaph in the Homersfield, Eng., Churchyard.)

As I walked by myself I talked to myself,
    And thus myself said unto me:
"Look to thyself and take care of thyself,
    For nobody cares for thee."
So I turned to myself and I answered myself
    In the self-same reverie:
"Look to thyself or not to thyself,
    The self-same thing it will be."

Isaac Ross.

INDEX OF FIRST LINES.

INDEX OF FIRST LINES.

———————•———————